P9-CQP-548

DISCARDED BY
DURHAM COUNTY
LIBRARY

DURHAM COUNTY LIBRARY

Jul 31 2014

DURHAM NC

UNREASONABLE MEN

UNREASONABLE MEN

THEODORE ROOSEVELT AND THE
REPUBLICAN REBELS
WHO CREATED
PROGRESSIVE POLITICS

MICHAEL WOLRAICH

palgrave
macmillan

UNREASONABLE MEN
Copyright © Michael Wolraich, 2014.

All rights reserved.

First published in 2014 by
PALGRAVE MACMILLAN®
in the United States—a division of St. Martin's Press LLC,
175 Fifth Avenue, New York, NY 10010.

Where this book is distributed in the UK, Europe and the rest of the world,
this is by Palgrave Macmillan, a division of Macmillan Publishers Limited,
registered in England, company number 785998, of Houndmills,
Basingstoke, Hampshire RG21 6XS.

Palgrave Macmillan is the global academic imprint of the above companies
and has companies and representatives throughout the world.

Palgrave® and Macmillan® are registered trademarks in the United States,
the United Kingdom, Europe and other countries.

ISBN: 978–0–230–34223–1

Library of Congress Cataloging-in-Publication Data:

Wolraich, Michael.
    Unreasonable men : Theodore Roosevelt and the Republican rebels who
created progressive politics / Michael Wolraich.
        pages cm
    Includes bibliographical references.
    ISBN 978–0–230–34223–1 (alk. paper)
      1. United States—Politics and government—1865–1933.
    2. Progressivism (United States politics)—History—20th century.
    3. Republican Party (U.S. : 1854–)—History—20th century. 4. Roosevelt,
    Theodore, 1858–1919. 5. La Follette, Robert M. (Robert Marion),
    1855–1925. 6. Cannon, Joseph Gurney, 1836–1926. I. Title. II. Title:
    Theodore Roosevelt and the Republican rebels who created progressive
    politics.

E661.W65 2014
973.91′1092—dc23   2013047104

A catalogue record of the book is available from the British Library.

Design by Newgen Knowledge Works (P) Ltd., Chennai, India.

First edition: July 2014

10 9 8 7 6 5 4 3 2 1

Printed in the United States of America.

For Tanya, all the way through

The reasonable man adapts himself to the world: the unreasonable one persists in trying to adapt the world to himself. Therefore all progress depends on the unreasonable man.

—George Bernard Shaw, 1903

CONTENTS

PREFACE

AT THE DAWN OF THE TWENTIETH CENTURY, AMERICA WAS IN CRISIS. THE GAP BETWEEN RICH and poor was growing. Natural resources were dwindling. Unregulated financial markets regularly succumbed to spectacular crashes. Workers labored long hours under hazardous conditions yet barely earned enough to get by.

Despite widespread discontent, congressional paralysis prevented the government from meeting the nation's challenges. Republican obstructionists maintained a chokehold on the House and Senate, blocking all but the most meager reform bills. The Democrats, weak and divided, had no hope of breaking their grip. Both parties catered to large corporations that lavished them with funding.

As the public's fury intensified, two unconventional Republican leaders tried to reform their own party and heal the country.

President Theodore Roosevelt was the pragmatist. He pushed for change one small step at a time. When congressional leaders wouldn't give him the legislation he wanted, he negotiated and compromised to get the best he could, operating under the premise that half a loaf is better than no loaf. "Nothing of value is to be expected from ceaseless agitation for radical and extreme legislation," he insisted.

Senator Robert Marion La Follette was the insurgent. "Fighting Bob" from Wisconsin never settled for half a loaf. He championed ambitious reforms that stood no chance of passing and refused to compromise with his Republican colleagues. When they voted down his bills, he went to their districts and campaigned against them in Republican primaries. Real progress would not be possible, he believed, until voters threw the obstructionists out of office.

Though Roosevelt and La Follette shared the same goals, they were never able to work together. Politically, their tactics were incompatible. Personally, they held each other in contempt. Their ferocious battle against the Republican establishment—and ultimately against each

other—traumatized the country and nearly destroyed the party, but it
finally broke down the barricades that had immobilized Congress. A new
political movement rose from the flames and triggered one of the greatest explosions of change in US history: income taxes, labor law, wom-
en's suffrage, campaign finance reform, environmentalism, industrial
regulation, the Federal Reserve, and other reforms that define modern
America.

With these changes, a new conflict emerged. The old North-South
rivalry that had divided the country since the colonial era began to slip
into the background. New battle lines, ideological rather than regional,
cut across American politics. Those who identified with Roosevelt or La
Follette called themselves progressives. Those who opposed their agenda
of reform called themselves conservatives.

A century later, we hear their echoes in our contemporary political battles. The protestors who occupied Wall Street and railed against
the capitalists took their words from Fighting Bob, though few of them
knew it. Tea Party rebels repeat the laissez-faire rationales of long-dead
Republican leaders while employing La Follette's tenacious grassroots
tactics in their insurgency against the Republican establishment.

I wrote this book to explain how it all began. By returning to the
moment when America broke into two ideological factions, we can see
more clearly what we're fighting about and better appreciate the stakes.

But clarity is not my only objective. History offers a solution to our
modern political dysfunction. The first progressives bequeathed us a case
study in how to reform a broken system. Theodore Roosevelt exemplified
conciliation and incremental change. Under the right circumstances, his
pragmatic approach has obvious advantages, but it failed to achieve much
progress in the face of entrenched opposition. Eventually even Roosevelt
abandoned incrementalism. Three years after his presidency, he reinvented
himself as the bellicose "Bull Moose," embraced La Follette's radical proposals, and assailed the conservative politicians with whom he had once
cooperated.

By then, the progressive movement was in full swing, driven forward by La Follette and his little band of Republican insurgents. Their
defiant, quixotic, "unreasonable" insurgency against their own party
inspired voters nationwide and catalyzed a historic political realignment
that decimated the obstructionists in Congress and opened the flood-
gates to reform. A century later, La Follette and his allies have left us a
rich legislative legacy and a timeless lesson in practical politics: to build
momentum, it is often necessary to lose in order to win.

1

THE BOLT

Oh, pshaw! It seems to be coming about that this country is divided into two parts—the republic of the United States and Wisconsin.

—Uncle Joe[1]

MADISON, WISCONSIN, MAY 18, 1904

Even without the barbed wire, the old brick gymnasium looked like a fortress. A fat red turret squatted at each corner of the building; six slender ones overlooked the parapets and gables. The huge wooden doors that sealed the entrances were tall enough for giants and studded with nails. Standing at the edge of a broad blue lake, the "Red Gym" seemed sturdy enough to protect the University of Wisconsin from Vikings, sea monsters, and other menaces.[2]

Politicians were another matter. They stormed the gymnasium by land one sunny spring day in 1904. Lightly armored in straw skimmer hats and convention badges, the "Stalwarts" advanced toward the citadel, hoping to overwhelm the enemy by force of numbers. Curious housewives stepped out in their aprons to watch them march down the road, four abreast waving two large American flags.

The "Half-Breed" defenders were ready for them. Two parallel fences tipped with barbed wire formed a narrow corridor into the gymnasium. A phalanx of large men guarded the entrance—football players, blacksmiths, cops, and Evan "the Strangler" Lewis, a world champion wrestler. When the Stalwart vanguard reached the perimeter, their ranks broke in confusion. Only those with proper credentials to the Wisconsin Republican convention were allowed to enter the building. Many would-be invaders carried counterfeit badges; a missing stroke in the signature gave them away. They shouted and scuffled as the Half-Breed gatekeepers shoved them aside.[3]

The Stalwart delegates with legitimate badges filed through the passage and took their seats on the gym floor. They were outnumbered now, but the Half-Breeds took no chances. More musclemen moved into position around suspected Stalwart rabble-rousers and made sure that they didn't leave their seats. Governor Robert Marion La Follette[4] had ordered a peaceful convention—no riots, no stampedes.

Another wire fence separated the delegates from a mass of roaring spectators crammed shoulder-to-shoulder on the far side of the gym. Intrepid university students perched on the ceiling girders and roared out a football cheer:

> *Cheer! Boys, cheer! La Follette's got the ball!*
> *U-rah-ah! Oh, won't they take a fall?*
> *For when we hit their line they'll have no line at all!*
> *There'll be a hot time in Wisconsin tonight, my baby!*[5]

The man they celebrated was no football star. Five-foot-five and nearly 50 years old with a slight paunch, his only helmet was a thick reddish-brown pompadour that sprouted mushroomlike from his scalp. "Fighting Bob" La Follette was the governor of Wisconsin, champion of the Half-Breeds faction, and, in the eyes of his Stalwart enemies, a dangerous radical.

Wisconsin's governors were expected to defer to the state's powerful party bosses and wealthy industrialists, but Governor La Follette was not like the others. Instead of relying on Republican bosses to nominate him at state conventions, he wanted the voters to select candidates in primary elections. Instead of granting favors to the railroad and lumber industries, he endeavored to tax their profits, regulate their activities, and prevent their lobbyists from meddling in politics.

Such radical ideas did not sit well with the bosses of the Republican machine. Wisconsin was booming. As America's industrial expansion devoured the state's abundant natural resources, some of its citizens had grown rich. Closely connected to the political establishment, they feared any disruption to the economic juggernaut or the Gilded Age political order that had governed Wisconsin for decades. During La Follette's first four years in office, Republican bosses succeeded in blocking his legislative initiatives, but he was popular, and his power was growing. In 1904, on the verge of obliteration, the old guard threatened an unbridled fight to prevent his nomination for a third two-year term.

The split in the Wisconsin Republican Party was different from any that had preceded it, and the press struggled to label the warring factions. It did not occur to people to call the two sides *progressive* and *conservative*. Americans did not yet associate these words with politics. Instead, journalists reached back to an earlier Republican schism from the days of Ulysses S. Grant. They called the Republican bosses and their supporters Stalwarts because of their fealty to tradition. They called La Follette and his allies Half-Breeds as in half-Republican—even though the Democratic bosses detested them as much as the Republican bosses did.

The decisive battle unfolded in the Red Gym on May 18, 1904. La Follette's Half-Breeds held a narrow lead in the delegate count. The Stalwarts hoped to swarm the convention and force a challenge to the delegate roll. If that failed, they could disrupt the proceedings by threat of force. But La Follette's football players thwarted both schemes. In vote after vote, the delegates rejected the Stalwarts' parliamentary challenges. By the time the sunrays streaming through the windows began to fade, it was clear that the Half-Breeds had won. La Follette would be nominated for a third term.

At 5:45 p.m., one of the Stalwart captains jumped from his chair and shouted, "I ask the privilege of announcing that all anti-third-term delegates in this convention are requested to meet in caucus at the Fuller Opera House at 8 o'clock tonight!" A crowd of Stalwarts followed him as he stormed out of the chamber.[6]

THE NEXT DAY, FRONT-PAGE HEADLINES FROM New York City to the Arizona Territory announced the sensational news: "BOLT IN WISCONSIN." The Stalwarts had bolted the Red Gym and were holding a shadow convention to nominate their own candidates at the opera house. The story was hot. Newspapers reveled in the feud and speculated feverishly about its effect on President Theodore Roosevelt's election chances. But none of them recognized its significance.[7]

The schism in Wisconsin was the first crack in the Republican Party's hegemony. Over the next eight years, the rupture would fissure across every state and territory in the Union. By the time the earth stopped shaking, the old political order would lie shattered on the ground. New battle lines would divide the voters. New rules and institutions would govern their lives. New visions would inspire them. The greatest period of political change in American history was about to begin.

WASHINGTON, DC, MAY 30, 1904

From Theodore Roosevelt's point of view, Governor La Follette was a nuisance. Roosevelt's eyes were fixed on the next election, six months away. Winning was not just a political goal; it was a point of honor. His accession to the White House had been a fluke, an accidental consequence of President McKinley's assassination. He wanted to prove that he could win the presidency in his own right.

The schism in Madison threatened this prize. His friend Nicholas Murray Butler, president of Columbia University, advised him that the Wisconsin situation was dangerous. If one of the factions bolted the national Republican ticket, he might lose the state's 13 electoral votes. Butler blamed La Follette for the turmoil, adding, "He is more or less of a fanatic and cannot be conciliated by any ordinary methods."[8]

Roosevelt concurred. "I absolutely agree with you that the Wisconsin situation is very, very ugly," he replied. "I am at my wits' end how to keep out of it. In my judgment you read La Follette exactly right..." He did not oppose Wisconsin's political reforms. To the contrary, he had established a reputation for taking on corrupt political bosses and powerful corporations. But he neither liked nor trusted Governor La Follette, whom he regarded as unbalanced and dangerous to the Republican Party.[9]

For Roosevelt, balance was paramount. In any controversy, he invariably positioned himself between the poles. If he gave a speech criticizing rich "plutocrats," he qualified it by censuring the "mob" as well. When he attacked "bosses" and "political machines," he made sure to denounce "demagogues" and "fanatics" in the next sentence. Born into old New York money, he disdained the populist agitation that was sweeping the West. "I have a horror of hysterics or sentimentality," he explained. "All I want to do is cautiously to feel my way to see if we cannot make the general conditions of life a little easier, a little better."[10]

In addition to his temperamental aversion to populism, Roosevelt also had a practical reason to be cautious. He knew the Republican-controlled Congress would never agree to radical changes. To pass legislation, he had to compromise with congressional leaders. "The reformers complain because I will not go to the absurdity of refusing to deal with machine Senators," he protested to journalist Ray Stannard Baker, "but I must work with the material that the states send me."[11]

Even Roosevelt's celebrated trust-busting exemplified his pragmatism. In the late 1800s, a rash of corporate mergers had concentrated the nation's thriving industries into giant holding companies known as trusts. Like many Americans, Roosevelt worried about the trusts' political influence and anticompetitive practices. Taking advantage of an antitrust law from 1890, he shocked the business community by suing the Northern Securities Company, the largest railroad corporation in the world. The pioneering lawsuit established his reputation as a legendary trust-buster, but after breaking up Northern Securities, he eased off his assault. Employing the threat of litigation as a "big stick," he worked quietly with corporate executives to reform rather than to dissolve other large conglomerates.[12]

His interactions with congressional leaders were similarly accommodating. In return for a free hand to conduct foreign diplomacy, he refrained from challenging Congress's purview over domestic legislation. His first term was not without legislative accomplishments, including the establishment of the Department of Commerce and Labor, but he achieved them by cooperating with recalcitrant Republican leaders, and the legislation's impact was modest. For the most part, he left Congress to plod along as it had for years, complacently passing small-bore appropriations and other minor legislation while substantive reform bills strangled silently in committee.[13]

Among the Republican legislators, Roosevelt held a particularly high regard for John Coit Spooner, the Wisconsin senator who led the Stalwart faction. Spooner's wire-rim pince-nez and thick mat of hair gave him the appearance of an absented-minded professor, but Roosevelt knew him to be one of the sharpest minds and most powerful politicians in Washington. He was indebted to him for helping to pass the Panama Canal treaty and other diplomatic initiatives. "What a trump Spooner is," he wrote. "He has done so much for me."[14]

One week after Wisconsin's Republican convention, Spooner visited the White House to ask a favor of his own. The Stalwarts had elected him to represent them at the Republican National Convention in Chicago. La Follette's Half-Breeds had selected their own representatives. There could only be one Wisconsin delegation, so the Republican National Committee would have to choose between the two factions. Spooner urged Roosevelt to stay out of the contest, arguing that presidential dignity required him to remain above the fray. Roosevelt, who was anxious to avoid entanglement in the affair, agreed.

A few days later, a Half-Breed delegation arrived in Washington, begging for his assistance. They pointed out that the Republican National Committee was biased against them. The committee chairman, Postmaster General Henry C. Payne, was a Wisconsin Stalwart, and the other members were on his side. Without presidential intervention, the committee would certainly authenticate the Stalwart delegation. But Roosevelt declined to interfere. Echoing Spooner's argument, he insisted that the President should not involve himself in state politics.[15]

His hands clean, he hoped that the matter would soon be put to rest. Years later, he would come to see the conflict in another light. By then, he would be a different man. And America would be a different country.

CHICAGO, ILLINOIS, JUNE 23, 1904

An angular old man stood on the stage beneath the great arched ceiling of the Chicago Coliseum, shaking and shouting. His arms made circles, his legs vibrated, and his toes worked up and down in their shoes. An ill-fitting coat bunched and puckered across his narrow frame, and he wore his white beard with no moustache, a throwback to the days of Abraham Lincoln. As he cavorted across the stage, the old man did not look like a statesman. Out of context, he might have been taken for an ignorant old farmer with "hayseed in his hair," as city folk said of country folk in his day.[16]

That was what they had assumed when he arrived in Washington, DC, back in 1873. After his first speech in the House of Representatives, a congressman from New Jersey sneered that he must have "oats in his pocket." But the Illinois freshman turned the jibe to his advantage. "Yes, I have oats in my pocket and hay-seed in my hair," he drawled, "and the western people generally are affected in the same way; and we expect that the seed, being good, will yield a good crop..." The other congressmen laughed; they appreciated wit. This man would do well in the House.[17]

And he did do well, though he never relinquished his western ways. On the contrary, he exaggerated his country manners and wrapped himself in the aura of the homespun American pioneer. When he cursed and shouted, swung his fists, swigged his whiskey, and chewed his cigars, well that was all part of his rugged charm. The legislators embraced his idiosyncrasies and hardly noticed as he worked his way up the Republican Party ranks. Soon they were calling him "Uncle Joe" and coming to him for favors. When the Speaker of the House stepped down in 1903, everyone knew who would succeed him: Joseph Gurney Cannon of Danville, Illinois.

The House Speaker held considerable authority in those days. He selected members of the congressional committees in which legislation was forged. He dictated the voting schedule, determining which bills reached the floor for a vote and which ones died quietly at the end of the session. He decided who would speak on the House floor on any given day. Cannon did not create the rules that concentrated such power in his office, but he applied them more zealously than his predecessors. He packed the important House committees with loyal supporters and blocked bills he disliked from coming to a vote, using his authority to enforce discipline among the Republican ranks and even among many Democrats. Congressmen who hoped to obtain prominent committee positions or federal projects for their districts had to win his favor. Each morning, they gathered at his office like supplicants, appealing to old Uncle Joe for the privilege of speaking on the record that day.[18]

Never before or since has one man exercised such supremacy in the House. Had he wished, Joseph G. Cannon might have been the most prolific Speaker in American history. But moving legislation was not his ambition. He liked the country just the way it was. "This talk about the country going to the devil is the mere raving of demagogues," he snorted. "The average man was never so profitably employed in the history of the world." Cannon's personal success had made him an inveterate optimist. Having raised himself from the dirt floor of a log cabin to the pinnacle of power, he saw no reason why any hard-working American who put his mind to it should not do the same. As long as the government kept its nose out of peoples' business, America would do just fine. He wasn't concerned about political bosses or robber barons, monopolies or bank runs, child labor or tainted food. He didn't like the idea of women voting, and he abhorred government regulation. "I am god-damned tired of listening to all this babble for reform," he said, "America is a hell of a success." He promptly quashed the few reform bills that occasionally peeped out from his congressional committees.[19]

Yet for all his reactionary authoritarianism, it was hard to hate Uncle Joe. His straightforward manner, his folksy humor, and his irrepressible optimism endeared him to congressmen on both sides of the aisle. Even his enemies could barely get through their denunciations without confessing how much they loved the man. As for the Republican rank and file, they adored him. The party had good reason to choose him to chair the Republican National Convention.

The convention was the media kick-off for the presidential campaign; the whole country would read about what went on in the Chicago Coliseum. The party leaders hoped to project confidence and enthusiasm. They wanted hordes of screaming delegates exploding with partisan fervor. Uncle Joe was the perfect man to rouse the troops. He bounded back and forth across the platform like a man half his age, bringing the ecstatic delegates to their feet. They roared with delight as he took up a tattered old American flag and brandished it over his head, shouting above the din, "Get up boys, and yell!"[20]

From behind the stage, two men hurried forward with a huge crayon portrait of a man's face. As it swayed precariously in their hands, two more rushed over to support it. The four gently rotated it to exhibit the picture to all sides of the hall while the crowd cheered and whistled. The face in the portrait was thick and blocky, almost square. A gold pince-nez, too small for the broad face, roosted on the nose. A bushy mustache hung from the upper lip, barely veiling two rows of enormous white teeth.[21]

As the cheering continued, a young man came forward to relieve the Speaker of his tattered flag, a relic from Lincoln's nomination. The young man waved the talisman back and forth over the heads of the crowd. With each swing he cried out through a megaphone, "Roosevelt!" The men surrounding the dais took up the refrain: "Roosevelt! Roosevelt!" The chorus rippled out through the crowd, surging and swelling until it shook the enormous hall with each triumphant blast: "Roosevelt! Roosevelt! Roosevelt! Roosevelt!"[22]

IN TRUTH, THE ENTHUSIASM FOR THEODORE ROOSEVELT may have been slightly forced. Newspaper accounts of the previous days' proceedings described listless speeches and empty seats. Some speculated that the convention would finish with a whimper after only two days. Party leaders fretted that the apathy could hurt turnout in the November elections. But Uncle Joe assuaged their fears. To make sure the convention lasted a full three days, he manufactured a dispute over the number of delegates accorded to the territory of Hawaii. The ensuing debate pushed the presidential nomination to the third day, which gave him plenty of time to prime the crowd for a proper presidential ovation.[23]

One factor in the earlier lethargy was the unity of the Republican Party. Enthusiasm, Cannon observed, requires a fight, and the delegates simply had nothing to fight about. The party platform and nominations had been fixed for months. After a string of unanimous votes, one bored delegate exclaimed, "Great Scott, what are we here for?"[24]

But there was another factor, seldom spoken in public. The Republican leaders didn't much like their nominee. They still hadn't forgiven Roosevelt for breaking up Northern Securities. Traditionalist Republicans did not believe that a company could be too large, and they certainly did not believe that the government had any business telling private corporations how to manage their affairs. In their view, the federal government had no authority outside the limited powers explicitly stated in the Constitution. "The function of the Federal government is to afford protection to life, liberty, and property," Uncle Joe expounded, "When that is done, then let every tub stand on its own bottom, let every citizen 'root hog or die.'"[25]

For ten years, the Republican leaders had used their congressional dominance to suppress antitrust laws, currency reforms, food safety inspections, an eight-hour workday, a federal income tax, and other proposals that would have expanded the size and power of the federal government. In 1901, Senator Mark Hanna of Ohio had aptly captured their philosophy when he urged his colleagues to "stand pat" against any changes to the federal tariff system. The phrase came from poker lingo; players who did not want to trade in any cards would declare their intention to stand pat. After Hanna's campaign, a new word entered the political lexicon. While conservative Republicans were called Stalwarts in Wisconsin, the national Republican leaders wore a different label: Standpatters.[26]

When Roosevelt launched his antitrust lawsuit against Northern Securities, the Standpatters braced for war. They still controlled the House and Senate, and the courts were on their side. They were determined to keep their disagreeable President bottled up in the White House. But the blows they anticipated never arrived. For all his talk of big sticks, Roosevelt proved more agreeable than they'd anticipated. "With the first year of his administration the uneasiness was relieved," Cannon reflected. "Roosevelt, business found, had a bark that was considerably worse than his bite, although often his bark was annoying enough."[27]

Nonetheless, they still didn't particularly like him. At the beginning of 1904, many hoped that Senator Hanna of Ohio would challenge him for the nomination, but Hanna died a few months before the convention, leaving no one of sufficient stature and popularity to defeat Roosevelt. So the Standpatters hung a picture of the late Hanna from the ceiling of the Coliseum and lined up dutifully behind the President. Some of them even boasted of his antitrust exploits to the public, which adored Roosevelt's swashbuckling assault on Wall Street. When Uncle Joe called on his allies to get up and yell, they got up and yelled as if they loved Theodore Roosevelt more than any man alive.

After 25 minutes of sustained cheering and a succession of glowing paeans to the President and party, the roll call finally began. One after another, representatives from 45 states, 8 territories, and the District of Columbia announced their delegations' enthusiastic endorsement of the President. "Theodore Roosevelt has 994 votes," pronounced Cannon after the Puerto Rican delegation completed the unanimous sweep, "It only remains for me to announce that Theodore Roosevelt of the state of New York is your candidate for the presidency for the term commencing on March 4, 1905."[28]

There was no acceptance speech at the convention; Roosevelt wasn't even in the same state. It was considered inappropriate for presidents to engage in politics, so everyone proceeded under the fiction that the nominee had nothing to do with his own nomination. Though Roosevelt had been closely monitoring the convention via telephone and telegraph, the Republican Party would not officially notify him of his nomination until the end of July.

Next, the delegates proceeded to select a vice presidential candidate. In those days, presidential nominees did not have the privilege of selecting their own running mates, and the Standpatters were not inclined to

honor Roosevelt's preferences in the matter. They arranged to nominate one of their own. Senator Charles W. Fairbanks of Indiana was the
opposite of the presidential nominee in every way: tall and lanky where
Roosevelt was thickset and muscular, dour and bland where Roosevelt was
vibrant and volatile—"The hot tamale and the Indiana icicle," quipped
one political wag.[29]

As with the presidential nomination, the vote was unanimous: 994
delegates for Fairbanks. After the vote, calls for an acceptance speech
arose from the crowd, but the vice presidential nominee had also made
himself scarce, hiding out at a nearby hotel and refusing his supporters'
entreaties to return to the Chicago Coliseum on the back of a circus
elephant they had hired. "No, no, boys—that wouldn't be dignified," he
demurred.[30]

Meanwhile, the convention delegates wrapped up their business and
headed for home, roused and ready for battle. Their candidate was strong,
and the Republican Party was united behind him. All signs pointed to
four more years of political supremacy.

EXCLUDING CANNON'S ARTIFICIAL DISPUTE over Hawaiian delegates, there had been
only one instance of serious discord at the convention. A few days before
the general assembly convened, two delegations representing the Half-
Breed and the Stalwart factions arrived from Madison and appealed for
recognition from the Republican National Committee. Chairman Payne,
the postmaster general and Wisconsin Stalwart, recused himself from the
hearing to avoid the perception of bias, but it didn't matter. After listening to several hours of testimony, the other members of the committee
delivered a verdict without pausing to review the voluminous documen-
tation submitted by each side: unanimous for the Stalwarts. Afterward,
some of the committee members explained their rationale to a *Baltimore
Sun* reporter, variously calling La Follette a "socialist," a "Cossack," and
a "bashi-bazouk."[31]

The Half-Breeds then appealed to the Committee for Credentials
but soon concluded that the second committee had also prejudged the
case. On the day of the hearing, they withdrew their case, charging that
the committee's members had been "approached." They did not say who
had approached them, but Walter Wellman of the *Chicago Record-Herald*
volunteered an explanation. "Appeals went out from the presidents of railroads in Wisconsin to their brethren all over the country to help down
this political train-wrecker of the Badger State," he reported. "This was
an opportunity to dispose of him which must not go neglected."[32]

La Follette called his delegates home to Wisconsin, but the Committee
for Credentials ruled on the case anyway and delivered its unanimous

repudiation of the governor to the convention delegates in Chicago. The crowd responded with prolonged cheers and applause. A voice vote was called to ratify the committee's recommendation, and a chorus of "yeas" gave the answer, burying the single audible "nay" that floated up from some lonely corner of the hall. And with that, the convention moved on to the next matter of business.[33]

MADISON, WISCONSIN, JUNE 28, 1904

The governor's residence was a stolid block of pitted yellow limestone seated on a grassy bluff with its back to one of Madison's lakes. Lincoln Steffens, the world-famous reporter from *McClure's Magazine*, stepped onto the front porch with some hesitation. He wasn't sure that it had been a good idea to accept Governor La Follette's dinner invitation. Too much familiarity with his subject might undermine his objectivity. He resolved to maintain a clinical distance during the visit.

Steffens was a new kind of journalist. Most newspapers of the era openly affiliated with one party or the other. Many reveled in scandal and sensationalism like modern-day tabloids. By contrast, Steffens and his colleagues at *McClure's* delivered serious, thorough investigations of the country's leading politicians and corporations. Ida Tarbell exposed the monopolistic abuses of John D. Rockefeller's Standard Oil Company. Ray Stannard Baker took on J. Pierpont Morgan's United States Steel Corporation. Steffens focused on the politicians. The charming and debonair journalist with a devilish goatee had a way of ferreting out the sordid schemes that greased the gears of government. Over the course of his career, he had exposed dirty cops, corrupt officials, robber barons, swindlers, bribers, boodlers, and card cheats.

As he penetrated the underbelly of American politics, his ideas began to evolve. He came to see the petty bribes and minor frauds as fragments of a much larger mosaic. A system, he called it, and later, The System. Crooked cops and venal officials were small cogs in The System. Much more dangerous were the party bosses, unofficial powerbrokers who oversaw the vast apparatus that delivered votes each election day. Some bosses were elected officials. Others held seemingly innocuous administrative posts and conducted party business behind the scenes.

Yet for all their power, the bosses were themselves beholden to others—the businessmen who financed their political operations. Campaigns cost money, more and more these days. Neither the spellbinders who went from town to town speechifying nor the ward-heelers who used less savory methods in the cities worked for free. Businessmen were willing to provide the capital—for a price. Such exchanges were entirely legal. The businessmen made lawful campaign donations; the politicians passed laws that benefitted their patrons. There was no crime to prosecute. Without new legislation, The System was impervious.

Steffens had been cautiously optimistic when his friend Theodore Roosevelt became president. They'd met in 1895 when Roosevelt became a New York City police commissioner. Steffens recalled how the hotshot blue-blood politician had invaded NYPD headquarters on his first day. "Where are our offices?" Roosevelt had shouted, "Where is the board room? What do we do first?" He wanted to know everything—the good cops, the bad cops, and how it all worked. Steffens became one of his trusted advisers on police corruption. Roosevelt used to lean out the window of his second-story office and summon him with a cowboy yell that he'd learned in the Dakota Territory, "Hi yi yi!"[34]

Steffens liked Roosevelt, and they became friends, but he never quite trusted him to fulfill his promises. Too many of Roosevelt's initiatives fell short of what was needed. As he got to know him better, Steffens could see that Roosevelt's mind was committed to reform but not his hips, and it was those hips that made the decisions. Whether he was charging up a hill under enemy fire or running for governor, Roosevelt always seemed to act before he had even made up his mind to act. "You don't think with your brains, do you?" Steffens asked him once. Those brains wanted reform, Steffens reckoned, but the hips hung back closer to the old guard. The hips were happiest right in the middle with one foot in each camp.

"You're a practical man," Steffens teased him.

Roosevelt took it as a compliment. "I am, you know," he replied, "I'm a practical man." He repeated it several times, and it became a watchword for him in the years to come.[35]

But Steffens thought he was a little too practical. Roosevelt denounced the patronage system—which rewarded political supporters with government jobs—but took advantage of it at election time. He criticized the Standpatters but allowed them to water down his legislative initiatives. He railed against the trusts but quietly negotiated deals with them. As president, Roosevelt had drawn the public's attentions to corporate abuses and enacted some modest reforms, but he did not fundamentally threaten The System.

So Steffens continued his investigations. He started with city governments, devoting an article each to St. Louis, Minneapolis, Pittsburgh, Philadelphia, and Chicago. Then he moved on to the states. It was a railroad executive, of all people, who gave him the idea of going to Wisconsin. During his investigation of Illinois, Steffens had interviewed the man about his connections with state politicians. The executive explained that railroad owners only meddled in politics as a precaution. They had to protect their interests from radical populists "like that we are suffering from in Wisconsin."

"Wisconsin? La Follette?" Steffens asked.

"Yes, that blankety-blank-blank demagogue, Bob La Follette," the man answered. "Why don't you ever show up such fellows as La Follette...?" he asked, "Why always jump on us?"

Steffens thought he had a point. After exposing the party bosses and the businessmen, it seemed only fair to take on a populist rabble-rouser. He pegged Governor La Follette for a typical politician, that is to say, a charlatan and a crook. The railroad man offered to put him in touch with some colleagues who would give him some dirt on the governor. A few weeks later, Steffens slipped up to Milwaukee to interview them.[36]

"He's a fanatic," charged a corporate attorney, "and the way that man goes around spreading discontent is a menace to law, property, business, and all American institutions. If we don't stop him here he will go out and agitate all over the United States. We're getting him now; you'll get him next. That man must be blocked."

"Yes," added an indignant banker, "La Follette will spread socialism all over the world."

Steffens listened as they presented their case against the governor, enumerating a long list of outrages that he had committed against the state. They seemed to regard his crimes as self-evident, but what they accused him of doing didn't seem so offensive to Steffens. In fact, he found the governor's ideas rather admirable. For his article, he would need something more sordid. What about corruption, he asked the two men, what about dishonesty?

"Oh, no, no," replied the attorney, "You are getting off wrong. La Follette isn't dishonest. On the contrary, the man is dangerous precisely because he is so sincere."

That wouldn't do. Steffens needed evidence of improprieties. These men offered him nothing but indignation. He spent the next two days interviewing other friends of the railroad executive, but none of them gave him anything more substantial. He was beginning to think that La Follette was not such a charlatan after all.[37]

At the end of June, Steffens went to Madison to meet the "little giant" himself. He spotted him right way: La Follette's height and enormous pompadour were unmistakable. "[A] powerful man," he thought, "short but solid, swift and willful in motion." One of the governor's aides saw Steffens and whispered in his boss's ear. La Follette came over at a run and greeted him with an eager handshake. He had read Steffens's work, he said, and was delighted to meet him. Would he like to come for dinner at the governor's residence?[38]

Later that evening, Steffens arrived on the doorstep of the old yellow house. His attempt to maintain emotional distance didn't go very well. Belle La Follette, the governor's wife, welcomed him like a shining hero come to rescue her husband from a terrible siege. Her enthusiasm was more than he could bear. Years later, he would ruefully recall, "I stood it for a while, then I repelled Mrs. La Follette with a rebuke that was rude and ridiculous, so offensive indeed that I find that I cannot confess it even now."[39]

Having insulted his hostess and sunk the house into an awkward silence, he tried to make amends. Soon the warmth of the La Follette family began to work through his skin. For all Bob's reputation as a rabble-rouser, he was humorous and self-deprecating in person while Belle was charming and intelligent. Steffens could not help but admire their struggle against the establishment—The System. He arranged to meet the governor again for an extended interview at the St. Louis world's fair. In the meantime, he returned to Chicago to finish his article on corruption in the state of Illinois.[40]

ST. LOUIS, MISSOURI, JULY 4, 1904

The Louisiana Purchase Exposition of 1904 was larger than any world fair in previous history, a 1,200-acre "ivory city" of chalky plaster palaces laced by 75 miles of roads and walkways. Nearly 20 million people came to St. Louis to see the world in miniature. For 25 cents each, they could visit Paris, Dublin, Tokyo, Cairo, ancient Rome, and "Mysterious Asia." For another quarter, they could ogle "queer people from all over the globe" at the Anthropology Exhibit. They marveled at new inventions—x-ray machines, dishwashers, and electric potato mashers—and snacked on curious concoctions—cold tea with ice, a buttery spread made from peanuts, and ice cream cradled in wafers that had been curled into cones.[41]

Lincoln Steffens had not come to see strange peoples or marvelous inventions. He had an appointment with a governor. When he arrived at La Follette's room, he found his subject well prepared. La Follette had stacked the table with books, documents, bills, and newspapers— evidence of the path he had cut through the world. Steffens listened and took notes while La Follette recounted the story of his political career.[42]

HE WAS NOT A "DANGEROUS RADICAL" in the beginning, just a young and ambitious district attorney in Madison. When a congressional seat opened up in his district in 1884, he resolved to win it. He was popular and thought he had a good shot, but there was a problem: it wasn't his turn. According to the unwritten rules of Gilded Age politics, aspiring politicians had to serve their party bosses and wait to be anointed for political office. The local bosses had arranged to nominate someone else for the seat. When La Follette broke the rules by initiating his own campaign, he received a stern reprimand from Senator John Spooner's brother, Philip.

"What's this I hear about you being a candidate for Congress?" La Follette recalled Phil Spooner telling him. "Don't you know nobody can go to Congress without our approval? You're a fool."[43]

But Phil Spooner was about to discover what many other politicians would learn in the years to come: Bob La Follette would not be bullied. There was some kind of coil in him that launched him headfirst at any authority who barred his way, forcefully and repeatedly. Many ambitious young men in his position would have followed orders and worked their way up the chain, absorbing the cynical ethos of machine politics along the way. A few idealists might have gone the other way, rejecting both major parties in favor of radical third parties like the Socialists or the Populists. But La Follette simply charged straight ahead. "[H]is strongest trait is a delight in overcoming obstacles," recalled a former classmate, "if two ways to the same end were open to him, one without and the other with opposition, he would deliberately choose the road with opposition."[44]

With the assistance of a disaffected Republican elder and a small army of college activists, La Follette won the nomination in spite of Phil Spooner and the bosses. Then he won the general election. In 1885, the 29-year-old congressman went to Washington.

His first few years in Congress were heady ones. Republican leaders overlooked his electoral insubordination, and the press celebrated the youngest member of Congress. He developed a reputation as an eloquent orator and an up-and-coming Republican star. During his third term, he befriended another young luminary, Theodore Roosevelt, who was serving in President Harrison's Civil Service Commission. At a New Year's Party, the exuberant Roosevelt spilled coffee over Belle La Follette's dress. Mortified, he sent her flowers the next day.[45]

As time went on, La Follette began to suffer doubts about his party. He clashed with his Wisconsin compatriots: Senator Philetus Sawyer, the boss of the "Milwaukee ring," and Henry C. Payne, the future postmaster general and chairman of the Republican National Committee. Sawyer was a lumber tycoon, Payne a railroad lobbyist. When they pressed La Follette to do favors for their respective industries, his stubborn streak returned. He was not yet a passionate crusader, but he took immense pride in his own virtue. Rebelliousness fused with self-righteousness, an explosive combination. He angrily rejected their demands.

"La Follette is a damned fool," Payne was heard to say after one confrontation. "If he thinks he can buck a railroad with 5,000 miles of continuous line, he'll find he's mistaken. We'll take care of him when the time comes."[46]

But it was neither the railroads nor the Republican machine that ended La Follette's congressional career. In 1890, the Democrats swept the Wisconsin elections in a rare victory, and he found himself back at his law practice in Madison.

His political hiatus did not last long. One day in the autumn of 1891, Senator Sawyer invited La Follette to a private meeting at a Milwaukee hotel. An embezzlement case brewing in the courts had snared some of Sawyer's associates and threatened to entangle the senator himself. La Follette's brother-in-law was the presiding judge in the case. Sawyer pulled out a roll of bills.[47]

Later, after the story became public, Sawyer insisted that he had only meant to retain La Follette's legal services for $50, but La Follette believed otherwise. His public allegations of bribery against the powerful Republican boss nearly wrecked his law practice as he lost clients and friends. Threatening letters warned him against trying to revive his political career. But adversity once again brought Fighting Bob to life, and that stubborn coil launched him into his next crusade.

This time he set a more ambitious course. Sawyer's final attempt to manipulate him crystalized the doubts that had troubled him in Washington. Sawyer was not the problem, he realized. The whole system was rotten. Wisconsin's government did not represent the people; it represented the party bosses and the powerful industries they served. "So out of this awful ordeal came understanding," he recalled, "and out of understanding came resolution. I determined that the power of this corrupt influence, which was undermining and destroying every semblance of representative government in Wisconsin, should be broken."[48]

Once again, he charged straight ahead by challenging the Republican leadership rather than mounting a third-party campaign. To succeed, he had to recruit enough Republican delegates to outvote the old guard at the biennial state conventions. If they achieved a majority, they could select the Republican nominees for governor and senate. They could also cripple the party machine by destroying the patronage network that the bosses used to deliver jobs to their supporters.

With few financial resources, La Follette began barnstorming the state, using his celebrated eloquence to attract reform-minded supporters. His condemnation of machine politics resonated with Wisconsin's disaffected citizens, who were fed up with political corruption and corporate arrogance. In 1896, he arrived at the Republican state convention with enough pledged delegates to win the gubernatorial nomination. As if to prove his point about corruption, Stalwart opponents bribed some of his delegates into switching sides, depriving him of victory. In 1898, it happened again. Defiant and undeterred, La Follette prophesied that "temporary defeat often results in a more decided and lasting victory than one which is too easily achieved."[49]

In March of 1900, Philetus Sawyer died at the age of 83, and the Stalwart embankment finally cracked. At the convention in August, the Half-Breeds overcame the old guard, and the Republican Party nominated Bob La Follette for governor. In November, Wisconsin voters elected him by a landslide.

Yet the struggle continued. Over the next four years, Governor La Follette battled the remnants of the Stalwart loyalists, who retained sufficient strength to frustrate his legislative initiatives. He might have passed more legislation by compromising with them, but he refused to dilute his proposals. There was that stubbornness again but also strategy. La Follette took a long view of political change. In contrast to Roosevelt, he believed that temporary defeat was preferable to compromised legislation, which would sate public demand for reform without making genuine progress. "In legislation no bread is often better than half a loaf," he argued. "Half a loaf, as a rule, dulls the appetite, and destroys the keenness of interest in attaining the full loaf." Legislative defeat, on the other hand, served a useful political purpose. He would use the defeat of a popular bill to bludgeon his opponents in the next election, and he would keep assailing them with it until they yielded or lost their seats.[50]

La Follette did achieve one partial victory in his second term. He was a passionate advocate of direct primaries. Under the old system, party members selected local delegates at informal caucuses. In practice, most of these delegates were loyal to party bosses—or at least receptive to the bosses' encouragement. Bribery in the form of cash or jobs was common. A primary system would allow voters to choose party nominees without mediation by faithless delegates.

The Stalwarts, anxious to preserve the elite power of the establishment, fought La Follette's popular initiative. "I think a primary election law as he wants it would destroy the party machinery," warned Senator Spooner, "and would build up a lot of personal machines, would make every man a self-seeker, would degrade politics by turning candidacies into bitter personal wrangles and quarrels, etc." Spooner's allies in the Wisconsin Senate succeeded in blocking La Follette's bill, but their majority was narrow, and the popular pressure was intense. Under duress, they agreed to put the question to the voters in a referendum in the upcoming election.[51]

The stakes were high. Knowing that 1904 might be their last chance, the Stalwarts mounted an aggressive campaign to defeat La Follette and his primary bill once and for all. When they failed to take control of the convention at the Red Gym, they bolted to the opera house and nominated their own candidate for governor. The Democratic bosses fielded a candidate as well, creating a tight three-man race.[52]

OVER THE COURSE OF A WEEK, CLOISTERED in St. Louis, Lincoln Steffens recorded La Follette's story with fascination and growing admiration. Perhaps too much admiration. La Follette may have been principled and sincere, but he tended to embellish. Steffens was thorough, though, and he returned to Wisconsin to corroborate the story. The Stalwarts, who still thought he intended to expose the governor, cooperated with his investigation. "Mr. Steffens' evident purpose always has been to speak the truth on all occasion," praised the Stalwart-owned *Milwaukee Sentinel*. "This is the kind of an investigation that Wisconsin needs at this time…"[53]

But Steffens had a new quarry. He was now determined to expose the antidemocratic methods of the governor's enemies. In Bob La Follette, he had finally found his champion: a political leader with the steadfast principles and strength of purpose to wage an open and relentless war against The System itself.

ST. LOUIS, MISSOURI, JULY 6, 1904

The Democrats held their national convention in downtown St. Louis, a few miles from the fairgrounds. In contrast to the Republicans, they had no trouble generating enthusiasm. The Democratic delegates shouted for former President Grover Cleveland—despite his disastrous second term. They shouted for William Jennings Bryan—who had lost the last two presidential elections to William McKinley. They shouted so lustily when the band played "Dixie" that no one could hear the song.[54]

They also shouted for Judge Alton Brooks Parker, if not quite as loudly. Parker was a soft-spoken judge from upstate New York, six-feet tall and balding with a dignified handlebar mustache. He had spent nearly two decades on the bench. In all that time, no one could recall his venturing an opinion on a matter of political importance. Even after party leaders began to promote him for the presidency, he avoided uttering anything that might be construed as a political position. The *New York Sun* quipped that he had "all the salient qualities of a sphere."[55]

But a sphere did have some advantages in the volatile soup that was the Democratic Party. From the South came the race-baiters who defended white privilege and suppressed black voters. From the West came the populists who championed small farmers and vilified East Coast moneymen. From the great cities came the machine politicians who cared only for patronage and graft. Sprinkled throughout were the conservative Bourbon Democrats, the Democratic equivalent of the Standpatters. At the national convention in St. Louis, they all swirled together, shouting and squabbling as they coalesced in mutual contempt for President Roosevelt and the Republican Party.

The populist faction had dominated the conventions of 1896 and 1900, twice nominating William Jennings Bryan, the "Great Commoner" from Nebraska. But he lost both elections, and his crusade to unhook the dollar from the gold standard flopped. In 1904, the Democratic bosses hoped to replace him with a "safe and sane" candidate who would appeal to a wider range of voters without antagonizing the populists. They settled on the spherelike Judge Parker, who had never antagonized anyone.[56]

Parker received the news of his nomination from a reporter as he emerged dripping and shivering from his regular morning swim in the Hudson River. "Is that so?" he replied with a grin as he made his way up to his house overlooking the river. "No," he replied to the journalists' requests for comments, "I will reserve anything I have to say until I am officially notified."[57]

OYSTER BAY, NEW YORK, JULY 27, 1904

One bright day at the end of July, a small passenger train rumbled into the hamlet of Oyster Bay, which rested quietly beside its namesake on the north shore of Long Island. When Uncle Joe bounded out with a flock of Republican dignitaries in tow, the assembled townspeople greeted them with cheers. Every available carriage in the village stood ready for service. The Republican officials climbed into the vehicles, pausing long enough for the press to snap photographs. As they rattled up the road past green lawns festooned with American flags and pictures of the President, an old fireman saluted them with joyful blasts from a little brass cannon.[58]

Half an hour later, the carriages came to a rambling country house at the crest of a small hill. President Roosevelt and his wife, Edith, stood waiting for them at the entrance, their children arrayed about the long veranda overlooking the bay. The visitors greeted their hosts and dispersed across the manicured lawn. The women relaxed in white gauzy dresses; the men roasted in dark wool coats. Even Uncle Joe dressed up for the occasion, forsaking his usual rumpled suit for a pressed and tailored frock coat that extended to his knees. He circulated among the crowd, leaving a trail of laughter wherever he went. Someone asked if he planned to speak extemporaneously as he had at the convention.[59]

"No, Sir," he replied, "I'm going to read my speech. It's seven minutes long—first time I read anything seven minutes long in my life." In lieu of a rostrum, he climbed on a chair to deliver the speech. He devoted the majority of his seven minutes to lambasting Democrats and venerating Republicans. His brief praise for Roosevelt's record was warm but vague. "You have recommended legislation to Congress from time to time," he said, "as it was your duty to, and when it was passed by Congress, have approved it." He did not specify the legislation.[60]

Roosevelt did not appear to notice the omission. "That's perfectly true," he murmured when Cannon attacked the President's critics, "That's perfectly true." At the conclusion of the speech, Cannon formally notified Roosevelt what he had already known for a month: the Republican Party had nominated him for president.[61]

Then Roosevelt mounted the chair to deliver his acceptance speech. He had a high, thin voice and spoke in the peculiar cadence of old-money New York, fiercely enunciating every consonant except Rs and Ls, which he rolled with a dramatic flourish. He measured out his speech line by line like a typewriter, pausing briefly after each clatter of syllables. When he became animated, he chopped the air with one hand, smashing it against the upraised palm of the other.[62]

The actual content of the speech did not quite measure up to the vigorous gesticulation. Roosevelt avoided aggravating the divisions within his party, emphasizing instead his foreign policy successes and America's booming economy. "Assuredly it is unwise to change the policies which have worked so well and which are now working so well," he urged, "Prosperity has come at home. The national honor and interest have been upheld abroad." Of his plans for the future, he offered only generalities. Of the great controversies of the day—the railroads and the suppression of black voters in the South—he said nothing. On the protective tariff, the time bomb that would eventually shatter the Republican Party, he stood pat.[63]

ESOPUS, NEW YORK, AUGUST 10, 1904

Judge Alton Parker greeted the opening of Roosevelt's campaign the same way he had received the news of his nomination: without comment. All through the long hot month of July and the first half of August, he behaved as if nothing unusual was happening. He rose each morning at seven for his daily swim, ate breakfast, rode his horse, tended his farm, read the mail and the papers, ate lunch. In the afternoons, he entertained reporters on his front porch but never discussed politics. Sometimes Democratic leaders came to meet with him, but Parker shared nothing of what they had discussed with the bored journalists. To begin the campaign before his nomination was official would have been improper.[64]

Finally, one rainy August afternoon, the moan of a steam whistle announced the arrival of the notification committee. A riverboat materialized from the drizzle that veiled the Hudson River. The red, white, and blue bunting that garnished its decks hung wet and limp; its passengers crowded into the sheltered lower deck. When the ship docked, they filed out onto the pier and trudged up the muddy slope to Parker's house. "It's a sure thing that Roosevelt couldn't charge up this hill," grumbled one dignitary as he struggled up the incline.[65]

When all the guests had reached the house and duly shaken the hand of their host, Representative "Champ" Clark of Missouri mounted a podium that had been installed beneath the trees. Rivulets of rain streamed down his bare scalp as he delivered an abridged version of his prepared speech to the sodden spectators. At last, he pushed the soggy notification papers into the hands of the judge and proclaimed, "May the God of our fathers guide, protect and bless you, both as a candidate and as Chief Magistrate of the Republic!" Cameras crackled as Judge Parker received his formal notification at last.[66]

Freed from his self-imposed silence, the judge delivered his long-awaited acceptance speech. It was as damp and dreary as the day itself, offering little more than a recapitulation of the platform that the splintered Democrats had settled on the previous month in St. Louis. On the protective tariff, Parker proposed a "reasonable reduction" but gloomily conceded that since Democrats "cannot hope to secure a majority in the Senate," there was no possibility of tariff legislation unless the Republicans initiated it. The only surprise was his promise not to seek a second term in order to resist the "temptation" of political self-interest, which provoked a rare swell of moist applause. After the speech, hands were shaken, photos were taken, and the campaign floundered into motion.[67]

It did not go far. During the next two months, Parker rarely left the little town of Esopus, preferring to let the voters come to him. "Judge Parker has no faith in the utility of speechmaking for its own sake," a campaign representative explained. "He believes a stumping tour by a presidential candidate to be improper, and he will undertake no such tour."[68]

At that time, it was not unusual for presidential challengers to forgo the stump. William McKinley's successful front porch campaign had attracted visitors from across the country in 1896. But Parker lacked McKinley's name recognition and formidable campaign operation. Few people made the trip to Esopus to hear Parker's wooden sermons. As the campaign began to collapse of its own weight, the *Los Angeles Times* called Parker's nomination the "crowning blunder" of the Democrats' failed electoral strategy. One demoralized supporter put it more plainly, "I reckon that the Jedge hain't quite riz to the occasion."[69]

MADISON, WISCONSIN, SEPTEMBER 1, 1904

Meanwhile, Governor La Follette ran a very different campaign in Wisconsin. Statewide politicians rarely visited Wisconsin's hinterlands, relying on their subordinates to campaign in far-flung towns. La Follette had another idea. In keeping with his populist impulses as well as political expediency, he resolved to personally address as many voters as possible. The only difficulty was the travel logistics. He didn't trust the railroad companies, and many small towns lacked rail access in any case, so he took a novel approach. At the beginning of September, a red Winton 5-seater with a 20-horsepower engine rumbled up to the old yellow house, much to the delight of La Follette's two young boys who accompanied their father on the first leg of his journey.[70]

For the next 48 days, he and his aides chugged across the farm-speckled countryside, speaking and traveling from 9 a.m. until late in the evening, and taking light meals where they could get them. La Follette, a vegetarian, was generally satisfied with a couple of eggs and some bread from a friendly farmhouse. When Wisconsin's mud-glutted roads thwarted the Winton touring car, he would switch to a second car that the campaign had acquired or else hitch a ride with a supporter. Even so, he would often arrive hours late, dirty and bedraggled, to find a crowd of farmers still waiting for him. If a meeting hall was available, he would speak to them from a podium. If not, he would climb onto a wagon or other convenient platform and address the group from there.[71]

Bob La Follette had a gift. He could mesmerize an audience on any subject—whether he was denouncing corporate power, interpreting *Hamlet,* or reading off a long list of shipping rates. He carried his listeners like twigs in a stream. At first his sonorous baritone drew them along leisurely with a gentle rhythm. As the flow of words grew swifter and choppier, the audience began to sense something coming, an ominous rumble in the distance. Suddenly they were in it, hurtling through a cataract as La Follette swept his hands through the air and roared out his passion. And then they were through, bobbing lightly in an eddy until he tugged them on again.[72]

La Follette's speeches were rich in facts and fables. He came by his facts through meticulous research and applied a lawyer's hand to shape a sturdy case from the mass of information, reading off statistics as if submitting evidence to a jury. But he fit the facts into morality tales as old as the Bible. The good guys shone with unimpeachable integrity; the bad guys lurked in the shadows with sinister intent. He drew his stories from the populist mythology of the era: honest farmers and laborers thrashing helplessly in a web spun by greedy industrialists and corrupt politicians.

La Follette argued that Wisconsin's powerful railroad companies had deliberately misrepresented their profits to evade state taxes, and he enumerated shipping rates between towns to expose the prejudicial favor of an industry that set its prices by the relative power of its customers rather than its operating costs. The congregated farmers received La Follette's accusations with nods and cheers, for there was truth behind the fables even if the characters were coarsely drawn in black and white. The railroads had a long history of misrepresenting their assets and their profits, and many a small farmer had been driven into bankruptcy by capricious shipping rates that favored big cities and large producers.

During his first four years as governor, La Follette tried to establish a state commission with the power to regulate shipping rates, but an alliance of Democrats and Republican Stalwarts in the legislature thwarted his plans. So La Follette took his railroad fight directly to the voters. He traveled to the home districts of his opponents and laid out his case to their constituents. Once the crowd was primed, he said matter-of-factly, "Now, I think you are entitled to know how your representative voted on this question."

And then he simply read out the entire roll call, stating the name of each legislator and whether he had voted yea or nay on the railroad bill. He spoke in a monotone, reading out the votes like a congressional clerk. As he neared the name of the local representative, the crowd would tense up and go quiet. Then he would state the representative's name and his vote, and the jeers would erupt. Sometimes, the legislator in question was actually present, not anticipating an assault from a member of his own party. But in this election La Follette targeted Republicans and Democrats alike, and those who found themselves in the glare of their constituents' contempt often made for the exit. "Put the men who betrayed you on the retired list!" La Follette would cry, and the crowd would roar its assent.[73]

SEPTEMBER 23, 1904

Halfway into La Follette's seven-week marathon, the October issue of *McClure's Magazine* landed in the newsstands. It sold out immediately as readers rushed to discover Lincoln Steffens's take on the radical governor who was making so much trouble in Wisconsin. In 17 spellbinding pages, he broke down the situation with the colorful cynicism and wry wit for which he was famous.[74]

Wisconsin's political system was rotten, Steffens concluded. The two major political parties did not answer to the voters. They served the interests of the state's two powerful industries: lumber and railroads. He described how railroad companies offered free travel passes to influence politicians, how party bosses bribed delegates to influence nominations, how Postmaster Payne, Senator Spooner, and the late Senator Sawyer had smoothed the way for the lumber and railroad industries to exploit the state's natural resources.

The remedy for Wisconsin's political affliction, he urged, was Governor Robert Marion La Follette and his direct primary initiative. The governor had defied the party bosses, defied the railroads, and taken his appeal directly to the voters. "His long hard fight has developed citizenship in Wisconsin—honest, reasonable, intelligent citizenship," Lincoln Steffens concluded, "And that is better than 'business'; that is what business and government are for—men."[75]

BELLE LA FOLLETTE READ STEFFENS'S ARTICLE with joy and gratitude. Her husband had finally received vindication and unequivocal support in a national publication from one of the most famous journalists in America.[76]

The Stalwarts responded to the article with venom and rage.

"Its inspiration is unmistakable, and its purpose evident," wrote Senator Spooner.[77]

"He maligns the fair name of the state," shouted his colleague Senator Joseph Quarles.[78]

"A more brazen, disreputable prostitution of the power of the press has never been recorded in this country," editorialized the *Milwaukee Sentinel*, the Stalwart-owned paper that had once praised Steffens's integrity.[79]

"Poor Payne is sick either unto death or nigh unto death," worried President Roosevelt, for his postmaster general had fallen fatally ill. "The attack on him in *McClure's Magazine* by Steffens was, I think, the immediate cause of breaking him down; and I am convinced that it is an infamously false attack."[80]

Bob La Follette kept on driving. On October 5, he received another burst of good news. Wisconsin's Supreme Court rebuffed the Republican National Committee, ruling that La Follette's Half-Breeds represented the legitimate Republican Party in Wisconsin after all. The official designation meant that election ballots would list La Follette and his allies under the Republican slate instead of the Stalwart candidates.

The next day, the Stalwart nominee for governor withdrew from the race. Another candidate replaced him, but it was clear that the cause was lost. Many Stalwarts threw their support to the Democratic candidate in a desperate attempt to bring down La Follette.

President Roosevelt, now fearing that Stalwart bolters threatened his chances in Wisconsin, endorsed the Half-Breeds at last. "Under the decision of the Supreme Court any weakening of the La Follette ticket is a weakening of the national ticket," he wrote to his campaign chief. "The 'stalwart' crowd have acted badly from the beginning, and the National Committee had no business to take sides," he added belatedly.[81]

ESOPUS, NEW YORK, OCTOBER 23, 1904

As Wisconsin churned, Judge Parker finally showed signs of life. Two weeks before the election, a group of supporters came up by train from New York City to hear him speak. They received a surprise.

"A startling change has taken place in the method of conducting campaigns," he announced, "a change that has introduced debasing and corrupt methods, which threaten the integrity of our Government, leaving it perhaps a republic in form, but not a republic in substance, no longer a government of the people, by the people, for the people, but a government whose officers are practically chosen by a handful of corporate managers..."[82]

His implication was clear: President Roosevelt had been bought.

WASHINGTON, DC, OCTOBER 25, 1904

Roosevelt was furious. He had built his reputation on clean government. Parker's charges of corporate influence stung, and he itched to retaliate. "I could cut him into ribbons if I could get at him in the open," he wrote to his son Kermit, "But of course a President can't go on the stump and can't indulge in personalities, and so I have to sit still and abide the result."[83]

The trouble was that Roosevelt's campaign had, in fact, received a great deal of corporate money—hundreds of thousands of dollars from John D. Rockefeller, J. Pierpont Morgan, and Henry Clay Frick, to name a few. Some of the biggest donors had been targets of Roosevelt's antitrust actions, but their losses had not been severe enough to keep them from backing his reelection. And though he had not promised any favors in return for their generosity, his campaign aides had not always been so circumspect. It didn't look good, and Roosevelt knew it.

Political protocol prevented him from responding publicly to the accusations, but he made sure to cover his back. Two days after Parker's speech, he dictated a letter to his campaign manager: "I have just been informed that the Standard Oil people have contributed $100,000 to our campaign fund. This may be entirely untrue. But if true I must ask you to direct that the money be returned to them forthwith."

As he was dictating, Attorney General Philander Knox entered the office. "Why, Mr. President, the money has been spent," Knox protested, "They cannot pay it back—they haven't got it."

"Well," Roosevelt replied, "the letter will look well on the record anyhow."[84]

He did not attempt to return contributions from any other donors, however, perhaps because the other donors were not as notorious as Rockefeller, or perhaps because he could not claim ignorance since he had personally solicited contributions from some of them.[85]

NEW YORK, NEW YORK, OCTOBER 31, 1904

Meanwhile, Parker finally overcame his aversion to the stump, traveling as far as New York City, New Jersey, and Connecticut. Soon, he was electrifying thousands at Madison Square Garden and other large venues, railing against corporate power like a vengeful populist. "We, the plain people of the United States, stand ranged on one side," he declaimed. "Upon the other, as I view it, stand the forces which make for evil to the United States."[86]

But like a lifelong teetotaler reeling from his first gulp of whiskey, he lost all sense of proportion. His speeches became shrill, and he hurled outrageous accusations against the White House, insinuating that Roosevelt had created the Department of Commerce and Labor in order to dig up dirt on the trusts and then blackmail them into contributing to his campaign.[87]

WASHINGTON, DC, NOVEMBER 4, 1904

Parker's blackmail accusations were too much, and Roosevelt could stand it no longer. Defying presidential precedent, he let fly a furious blast at his opponent four days before the election, daring him to produce evidence of his accusations. "The statements made by Parker are unqualifiedly and atrociously false," he roared through the typewritten pages of a press release. "If elected, I shall go into the Presidency unhampered by any pledge, promise, or understanding of any kind, sort, or description, save my promise, made openly to the American people, that so far as my power lies I shall see to it that every man has a square deal, no less and no more."[88]

WASHINGTON, DC, NOVEMBER 8, 1904

On the eve of the election, President Roosevelt took a midnight train from Washington to Jersey City, transferred to a tugboat to cross New York Harbor, boarded a second train in Long Island City, and arrived at Oyster Bay at 9:50 a.m. He cast his ballot, stopped briefly at Sagamore Hill, and then started back the other way, returning to the White House around 6:30 p.m. The first election results had just come in.[89]

Roosevelt joined his family and a few friends in the Red Room to await more results, which soon surged from a trickle to a stream. As the telegraph machine rattled out win after win, Roosevelt strode up and down the room exclaiming, "How they are voting for me! How they are voting for me!"[90]

At 8:30, the telegraph operator announced a message from Judge Parker: "The people by their votes have emphatically approved your administration and I congratulate you."[91]

At 10:15, Roosevelt left his guests and crossed over to the Executive Offices—what we now call the West Wing—where the Washington press corps waited in the lobby. He invited them into his office for he had a statement to make. The newsmen filed after the President and ranged themselves in a semicircle around his desk. He took up a scrap of paper from the desk and studied it for a moment. The room was silent but for a clock ticking pensively on the mantel. Then Roosevelt tilted back in his chair and began to dictate.

"I am deeply sensible of the honor done me by the American people in thus expressing their confidence in what I have done and tried to do," he began. "On the Fourth of March next I shall have served three and one-half years, and this three and one-half years constitutes my first term. The wise custom which limits the Presidency to two terms regards the substance and not the form. Under no circumstances will I be a candidate for or accept another nomination."[92]

And so the word went out to the nation. Roosevelt had promised that his second term would be his last, a decision that would have momentous consequences four years later.

The final elections results were tallied a few days after. Roosevelt won 56.4 percent of the popular vote to Parker's 37.6. He captured every state north of the Mason-Dixon line plus Missouri, amassing a record-breaking 336 electoral votes out of 476.

MADISON, WISCONSIN, NOVEMBER 8, 1904

A man with a telephone to his ear tried to hush the boisterous crowd jammed into the governor's office, but it was no use. The shouting and shoulder-slapping drowned out any details about the latest county to fall to La Follette. The supporters who had gathered round the governor grew more exuberant with every phone call. By midnight, his reelection was assured.[93]

In the final count, La Follette captured just over 50 percent of the vote, easily defeating his Democratic opponent with 39 percent. The Stalwart candidate took fewer than 3 percent, having urged his own supporters to vote for the Democrat. President Roosevelt's fears of losing Wisconsin proved groundless; he won the state by a 35-point margin.

Roosevelt's assistant secretary of the Treasury, a Wisconsin man, voiced the feelings of many Stalwarts when he attributed La Follette's win to the President's popularity. "A yellow dog would have been elected on the Republican ticket in Wisconsin," he groused, "just because the people were crazy to vote for the President…not because La Follette and his men were possessed of any popularity of their own."[94]

Like other Republican candidates, La Follette certainly received a boost from Roosevelt's landslide, but it took particularly sour grapes to credit his 11-point margin of victory to presidential coattails. Nor did Roosevelt's success explain the Stalwarts' wholesale collapse. La Follette's roll-call campaign had decimated his opponents in the legislature and finally given him a legislative majority that would support his reforms. The direct primary referendum he championed passed with an even larger majority, eliminating the state delegates that the party bosses had found so pliable. Under the direct primary system, which would become a model for the nation, the Wisconsin bosses would never again wield the influence they had exercised in the nineteenth century.

NOVEMBER 9, 1904

The day after the election, paperboys bawled out the news of Roosevelt's victory from street corners across the country. Within the inky pages, political reporters tallied up votes and forecast the results of contests still too close to call. Others ruminated over what was to come in the years ahead. Would Roosevelt push for railroad regulation? Would he finally take on the tariff? Who would succeed him in 1908? Would

Governor La Follette run for the Senate? Would he even finish his term as governor?[95]

Some journalists tried to ascertain what it all meant. There was something unsettling about the 1904 election, a creeping sense that the old ways were breaking down—the Democrats splintered, Wisconsin divided, Roosevelt at odds with his own party. The *Chicago Daily Tribune* took a stab at a synopsis in a short editorial with an ambitious title, "The Beginning of a New Era." Focusing on the divisions in the Democratic Party, the editor predicted, "The political warfare of the future in the United States will be between conservatives banded together and radicals banded together. The two kinds of minds will not much longer be found in the same party. The wreck of the Democratic Party as at present constituted was necessary to this development. That wreck is complete."[96]

The editor's prescience was impressive, but he had overlooked one half of the equation. A second wreck would also be required before his prophecy could be realized. The Republican Party was as yet still whole.

2

THE RAILROAD

If the Federal Government continues to centralize, we shall soon find that we have a vast bureaucratic government, which will prove inefficient if not corrupt.

—Uncle Joe[1]

BALTIMORE, MARYLAND, JULY 4, 1828

It was a fine day, and the sun shone big and bright over Baltimore. Thousands crammed the streets of the nation's third-largest city to celebrate the 52nd anniversary of American independence. A column of soldiers, tradesmen, schoolchildren, and horse-drawn floats parted the crowd while a military band beat the rhythm. The procession rolled down the road to a sprawling plantation that nudged up against the city limits.

When they arrived, dignitaries in top hats and breeches stepped down from their carriages and moved into position beneath a ceremonial pavilion. The mayor was there with a delegation of businessmen. Congressmen and governors had come from as far away as Indiana. The luminaries waited patiently for the guest of honor to shuffle up to the pavilion: Charles Carroll, 90 years old, the last surviving signatory of the Declaration of Independence.

When everyone had arrived, the Masonic grand chaplain delivered a prayer, and the Declaration of Independence was read aloud. Then, one of the businessmen came forward to address the audience. "Fellow citizens," he called out, "The occasion which has assembled us, is one of great and momentous interest. We have met to celebrate the laying of the first stone of the Baltimore and Ohio Railroad."

Even then, two years before inventor Peter Cooper built America's first locomotive from musket barrels and spare parts, people could see that the rails would reshape their rustic little nation. The businessman continued, "The result of our labors will be felt, not only by ourselves, but also by posterity—not only by Baltimore, but also by Maryland and by the United States…We are in fact commencing a new era in our history."

Upon the conclusion of the address, Charles Carroll was presented with a spade, which he pressed into the ground "with a steady hand." Then a group of masons heaved forward a 700-pound block of marble and nestled it into place. The grand marshal of the Baltimore Masonic Order stepped up to examine the stone. Pronouncing it "well-formed, true and trusty," he consecrated it with wine, oil, and kernels of corn.[2]

DURING THE NEXT TWO YEARS, 13 MILES OF iron-plated wooden rails sprouted from the celebrated block of marble and crept through yellow wheat fields to the town of Ellicott's Mills, Maryland. In a few more years, railroads bloomed from all the great eastern cities and began weaving through the interior. By the turn of the century, nearly 200,000 miles of iron and steel reached across the continent, conveying people and products to every corner of the bursting nation—cotton, coal, corn, cattle, bricks, butter, leather, linens, timber, tables, shoes, shirts, and new inventions like telephones and light bulbs.[3]

As the rails unfurled like the tendrils of an immense vine, the number of railroad owners dwindled to a handful. The ambitious entrepreneurs who laid the first railroads gave way to rapacious industrialists like Jay Gould and Cornelius Vanderbilt, whose predatory tactics inspired the epithet "robber barons"—a reference to feudal lords who demanded exorbitant tolls for river passage. The railroad tycoons initiated a series of consolidations that absorbed smaller lines into larger corporations. In the late 1800s, investment banker J. Pierpont Morgan accelerated the process by combining railroad concerns into trusts. By the time he and two other railroad magnates merged their holdings to create the Northern Securities Company, J. P. Morgan & Co. had acquired control of half the railroad mileage in the United States and substantial holdings in sea transport. "You can now ride from England to China on regular lines of steamships and railroads without once passing from the protecting hollow of Mr. Morgan's hand," wrote *McClure's* journalist Ray Stannard Baker in 1901.[4]

The consolidations helped stabilize the turbulent railroad industry, but they smothered competition. Towns that had blossomed when the rails arrived suddenly found themselves captive to monopolies, with no recourse when their shipping rates shot up. Even cities with competitive lines suffered when the railroad companies colluded to fix the rates. The higher rates wrecked havoc on businesses that could no longer compete due to increased shipping costs. Small farmers, whose earnings were meager enough under the best conditions, were particularly vulnerable. Many were ruined when crop prices dropped and shipping fees wiped out their profits. Meanwhile, huge industrial trusts like Standard Oil negotiated secret shipping rebates from the railroad companies that helped them bankrupt and buy out their competitors, accelerating the relentless momentum of corporate consolidation.

As popular resentment started to simmer, the railroad companies insulated themselves against government interference by manipulating local political machines and wooing legislators and journalists with free travel passes for their families and friends. Rate regulation bills were watered down or smothered completely. Labor strikes by railroad workers were ruthlessly crushed, often with government support.

With the two major political parties beholden to the railroads, frustrated voters turned to populist third parties that burst like Furies from the prairies and plains. But the populists made little headway in the country's rigid two-party system, and the railroads remained virtually impervious to regulation.

In 1887, Congress roused itself long enough to establish the Interstate Commerce Commission (ICC), an executive agency designed to investigate and penalize railroads that charged excessive freight rates. But the courts stripped the commission of its enforcement powers, rendering it impotent. Year after year, the ICC held hearings and issued warnings about abusive and discriminatory rates, but its efforts produced little more than a stack of government reports.

When Theodore Roosevelt arrived in the White House, antirailroad hostility had reached a boiling point. Roosevelt worried that a populist backlash was imminent unless the government quickly remedied the situation. The freight discounts obtained by the trust companies particularly offended his sense of fair play, and he called for legislation to outlaw rebates for favored customers. Congress obliged with the Elkins Anti-Rebate Act of 1903, which ostensibly banned the practice. But the penalties it imposed were negligible, and the trusts found ways to work around the rebate restrictions. A railroad industry insider later testified that the general counsel for the Pennsylvania Railroad had drafted the bill.[5]

After the 1904 elections, President Roosevelt determined to take another crack at railroad reform, particularly the shipping rebates that the Elkins Act had failed to prevent. In his view, the railroad was no ordinary industry. At the time, trains were the only efficient means to convey goods over land. The railroads had become the nation's "highways of commerce," as he put it in his annual address to Congress in December of 1904. To ensure that the rails remained "open to all on equal terms," he urged Congress to grant enforcement powers to the feeble ICC.[6]

The founding of the first commercial railroad in 1829 had initiated one new era; President Roosevelt's 1904 request for railroad legislation inaugurated another. The politicians who lined up on either side of the issue did not reflect familiar ethnic divisions or the North-South rivalry that characterized America's first century-and-a-quarter. Instead of pitting northern Republicans against southern Democrats, Roosevelt's proposal split each party in half. On one side, reformers fought to protect the people from industrial excess. On the other, Standpatters and Bourbon Democrats fought to protect industry from federal regulation.

For the first time, two fundamentally distinct visions of American government crashed head-on in the Capitol with a boom that would reverberate into the modern day.

WASHINGTON, DC, JANUARY 7, 1905

Nine men arrived at the White House one flurry-flecked afternoon in early January. Speaker Cannon came with four of his lieutenants from the House of Representatives. Four powerful Republican senators filled out the delegation: Nelson Aldrich of Rhode Island, W. B. Allison of Iowa, Orville Platt of Connecticut, and John Spooner of Wisconsin.[7]

The presence of so many bigwigs at the White House attracted attention. While Roosevelt met with the congressmen, reporters loitered outside the Executive Office and speculated about the purpose of the meeting. The four senators were all members of the Finance Committee, leading some to conclude that Roosevelt had summoned them to discuss tariff revision.

But veteran Washington correspondents knew that the senators' authority extended well beyond finance. The "Big Four" had been running the Senate for the past eight years, ever since they had seized control of the powerful Republican Steering Committee in 1897. They chaired most of the Senate's major committees themselves and placed loyal allies in charge of the rest. According to a *New York Times* correspondent, the public debates on the Senate floor amounted to little more than dramatic performances for "eager-eyed tourists." The real debates took place in private meetings between these four men and a few privileged subordinates. No matter what legislation Roosevelt was after, he would need the cooperation of the Big Four to get it through the Senate. As for the

House, only one man really mattered. Uncle Joe put on a show of consulting his colleagues, but his authority was absolute, and Roosevelt could accomplish nothing without his support.[8]

The congressional leaders spent two hours cloistered with the President. When they finally emerged, the waiting reporters pressed them for details, but Cannon just shook his head and laughed. "I haven't a thing to say, boys," he declared, "I don't deny that some things were said in that room yonder, but I can't tell you what they were."

"You are respectfully referred to the President," added Senator Spooner with a smile.[9]

But the President wasn't talking either. He had sworn the participants to secrecy in order to conceal any divisions within the Republican Party. Such "smoke talks" between the party leaders were not unusual. During Roosevelt's first term, he had arranged a number of confidential meetings with Cannon and the Big Four to coordinate policy on the Panama Canal, the Elkins Act, and other matters. "With every one of these men I at times differ radically on important questions," he had written to his friend William Taft in 1903, "but they are the leaders, and their great intelligence and power and their desire in the last resort to do what is best for the government, make them not only essential to work with, but desirable to work with." He added that his dealings with the Republican leaders were much more satisfactory than his attempts to work with "the alleged radical reformers."[10]

But Roosevelt's meeting with congressional leaders in January of 1905 was not quite as satisfactory. They had been amenable enough to his foreign policy requests, but they objected to his plans for tariff revision and interstate railroad regulation. After the meeting, he wrote a friend, "I am having anything but a harmonious time about the tariff and about the interstate commerce." Given the force of the opposition, he concluded that he would not be able to achieve both objectives without shattering the Republican Party. "On the interstate commerce business, which I regard as a matter of principle, I shall fight," he decided. "On the tariff, which I regard as a matter of expediency, I shall endeavor to get the best result that I can, but I shall not break with my party."[11]

Two days later, he sent a letter to Cannon. "Stop in here as soon as you can," he requested, "I do not want the people of the country to get the idea that there will be any split or clash between you and me on the tariff or anything else." The details of their subsequent negotiations never became public, but it was widely assumed that the two leaders had struck a bargain.[12]

"The President is to keep his mouth shut about tariff revision," surmised Representative Henry Adams of Wisconsin, "and Mr. Cannon is to carry through the railroad rate legislation and the joint statehood schemes, which are pet projects of the President."[13]

The following week, Speaker Cannon publicly committed himself to fulfilling his part of the deal. "We will pass some rate legislation at this session," he pledged to reporters. Given his dominance in the House, few doubted that he would deliver on the promise. The Senate was another matter. "When I said 'we,' I meant the House," Cannon added quickly. "I never assume the responsibility of saying what the Senate will or will not do. No man can say."[14]

PROVIDENCE, RHODE ISLAND, JANUARY 17, 1905

On January 17, Nelson Wilmarth Aldrich won again. The State General Assembly of Rhode Island elected him to his fifth consecutive term in the Senate, extending his 24-year tenure by another six. Thirteen other US senators were elected or reelected by their respective state legislatures on the same day. Half of them were millionaires. Aldrich was the richest among them.[15]

America's Founding Fathers did not fully trust the principle of democracy. In 1787, most delegates to the Constitutional Congress agreed with James Madison that one branch of the new legislature should be popularly elected by the citizens, while the other should be composed of wealthy landholders who would govern with "more coolness, with more system, and with more wisdom, than the popular branch." They hoped to emulate the British Parliament, which divided power between the popularly elected House of Commons and the hereditary House of Lords. But the American colonies had no official aristocracy, and the delegates puzzled over how to apportion seats in the *upper* branch.[16]

John Dickinson of Delaware proposed a solution: State legislatures should elect the representatives. He reasoned that legislators would be wiser than ordinary citizens and would choose only "the most distinguished characters, distinguished for their rank in life and their weight of property." That way, the chamber would bear "as strong a likeness to the British House of Lords as possible."[17]

Dickinson's proposal was sustained and his intentions realized. Over a century after the signing of the Constitution, most senators retained ample weight of property, so much of it that populist critics derided the Senate as a millionaire's club. While the House was filled with country lawyers, small businessmen, and farmers, many of the senators had founded, represented, inherited, or invested in the country's largest industrial concerns—railroads, oil, coal, marble, steel, insurance, and sugar. Unlike the rough-hewn congressmen who wore loose-fitting sack coats and felt hats to avoid being labeled "dudes" by the folks back home, the senators generally dressed in fashionable Prince Albert frock coats and silk top hats. They didn't have to worry about the folks back home; the folks back home hadn't elected them.[18]

MADISON, WISCONSIN, JANUARY 24, 1905

Governor La Follette faced a dilemma. Wisconsin's new direct primary law changed the old Senate selection process. Going forward, primary voters would elect each party's Senate nominees. Whichever party controlled the state legislature would be obligated to elect the winner of its primary. But the new rules would not go into effect until 1906. In the meantime, Senator Quarles's term had expired, and Wisconsin legislators were free to elect whomever they wished to replace him. La Follette's Half-Breeds now controlled the legislature, so there was no question of returning Quarles to the Senate, but who to send in his place?

After the November elections, La Follette received a number of congratulatory letters urging him to seek the Senate seat himself. With President Roosevelt promising to push for railroad regulation, reformers hoped for an aggressive advocate to lead the charge in the Senate. The letters pricked at his sense of ambition, and he was sorely tempted to take his railroad fight to Washington, but the Wisconsin voters had just reelected him governor with the legislative majority he needed to finally pass his state reforms, and he felt obligated to fulfill his campaign promises.

After weeks of deliberation, he finally decided to have it both ways. He would accept the Senate nomination but skip a special spring session. The first regular session would not begin until December 1905—eleven months away—and he was confident of realizing all his campaign promises by then. On January 21, his spokesman announced, "Gov. La Follette will accept the honor if it is bestowed upon him." Three days later, 101 of 123 legislators elected him to the United States Senate. Even many of the Stalwarts voted for him, perhaps consoling themselves that his Senate duties would keep him far away from Wisconsin.[19]

The *Baltimore Sun* lauded La Follette's election as a harbinger of change within the Republican Party. "It may not be long before there will be a pronounced division in the President's party on economic reforms," the editor predicted, "But what will Senator Aldrich, of Rhode Island, have to say...? Can the conservatives—the Senators who would 'stand pat' on corporations, tariffs, and railroads—control a President like Mr. Roosevelt? Do they fail to see the significance of Governor La Follette's election to the Senate?"[20]

JANUARY 27, 1905

"What sort of man is Senator Aldrich?" asked Lincoln Steffens in the opening pages of the February issue of *McClure's*.[21]

Nelson Aldrich was a different breed from his colleagues. He didn't wear Prince Albert frock coats or deliver theatrical speeches from the Senate floor. He preferred the trim suits popular on Wall Street and sat quietly aloof while the Senate's renowned orators held forth on pressing matters of state. Unlike Uncle Joe, he did not smoke, rarely drank, and never lost his temper. He was soft-spoken and courteous, clean-cut and handsome "with piercing eyes and a flowing white mustache."

On the surface, Aldrich seemed friendly enough, but there was something unnerving about him. "While he smiles with his mouth, he watches with his eyes," one reporter wrote, "He seems to be able to look on all sides and behind without turning his head or disturbing the fascinating smile that plays delicately about his lips." Another journalist described him as "a man of pleasant address and with a voice agreeable to hear; but there is about him a constant indefinable impression of power and command, the product of long habit in ruling men."[22]

The position of Senate majority leader did not exist at that time, and Aldrich's only official leadership position was chairman of the Finance Committee, but he was the undeclared ringleader of the Big Four and the de facto master of the Senate. He exercised authority from the smoky obscurity of committee offices and private social clubs, in which it was said that he could kill a bill with a whisper. "We used to sit there in the Senate," recalled former Senator Quarles of Wisconsin, "and we used to see our friend move about there, as quietly...as a spirit. He made no noise. He was always a silent member. His influence was never reinforced by oratory. But when we saw him moving about, and whispering to Senator Allison, and just giving a little wink at Senator Hale and Senator Platt of Connecticut, we knew our cake was dough."[23]

In his *McClure's* article, Lincoln Steffens rattled off Aldrich's nicknames: "the boss of the United States," "the power behind the throne," "the general manager of the United States." He traced the senator's path from humble origins to the pinnacle of American power. His father had been a poor millworker from a minor town in Rhode Island. With modest prospects, young Nelson Aldrich began his career as a clerk in a wholesale grocery business. But he was a man of uncommon ability, and he soon worked his way up to partner in the company.[24]

He was also a man of uncommon ambition. The wholesale business bored him, and he regarded the grocery company as little more than a stepping-stone. In 1866, 24-year-old Aldrich wrote to his fiancée that he hungered for more—"willingly or forcibly wrested from a selfish world. *Success* (counted as the mass counts it, by dollars and cents) shall be mine." And so Nelson Aldrich entered politics.[25]

Rhode Island differed from the western states that Steffens had previously investigated. The population was small, and stringent voting restrictions made the electorate even smaller. Instead of bribing delegates and legislators, Rhode Island's bosses could afford to compensate voters directly, openly paying them "for their time." In some towns, Republicans and Democrats bid for votes, with the better-financed Republicans usually prevailing.

"My town is all right," one Democratic operative told Steffens. "The Republicans can come in there with more money than I have, and I still can hold it. Suppose they have enough to pay ten dollars a vote and I can give but three; I tell my fellows to go over and get the ten, then come to me and get my three; that makes thirteen, but I tell them to vote my way. And they do."[26]

Rhode Island's bosses directed the slush funds and thereby commanded the loyalty of the politicians, who needed the money to get elected. When Aldrich began his political career, the Republican boss of Rhode Island was an old wispy-bearded senator named Henry B. Anthony. Anthony saw potential in the ambitious young grocer. Nelson Aldrich was a poor public speaker and an indifferent campaigner, but these were not essential qualities in the mercenary political culture of Rhode Island. More importantly, he excelled at the backroom dealing that greased the gears of the Republican machine. With Anthony's help, Aldrich climbed the ladder from city councilman to state legislator to US congressman. When Senator Ambrose Burnside, the mutton-chopped namesake of the sideburn, died in 1881, the Republican-controlled legislature elected Nelson Aldrich to take his place.[27]

Once Aldrich arrived in the Senate, Senator Anthony shepherded him into the Finance Committee, where he soon mastered the arcane mysteries of the federal tariff system. The tariff proved a useful instrument for a politician on the make. Businessmen petitioned Aldrich for favors. Some sought higher tariffs to insulate their products against foreign competition. Some sought lower tariffs on the raw materials they had to import. Some wanted both. Aldrich played the maestro, deftly orchestrating complex tariff adjustments to suit the needs of well-placed industrialists. The financial community took notice, and Aldrich soon developed relationships with America's richest men. He became a confidant of J. Pierpont Morgan and other industry titans.[28]

Despite his new connections and political influence, the wealth Aldrich craved still eluded him, though not for long. Lincoln Steffens described how a group of Rhode Island investors hatched a plan to consolidate and electrify Providence's horse-drawn trolley routes in the 1890s. To obtain the requisite licenses and tax abatements, they needed help from above. And so Nelson Aldrich became the president of the United Traction and Electric Company. He was not required to invest any of his own modest wealth in the enterprise. The American Sugar Refining Company—popularly known as the Sugar Trust—had profited handsomely from Aldrich's tariff work. Its officers put up the millions needed to build the infrastructure. The Rhode Island legislature granted United Traction a 999-year franchise. Soon, power lines began to spider over Providence's cobblestone streets.[29]

Meanwhile, ten miles south of the city, a granite water tower rose up over the rocky shore of Narragansett Bay. It gazed across a splendid stretch of coastline, one of the largest properties in Rhode Island, and bore silent witness to the upheavals at its feet. Men cut away the shrubs and trees poking from the soil and replaced them with a smooth blanket of lush grass. They pried giant stones from the earth and settled them into a long gray seawall that stretched along the graveled shore. A sturdy stone dock reached into the sea to welcome the graceful steam-driven yacht that came so often. Buildings arose, a boathouse and a domed tea house with its own ballroom. One autumn evening, the tea house filled up with people dressed in the finest French fashions. The Rockefellers had come from across the water to marry their son, John D. Rockefeller Jr., to Nelson Aldrich's eldest daughter, Abigail.[30]

The mansion would come later, after Aldrich sold his trolley company. "I will build it when I get money enough," he promised. It would resemble a grand chateau from the French countryside. European artisans would adorn its many rooms with Italian marble fireplaces, oil frescoes, and woodcarvings. It was to be his palace, a monumental testimony to his emergence as an American multimillionaire, the proof that Nelson Aldrich had achieved *Success* (counted as the mass counts it).[31]

But with the publication of Lincoln Steffens's article, Aldrich gained something that the mass did not value so highly: notoriety. Critics called his looming mansion "the house that sugar built." They derided his cabal of powerful senators as an oligarchy—rule by the few.

Aldrich did not respond to the detractors. He rarely spoke to reporters and did not need to. Safely ensconced in the Senate by a corrupt state government, the immense power that he had "forcibly wrested from a selfish world" was secure. Or so it seemed. Aldrich's domain was starting to tremble, ever so slightly. New opponents, the likes of which he had not encountered in his early career, were rising to challenge his dominion.

WASHINGTON, DC, JANUARY 28, 1905

"My Dear Mr. Baker," the President wrote to his friend Ray Stannard Baker, "I think your last article in *McClure's* is far and away the best discussion of lynching that I have seen anywhere. You know how much I admire your treatment of labor matters; but upon my word I think this is even superior. I am anxious to see you. Come down some time when you can take lunch with me. Sincerely yours, Theodore Roosevelt."[32]

In a photo portrait from his *McClure's* days, Baker stares straight at the camera as if he were scrutinizing the viewer, his chin forward, hair combed tight against the scalp, scholarly spectacles, no-nonsense mustache. His writing was much the same—focused, earnest, intense. Baker eschewed the stylistic flourishes and rhetorical barbs favored by his colleague Lincoln Steffens. He bored straight into his subjects like a drill.[33]

Like Steffens, Baker had known Roosevelt from the early days. One of his first assignments at *McClure's* was to interview the celebrated army colonel from the Spanish-American War who had enthralled the nation by leading the Rough Riders so fearlessly up Cuba's San Juan Hill. Colonel Roosevelt impressed the young journalist. Baker composed a glowing biographical article that recounted Roosevelt's metamorphosis from a pale and pampered aristocrat into a furious force of nature. Whether he was corralling cattle in the Dakota territories, chronicling British naval history, or overhauling the New York City police department, Baker's Roosevelt approached every task with heroic vigor.[34]

Roosevelt returned Baker's admiration, often praising the journalist for the fairness of his reporting and his dedication to the truth. Through the years, he maintained a friendship with Baker that was less chummy than his relationship with Steffens but always characterized by mutual esteem.

On January 28, Ray Stannard Baker answered the President's summons, arriving at the White House for an informal lunch with the First Family. "The President is fond of laughing out in a big, hearty way and of joking with his boys," he jotted in his notebook.

After lunch, Roosevelt drew Baker aside for a private talk, during which he tried to justify his relations with the Standpatters. That very morning, Roosevelt told Baker, Orville Platt of the Big Four had come to the White House to ask him for six favors. He had granted five of them in order to cultivate goodwill. "The sixth I refused because it was not just," he said proudly.

The discussion soon turned to railroad reform. Roosevelt laid out his philosophy to Baker: "One must proceed in this railroad legislation by evolutionary methods, not by revolution." But Baker was not so sure. He was preparing to write a railroad series for *McClure's* that would lead to a somewhat different conclusion.[35]

WASHINGTON, DC, FEBRUARY 3, 1905

Speaker Cannon was having some trouble with a few Pennsylvania congressmen who balked at the President's railroad bill.

"I won't vote for that bill if I have to retire from Congress for voting against it," vowed Representative Thaddeus Mahon, president of the Baltimore & Cumberland Valley Railroad. "Do you propose to take the property of Pennsylvania and other States and put it entirely in the hands of this Interstate Commerce Commission?"

"The giving of seven men the power to make rates will ruin the railroads of the country," agreed Representative George F. Huff, coal magnate. "I am not willing to impoverish my stockholders, many of whom are widows and orphans."[36]

But Cannon was committed. He needed a railroad bill before the end of the session, and he didn't particularly care what was in it. His counterparts in the Senate would take care of the details. So when the Pennsylvanians threatened to revolt during a meeting of the Republican caucus, Uncle Joe hitched up his coat sleeves and sauntered to the front of the chamber. He leaned over a desk and glared at his colleagues, a half-chewed cigar hanging out of a corner of his mouth.

"But we've got to pass this bill," he said, "or we've got to pass some other bill. We have got to put this legislation through. Now, if there is anybody who can draw a better bill let's have it. If there is no one who wants to draw a better bill, then let's take this one. We've got to pass some kind of bill and we've got to pass it right away."

That did it. Few Republican congressmen were bold enough to defy the Speaker to his face. Uncle Joe had his reasons, and they would have to yield to his will or face his wrath. Only Representative Mahon refused to stand down.

"Pennsylvania has four billion dollars invested in the railroad properties," he shouted, "and I will be damned if I will vote to make that property any less valuable!" He grabbed his hat, jammed a cigar in his mouth, and stormed out of the chamber. The remaining congressmen affirmed the bill in a voice vote.[37]

A week later, the Esch-Townsend Railroad Rate bill passed the House by a bipartisan vote of 326 to 17. George Huff, defender of widows and orphans, voted nay. Thaddeus Mahon, the railroad president who had vowed to vote against the bill even if he had to leave Congress, did not vote.[38]

After passage in the House, the bill moved on to the Senate with two weeks remaining in the congressional term.

WASHINGTON, DC, FEBRUARY 21, 1905

Senator Aldrich was not in Washington when the Esch-Townsend bill reached the Senate. He and his wife had embarked on a four-month European vacation. During his absence, he entrusted the railroad legislation to his ally Stephen Benton Elkins, a white-haired cherub-faced senator from West Virginia.

Elkins was even wealthier than Aldrich. He had made his fortune as a Wild West carpetbagger after the Civil War. New Mexicans knew him as "Smooth Steve," the most prominent member of the Santa Fe Ring, a loose syndicate of state officials, land speculators, and outlaws accused of defrauding the federal government, Indian tribes, and incoming settlers. After enriching himself in the West, Elkins moved back east to conquer the fertile coalfields of West Virginia. He took the state by storm, strong-arming rivals as he amassed mines and railroads. In the 1890s, he subjugated West Virginia's Republican machine and became its senator.[39]

The Big Four welcomed Elkins as a kindred spirit and put him in charge of the powerful Senate Committee on Interstate Commerce— not to be confused with the executive branch's Interstate Commerce Commission. When President Roosevelt demanded antirebate legislation in 1903, Elkins worked closely with railroad executives to draft a tepid bill that would not overly inconvenience the industry.

But for all his influence, Elkins remained subordinate to the Big Four, a junior partner in their consortium. Senator Aldrich also sat on the Interstate Commerce committee. As chairman, Elkins outranked Aldrich on the committee, but he dared not risk his position by defying the most powerful man in the Senate. "I voted for nearly everything prepared by the Senator from Rhode Island to get what I did for my state," he would later confess.[40]

With a man like Elkins at the helm, there was no need for Aldrich to cancel his vacation plans when the House passed the Esch-Townsend Act in winter of 1905. The distinguished senator from West Virginia knew what was expected of him.

"The committee has given the best attention possible to the bill," Smooth Steve told the press, "but there has been no time to consider the amendments, and there are several believed to be important. No decision as to an effort to pass the bill this session has been reached, but with the limited time at their disposal it would seem that there is very little prospect of that result before adjournment, with only 10 days of the session left and with much other imperative business to be performed."[41]

WASHINGTON, DC, MARCH 4, 1905

Theodore Roosevelt's first inauguration had taken place at a private home in Buffalo, New York, before a handful of witnesses a few hours after President McKinley's death. The second was entirely different. Now he stood at the East Portico of the Capitol, looking out over thousands upon thousands of cheering citizens. Neat lines of soldiers and sailors ringed the grand staircase, shielding the plaza from a formless throng of civilians pressing hungrily against the perimeter. Faces peered from every window in the Capitol and the nearby Library of Congress. A number of men and a few intrepid women perched on tree branches. In the distance, they looked like giant birds.[42]

Beside him, old Chief Justice Melville Fuller struggled against the gusts that billowed his black gown and yanked on his long white locks. The breeze whipped the words from the old man's mouth as he administered the oath, but Roosevelt could hear him well enough. He repeated each phrase distinctly, biting through the syllables and discharging them one by one into the wind. "I will faithfully execute the Office of President of the United States," he swore, "and will to the best of my ability, preserve, protect and defend the Constitution of the United States."[43]

And then it was done. He was no longer a vice president elevated to high office by an assassin's whim. He was finally President *in his own right*, duly elected—by a landslide no less—and sworn in according to a century of tradition. He pulled out the notes for his inaugural address, but when he looked up at the mass of people splayed out at the far end of the plaza, he saw that they had no hope of hearing him through the wind. So he turned his back to them and faced the congressmen and officials sitting on the Capitol steps. But then he paused again. That was not the way to do it. He turned back around to face the crowd and began to speak.[44]

The address was brief and somewhat hazy; he would worry about the policy details later. The point was clear enough. With the mandate of a popular election behind him, Roosevelt was ready to put his muscle into domestic legislation. "Modern life is both complex and intense, and the tremendous changes wrought by the extraordinary industrial development of the last half century are felt in every fiber of our social and political being," he declared. "The conditions which have told for our marvelous material well-being...have also brought the care and anxiety inseparable from the accumulation of great wealth in industrial centers." His lower jaw jutted out, and he bared his teeth in challenge. Several of the Republican senators exchanged glances. Speaker Cannon, slumping lazily in his seat, looked up with a slight smile.

Roosevelt carried on, "There is no good reason why we should fear the future, but there is every reason why we should face it seriously, neither hiding from ourselves the gravity of the problems before us nor fearing to approach these problems with the unbending, unflinching purpose to solve them aright."[45]

He concluded his speech with a bow and the crowd cheered wildly, though few could have heard anything but the wind. The congressmen converged onto the platform to shake his hand. There was still much for Roosevelt to do that day—the luncheon, the parade, the ball, and other social obligations, but they would pass quickly. And in a month, he would gallop off into the wilderness he loved so much for a long vacation from all of this. "As regards internal affairs," he reasoned, "there is no reason why I should not be gone for the six weeks."[46]

WASHINGTON, DC, MARCH 7, 1905

The week after the inauguration, Elkins reconvened the Senate Committee on Interstate Commerce. According to "almost universal testimony," he boasted, the Elkins Act of 1903 had been very effective in preventing the trusts from obtaining special shipping rebates. "Now I want a law for the regulation of rates that will be just as effective and just as fair to all concerned, as that rebate law is," he declared.[47]

In order to craft such an effective law, he invited railroad executives from across the country to testify at committee hearings. In earlier hearings, he explained, only reform proponents had spoken, and a balance of testimony was required for such important legislation. After the railroad representatives testified, the shipping companies sent their people to speak to the committee. As March plodded into April, the papers speculated that Elkins was deliberately stalling until Aldrich returned from Europe. Elkins denied it. "There is no disposition to delay the hearings or to prolong them," he assured reporters. "This is a question which must be met, and we are here for the purpose of getting the information to meet it."[48]

ROME, ITALY, APRIL 21, 1905

Aldrich was making the most of his Roman holiday, exploring the hill towns with his daughters, shopping for art for his collection, and spending time with his friend Pierpont Morgan, who was also vacationing in Europe. Both men had audiences with the King of Italy. Aldrich had one with the Pope too, though he was not Catholic.

He had paid little attention to Steffens's article or the affairs of Washington. Aldrich rarely read the newspapers even when he wasn't on vacation. But there was no escaping news of the tragedy in Connecticut. Senator Orville Platt was dead of pneumonia at 78. The Four had become Three.

Aldrich cabled Platt's wife immediately, "We are shocked and pained by the sad news. I have lost a dear friend, the best man I ever knew."[49]

MADISON, WISCONSIN, MAY 18, 1905

While Aldrich hunted art in Italy and Roosevelt hunted bear in Mississippi, Bob La Follette hunted votes in the Wisconsin senate. He had proposed railroad legislation similar to the Esch-Townsend bill that was stuck in Elkins's committee. It would authorize a state commission to investigate in-state shipping rates. If the commission found a particular rate to be abusive, it could substitute a "reasonable" alternative.

The Wisconsin assembly approved the bill in early April, but the state senate deliberations lingered into May as the end of the session approached. Running short on time and patience, La Follette did what he had vowed never to do: he compromised. The concessions were small, he rationalized, enough to allow his opponents to retreat gracefully without jeopardizing the bill's intent. Yet, even after the compromise, the Stalwarts continued to propose amendments to dilute the bill and delay its passage. They haggled over how the commissioners were appointed and tried to force court oversight of the commission's rulings.

At last, La Follette decided to press the issue. He let it be known that if the railroad bill did not pass by the end of the session, he would relinquish his Senate seat and run for reelection as governor in 1906. That did it. The Stalwarts had clearly had enough of La Follette's ferocious campaigns. On May 18, they passed the bill by unanimous vote.[50]

Before he had even signed it into law, La Follette introduced two more bills, one to regulate corporate lobbyists and another to require railroad companies to open their books to state tax auditors. Within two weeks, these also passed, and the Wisconsin legislature adjourned for summer.[51]

NEW YORK, NEW YORK, SEPTEMBER 8, 1905

Ray Stannard Baker admired La Follette's methods. "He went at it as a scientist would have done," he wrote. "He had to interview shippers, farmers, small manufacturers, many of whom, although suffering from the inequitable practices, were so dependent upon favors from the railroads that they dared not give their names...He labored prodigiously. I have never known any other public man who worked year after year with more dogged determination than he."[52]

Baker was laboring prodigiously himself. He had spent the spring and summer investigating the railroad business for his upcoming *McClure's* series. He wanted to tackle the rate problem in "some big, important, impressive way," he wrote to Roosevelt. After completing the first article, he sent the proof to the President. It blasted the railroad industry. Baker described the bizarre inconsistencies that led farmers in Iowa to ship produce west to Omaha in order to take advantage of cheaper rates to ship back east again. He explained how J. Pierpont Morgan's Southern Railway bought up a competing line in the city of Danville, Virginia, and brought the once thriving industrial town to its knees. He documented the blatant price-fixing between rival railroad companies, the favoritism granted to particular towns and regions, the free rail passes offered to politicians, and the private rail cars that the trusts used to circumvent the Elkins Act.

"No sensible person," Baker concluded, "who beholds the utter chaos, the injustice and immorality of the present system, will assert that this is the best we can do for ourselves."[53]

OYSTER BAY, NEW YORK, SEPTEMBER 13, 1905

President Roosevelt liked what he read. Baker's critique of industrial favoritism appealed to his sense of fairness, and the publication schedule fit perfectly into his political calculations. "I haven't a criticism to suggest about the article," he replied by letter, "You have given me two or three thoughts for my own message."[54] He then surprised Baker by sending him an early draft of his annual message to Congress.

NEW YORK, NEW YORK, OCTOBER 16, 1905

Baker's delight at the unexpected honor slipped into dismay when he read the draft of Roosevelt's address. "I confess that I was much disappointed," he wrote in his autobiography. "I was terribly afraid that he was plumping for a solution that, while it might help a little, and look good politically, would fail to reach the heart of the matter."[55]

The first installment of Baker's railroad series came out at the end of October to wide acclaim. Though the tone was measured, his indictment of railroad industry practices and his demand for government intervention were considerably sharper than the language Roosevelt had chosen for his annual message. "The Railroad is, indeed, the essential tool of industry throughout the world," Baker wrote, "It is the regulator of business. It holds the scales of destiny. It decides where cities shall be located, and how fast they shall grow...It is terrible power to place in the hands of a few men—fewer every year—about ten men, now, sitting in Wall Street."

"The people," he continued, "believe that such great power is better in the hands of the Government than in the hands of individuals. This demand the railroad owners are opposing with all the ability, legal acumen, money power, and political influence that they can command."[56]

Though he maintained a tight focus on the railroad question, Baker endeavored to place the dispute within the context of the larger political struggle that had consumed Wisconsin and other western states and that now threatened to inflame Washington.

"We are at this moment facing a new conflict in this country, the importance of which we are only just beginning to perceive," he wrote. "It lies between two great parties, one a progressive party seeking to give the government more power in business affairs, the other a conservative party striving to retain all the power possible in private hands. One looks toward socialism, the other obstinately defends individualism. It is industrialism forcing itself into politics. And the crux of the new conflict in this case, recognized by both sides, is the Railroad Rate."[57]

By "two great parties," Baker did not mean the Democratic and Republican parties, which were ideological mélanges delineated by geography and the legacy of the Civil War. He was referring to the factions that had recently emerged within each of the old political parties. Baker knew that Americans were unfamiliar with the words *progressive* and *conservative* in this context. The newspapers of the day called men like Roosevelt and La Follette reformers or radicals, not progressives. When they referred to conservatives, they meant the word in the traditional sense of politicians who oppose change. But Baker used the words *progressive* and *conservative* to describe something deeper than support for reform and opposition to change. In his parlance, each label stood for a comprehensive set of ideas and principles, a political ideology.

MADISON, WISCONSIN, DECEMBER 5, 1905

La Follette was ready. He had called the state legislature back into session in December in order to push for a few last reforms, but after that, he would leave the field to his successor. Come January, he would head for Washington to introduce the nation to what the press was calling "The Wisconsin Idea."

"I shall transmit to you my resignation as governor," he announced to the legislators and a crowd of spectators, "and accept your high commission as United States Senator."[58]

La Follette did not anticipate a warm welcome in Washington. The Senate was the Standpatters' citadel, and his nemesis Senator Spooner was one of its masters. They would likely do their best to shut him out. The *Chicago Tribune* warned, "[W]henever he undertakes to make a sensational speech the older members of the senate, both republicans and democrats, will find it convenient to stroll out into the cloakrooms or down to the restaurants." The *Washington Post* joked that La Follette would be relegated to the basement of the Capitol, where he would be permitted to pontificate on the "Committee on Ventilation and Acoustics" and the "Committee on the Disposition of Waste Papers in the Executive Departments."[59]

But La Follette was not overly concerned about such prophecies. He had played the underdog before. It was his favorite role.

WASHINGTON, DC, DECEMBER 5, 1905

On the day of La Follette's announcement, President Roosevelt submitted his annual message to Congress—what we now call the State of the Union address. In those days, presidents did not speak to the legislators in person. Ever since Thomas Jefferson dismissed presidential speeches to Congress as too monarchical, American presidents had sent written copies of their speeches to the Capitol, where congressional clerks read them aloud. In Roosevelt's case, the clerk's task was not easy. His address was 26,000 words and took two-and-a-half hours to present.[60]

The message was vintage Roosevelt. He bookended each proposal with a variation of the same refrain: a strident call for government intervention to curb industrial abuses followed by a stern warning against "radical or hasty action." "This Government is not and never shall be government by a plutocracy," he proclaimed, "This Government is not and never shall be government by a mob."

The railroad question occupied the centerpiece of the address. "The first thing to do," Roosevelt urged, "is to deal with the great corporations engaged in the business of interstate transportation." In order to combat rate discrimination, he proposed to authorize the ICC to hear rate cases and set a maximum shipping rate if it found evidence of abuse.[61]

No sooner had the message been read than Senator Elkins went to meet the press. "I consider President Roosevelt's message throughout as one of the ablest, most comprehensive, and best composed state papers ever sent to Congress," he beamed. He assured the assembled journalists that contrary to reports, he had favored the President's railroad proposals all along and indeed had already prepared his own bill along those lines. "As I understand the President," he continued, "he does not desire to vest in the commission arbitrary and uncontrolled power to fix rates."

In order to protect the railroad companies from such injustice, Elkins proposed a slight addition to the President's recommendation: The ICC would only be empowered to reduce a rate if the courts first determined that it violated federal law. In order to challenge an abusive rate, a shipper would have to sue the railroad before the ICC could consider the case. If the lawsuit were successful, then and only then would the government be able to force the railroad to lower its rate.[62]

WASHINGTON, DC, DECEMBER 18, 1905

Roosevelt was not impressed by Elkins's interpretation of his wishes. The shippers already could sue the railroads under the Elkins Act of 1903, but the courts had proved extremely slow and inclined to favor the railroads. If a lawsuit were required for the ICC to act, the railroad companies would simply bury shippers' complaints in legal proceedings. The plaintiffs would have to wait years and pay considerable legal expenses for the uncertain prospect of relief.

Having seen one example of Elkins's regulatory handiwork, Roosevelt was not about to give him another opportunity. Instead, he decided to enlist one of the junior Republicans from the Committee on Interstate Commerce to write a new railroad bill. Senator Jonathan Dolliver was a big broad-shouldered lawyer from Iowa, renowned for his hammering oratory. His Republican pedigree was impeccable. He had entered the Senate in 1900 as the celebrated protégé of Senator W. B. Allison, the grand patriarch of Iowa politics and Aldrich's partner in the Big Four. But while Dolliver remained loyal to Allison, he had begun to exhibit discomfort with the Standpatters' agenda. Whether he was experiencing a genuine change of heart or simply reacting to the shifting political conditions back in Iowa, Roosevelt didn't know. But either way, he could make use of Dolliver.

He invited the senator to a White House conference on December 18. The next day, Dolliver introduced legislation to grant the ICC power to set maximum shipping rates—a slightly weaker version of the moribund Esch-Townsend bill. The wording conformed precisely to Roosevelt's wishes. The gauntlet had been thrown.[63]

WASHINGTON, D.C., DECEMBER 19, 1905

As the gales of December swept across the eastern seaboard, the Standpatters girded for assault. Senators grumbled that the President was exceeding his constitutional authority. The conservative *New York World* warned that Roosevelt schemed to become "the political boss of the United States." Senator Spooner expressed his concerns in a forceful speech about the dangers of executive power: "The only fear I have ever entertained...for the future of our government has arisen from apparent popular toleration of or encouragement to invasions by one department of the government of the functions of another—in the nations or in the states...And when the people of any state permit, under any pretext, those three branches of the government to be reduced to two, they tolerate treason to our constitutional system."

Spooner pointedly avoided identifying any particular executive—whether a president, a governor, or both.[64]

3

THE MUCK RAKE

*Our people are too busy to be disturbed by professional agitators. They just go
ahead attending to business and let the agitators howl.*

—Uncle Joe[1]

WASHINGTON, DC, JANUARY 3, 1906

Bob La Follette arrived in the evening. A cold mist touched his skin as
he stepped down to the rain-spattered platform. Farther up the track, the
heaving locomotive coughed and hissed. All about him, black porters in
blue uniforms heaved pinewood trunks for white passengers staggering
wearily from Pullman sleeping cars. Belle was at his side; the children
had stayed behind at boarding school while they settled themselves in
Washington. They had left Madison the day before with a couple of aides
and a collection of trunks. The trains were faster than they used to be—
only twenty hours from Chicago to Washington.[2]

The capital had changed since their first arrival, two decades earlier.
Rumbling automobiles and clanging trolleys jostled horse carriages on
asphalt-coated streets. Electric lights had replaced the gas lamps; black
cables hung lazily from wooden poles, conveying power and telephone
service to the glowing townhouses. Behind them, low-slung tenements
without electricity or running water hunched over dark alleyways like
sores below the skin.[3]

The blaring, bustling Washington of the new century received La
Follette in a different manner this time. In 1885, he was just another

freshman congressman, distinguished only by his relative youth. Now he was *notorious*. Half the newspapers expected him to set his colleagues' hair afire. The other half predicted that the other congressmen would lock him in an icebox in the basement of the Capitol. The reporters caught up to him at his hotel that evening, but La Follette declined their interview requests. They would want to know about Spooner. Tradition dictated that new senators be formally introduced by the senior senators from their respective states. All year long, the papers had gossiped about whether he and John Spooner would walk arm-in-arm down the aisle at his swearing in. The press loved a good feud.[4]

La Follette read their eager bulletins with amusement. He made a point of avoiding personal attacks and never named Spooner in his speeches—or any other opponent except during the roll-call campaigns. And while he did not like the man, Spooner was not as venal as old Senator Sawyer or some of the other Standpatters. Still, he defied tradition by neglecting to ask Spooner to escort him, and he took some pleasure in the public consternation this omission produced.[5]

WASHINGTON, DC, JANUARY 4, 1906

The next day, onlookers thronged the wide galleries that looped above and around the Senate chamber. "Necks were craned and eyes protruded in the spectators' efforts to get a glimpse of the man who has fought to their knees the railroad and other big corporations of Wisconsin," a *Washington Post* journalist reported. The crowd's anticipation boiled up as a rumor went round that La Follette had arrived at the Capitol. When the sergeant-at-arms rushed through the empty assembly floor into the cloakroom, someone whispered, "He's looking for Spooner." Sure enough, he returned with the senator a moment later, and the two disappeared into the office of Vice President Fairbanks, presiding officer of the Senate.[6]

Meanwhile, the floor of the chamber slowly filled with middle-aged men in black and gray frock coats, sober hues befitting the nation's upper chamber. Even the neckties and the handkerchiefs peeping out of coat pockets were respectably demure. Only a few bright carnations perching in buttonholes dared to challenge the gravity of the assembly.

An excited murmur rolled through the gallery as three men emerged from the cloakroom—Spooner and La Follette with the sergeant-at-arms between them. The other senators ambled over to shake the hand of their new colleague as Spooner conducted La Follette down the aisle. After Vice President Fairbanks rapped his gavel to call the Senate into session, Spooner requested the floor.

"Mr. La Follette, the senator-elect, is now in attendance," he announced, "I ask that the oath of office be administered to him." With that, he bowed gracefully to La Follette, La Follette bowed gracefully back, and the two short senators marched grandly down the aisle arm-in-arm to the vice president's desk. Senator Robert Marion La Follette then placed his hand on a Bible and solemnly swore to support and defend the Constitution of the United States against all enemies, foreign and domestic.[7]

"LA FOLLETTE AND SPOONER IN TRUCE," crowed the *Chicago Daily Tribune* the next day, recounting their subsequent lunch together with their wives. The vaunted dignity of the Senate was, for the moment, preserved.[8]

THE EVENING OF LA FOLLETTE'S INAUGURATION, he and Belle attended a gala soiree at the White House. The annual reception for the diplomatic corps was the grandest pageant in Washington. Ambassadors and attachés draped themselves in full regalia for the event—swords, sashes, furs, feathers, jewels, medals, and ribbons galore. Americans were fascinated by the spectacle—on the one hand, awed that the world's great powers had privileged their young nation with so much pomp and finery, on the other hand, boastful of their contrasting republican simplicity.[9]

All the well-connected families in Washington turned out for the event. The men dressed conventionally enough, but the women indulged in ostentatious satin and lace, diamonds and gold. The papers catalogued their costumes as breathlessly as modern-day tabloids describe Hollywood celebrities on the red carpet. Belle La Follette's modest gown did not make the society papers, but Bob was conscious of the fascination he and his wife provoked among the guests. "We were quite observed during the evening," he confided to a friend afterward. "I think if I had been a wild boar, led about by Mrs. La Follette with a rope fastened to my hind leg, as a pair, we would not have been more observed."[10]

At 9 p.m. sharp, the bugles sounded, and the Marine Band played "Hail, Columbia." A grinning President Theodore Roosevelt descended the massive marble staircase with his wife, Edith, resplendent in a blue satin gown and diamond necklace, a bouquet of lilies and violets in her hand. The cabinet members and their wives followed in procession as the Roosevelts took their appointed places in the Blue Room, decked with blue wallpaper, blue curtains, and blue furnishings. As hundreds of distinguished guests passed through the receiving line, the President chirped to each in turn that he was "Dee-lighted!" to see them.[11]

When the La Follettes' turn came, Roosevelt's enthusiasm bounded even higher. He declared himself "dee-lighted, overjoyed!" proclaiming that it was one of the greatest pleasures of his life to see his old friends again. He introduced Belle to Edith and recalled their old camaraderie from the 1880s, when La Follette was a young congressman and Roosevelt a civil service commissioner.

Later that evening, the La Follettes met another old acquaintance. Big Bill Taft came barreling across the room to greet them. It had been 15 years since they had seen him. Belle noticed that he had grown about one-third larger since then. He had recently returned from the Philippines, where he had served as governor-general, to become the US secretary of war. There were rumors that Roosevelt was grooming him for the presidency.[12]

WASHINGTON, DC, JANUARY 9, 1906

The pomp and celebration did little to mitigate the tension that had enveloped Washington that winter. In the Senate, Jonathan Dolliver struggled to get his railroad bill through the Committee on Interstate Commerce. Nelson Aldrich and Stephen Elkins refused to let him report it out without amendment. They wanted language to require court review of the Interstate Commerce Commission's (ICC) proposed shipping rates. Dolliver refused. So did Roosevelt. "I will not accept it," the President declared, "under any circumstances."[13]

With the Dolliver bill mired in the Senate committee, Roosevelt turned to the House, in which his agreement with Speaker Cannon still held. On January 9, the Republican members of the House Committee on Interstate Commerce held a secret conference at which they agreed to draft an identical bill to Dolliver's. Committee chairman William Hepburn, a veteran congressman from Iowa, would sponsor it. His close relationship with the Speaker and his reputation as a Standpatter would ease its passage in the House. But it would still have to survive the Senate to become law.[14]

WASHINGTON, DC, JANUARY 28, 1906

As the newest senator in Washington, Bob La Follette was last in line to choose a seat. Republicans so outnumbered Democrats that junior Republican senators had to sit across the aisle in a slice of seats dubbed the Cherokee Strip after a thin belt of Indian territory in Oklahoma. At Senator Spooner's urging, he took a seat at the back to avoid drafts from the door.[15]

His office was even more remote. To reach it, he had to descend several dim flights of stairs into the subcellar of the Capitol. As he navigated a narrow winding passage stacked with cordwood, the air became warm, then hot. A boiler roared and hissed in its lair behind the wall. Then there was a door and a prim little sign: "Committee on the Improvement of the Potomac River Front." When Bob learned that he was to chair the committee, he assumed that it would be responsible for cleaning up the entire Potomac, but he soon discovered that the committee had never actually met or had a bill referred to it.[16]

He busied himself with the Committee on Indian Affairs, his only notable committee appointment, but itched to join the railroad fight. He was not impressed with the Dolliver-Hepburn bill. The legislation would empower the ICC to correct specific instances of rate discrimination between competing shippers, but it would do little to reduce overall shipping rates. He believed that the railroads were gouging customers across the board, generating tremendous profits for shareholders at the expense of ordinary consumers who had to pay inflated prices for goods due to high shipping costs. The Dolliver-Hepburn bill, he argued, "never touched the heart of the matter, namely, whether the commission should be given the power to determine what was a reasonable rate and to enforce its decisions."

He had some ideas about how to improve the bill, but no one seemed to want to hear them. He had hoped that Roosevelt would consult him because of his legislative experience in Wisconsin, but he hadn't received any White House invitations since the diplomatic reception. He was convinced that the President had been warned about his "dangerous and extreme" ideas.[17]

In late January, Lincoln Steffens came to Washington. Since meeting La Follette, he seemed to have shed some of his world-weary cynicism. His recent articles were more hopeful, less caustic. He joined Bob and Belle for dinner one night with a few friends. The discussion soon turned to the railroad problem, and Bob expressed his concerns about the pending rate bill.

"I have been seeing the President," Steffens volunteered, "and I am going to suggest to him that you have gone all over this question in Wisconsin, that you have been at it for years up there, and it will do no harm for him to have a talk with you about it."[18]

Before long, Bob La Follette received an invitation to the White House. He arrived at 10 p.m. on a Sunday evening in late January—"when newspaper reporters were not about," he quipped, "and there was no one to take note of the fact or publish to the country that the President was conferring with so dangerous a person."

According to his recollection, the discussion lasted two hours. He tried to impress on Roosevelt his conviction that the Dolliver-Hepburn bill would do little to reduce overall shipping rates. To strengthen the legislation, he urged the President to push for additional ICC authority to audit the railroad companies' books and to set and enforce "reasonable rates" based on a physical valuation of the businesses.

"But you can't get any such bill as that through this Congress," Roosevelt objected.

"That is not the first consideration, Mr. President," La Follette recalled telling him. He laid out a strategy for broad political reform that differed fundamentally from Roosevelt's gradual approach. "If you will send a special message to Congress right now," he advised, "you may not get it through this session, but you have got an organized sentiment that has been building up for nine years; and if you lay down clearly, so the public can understand just what ought to be done, and this Congress fails to act, in the next Congress you will have the people back of you more strongly than ever."[19]

In his autobiography, La Follette recorded that he departed the White House at midnight. At 2 a.m., Lincoln Steffens telephoned him at home to congratulate him. "I have just left the President and he said you did a bully job," he said.[20]

But Steffens remembered the incident differently. In his own autobiography, he wrote that he had as much trouble persuading La Follette to come to the meeting as he did Roosevelt. Their eventual encounter, he recalled, was brief and awkward. "When they met at the White House," he wrote, "it was comic. They began to back off from each other before they met; their hands touched, but their eyes, their bodies, their feet walked away. I don't recall a word that either of them said; they probably said nothing but 'glad to meet you.' It was all over in a second, and I was outside with La Follette, who hurried away."[21]

It is difficult to reconcile these two different accounts. Both were recorded without notes years after the encounter. La Follette's recollections were much more specific in terms of chronology and content. On the other hand, he described Roosevelt as a "very good listener," perhaps the only time in history that such a compliment was paid to a man who famously never stopped talking.

Despite the inconsistency, both accounts speak to the fundamental divisions between the senator and the President. One addresses their contrasting political strategies. The other illustrates their personal friction. Each would play its role in the days to come.

WASHINGTON, DC, FEBRUARY 9, 1906

Ray Stannard Baker had some advice for the President as well. Roosevelt had scheduled him in during his morning shave—one of his tactics for

making use of every minute in the day. While the barber applied the
lather, Roosevelt held forth on the railroad situation. He was delighted
that the Hepburn bill had passed the House. Even the recalcitrant
Pennsylvanians had voted for it this time. But over in the Senate, the bill
was still trapped in committee. He concluded that the Standpatters were
not negotiating in good faith, and he pinned his hopes on Democratic
support for the Dolliver bill.[22]

While the President pontificated, Baker waited patiently for the barber to apply the razor. The threat of laceration finally quieted the oration
long enough to permit an interruption. He complimented Roosevelt on
his success in the House and called the railroad bill "the most important"
legislation of his presidency, but he added that it was only a first step.

Roosevelt swiveled his head in agitation, confounding the barber. "If
this is the first step," he demanded, "where do you think we are going?"

"You may not agree with me, Mr. President," Baker replied, "but
I believe that we cannot stop short of government ownership of the
railroads."

Heedless of the razor, Roosevelt objected furiously. No one knew
better than he how "inefficient and undependable" federal employees
were. Government ownership of free enterprise would be "a disaster," he
warned.

But Baker remarked that popular opinion was moving in that direction, particularly in the western states. "The people out there are getting
beyond you on these questions," he ventured.

"Here is the thing you must bear in mind," Roosevelt retorted indig-
nantly, "I do not represent public opinion: I represent the public. There
is a wide difference between the two, between the real interests of the
public and the public's opinion of those interests."[23]

WASHINGTON, DC, FEBRUARY 21, 1906

Such paternalistic sentiments were not far from those of Nelson
Aldrich, who believed "that the masses of people did not know
what they wanted or what was best for them in the way of legislation." Aldrich's approach to government-industrial relations was also
remarkably close to Roosevelt's. In contrast to the "root hog or die"
laissez-faire principles that Uncle Joe glorified, Aldrich believed in
collaboration between government and business. He just insisted
that government play a subordinate role—an eager helper not a stern
overseer. The tariff system offered a prime example of such collaboration. Before writing a tariff bill, Aldrich would consult with industry
experts, who would recommend import duties to benefit their respective industries. Then he would follow their recommendations to the

best of his ability. By contrast, the Dolliver-Hepburn rate bill did not serve the railroad companies, it shackled them, and so Aldrich fought it with all his power.[24]

Railroad regulation was not the only threat to corporate autonomy. A persistent piece of legislation known as the Pure Food and Drug bill was also pending before the Senate. Pure food advocates had been clamoring for years about mislabeled and adulterated substances—whiskey blended with ethyl alcohol, domestic cottonseed oil sold as virgin Italian olive oil, rancid meat deodorized with chemicals, and patent medicines mixed with toxic ingredients. Such deceptions were not new, but they had become more prevalent as the country industrialized. German-trained chemists employed the latest scientific advances to treat foods with undisclosed additives. States and municipalities struggled to regulate industries that increasingly transcended state lines.[25]

Aldrich, who knew more about the grocery business than anyone in the Senate, was more concerned about crusading federal regulators than mislabeled food. In a rare speech from the Senate floor, he warned that the pure food bill jeopardized "the liberty of all the people of the United States…Are we going to take up the question as to what a man shall eat and what a man shall drink," he asked rhetorically, "and put him under severe penalties if he is eating or drinking something different from what the chemists of the Agricultural Department think it is desirable for him to eat or drink?"[26]

With the assistance of Senator Spooner, Aldrich kept the pure food legislation bottled up for three years straight, but its advocates kept pushing. In 1905, pure food advocates persuaded Roosevelt to endorse their cause. He obliged with an explicit request in his annual message. Senator Weldon Heyburn of Idaho answered the request with yet another pure food bill, though there seemed little prospect of success.[27]

But in February 1906, Aldrich astonished everyone with a sudden about-face. Senator Albert Beveridge of Indiana recounted the circumstances years later. "The Senate was in a jam and public feeling had become intense," he recalled. "Aldrich came to me one afternoon and said: 'Tell Heyburn if he asks consideration for the Pure Food bill there will be no objection.'" Aldrich offered no explanation for his change of heart; Beveridge assumed that he wanted to focus on the railroad bill and was counting on the House to kill the pure food bill later. "So I went to Heyburn," he continued, "and told him to bring up the Pure Food bill instantly and the Old Guard would not block him. Heyburn could not believe it and said he was tired of being made a fool of by asking useless consideration which he had asked so many times before. However, I insisted, for I never knew Aldrich to promise anything that he did not make good. I told Heyburn there was no time to waste, and to act without any questions."[28]

On February 21, the Pure Food and Drug bill passed the Senate 63 to 4. Aldrich abstained. The legislation then moved over to the House Committee on Interstate and Foreign Commerce, where old William Hepburn of Iowa took charge of it. And there it would remain, quietly fermenting for the next four months.

WASHINGTON, DC, FEBRUARY 24, 1906

At the end of February, Senator Dolliver finally convinced the Democratic members of Committee on Interstate Commerce to help him report out the railroad rate bill. Without a committee majority, Aldrich couldn't stop them, but he still had cards to play. If the bill had to go to the Senate, he would make sure that the double-crossing Dolliver was not in charge of it. After the committee voted in favor of the bill, Aldrich announced, "This bill is being reported by the vote of the four Democrats and two Republicans present. It's a Democratic measure, and, if Senator Elkins cannot report it as chairman of the committee, I move that Mr. Tillman, the senior Democrat, report it."[29]

The Democrats, who had sided with Dolliver to report out the bill, now sided with Aldrich to turn it over to Benjamin R. Tillman.

The trick brought tremendous amusement to Roosevelt's opponents, for everyone knew how much the President detested "Pitchfork Ben," the one-eyed, thick-necked bulldog from South Carolina. Tillman had earned his nickname by threatening to plunge a pitchfork through President Cleveland's ribs in 1896. He was a radical populist—precisely the kind of man Roosevelt kept warning people about. He was also an unbridled racist. "We have done our level best," Tillman boasted of his state's success at disenfranchising black voters, "We have scratched our heads to find out how we could eliminate the last one of them...We stuffed ballot boxes. We shot them. We are not ashamed of it."[30]

Roosevelt openly despised Tillman for his racism as well as his demagoguery, and he refused to let him in the White House.

"Is it not most appropriate," Aldrich smirked when his motion passed, "that this administration bill should be placed in the hands of the president's dearest friend, Senator Tillman?"[31]

WASHINGTON, DC, MARCH 1906

As the tardy winter of 1906 hurled late snowstorms at the capital and spread a thin blanket of ice over the Potomac, Senator Tillman gathered Democratic votes for the Hepburn railroad bill that no longer bore Dolliver's name. It was a daunting task, for the Democrats were as divided as the Republicans. Meanwhile, the Standpatters launched their counterattack with John Coit Spooner and Philander Knox of Pennsylvania leading the charge. Following Aldrich's and Elkins's strategy, they proposed amendments to subject the ICC rulings to court review.[32]

"The political pot is boiling frantically," Roosevelt wrote to his son Kermit, "which is another way of saying that the fight on the rate bill is growing hot. I cannot tell how it will come out yet; but inasmuch as the Republican leaders have tried to betray me and it, I am now trying to see if I cannot get it through in the form I want by the aid of some fifteen or twenty Republicans added to most of the Democrats."[33]

For the sake of the bill, he swallowed his enmity and dispatched an emissary to treat with Pitchfork Ben. Tillman proved receptive; he and Roosevelt began quietly collaborating to build a bipartisan majority. To appease the Standpatters and ensure the bill's constitutionality, they agreed to wording that would allow for some kind of court oversight, but they determined to limit it as much as possible.

The Senate battle then shifted to how much oversight the courts should have. The Standpatters pushed for *broad review* that would grant railroad-friendly judges the final say on the ICC's rate reductions. Reformers argued for *narrow review* so that the ICC could determine rates with minimal interference from the courts. For weeks, the senators took turns launching rhetorical missiles into each other's camps, but neither side could muster a majority.[34]

Journalists puzzled over the odd alliances that had produced the stalemate. Roosevelt had teamed up with Tillman. Republican Standpatters had joined with Bourbon Democrats.

"A political realignment is going on here," Lincoln Steffens remarked thoughtfully. "There is a great slanting crack across the face of both the old parties." The new schism differed from the old ethnic and regional rivalries, but no one was quite sure how to articulate the essential disagreement, not even the leaders of the alliances. "Mr. Aldrich had names for the two sides," Steffens continued, "it was he that first used the word 'conservatives' for those who stood with him in both the old parties, and he waved away all others as 'radicals.' He said that the division was not one of principle, but he couldn't or wouldn't describe what it was. And neither could the President. Yet these two men are the leaders at present of what may turn out to be two new American' parties."

"And we need two new political parties," he added, "One isn't enough."[35]

WASHINGTON, DC, MARCH 15, 1906

President Roosevelt did not share Steffens's enthusiasm for any new parties. He was struggling to keep his Grand Old Party in one piece, and Steffens's speculations did not help matters. He was coming to think that these "exposure journalists" had gone too far. Steffens and Baker were all right, but they had inspired a gang of imitators who reveled in sensationalism and slander. There was Upton Sinclair, the socialist, who had written that novel about the meatpacking industry. Roosevelt thought there was some truth in it, and he planned to investigate, but the socialist propaganda disturbed him almost as much as Sinclair's nauseating descriptions of mass-produced beef. Then there was David Graham Phillips, another novelist. He was methodically smearing the reputations of US senators for one of William Randolph Hearst's rags in a sensationalist series called "Treason of the Senate." Roosevelt worried that such articles had contributed to "a very unhealthy condition of excitement and irritation in the popular mind."

He expressed his concerns to Bill Taft in a letter. Something should be done, he wrote, "to combat the great amount of evil which, mixed with a little good, a little truth, is contained in the outpourings of the *Cosmopolitan*, of *McClure's* . . . of David Graham Phillips, of Upton Sinclair. Some of these are socialists; some of them merely lurid sensationalists; but they are all building up a revolutionary feeling which will most probably take the form of a political campaign."

To overcome such demagoguery, he believed the Republicans must nominate a strong, levelheaded presidential nominee in 1908. "Under such circumstances," he urged Taft, "you would be the best possible leader, and with your leadership we could rest assured that only good methods would prevail." Though Roosevelt was willing to appoint Taft to the Supreme Court if that's what he wanted, he urged him to forgo the opportunity and run for president instead.[36]

NEW YORK, NEW YORK, APRIL 7, 1906

Ray Stannard Baker bumped into a friend on the street one spring day. "Hello, Muckraker," teased the friend. Baker wondered what he was talking about. What was a muckraker?[37]

He found out soon enough. President Roosevelt had coined the term in a speech at the Gridiron Club in Washington on March 17. According to club rules, journalists were prohibited from publishing anything spoken within, but news of the speech had leaked out. Baker learned that Roosevelt had denounced investigative journalists, comparing them to a character from John Bunyan's *Pilgrim's Progress* who was pathologically obsessed with sweeping up dust and filth—the Man with the Muck Rake.[38]

Baker was aghast. Hadn't he done the President a great service by stoking public interest in railroad abuses? Why had Roosevelt so often praised his investigative work only to denounce exposure articles at the Gridiron dinner? To make matters worse, he learned that Roosevelt planned to repeat the speech for the general public at the upcoming dedication of a new congressional office building.

"My Dear President, I have been much disturbed at the report of your proposed address," he wrote. "Even admitting that some of the so-called 'exposures' have been extreme, have they not, as a whole, been honest and useful?" Baker protested that if Roosevelt used his authority to attack the magazines, he would end up destroying the honest journalists who endeavored to expose misconduct to "light and air."

"My Dear Mr. Baker," Roosevelt replied, "I want to 'let in the light air,' but I do not want to let in sewer gas. If a room is fetid and the windows are bolted, I am perfectly contented to knock out the windows; but I would not knock a hole into the drain pipe."[39]

ROOSEVELT WENT AHEAD WITH HIS ANTICIPATED address on April 14. Baker read about it the following day. The entire Congress had assembled outside to hear the speech along with the Cabinet, Supreme Court, diplomatic corps, military officers, brothers of various Masonic orders, and thousands of spectators. Baker could picture his friend the President standing on a rostrum next to the huge marble cornerstone of the future Cannon House Office Building, smashing fist on palm as he hurled lightning bolts at the mortals who had dared to violate his justice. He charged Baker's colleagues with "knavery," "mendacity," "hysterical sensationalism," "violent emotionalism," and "gross and reckless assaults on character." He called exposure articles "one of the most potent forces for evil" and blamed them for inflicting "untold damage to the country as a whole." As he fulminated, the senators and congressmen answered the presidential rebukes with laughter and applause.

Roosevelt did not limit his opprobrium to journalists, however. By the end of his half-hour speech, he had also denounced the "hot-headed zealot," the "impracticable visionary," "the politician who betrays his trust," "the big businessman who makes or spends his fortune in illegitimate or corrupt ways," and "the wild agitators against the entire existing order." He again called for regulation of the railroads, provoking more laughter from the congressmen. But then he shocked them into silence by proposing income and inheritance taxes to reduce "fortunes swollen beyond all healthy limits."[40]

Roosevelt's new reform proposals did little to mollify Baker, however. Crushed by what he saw as betrayal, he lost his faith in his friend. "I met the President many times afterward and there were numerous exchanges of letters," he wrote, "but while I could wonder at his remarkable versatility of mind, and admire his many robust human qualities, I could never again give him my full confidence, nor follow his leadership."[41]

WASHINGTON, DC, APRIL 17, 1906

Belle Case La Follette fidgeted on a wooden pew in the Family Gallery, watching her husband on the Senate floor below. He sat at his desk at the rear of the Cherokee Strip, nurturing a stack of papers. It had been only three months since he swore the oath of office, too soon for a freshman senator to take the floor, but Bob cared little for the Senate's rigid traditions. The galleries were crowded; people knew that Fighting Bob was scheduled to speak.[42]

"Mr. President," he began, addressing the Senate's presiding officer by formal title, "The opponents of the regulation of railway rates and services have skillfully conducted this debate almost from the beginning upon constitutional grounds." By focusing on legalities, he argued, they had distracted the Senate and the public from the heart of the matter: the government's sovereign obligation to maintain public highways open to all.[43]

While he spoke, the other senators stood and sauntered toward the cloakroom. Were they deliberately hazing him, Belle wondered. Perhaps they were just distracted. There had been news over the wire of a dreadful earthquake in San Francisco. But so many senators had left, and their departures seemed so ostentatious. Soon, only a few Democrats and two Republicans remained in chamber. Bob paused and looked around at the vacant seats. When he resumed, his voice was so low that it was hard to hear him. "Mr. President," he said, "I can not be wholly indifferent to the fact that Senators by their absence at this time indicate their want of interest in what I may have to say upon this subject. The public is interested. Unless this important question is rightly settled seats now temporarily vacant may be permanently vacated by those who have the right to occupy them at this time."

Belle froze, astonished that her husband dared to go so far. Then she breathed. Of course, he was right. He would hound his opponents from the Senate as he had in Wisconsin. All around her, people applauded in the galleries. Below, she could see the remaining senators jump to their feet. John Kean of New Jersey, an Aldrich man who seemed to have been left on guard, demanded that the galleries be cleared, but the presiding officer only admonished the visitors to remain quiet.[44]

La Follette continued his speech. He enumerated the flaws of the Hepburn Bill and promised amendments to address them. In particular, he insisted that the ICC should have authority to fix reasonable rates based on a comprehensive valuation of the railroad properties. After a while, the senators began to drift back into the chamber. Some read or talked among themselves, but others began to pay attention, particularly Senator Dolliver of Iowa. When La Follette concluded his maiden speech, the applause again flooded down from the galleries, but this time, the chamber was full of senators, many of whom shook his hand and congratulated him.

Belle wrote to her daughter, "Papa was as free and at home as though he had been in the Senate twenty years...Whatever comes, he has established himself right in the beginning, as the peer of any man on the floor of the Senate, and a *new kind* of leader."[45]

WASHINGTON, DC, MAY 4, 1906

Theodore Roosevelt wanted no more accolades for Senator La Follette. The constant plaudits from Steffens and Baker were bad enough. Now Dolliver had come to the White House singing about how La Follette's speech would help pass the Hepburn bill. Even the *New York Times*, of all papers, had praised La Follette's long-winded screed. Were they blind to the man's rank self-interest? The Standpatters would never accept any of his proposed amendments, as La Follette surely knew. Roosevelt surmised that his real motive was not "to get something good and efficient done, but to make a personal reputation for himself by screaming for something he knew perfectly well could not be had."[46]

Roosevelt had enough problems without that "shifty self-seeker" stirring the pot. The Hepburn bill was in trouble. Senator Tillman had failed to gather enough Democratic votes to defeat the opposition, and the bill had stalled. With only a few weeks left in the session, it looked as if there would be no bill at all. Roosevelt decided that there was no point in traveling any further down the road with Tillman. He would have to take what he could get from the Standpatters.

Not long after La Follette's speech, Roosevelt quietly reached out to Senator W. B. Allison. The elder patriarch of the Big Four was more flexible than Aldrich on these matters. His home state of Iowa had turned radical, and his protégé, Dolliver, had defected to the reformers. During the rate bill deliberations, Allison unexpectedly broke with Aldrich to support narrow court review, and he seemed anxious to come to an arrangement that would preserve Republican unity. "I am not at all sure," Roosevelt wrote to him, "but that the easy way will be to come right back to the bill as it passed the House, and with very few unimportant amendments to pass it as it stands."[47]

The two men discussed a preliminary compromise on the court oversight question. But it was not Allison who showed up at the White House at the beginning of May with a proposal in hand. It was Aldrich. The senator from Rhode Island explained that Allison was ill, so he had come to deliver the compromise amendment that his friend had drafted. The new wording empowered the courts to "enjoin, set aside, annul, or suspend any order" of the ICC.[48]

On May 4, Roosevelt telephoned the press gallery. He wanted the newsmen to come to the White House at 3 p.m. for a statement. When they arrived, he proudly announced his support for the Allison amendment, which would allow the Hepburn bill to proceed at last. He explained that the new court review proviso was precisely what he had wanted all along. As he was elaborating, Richard Lindsay of the *Kansas City Star* interrupted him, "But, Mr. President, what we want to know is why you surrendered."

Roosevelt was flummoxed. He hadn't expected that, not from an admirer like Lindsay. He resumed his statement without answering the question directly. Though he allowed that the Allison amendment left some of the details vague, he was confident that the judges would limit themselves to narrow oversight.[49]

THE NEXT DAY, CHAOS ENSUED. AS ALDRICH AND Spooner cheerfully distributed the text of the amendment to the other senators, Dolliver went to see Allison, who was still recovering at home from his illness. He reported back that Allison knew nothing about the amendment and denied writing it.[50]

Meanwhile, Tillman complained about surrender and betrayal. He told the press that he had been a few days from winning a better bill—if Roosevelt had only kept his mouth shut. His ally, Senator Joseph Bailey of Texas, was even more insulting. "I love a brave man," Bailey drawled, "I love a fighter, and the President of the United States is both on occasion, but he can yield with as much alacrity as any man who ever went to battle...Let us have no more talk in the Senate and in the country about this 'iron man.' He is clay, and very common clay at that."[51]

Tillman and Bailey revealed their secret negotiations with the President—how he had conspired with them to outflank the Standpatters and then double-crossed them. The allegations were detailed and sensational. Roosevelt fiercely denied them, calling the account a "deliberate and unqualified falsehood." The imputations would have been an affront to any president but none more than Roosevelt, whose reputation was founded on his upright character. He also had to repair his relations with

Spooner and Knox, who were said to be furious over his alleged remarks about them.[52]

But for all the fuss, the Hepburn bill went through in the end. After some haggling over terminology, the Senate passed the mysterious "Allison amendment," which its namesake continued to disown. The senators also had to deal with La Follette's numerous amendments, which they dismissed so abruptly that the chamber seemed to ring with their obliteration. Even Spooner was moved to protest the harsh treatment of his junior colleague, but that did nothing to save the amendments.[53]

On May 18, the bill finally came to a vote, passing the Senate 71 to 3. Only one Republican, Joseph Foraker of Ohio, opposed it. Roosevelt pronounced himself well satisfied with the result. "The rate bill is a fine piece of constructive legislation," he wrote to his son Kermit, "and all that has been done tends toward carrying out the principles I have been preaching."[54]

Roosevelt had reason enough to celebrate. Notwithstanding complaints that he might have pushed for stronger legislation, even Tillman acknowledged that without the President's strenuous efforts, there would have been no rate bill at all. A few years later, Roosevelt's gamble on vague language in the court oversight clause would also be vindicated. As he had predicted, the courts chose to refrain from any comprehensive supervision of ICC rulings. The commission was no longer a helpless appendage of the executive branch. It had teeth.[55]

Yet, its authority proved limited. Over the next few years, the ICC would alleviate some of the most egregious discrimination between competing shippers, but, as La Follette had anticipated, the Hepburn Act would do little to address the deeper structural imbalances in the industry and would not reduce railroad rates overall. That would take additional legislation.[56]

Two other bills pending that spring, however, would leave more enduring legacies.

WASHINGTON, DC, MAY 25, 1906

Senator Albert J. Beveridge of Indiana was one of those who believed that Roosevelt had capitulated to Aldrich. He was a recent convert to the railroad reformers' cause; his sudden defection from the Standpatters in February had surprised his colleagues. "We'll get you for this," Aldrich hissed under his breath when Beveridge announced his support for the Tillman bill.[57]

But Beveridge no longer saw Aldrich as the future of the Senate or the nation. He was young for a senator, only 43, and the gulf separating him from the party elders seemed to grow wider every session. He did not hate the Standpatters; he pitied them. "[T]he older politicians are like a bunch of belated travelers," he wrote to Roosevelt, "who have come to catch a train and stand on the platform waiting for it, when as a matter of fact the train has passed on a long while ago. Their watches are bad, that is all."[58]

Aldrich dismissed the western states' unrest as a temporary hysteria that must be quarantined until the fever passed. Beveridge believed otherwise. "I am coming to the conclusion that it is not a passing whim," he wrote to a friend, "but a great and natural movement such as occurs in this country, as our early history shows, once about every forty years." He dreamed of riding at the vanguard of this new movement and making a name for himself as a great reformer. To do that, he needed a cause of his own, some glorious crusade for the history books. He found it in a novel.[59]

The Jungle by Upton Sinclair was not a pleasant read. The prose sagged under its grim duties as Sinclair shoveled misery after misery onto the wretched heads of his characters—a family of impoverished meatpackers—in order to prod his readers into a revolutionary fervor. But it was not the sad plight of the meatpackers that shocked American readers. It was the meat. Sinclair had spent weeks exploring the stinking Packingtown district of Chicago, touring the facilities and interviewing the workers. He recorded the revolting underside of industrial meat production and presented it in sickening detail to his readers: diseased animals, rotten meat, cartilage, offal, and even poisoned rats chopped up, colored, deodorized, and shunted into cans or sausage casings for Americans' unknowing consumption.

The book was a sensation. It may not have persuaded many readers to overthrow the bourgeoisie, but it catalyzed a popular backlash against the meatpacking industry. Beveridge could harness that anger and turn it into legislation. He sent a copy of *The Jungle* to the White House.

Roosevelt, it turned out, had already read it. The President did not like Upton Sinclair, and he despised the book's socialist agitation, but he took the meatpacking allegations seriously and had sent two investigators, Charles Neill and James Bronson Reynolds, to corroborate the account. "Bully," he replied when Beveridge told him of his interest in an inspection bill, "but you'd better wait until Neill and Reynolds get back from Chicago."

Beveridge did. He also met with the secretary of agriculture, but he refused to let anyone else write the bill. He redrafted the legislation more than twenty times before introducing it to the Senate on May 21, three days after the passage of the Hepburn bill. The exhausted senators attached it to an agricultural appropriations bill and ushered it through the same week without a single dissenting vote.[60]

The agriculture bill then trundled down the hall and nestled itself into the welcoming arms of the House Committee on Agriculture—not far from the Pure Food and Drug bill, which was still buried in the embrace of the House Committee on Interstate and Foreign Commerce.

WASHINGTON, DC, MAY 26, 1906

"My Dear Mr. Wadsworth," Roosevelt wrote to the chairman of the House Agriculture Committee, "I am anxious to see you about the agricultural appropriation bill, providing for effective inspection and control over the packing industry." He informed Representative James Wadsworth of New York that he had recently read a "hideous" report from his investigators, Neill and Reynolds, which he was tempted to release to the public. He would hold off in order to avoid serious harm to the country's meat exports—provided that the House passed the agriculture bill. In case Wadsworth missed the threat, he repeated it. "I do not believe that you will have any doubt on the matter," he concluded. "If you have, I earnestly hope you will see me at once."[61]

Roosevelt had cause for concern. Wadsworth, a cattle rancher, had already made clear his objections to the bill. But Wadsworth was not his chief worry. Speaker Cannon had come to the White House with a couple of disgruntled Chicago congressmen in tow. They complained that the inspection bill would crush the meatpackers, who would be forced to pass the costs onto consumers. Higher prices would threaten US exports, they warned, which would hurt everyone.

Roosevelt could barely conceal his exasperation. Nothing, he warned them, would damage meat exports as much the Neill-Reynolds report. If European consumers found out what went on in the packinghouses, the meatpackers would certainly discover the meaning of hardship. He again threatened to publish the report if the House didn't pass the Senate bill. The meeting was over in half an hour.[62]

Roosevelt had more on his mind than the meat inspection bill. During his first term, the House had passed two variations of the pure food bill only to see them die in a Senate committee. Now that the Senate had finally passed pure food legislation of its own, the bill was stuck in a House committee. It was like some kind of shell game. The *Chicago Daily Tribune* warned that the legislation had been "put to soak" until the end of the congressional session.[63]

Roosevelt did not need to wonder who had scheduled the soaking. The whole country had come to appreciate the awesome extent of the Speaker's powers. In a small indirect way, Roosevelt had contributed to the situation. Back in the 1890s, he had supported Thomas Brackett Reed for House Speaker. So had La Follette; they worked together on the campaign. It was Reed who first expanded the Speaker's authority.

In those days, the Democratic opposition was fiercer than the docile crew sitting tamely in its little section of House chamber. Democrats of old used to "vanish" whenever the clerk called the roll for a bill they didn't like. They remained in their seats, of course, but by pretending to be absent, they denied the Speaker his quorum, and the vote could not proceed. Such obstructive tactics would tie up the House for weeks, effectively killing the legislation.

Reed changed all that. With the assistance of his trusted lieutenant, Joseph G. Cannon, he rewrote the House rules to eliminate the disappearing quorum trick. But it didn't end there. Under subsequent alterations, the Speaker gained the authority to select committee members and chairmen, refer bills to committees, schedule votes, and control the floor debate. With these powers, he could suppress or advance legislation at will.

The first time Reed blocked the disappearing quorum, screaming Democrats rushed the podium. "Fighting Joe" Wheeler charged from the back of the chamber by leaping from desk to desk like a mountain goat. A huge Democrat from Texas sat in his seat whetting a bowie knife on his boot. But Reed prevailed, and the Democrats were silenced. They came up with a new nickname for him after that: Czar Speaker.[64]

Yet, Reed's regime was a model of egalitarianism compared to Cannon's. There were no violent outbursts in Uncle Joe's House. The legislative process ticked along smoothly and harmoniously. No one had an opportunity to challenge him, even if they dared. "Every day there is a pretense of 'catching the Speaker's eye,'" the New York Times reported. "Men crowd around the desk and call for recognition, and the Speaker recognizes first one and then another to move the passage of a bill. This is a mere sham." According to the correspondent, Uncle Joe kept a pre-arranged list of all the congressmen he would recognize each day. Only those who were "subservient to the machine" made the list.[65]

President Roosevelt was no supplicant, but he could get no legislation through without the Speaker's approval. When he queried Cannon about the status of the Pure Food and Drug bill, the Speaker calmly replied that the bill was on the calendar, and the House would consider it any day that the majority wished to do so—as if he were nothing but the humble executor of the greater congressional will.[66]

WASHINGTON, DC, JUNE 4, 1906

At first, Roosevelt seemed to have more luck with meat inspection. After he threatened to release the Neill-Reynolds report, Cannon agreed to pass an inspection bill, and Representative Wadsworth went straight to work on it. But the draft he sent Roosevelt the following week made a number of alterations to Beveridge's bill: the government would pay for the inspections, not the meatpackers; canned food would not have to be dated; the courts would have oversight over the inspectors.

Roosevelt responded with cold fury, "I went over the changes stated to have been proposed by you very carefully," he wrote to Wadsworth, "I am sorry to have to say that it seems to me that each change is for the worse and that in the aggregate they are ruinous, taking away every particle of good from the suggested Beveridge amendment."[67]

Concluding that the House needed a harder shove, Roosevelt sent Congress a preliminary version of the Neill-Reynolds report. He prefaced it with a characteristic burst of presidential obloquy: "The conditions shown by even this short inspection to exist in the Chicago stock yards are revolting. It is imperatively necessary in the interest of health and of decency that they should be radically changed."

But after all the well-publicized threats and media leaks, the report itself seemed anticlimactic. Its account of filth and diseased animals in the packing plants was still disturbing but no longer surprising. Cannon shrugged them off with studied nonchalance. "I have not given much consideration to the proposed legislation," he told reporters, "Under the rules of the house it was referred to the committee on agriculture. My information is that that committee is giving it vigorous and careful consideration."[68]

As the committee proceeded to approve Wadsworth's changes, Roosevelt cast about for another big stick. He threatened to release more shocking details from the Neill-Reynolds report. He published his scathing letter to Wadsworth in the newspapers. He hinted that he might veto the bill and call a special congressional session to enact another one. But Wadsworth ignored his threats and publicly mocked his letter.[69]

WASHINGTON, DC, JUNE 18, 1906

After the public contretemps between Roosevelt and Wadsworth, Cannon reckoned that the quarrel had gone on long enough. The midterm elections were coming up. If the Republicans couldn't resolve their differences and settle the meat business, they would have some trouble come November.

Wadsworth was out of town when the Speaker went to the White House late one evening. He sat down alone with the President, and the two men haggled away the remaining elements of contention. The cans would not be dated, and the packers would not pay for inspections, but Cannon gave up court oversight and promised to pass the pure food bill. Forty-five minutes later, he emerged from the President's office with a deal. "I never felt better in my life," he beamed to the reporters waiting outside, "I do not think that we are going to have any trouble about meat—by meat I mean the agricultural bill. We will undoubtedly pass a satisfactory bill, and I hope that we will pass it this week."[70]

They passed it the next day with little debate and only one dissenting vote. As the bill sailed past, Democratic Minority Leader John Sharp Williams sardonically observed, "Of course, this legislation could not be defeated if I wanted to defeat it, and I do not, because, as I understand, the two real ruling authorities under this boasted American form of free government have consulted together about it and determined upon and here prescribed just exactly what shall be done, to wit, the President of the United States and the Speaker of the House of Representatives."[71]

WASHINGTON, DC, JUNE 30, 1906

The Pure Food and Drug bill passed a few days later, 240 to 17. Both bills went out to the joint committees, which briskly resolved the differences in favor of the House versions. The bills returned to the chambers and passed handily on June 30, the last day of the session.

In a parting press conference, Speaker Cannon lauded the legislation to which he had so recently and reluctantly consented, singling out the railroad rate, meat inspection, and pure food acts for praise. "In my judgment," he boasted, "the work done and the legislation enacted in the session just closed exceeds in importance, for the best interests of all the people of the republic, the work of any session during my thirty years of public life."

President Roosevelt also tipped his hat to the Congress with which he had grappled all term. "I would not be afraid to compare its record with that of any previous congress in our history," he enthused, "not alone for the wisdom, but for the disinterested high-mindedness which has controlled its action."[72]

All in all, it had been the most productive legislative term of his presidency, and he recognized that there would not be another like it during his tenure. "I do not expect to accomplish very much in the way of legislation after this Congress," he wrote to Kermit. "By next winter, people will begin to think more about the next man who is to be President; and then, too, by that time it is almost inevitable that the revulsion of feeling against me should have come. It is bound to come some time, and it is extraordinary that it has not come yet. So it is very satisfactory to me to have accomplished a good deal at this session."[73]

STOCKBRIDGE, MASSACHUSETTS, JUNE, 1906

Charles Sanger Mellen, president of the New Haven and Hartford Railroad, was accustomed to dealing with powerful men. They did not often show up at his house, though. At the beginning of the summer, Nelson Aldrich drove up to Mellen's sprawling estate on the banks of the Housatonic. He wanted to discuss the United Traction & Electric Company.[74]

Charles Mellen was a Morgan man. "I took orders from J. P. Morgan Sr.," he acknowledged. "I did as I was told." In the 1890s, he ran the Northern Pacific Railway, one of the properties Morgan tried to absorb into the Northern Securities Company. After Roosevelt broke up the trust, Morgan sent Mellen to the New Haven-Hartford with orders to forge a monopoly from various New England railroads and streetcar companies. In early 1906, Mellen began negotiating to acquire United Traction & Electric Company, Aldrich's trolley company in Providence. But the trolley directors' asking price was much too high, and Mellen pulled out of the negotiations.[75]

Aldrich came to Stockbridge to revive the deal. He stayed for half-an-hour. By the time he left, Mellen had agreed to resume negotiations. A few months later, the New Haven bought United Traction for $21 million, more than twice what it was worth. During a subsequent congressional investigation, Mellen conceded that the price was "unconscionable" but explained, "I was dealing with Nelson W. Aldrich. Do you think I got the stock of these railroads at par?"[76]

EVANSVILLE, INDIANA, JULY 7, 1906

When Washington's leaders decamped for the summer, La Follette returned to Wisconsin but only for a day. Income from his little farm and modest law practice would not cover his thousands of dollars in campaign debt. To supplement his government salary, he spent the summer speaking.[77]

It was the age of Chautauqua, an adult education movement that brought traveling speakers and musicians to towns across the country. Oblong tents with thick brown canvas skins sprouted from grassy fields like huge misshapen mushrooms. In contrast to the flashy white pavilions of circuses and hucksters, the drab Chautauqua tents promised to enlarge the mind and fortify the soul. Their distinguished lecturers held forth on weighty topics: science, literature, art, religion, and, of course, politics.[78]

In the summer of 1906, La Follette decided to experiment with a new format for his Chautauqua speeches. He wrote to Belle from Iowa, "I tried reading the roll calls on some of my amendments which were 'tabled' to see how it would go. It goes and some Senators will find a back fire to look after. I suppose they will think I am the meanest fellow ever to 'go and tell.'"[79]

Modern Americans are accustomed to political litmus tests. Organizers and fund-raisers often target lawmakers who fail to support their causes in key legislative votes. But a century ago, such tactics were unprecedented. Constituents often had no idea how their representatives voted on particular issues. To educate voters, La Follette revived the roll call strategy that had served him so well in Wisconsin. "I am going to read you a few roll calls to show you how your Senators voted," he would announce, "Some one ought to keep the public posted, and as no one seems to have the time, I am making a little tour around the country doing it myself." He traversed the Chautauqua circuit from New Jersey to Washington State, denouncing Republicans and Democrats alike who had voted against his amendments.

The *New York Times* chuckled over how La Follette hazed his hazers. "He carried Senatorial discourtesy so far that he has actually imperiled the re-election of some of the gentlemen who hazed him last Winter...When he got to Kansas he spread panic among the friends of [Senator] Long...In Minneapolis La Follette got Senator Nelson going around in circles and emitting loud cries...In New Jersey La Follette did his conscientious best to retire [Senator] Dryden to his chosen field of infant insurance."[80]

But La Follette was not after revenge. He was after legislation. The three bills that Uncle Joe had lauded as the most important in decades did not impress him, especially not the Hepburn Act. It seemed clear to him that the current Congress would never accomplish any serious reform. The way to achieve real change was to remake Congress. And the way to remake Congress was to educate and empower the people. "Publicity, discussion, and agitation," he maintained, "are necessary to accomplish any work of lasting benefit."[81]

NOVEMBER 4, 1906

Remaking Congress would require more than a summer's worth of agitation, however. The Republican Party so dominated the Legislature and the Standpatters so dominated the Republican Party that the prospect of building a viable reform coalition, let alone a reform majority, seemed infinitely remote in the autumn of 1906. In the November midterm election, the Republicans lost 28 seats in the House: a defeat but not a grievous one, for they still retained a large majority. The Senate elections would not be held until January, but it looked as if the Republicans might actually pick up some seats.

Nonetheless, the soil of American politics was unsteady. Another Republican feud had broken out into the open, in Iowa this time. At the state convention, the Progressive faction had prevailed over the Standpatter faction, reelecting La Follette's ally, Governor Albert B. Cummins. Representative James Wadsworth lost his seat in the House—the voters' reward for his resistance to meat inspection. Even Speaker Cannon faced an unexpectedly robust challenge. Samuel Gompers, president of the American Federation of Labor, named him an enemy of the workers because of his suppression of labor reforms and publicly campaigned for his removal. Though unsuccessful, Gompers' political offensive tarnished Uncle Joe's everyman image and signaled to the country that organized labor was developing into a potent electoral force.[82]

WASHINGTON, DC, DECEMBER 3, 1906

Into this uneasy stew, President Roosevelt poured his sixth annual message. He opened the address with a customary nod to America's unrelenting economic growth, but he tempered it this time with a warning. "As a nation we still continue to enjoy a literally unprecedented prosperity," he declared, "and it is probable that only reckless speculation and disregard of legitimate business methods on the part of the business world can materially mar this prosperity."

The caveat was so subtle that the press barely noticed. A sentence later, Roosevelt plunged into the body of the message, which included a raft of ambitious policy proposals—eight-hour workdays, a child labor law, income taxes, and currency reform—as well as the usual dose of moral censure—the "crafty corruptionist," the "sinister demagogue," the "violent agitator," the "wild and crooked savagery of a mob."[83]

Wall Street too paid little attention to Roosevelt's caveat. The Dow Jones average hovered confidently in the nineties, up ten points from a midyear slump. But at the very top of the banking hierarchy, a strange foreboding disturbed the House of Morgan. "There is plenty of money in the country everywhere except in New York," J. Pierpont

Morgan's son Jack wrote to his partners in London. He sensed something amiss but couldn't quite put his finger on it. "[T]he only really alarming thing about the situation," he added, groping for words, "appears to be a very undefined feeling that there is something wrong in New York."[84]

4

THE PANIC

What in hell does this howling in Wall Street amount to? The country don't care what happens to those damned speculators.

—Uncle Joe[1]

IT WAS HARD TO GET A LOAN IN OCTOBER. THE COTTON, TOBACCO, AND WHEAT FIELDS WERE bare and brown by then. The orchards had gone yellow-orange, shedding their apples and peaches to become ordinary groves of trees. In the still-green cornfields, farmers sheared the ears from their stalks, stripped the husks, and tossed the naked yellow cobs onto wagons. Mist-snorting horses dragged the loaded vehicles to market towns where laborers heaved the loads onto railcars and steamboats to join the great migration of fruits, vegetables, grains, and cloth fibers. The river of produce flowed to the cities for workers to bake into bread, roll into cigars, sew into clothing, crush into cans, or bundle into packages.[2]

Paper migrated in the opposite direction. All year long, great green stacks of it gathered in reservoirs in the steel vaults of New York banks. Come autumn, the paper began to flow, surging across the Hudson and branching out to regional banks in a torrent before splitting into a million forks and trickling into the pockets of farmers and merchants like some immense river delta.

By late October, New York's supply of available paper currency was nearly dry. The banks were solvent and held plenty of assets, but they had no cash to loan. If you needed money at that time, you would have to pay high interest rates to get it—if you could get it at all. If you couldn't get it, your business might collapse. If your business collapsed, your investors and creditors might need loans themselves, and they might have just as much trouble getting them, and their businesses might also collapse. As the contagion spread, the magnificent New York banks that seemed so healthy the week before might pale and swoon when their loans went bad one after another. Then everyone would go racing to recover the valuable paper they had given the banks for safekeeping.

But in October, there would not be a bank in New York with enough paper to satisfy everyone who wanted it. And that's when the panic would set in.[3]

WASHINGTON, DC, JANUARY 13, 1903

Representative Charles N. Fowler of New Jersey was obsessed with currency. He had been elected in 1894 at the peak of a terrible depression. A panic had started it. An ambitious rope company tried to corner the hemp market. It failed. The failure precipitated a stock market slump, which led to bank runs, which wrecked the economy and doomed Americans to four years of misery—the worst depression since the nation's founding.[4]

The source of the problem, Fowler believed, was *inelastic* currency. When the demand for money surged, there was no way to enlarge the supply to meet it. Banks might be flush with stocks, bonds, and other securities, but they couldn't lend without currency. Companies might be stable and prosperous, but without cash, they couldn't expand their operations or even pay their employees. Investors couldn't trade, and consumers couldn't buy. During currency shortages, the economy was particularly susceptible to bank panics, stock market crashes, and other disruptions.

In Fowler's day, there were four types of paper currency in circulation: gold certificates, silver certificates, US notes, and bank notes. Gold and silver certificates were essentially paper receipts for gold and silver coins. Holders could redeem them at face value from the Treasury. Since these certificates were backed by actual metal reserves, they did not fluctuate with the currency demand.

US notes, commonly known as *greenbacks*, made up a smaller portion of American currency. The federal government guaranteed the notes but did not explicitly back them with gold or silver. Greenbacks were elastic in principle—the Treasury could always print more—but Congress had fixed greenback circulation at $346 million, so these too were inelastic.[5]

Fowler certainly didn't want the government to print more greenbacks. If anything, he wanted to eliminate US notes entirely and take the federal government out of the money business. Instead, he focused on the fourth form of paper currency: bank notes. At that time, big banks still printed their own proprietary notes. The notes looked like greenbacks but bore the name of the issuing bank in bold block letters. They also exhibited the reassuring words, SECURED BY UNITED STATES BONDS DEPOSITED WITH THE TREASURER OF THE UNITED STATES. To issue legal tender, the banks had to back the notes by purchasing US bonds. In return, the federal government guaranteed the notes if the bank should fail.[6]

In theory, bank notes were more elastic than gold certificates and greenbacks. The banks could issue more currency by buying more bonds. But when interest rates were high, which happened whenever money was tight, the low-yielding government bonds were unprofitable, and the banks were reluctant to purchase more of them. Even when they were willing, the process took too long to address urgent crises.

In order to increase the elasticity of bank notes, Fowler proposed to release the banks from the federal bond requirement. Under his *asset currency* plan, banks could issue notes backed by various securities in the same way they backed their loans. When money was tight, the banks could issue new bank notes at will in proportion to their total assets.[7]

Fowler had introduced his first version of the bill in 1897, but it went nowhere. Three years later, he became the chairman of the House Committee on Banking and Currency, a much stronger position from which to advance the legislation. His committee reported out a second version of the bill in January 1903, the midpoint of Theodore Roosevelt's first term.[8]

But two formidable obstacles conspired to prevent the bill from becoming law. The first was Senator Nelson Aldrich.

WASHINGTON, DC, FEBRUARY 9, 1903

Aldrich's allegiances lay with the New York banking community, particularly J. Pierpont Morgan. Morgan and his colleagues also wanted a more elastic currency, but they were not enthusiastic about Fowler's solution. As America's largest federal bondholders, they effectively controlled the national supply of bank notes. Fowler's asset currency scheme would enable competitors in Chicago and other Western cities to issue more notes and possibly destabilize the currency.

So a few weeks after Fowler reported his bill to the House, Aldrich produced an alternative bill in the Senate. Instead of allowing more currency to be printed, his bill enabled the US Treasury to deposit its gold reserves in private banks. Though the bill did not create new currency, the gold deposits would free up cash that the banks were holding in reserve. It effectively increased the money supply by putting more currency into active circulation. "So necessary and important are its provisions," Aldrich declared when he introduced the legislation, "that I believe the bill will pass without material opposition."[9]

His prediction proved somewhat optimistic. Currency reform advocates condemned the bill as a feeble half-measure, noting that the Treasury could already deposit gold in private banks and in fact did so every autumn as a precaution. Western bankers objected that the legislation would exclusively benefit New York banks, the presumed recipients of the gold deposits. Populists attacked a provision that would allow banks to guarantee the gold deposits with railroad bonds, denouncing it as a giveaway to the railroad companies.[10]

But the coup de grace to both the Aldrich and Fowler bills came from another executioner.

DANVILLE, ILLINOIS, JULY 11, 1903

"As far as the currency is concerned the country is in very good condition just now," Representative Joseph G. Cannon told a reporter during an interview in his hometown of Danville. He would not be elected Speaker for another four months, but the papers were already introducing him as "the next speaker." Uncle Joe waved away Aldrich's concerns about waning business confidence and Fowler's premonitions of disaster. "Business conditions are splendid," he enthused, "crops are fine and our foreign markets are good...I cannot see anything but good times ahead."[11]

Over the summer and early fall, Roosevelt and the Big Four senators tried to coax Cannon into endorsing some version of Aldrich's bill, but he steadfastly refused to sanction any "rubber currency," as he called it. In November, the House elected him Speaker, and the other Republican leaders resigned themselves to the status quo. "The integrity of our currency is beyond question," Roosevelt announced in his December annual address, "and under present conditions it would be unwise and unnecessary to attempt a reconstruction of our entire monetary system."[12]

Those conditions persisted for another three years, and the economy grew vigorously despite seasonal currency shortages. But in 1906, something happened to upset the balance.

SAN FRANCISCO, CALIFORNIA, DECEMBER 14, 1906

First Assistant Secretary of the Treasury James B. Reynolds admired the Californians' pluck. Eight months after the great earthquake of 1906, San Francisco was swiftly rebuilding. "If I can be of service to you," he offered a group of businessmen, "let me assure you that I will do all in my power to assist you in rebuilding your city." His words echoed though the burned-out shell of the Merchants Exchange. Construction workers had been pounding away when he arrived, but they paused while he spoke. The San Franciscans behaved as it were normal to deliver an address in a blackened ruin, as if there had never been such a thing as fire in the whole city.

After the speech, they took Reynolds up to the roof so he could observe the rebuilding efforts from above. "I can scarcely comprehend how all this was accomplished," he told them. "It proves the courage and enterprise of the Californians." Reynolds was a customs officer, so disaster relief was outside his purview, but he could see that there was no shortage of money for reconstruction. For all its devastation, the inferno had brought one blessing to the stricken city. The insurance companies did not indemnify for earthquake damage, but they did cover fire. There had even been reports of people burning down their damaged homes in order to collect compensation.[13]

The consequence was a great movement of gold from east to west. Most of it came from British insurance companies. More than sixty million dollars worth had shipped from London since the quake—fourteen percent of Britain's gold stock. The gold deficit unsettled the Bank of England, which raised interest rates to shore up British reserves. Between the construction in San Francisco and the usual harvest outflow, the New York banks were also pinched for capital. The week before Reynolds arrived in San Francisco, the Treasury secretary had warned Congress about "world-wide money stringency" and pleaded for legislation to expand the money supply.[14]

But First Assistant Secretary Reynolds wasn't concerned. Imports were up and customs revenue was higher than ever. "Oh no," he assured a reporter who inquired about his boss's apprehensions, "I don't think there will be a panic. I will go further, and say that I do not believe there will ever be another big panic."[15]

WASHINGTON, DC, JANUARY 1, 1907

Others were less sanguine. When journalists looked back over the course of the year, they noted that despite a roaring economy, the stock market finished the year ¾ of a point lower than it began. To explain the inconsistency, experts concluded that the economic boom and the reconstruction of San Francisco had sucked all the money from New York and pushed interest rates so high that the cost of borrowing deterred investors.[16]

Some Wall Street men blamed President Roosevelt's policies for depressing the stock market. The *New York Sun*, which had never been kind to him, presented itself as the voice of disgruntled industrialists in a series of caustic broadsides. The paper denounced "Government harassments" of the railroads and accused Roosevelt of seducing workers with radical ideas that encouraged "social jealousy" and "hatred of wealth." "The logical end of such proceedings," the editors prophesied, "is not pleasant to contemplate."[17]

Roosevelt dismissed the accusations. He believed the industrialists had brought enmity upon themselves by ignoring and mistreating the workers. The only way to protect the rich from the violent impulses of the mob, he argued, was for the government to gently correct society's imbalances. "I have furnished a safety-valve for the popular unrest and indignation," he explained in a letter. "[U]nless we want to see very violent convulsions in this country, and the certainty of ultimate adoption of State ownership and of very drastic measures against corporations, there must be a steady perseverance in the policy of control over corporations by the Government which I have advocated."[18]

Nonetheless, Roosevelt was keenly sensitive to disapproval, and he found it difficult to ignore Wall Street's growing hostility. It gnawed him until he began to perceive the machinations of his enemies everywhere.

On New Year's Day 1907, the President shook 8,500 hands. With typical hyperbole, the papers described the traditional New Year's greeting as the "the most brilliant" in recent memory, but there was nothing unusual about this year's ceremony except for the near absence of African Americans. The three-hour ordeal was exhausting, even for a president as fit as Theodore Roosevelt, but he maintained his exuberance throughout. He even managed a toothy grin for Senator Joseph Foraker of Ohio, though reporters noticed a certain grimness in his expression.[19]

Senator Foraker was a true Standpatter, not one of Aldrich's toadies but a genuine laissez-faire diehard, the only Republican in the Senate to have voted against the Hepburn railroad bill. That was not why Roosevelt hated him, though. Nor was it because of Foraker's ambition to challenge Taft for the Republican nomination. It was because of Brownsville.

Brownsville was a dusty little port city at the southern tip of Texas. Five months earlier, black soldiers had rampaged through the town, killing a bartender and wounding a policeman. At least that was what the white townspeople had said, and Roosevelt did not doubt them. Yet, the Army investigators could not identify the perpetrators. None of the black troops stationed at Fort Brown admitted any knowledge of the attacks. The Army report blamed their silence on "the secretive nature of the race." Roosevelt agreed. He ordered all 167 black soldiers stationed at the base, including decorated war veterans, dishonorably discharged without trial.[20]

That should have been the end of it. The Democrats certainly had no objection. Black leaders complained, of course. They expressed their pique on New Year's Day by shunning the handshake ceremony, but the political impact was minimal. Roosevelt had made sure of that by releasing his order just after the November midterm elections.[21]

Then in December, Senator Foraker staged his assault. He sponsored a Senate resolution demanding all documents related to the Brownsville investigation. The resolution forced Secretary of War William Taft into the humiliating position of subordinating himself to Congress. Most people assumed that Foraker was courting the black vote for the upcoming Republican primary, but Roosevelt suspected an ulterior motive. He wrote to a friend, "I believe you are absolutely right in saying that Foraker has been representing Wall Street in attacking me on this issue."[22]

WASHINGTON, DC, JANUARY 10, 1907

Bob La Follette paid little attention to the financial unrest in New York. There would come a time when the titans of Wall Street would occupy his full attention, but in early 1907, he was still focused on the railroads. He had an idea for some new legislation. In those days, railroad employees often had to work twenty hours or more at a stretch. Exhausted workers made mistakes that contributed to hundreds of deadly railroad accidents. So La Follette drafted a bill to prohibit railroad employees from working more than sixteen consecutive hours. Given the public's concerns about rail safety and the senators' concerns about his roll call campaign, he thought it had a good chance of passing. To prevent the Standpatters from diluting the legislation, he introduced the core provision as a late amendment—after the Senate had finished debating an inferior version of the bill—and then pressed for a roll call on the amendment.

The gambit worked. With an apprehensive eye on their constituents, western senators backed the amendment, which succeeded by a narrow margin. After the vote, the *Washington Times* applauded La Follette's "sweeping victory," and the *New York Times* credited his "deadly roll call campaign" from the previous summer for intimidating the opposition.[23]

A few days later, La Follette received praise from another unexpected source. Since returning to Washington, he had become a frequent guest at the White House. Roosevelt always greeted him effusively at these meetings, but La Follette doubted his sincerity. "I never know how much he is really *dee*-lighted," he wrote to Belle.

ROOSEVELT HAD INDEED WARMED TO LA FOLLETTE, though he remained skeptical of his tactics. In a letter to Kansas journalist William Allen White, he wrote that he appreciated La Follette "when he stands against certain big corporation evil" but not "when he goes to a foolish extreme, or throws away the possible by demanding the impossible." Nonetheless, he praised La Follette's courage and acknowledged that his roll call campaign had served a "useful purpose" by forcing senators to go on the record.[24]

After the railroad safety bill passed, Roosevelt again invited La Follette to the White House and honored him this time with an unqualified tribute. "There was one of the Senators whom I was afraid of last session whom I didn't trust," Roosevelt told him. "But I was wrong. I trust him now and have every confidence in him—You are that Senator." He acknowledged that La Follette's criticisms of the Hepburn bill had angered him at the time but confessed that he now appreciated the value of the amendments he'd proposed. "I am going to support them next session," Roosevelt promised. "We cannot make it this session but I'll put all my force into it next December."[25]

THE FOLLOWING WEEK, LA FOLLETTE MET AGAIN with Roosevelt to discuss another bill he was preparing. Mining companies and land speculators had long taken advantage of lax federal land management by purchasing public land far below market value. Some companies filed mining claims on negligible coal reserves in order to cheaply acquire the timber on the surface. La Follette's bill prohibited the government from selling off public mineral land and required companies to lease the development rights instead. That way, the public would retain ownership while still allowing private industry to run the mines. The bill also stipulated a royalty fee and imposed liability for environmental damages. As La Follette explained each of the bill's provisions to the President, Roosevelt pounded the table and piped, "Admirable, admirable! That does the business!" When he had finished, Roosevelt declared his support and authorized him to introduce it as an administration measure. For a moment, it seemed as if the two Republican reformers would finally join forces.[26]

La Follette's coal bill provoked an immediate stir. Though the *Wall Street Journal* lauded the plan, the *New York Times* cautioned that it represented a "radical departure from any legislation ever proposed." Meanwhile, Roosevelt changed his mind even before the papers came out. Within hours after La Follette introduced the legislation, he became convinced that it would not pass and quietly withdrew his support. In a letter, he urged La Follette to endorse a compromise measure by Knute Nelson of Minnesota.[27]

La Follette refused. The Nelson bill lacked the safeguards of his own bill; he anticipated that companies would simply exploit mineral leases in the same way that they had previously exploited land sales. It was a typical half-a-loaf compromise, he believed, worse than no loaf at all. "The interests of the public will be better served by temporary defeat," he replied to Roosevelt, "than by compromising on a bill which sounds well in the title but is weak or silent on vital points. The enactment of a law that falls short of reaching the real evil will be a stumbling block for many years to a substantial protection of public interest."[28]

But La Follette's argument sailed straight past the President. Though Roosevelt was a brilliant tactician, he seldom looked beyond the next battle. "I know what I want to do now," he told Lincoln Steffens, "and I know what I'd like to do next. But after that, I don't know." It had been that way with the railroad fight. In 1906, La Follette's railroad valuation had seemed hopelessly out of reach, so Roosevelt refused to entertain it. Two years later, it seemed like the next logical step, and he endorsed it.[29]

So it was with the coal lands. He had sized up the enemy and concluded that La Follette's plan could not prevail. Therefore, the only sensible course was to sue for terms. The possibility that defeat would serve a long-term political purpose did not even register. It was beyond his horizon. From his perspective, losing would only waste time and squander the opportunity to accomplish something useful. To go into battle knowing that you would be annihilated seemed vain and stupid, another example of La Follette throwing away the possible by demanding the impossible.

Since he could see no sense in it, Roosevelt assumed that La Follette was impugning his courage as the Democrats had done after the railroad fight. "I do not see how any human being could have stood more firmly for effective legislation than I have stood," he replied irritably to La Follette's letter. Ignoring the argument that they would get a better bill in the long run, he warned of the consequences if no bill passed that session. Then he protested again, "I have stood as firmly as any human being can stand for effective legislation. I trust you and your colleagues will give it to me."[30]

La Follette, deeply disappointed, resolved to go his own way once more. He could no more understand Roosevelt's point of view than Roosevelt could understand his, so he concluded that the Standpatters had manipulated the President. "I think he knows—must know I am right," he wrote to Belle, "but the Senate crowd... as well as the House gang gave him to understand that no bill could pass with La F's name on it. If he would say so frankly to me I'd like him better. But I must take him as he is and do the best I can with him. Beveridge came to me today and told me that the Pres. told him day before yesterday that he the Pres. thought very highly of me & c & c. But you know 'Bev.' I shall always remember how the Pres. threw me down and govern myself accordingly."[31]

WASHINGTON, DC, JANUARY 24, 1907

Albert Beveridge had his own frustrations with the President. He had spent the summer preparing his next Senate crusade: a federal law to ban child labor in the United States. The stories he read were harrowing: hundreds of thousands of children as young as seven working twelve-hour shifts in the mines, factories, and sweatshops. Some states limited the hours children could work to eight or ten, but even these modest restrictions often went unenforced. In November 1906, Beveridge had sent Roosevelt a draft of his bill. "If it is not too late," he inquired, "I am hoping that you can make favorable mention of this proposed legislation in your Message."

Roosevelt did not answer him personally. Instead, his secretary conveyed his regret that he had not known of Beveridge's plans sooner. He had already incorporated a child labor recommendation into his annual December message.[32]

The reason for the brush-off became clear two weeks later when Roosevelt sent his annual message to Congress. He urged the congressmen to outlaw child labor—but only in the District of Columbia and US territories. Child labor was not particularly egregious in DC or the territories, neither of which had much industry. There was only one reason to single them out for labor regulation: they were not states. The Republican leaders had taken the position that child labor was deplorable but that the Constitution had tied their hands; the federal government had no authority over the states in the matter. Southern Democrats, who revered states' rights and doted on cotton mills that relied on child labor, agreed. In light of the opposition, Roosevelt had concluded that the District of Columbia and the territories were the only places that Congress would legislate against child labor.

Without the support of the President or Republican leaders, Beveridge found himself in an unfamiliar position: alone. Passing a national child labor law was impossible under the circumstances, but he had come to share La Follette's long view of political change. If his colleagues voted down the bill, they would pay for it at the ballot box. Eventually, the old Standpatters waiting at the station with their broken watches would lose their seats. Then his bill or one like it would become law. It had taken the British Parliament fifty years to ban child labor; Beveridge hoped to do it in five. Two days after Roosevelt's message, he introduced his legislation.[33]

The wording of the bill was clever. Rather than prohibiting child labor in the states, which everyone agreed to be unconstitutional, the legislation prohibited only the interstate transport of materials produced by children. Since the Constitution granted Congress the authority to regulate interstate commerce, and since most companies sold their goods out of state, the bill would effectively ban child labor nationwide without violating the Constitution. The *New York Mail* praised Beveridge's "ingenious means of invoking national action against an admitted evil" and suggested that it be applied to other causes, such as establishing an eight-hour workday and restoring black suffrage in the South.[34]

The Senate debate was scheduled for late January. Beveridge spent the intervening weeks preparing an arsenal of statistics and stories. On the day of his speech, he mustered them around his Senate desk, stacking three adjacent desks high with books, photographs, and affidavits. He had dressed even more fastidiously than usual, buttoning his fine frock coat all the way up. When the moment arrived, he stood at his desk with his chest out and shoulders back, just as he had learned in college oratory competition. He tucked his hand into his lapel and began to talk—quickly, vehemently, and sanctimoniously.[35]

He spoke of boys and girls, ten to twelve, rolling cigars fourteen hours a day. He described nine-year-old "breaker boys" in the mines who inhaled toxic coal dust as they picked out slate with cracked and swollen fingers. He quoted a bottle factory foreman to explain the purpose of a wooden stockade topped with barbed wire: "It keeps the young imps inside once we've got 'em for the night shift." When some congressmen laughed at his reference to a ten-year-old girl's "puny, stunted body," Beveridge chided them, "I do not think that you will find in this, as we go along, any particular materials for amusement."[36]

He tried to impress on his colleagues the inadequacy of state-by-state legislation. "If one State passes good laws and enforces them and another state does not," he argued, "then the businessmen in the former State are at a business disadvantage in comparison with the business men in the latter State."[37]

But the Standpatters saw only an unconstitutional expansion of federal power. A week later, the Judiciary Committee chaired by Senator Spooner ruled that since the Constitution did not enumerate federal authority over child labor, Beveridge's amendment was unconstitutional. The Senate never even had an opportunity to vote on it.[38]

Beveridge's five-year forecast proved optimistic. It would take another thirty years for the federal government to successfully prohibit child labor. That legislation, part of FDR's New Deal, would employ language much like Beveridge's bill to assert federal authority under the interstate commerce clause.

WASHINGTON, DC, JANUARY 27, 1907

Roosevelt seethed over his green-turtle soup. He sat at the midpoint of a narrow wooden table that ran the entire length of the New Willard

Hotel's opulent ballroom. The other tables extended out at right angles from the long one so that the arrangement resembled a huge gridiron. Senator Joseph Foraker sat at one of the central tables. He faced away from the head table and could not look at Roosevelt without turning his head, but Roosevelt could see him quite clearly.[39]

Foraker had been busy in January. After subpoenaing the Brownsville documents from Secretary Taft, he called for a congressional investigation into Roosevelt's order to discharge the black soldiers—a direct challenge to the authority of the commander-in-chief. At that point, Aldrich and Spooner intervened. They pressed Foraker into accepting a compromise measure that would investigate the incident without addressing the President's authority to dismiss the soldiers. But even that limited investigation offended Roosevelt, and he remained furious about the whole business.[40]

The Gridiron dinner was normally a jovial affair in which journalists roasted politicians good-naturedly, but Roosevelt was not in the mood. Perusing a booklet of caricatures of prominent guests, he found a sketch of Foraker. Underneath the picture was a crude poem:

> All coons look alike to me,
> Since 'mancipation set 'em free,
> Nigger vote hold de balance,
> All coons look alike to me

As he read it, his jaw tightened. He leaned over to the president of the club and said, "I would like to speak now, if it can be arranged."[41] Dinner service was paused while the President addressed the room.

He did not speak of Brownsville right away. Foraker was not his only rival in the room. A number of prominent businessmen also attended, including J. Pierpont Morgan and the vice president of Standard Oil. Roosevelt believed that these men or their associates were in cahoots with Foraker. He shook his finger at them. "If you gentlemen are not willing to accept the action of the conservative class," he warned, "which is ready to afford protection alike to the rich and poor, I will say to you now that you will find yourself face to face with a people which believes it has been deprived of its rights and a mob which does not have the least respect for riches. You can take your choice."[42]

As hungry guests waited in vain for the next course to be served, Roosevelt turned to Brownsville and vigorously defended his discharge order. The Senate investigation was "academic," he insisted, for Congress had no right to challenge the White House in the matter. Though he avoided mentioning Foraker by name, he made it quite clear whom he meant. "All coons look alike to me," he remarked, "and all white persons look alike to me also."[43]

But then it was Foraker's turn. Pale with rage, the senator rejected the insinuations that his purposes were political. Had not the President himself once said that no man was so high or so low that that he would not give him the full protection of the law if innocent? These soldiers, Foraker argued, were innocent men who had served their country honorably, and they deserved a fair trial. "No one in this country ever loved the President more than I did," he concluded. "That was when he was in the right; in the wrong I have opposed him and shall always do so. That is the way I see my duty to my conscience, my constituents and my country."[44]

As Foraker spoke, Roosevelt could barely contain himself. He kept motioning to rise as his tablemates restrained him. When the speech finally concluded to a crash of applause, he popped up to refute the attacks, but there was too much commotion. Between his own anger and the agitation of the dinner guests, he couldn't get in a proper rebuttal. And then Uncle Joe was speaking, trying to calm everyone down—something about how they all thought they were so mighty important, but the world would keep right on spinning even if an earthquake swallowed the whole roomful of them. And then it was midnight, and the club president called for dinner to be adjourned, though the long speeches had prevented the remaining courses from being served.[45]

The next day, despite the club's confidentiality rules, the papers could not resist reporting such a sensational event. The quarrel between the President and the senator became the talk of Washington. The hearings began a week later and lasted more than a year. In the end, a majority decision by the Military Affairs Committee validated Roosevelt's order, but the issue continued to dog him until the end of his presidency and remained a blot on his legacy. Sixty-six years later, when only two of the soldiers who had been discharged remained alive, the Army reinvestigated and cleared their records.[46]

WASHINGTON, DC, MARCH 4, 1907

They were supposed to turn back the clocks. By law, Congress had to adjourn before noon on March 4, but last-minute legislation frequently pushed the proceedings into the afternoon. Even when the proceeding ran late, the congressional record would register the adjournment before noon to comply with the law. To complete the fiction, someone was supposed to turn back the Senate's big wall clocks, but it hadn't happened this year for some reason.

That upset Senator Spooner. He and W. B. Allison conferenced with Fairbanks, but the vice president didn't seem to care, so Spooner scurried up the aisle and asked the correspondents in the press gallery to push back the minute hand on the clock over the balcony. But the journalists pointed out that the clock on the other side of the room had glass over it, and the hands could not be moved, so what was the point of changing just one clock? To Spooner's chagrin, both clocks showed 12:12 when the Senate adjourned.[47]

It was an ignominious finale to his last session. He had served sixteen years in the Senate, but this was no longer the same chamber it had once been. Orville Platt was dead, and the remaining members of the Big Four had drifted apart. He warned his friends that a "tidal wave of populism and radicalism" was washing away the old traditions. La Follette's direct primary law had already ruined Wisconsin; now other states like Oregon and Nebraska were following suit. Nothing good would come of it, he was certain. These new laws would simply replace the venerable party machines with "personal machines" that turned politicians into shame-less "self-seekers" like La Follette.[48]

Though he still had two years left in his term, he decided not to wait around for the inevitable. Unlike Aldrich, he'd never made much money as a senator. There was time yet to provide something more for his wife and children. He resolved to move to New York to resume his corporate legal practice. The day before the session ended, he sur-prised everyone by publishing a resignation letter thanking the people of Wisconsin for the honor they had done him. It was time for him to move on.[49]

DOWN THE HALL, UNCLE JOE WAS HIDING from the Democrats. It was customary for the minority party to praise the Speaker at the end of the session, so Cannon made a show of modesty by vacating the chamber. The Democrats hunted him down of course, and he "reluctantly" accompanied them back to the chamber where congressmen from both parties were clapping and shouting merrily. He and Minority Leader John Sharp Williams had had their differences earlier in the session, but Williams was a decent fellow, not the sort to let politics interfere with congressional courtesy. Cannon ordinarily let the Democrats choose their own committee members, but the man Williams had wanted was a prohibitionist, and the whiskey makers would never sit for a prohibitionist on the Judiciary Committee. Williams had been furious when Cannon overruled him, but he showed no sign of resentment today as he delivered the customary motion of thanks to the Speaker, praising him for "his big heart, his big brain, and his impartiality."

"He is nearly always wrong," Williams continued to raucous laugh-ter, "but there is no sham about him, there is no pretense, there is no hypocrisy. He is simply plain Joe Cannon, characteristically American, characteristically Western and characteristically Southern, for his old blood came from there."[50]

It was nearly twelve, so Cannon ordered the clocks turned back twenty minutes while the boys sang, "For He's a Jolly Good Fellow." Everyone was in good humor, and they got in a few rounds of "The Star Spangled Banner," "America," and "Good Night, Ladies" before the tampered clocks reached noon. Then Uncle Joe banged the gavel and offered the representatives his own thanks for their kindness, their friendship, and their "appreciation of my duty, even when it crossed some of your cherished purposes." He concluded with the traditional recitation, "I declare the Fifty-ninth Congress adjourned without day[, *sine day*]."[51]

All in all, the last session had been an easy one with none of the trouble from the year before. Fowler had come pleading to him about asset currency again, but he'd sent him straight off. The howling on Wall Street didn't worry him much. "The country doesn't care what happens to those damned speculators," he'd told Fowler, "Everything is all right out West and around Danville. The country don't need any legislation." Aldrich and Roosevelt were also anxious about the stock market of course. Cannon let them have their Treasury bill this time—he saw no harm in allowing the Treasury to deposit gold reserves in private banks—but he drew the line at currency reform.[52]

After much presidential prodding, he'd also let La Follette's railroad service bill through on the very last day. The other reform bills—child labor and coal lands—died quietly. He did not expect any more trouble from the President. The next session wouldn't start until December. By then, everyone would be focused on the presidential election, and Roosevelt would be just another lame duck. Foraker had played a neat trick with that Brownsville business. Not only did it distract Roosevelt from his endless preaching, it set up Foraker nicely for the Republican nomination. The only time anyone cared about the black vote was during the Republican presidential convention on account of the black delegates from southern states. But Foraker would have to fight uphill against Taft and Fairbanks, even if he got the black vote.[53]

Cannon reckoned that he had as good a shot at the nomination as any of them. He was careful not to give any encouragement to the folks who were pushing his candidacy—it was bad form to seek the presidency—but he let them know that he wouldn't turn down the honor if his party saw fit to offer it to him.[54]

Time would tell. In the meantime, he was looking forward to a long slow steam through the West Indies with a dozen of the other boys. The congressmen were ostensibly going to check up on the Panama Canal work, but, as Uncle Joe told the newsmen, he did not intend to allow business to interfere with pleasure.[55]

NEW YORK, NEW YORK, MARCH 13, 1907

The stocks had been slipping since the New Year. The economy continued to flourish, and nothing seemed amiss besides the persistent currency crunch, but investors were skittish. On March 13, the market stumbled hard. J. Pierpont Morgan had departed for Europe the night before, leaving his son Jack to manage the crisis. After a nerve-wracked day of damage control, Jack wrote to his London partners, "Here we are, still alive in spite of the most unpleasant panic which we are going through. The whole situation is most mysterious; undoubtedly many men who were very rich have become much poorer, but as there seems to be no one breaking, perhaps we shall get off with the fright only."[56]

It would be another couple of weeks before the market stabilized. The Treasury moved aggressively, depositing gold into New York banks to soothe investors' currency fears, and the disturbance did not appear to extend beyond Wall Street. The press dismissed it as a "rich man's panic" that only affected wealthy speculators. When it was over, Jack Morgan breathed with relief. "I am tired but hopeful," he wrote to London, "hopeful because of the simple fact that there is a tremendous productive capacity in this country, and that this productive capacity has not been one whit reduced by the colic we have all been having."[57]

But currency remained tight. In the middle of summer, the Bank of England imposed a prohibition on US finance bills to protect Britain's gold reserves. With Americans unable to borrow from British banks, the flow of gold suddenly reversed and started moving from New York to London. The timing could not have been worse, for America's farmers had already begun the harvest, and what remained of New York's currency reserves was about to begin its annual migration to the country's interior.[58]

NEW YORK, NEW YORK, OCTOBER 14, 1907

The Curb was crowded as usual. A swirling mass of men in top hats jostled one another in ragged clusters, thrusting their fingers into air, shouting pleas, and bellowing demands. A jumble of arms and heads protruded from windows several stories overhead, motioning to the chaotic swarm below. These were the brokerage clerks, communicating instructions to the traders down on the Curb. The traders worked the Curb in the rain and snow because their brokerages could not afford $95,000 seats on the

New York Stock Exchange and because the Big Board did not list the stocks they traded.[59]

The United Copper Company was a Curb stock. Fritz Augustus Heinze, one of the boldest and scrappiest of the "copper kings," had set up the corporation with his brothers, Otto and Arthur, a few years before. United Copper's share price had slumped in autumn of 1907, the work of short-sellers perhaps. Short-sellers made money whenever prices dropped. They borrowed shares and then sold them immediately, betting that they could buy them back at lower prices before the loans came due. When short-sellers were active in a stock, they drove the price down. On Saturday, October 12, United Copper closed at 37¾, far below its peak of 77¾ the year before.[60]

The following Monday, trading opened quietly—at least by Curb standards. Ten minutes after the opening, a broker from a prominent stock exchange house joined the United Copper crowd. He wanted 500 shares and bought the first hundred at $40 each. He bought the second hundred at 41, the third at 49 . As word got out, the clerks in the upstairs windows "wigwagged" to their traders to buy United Copper, and the price kept climbing: 51, 52, 53, 57, 59, 60.[61]

Veteran Curb traders noticed something odd about the trades. The mysterious broker and other buyers did not seem particularly anxious to acquire the stock. They bought shares methodically at the lowest prices they could get. The old-timers on the Curb reckoned the Heinze brothers were up to something.[62]

The next day, Otto Heinze showed his hand. He served notice to borrowers of United Copper that he wanted the outstanding shares returned immediately. This was a *bear squeeze*. Heinze had cornered the United Copper stock and driven up the price in order to wipe out the short-sellers. They would have to buy back the borrowed shares at much higher prices than they'd sold them. If unable to pay, they would have to settle with Heinze under steep terms.

Except that Heinze had miscalculated. There were not nearly so many short-sellers as he believed, and the borrowers returned the stock immediately—far more than he could handle. "Thousands of shares began to appear as fast as the mails could carry them," the *New York Times* reported. Unable to transfer all the shares to Heinze, the brokers dumped the rest on the market, and the price of United Copper plummeted. On Tuesday afternoon, it fell to 36. On Wednesday, it dropped down to 10. During the final hour, a crowd of brokers rushed up and down the street shouting and fighting. "Never has there been such wild scenes on the Curb," tutted the old-timers.[63]

Otto Heinze was ruined. But not just Otto. The brokerage house he had hired to lead the squeeze closed its doors after he refused to pay for the shares it had purchased on his behalf. Two thousand miles away, the State Savings Bank of Butte, Montana, which was as heavily invested in United Copper, announced insolvency and suspended operations. Though Fritz Augustus, the copper king, was not directly implicated in his brother's scheme, his reputation was stained. Nervous investors fled from anything he touched. There were runs on several banks with which he was affiliated.[64]

At another moment in history, that might have been the end of it. The failed squeeze would have become nothing but a footnote in the annals of financial recklessness. But it was October, and the farmers were shipping crops, and San Francisco was gobbling cash, and London was hoarding gold, and the great reservoirs in the vaults of New York City were nearly dry.

NEW YORK, NEW YORK, OCTOBER 22, 1907

On Tuesday, one week after the United Copper crash, a crowd gathered under the marble columns of the Knickerbocker Trust Company on the corner of Fifth Avenue and 34th Street, across the road from where the Empire State Building now stands. There were about a hundred people, mostly small depositors—shop owners, mechanics, and clerks. When the great bronze doors opened at 10 a.m., the crowd divided into two lines, one for men and one for women. The customers waited impatiently to reach the teller windows so they could withdraw their savings.[65]

The Knickerbocker Trust was not technically a bank. It looked like a bank—with marble walls and crystal chandeliers that bespoke abundant wealth. It acted like a bank—accepting deposits, making loans, and renting safety deposit boxes. But it was organized as a trust in order to avoid cumbersome financial restrictions. With lower reserve requirements, trusts were able to offer better terms than traditional banks. Lower reserves meant higher risk, but the impeccable pedigree of the Knickerbocker's president, Charles T. Barney, seemed to promise the best of both worlds: financial security with excellent returns.[66]

Unfortunately for the depositors, pedigree is not always what it seems. After the United Copper fiasco, it came out that Charles Barney had associated with some disreputable speculators, including Fritz Augustus Heinze. The board forced him to resign after United Copper's crash, but that was not enough to save the trust's reputation. The following morning, anxious customers came to retrieve their deposits. As soon as the doors opened, the staff tried to move everyone inside to avoid attracting attention from the street. Long lines soon coiled round the marble pillars and mahogany desks, traversing every square foot of the chamber. But there were too many people. Within minutes, the lines burst out the door, through the columns, down the steps, and along Fifth Avenue for all to see.

As word spread, horse carriages, automobiles, and battery-powered taxicabs began to appear at the front steps bearing men in frock coats and woman in silks. A richly gowned woman arrived with her poodle and went straight in to see the branch manager. Another man came with an attendant clutching an alligator-skin valise, which he filled with $60,000 in yellow-backed gold certificates once he finally reached a teller.

The biggest depositors were banks and investment firms. When their agents began submitting withdrawal checks for millions of dollars, the trust's managers realized that the Knickerbocker did not have enough cash in its vaults to meet depositors' demands. At 12:35, a vice president climbed on a chair and announced to the crowd that no more withdrawals would be allowed that day. "Payments of checks will be, probably, resumed in the morning," he assured them weakly. "The company is solvent." With that, the tellers shut their windows.[67]

NEW YORK, NEW YORK, OCTOBER 23, 1907

On Wednesday, New York started to unravel. The Knickerbocker did not open in the morning, and the panic spread. There were bank runs on the Trust Company of America downtown and the Dollar Savings Bank in the Bronx. Fearing an epidemic, the other banks and trusts prepared for the worst. They called in their outstanding loans to shore up their cash reserves, which put more pressure on the borrowers. Credit evaporated; interest rates soared. On Wall Street, the interest rate on call money— short-term loans that traders used to buy stocks—reached 96 percent. The stock market tumbled.[68]

As panic flooded the financial markets, frantic businessmen cast about for a savior. They did not find one in the White House. Theodore Roosevelt was en route from Louisiana, relaxed and tan after a week-long hunting trip. When news of the crisis reached him in Nashville, Tennessee, he did nothing to reassure investors. Instead, he made a speech denying that his policies "had any material effect in bringing about the present trouble" and delivered yet another tirade against the twin evils of demagoguery and dishonest capitalism.[69]

He had little more to add when he arrived in Washington the next day. As the Knickerbocker's collapse reverberated around the world, Roosevelt preferred to talk to reporters about the black bear he'd shot in the canebrakes. Nor did he show much concern in private. "Do I look as though those Wall Street fellows were really worrying me?" he boasted to a friend. "I've got them on the run," he snapped out through flashing teeth.[70]

In truth, there was little Roosevelt could have done about the crisis even if he'd taken it more seriously. Without a central bank or any means of expanding the money supply, without the ability to bail out failing banks or reduce interest rates, the federal government was ill-equipped to combat financial emergencies. Its only recourse was to shift more Treasury reserves into the New York banks to free up a little more capital in the market.

By the time Roosevelt returned to Washington, Treasury Secretary George Cortelyou had already traveled to New York for that purpose. He did not go at the President's behest, however. Another man had summoned him. That man had no affiliation with the government. He was neither elected nor appointed. But he was the only man in America who commanded the authority, the expertise, and the capital to confront the panic.[71]

JOHN PIERPONT MORGAN WAS NOT AN ATTRACTIVE MAN. His nose was grotesque—swollen and purple from chronic rosacea. The rest of his features arranged themselves deferentially around it. Thick brows straddled the bridge. Dark eyes glowered from cavities on either side. A ragged mustache drooped from the nostrils, nearly obscuring his mouth. His personality offered little to compensate for his appearance. Acquaintances described him as taciturn, gruff, and imperious. He barked at people. Even his business partner complained, "He is an impossible man to have any talk with. The nearest approach he makes is an occasional grunt."[72]

Yet for all his physical and temperamental flaws, Morgan radiated a kind of power that people responded to, an invisible force that inspired trust, awe, and loyalty. "You felt something electric," recalled a family friend. "He wasn't a terribly large man but he had a simply tremendous effect—he was the king. He was it." Pierpont Morgan seldom spoke, but when he did speak, everyone paid attention. And when he told them what to do, they usually obeyed.[73]

In the fall of 1907, Morgan was seventy years old. His white hair was thinning to nothing. He had trouble hearing and walked with a cane. On the morning after the Knickerbocker run, he could barely open his eyes and could not speak above a whisper. Late nights and long hours had exacerbated a severe cold. His personal physician was summoned and a dose of gargles and sprays prescribed, but it was coffee that finally revived him enough to go to work. When his cab turned onto Wall Street, Morgan saw a mass of spectators gawking at the main branch of the Trust Company of America as if the building were on fire. There were no flames issuing from its doors, only people. More than a thousand of them lined up around the block.[74]

When Morgan reached his office, he found a group of business-men waiting for him. Everyone was worried about the Trust Company of America. If it closed, the impact would shake the markets even more violently than the Knickerbocker's collapse. One of Morgan's deputies, a young man named Benjamin Strong, was already poring over the trust's books to see if it could be saved.[75]

Strong reported back to Morgan in the early afternoon. As he described his findings, they were interrupted by a series of increasingly desperate phone calls from the trust's president. At 1 p.m., the company had $1.2 million remaining in its vaults. Half an hour later, its reserves were down to $800,000. By 1:45, they had dwindled to $500,000. The tellers were supposed to stay open until 3, but the money could not possibly hold out that long. When the reserves dropped to $180,000, Morgan pressed Strong for a verdict. "Are they solvent?" he wanted to know. If the company owned enough assets to cover its obligations, then its immediate cash shortage was temporary. Strong believed the trust to be solvent. "This is the place to stop the trouble then," Morgan replied.[76]

He called back the trust president and told him to come immediately with the most valuable securities in his vaults. Minutes later, a long line of men carrying bags and boxes entered Morgan's office and laid out the trust's assets on the table. Morgan sat at the table tallying them with a pad and pencil. As he reviewed the collateral, he periodically instructed the presidents of the First National Bank and the National City Bank to deliver sacks of cash to the Trust Company. Less than one hour and three million dollars later, the tellers closed their windows on schedule at 3 p.m. The trust was saved...for a day.[77]

That evening, Morgan summoned ten presidents of New York's larg-est trusts and asked them to put together a ten-million-dollar pool to shore up the Trust Company of America. One president offered to con-tribute up to a million, but the rest hesitated. Some hoped to benefit by their competitor's downfall. Others feared for their own stability and did not want to risk their precious reserves.

Morgan silently smoked a cigar while they haggled. When it went out, his head dropped forward, and he fell asleep in his chair, exhausted. Thirty minutes later, he awoke and asked for a pen and paper. "Well, gentleman," he said. "The Bankers Trust Company has agreed to take its share and more of a loan." Then he went round the table asking each in turn how much he would contribute. Singling them out in succession, he received pledges for $8.5 million. He would make up the remaining balance through banks he controlled.[78]

Morgan's willingness to risk his own capital was not entirely altruistic. Though he was not nearly as rapacious as popular imagination would have him, he was nonetheless one of the shrewdest businessmen in American history. Many of his clients held stakes in the Trust Company of America—far more than in the Knickerbocker. Its failure would cut into the profits of J. P. Morgan & Co. And if the reverberations from its fall brought down the whole banking system, the catastrophe would swallow many great fortunes. J. Pierpont Morgan had a great fortune to protect.[79]

NEW YORK, NEW YORK OCTOBER 24, 1907

Despite the Trust Company of America bailout, the panic continued on Thursday morning. Waves of fear swept through immigrant communities, and community banks shut their doors one after another. In downtown Manhattan, the much larger Lincoln Trust trembled, and the ten-million-dollar pool for the Trust Company of America bled out rapidly. Other big trusts, anticipating trouble, called in more loans. Every last ounce of available credit vanished.[80]

At 1:30 p.m., Ransom H. Thomas, president of New York's Stock Exchange, came to see Pierpont Morgan. He rushed into the room and exclaimed, "Mr. Morgan, we will have to close the Stock Exchange."

"What?" Morgan asked sharply.

"We will have to close the Stock Exchange," Thomas repeated.

"At what time do you usually close it?" Morgan asked.

"Why, at three o'clock," he replied.

Morgan pointed his middle finger directly at Thomas. Emphasizing each word with a jab, he bellowed, "It must not close one minute before that hour today!"[81]

But Thomas was followed by a series of stockbrokers begging for help, many with tears in their eyes. They couldn't raise money to pay for the day's losses. They had collateral, but no one was lending. The moment of reckoning loomed at 2:20. That was when the Exchange compared the day's sales and adjusted brokers' accounts. If they couldn't settle their accounts, they would have to close.

Morgan immediately summoned the presidents of the city's largest banks to his office. As they filed in a few minutes after 2, he explained that fifty brokerage companies were doomed unless they raised a credit pool of $25 million in the next twelve minutes. By 2:16, he'd secured $23.6 million from 14 banks. When the news filtered out into hallway, jubilant brokers started cheering. One hurled his hat into the air, crying, "We are saved, we are saved!"

As soon as the money hit the market, brokers scrambled over one another in a frenzy. One of Morgan's men had his coat and waistcoat ripped off in the mayhem. The money poured out, $19 million in the space of thirty minutes. When the Stock Exchange closed at 3, "a mighty roar of voices" exploded from the floor. "What's the matter with Morgan!" some of the traders shouted. The rest rejoined, "He's all right!"[82]

NEW YORK, NEW YORK, OCTOBER 25, 1907

On Friday, it started all over again. Despite the $10 million bailout of the Trust Company of America and the $24 million pool for the stock exchange, despite $25 million from the US Treasury and another $10 million from John D. Rockefeller, the bank runs continued. The Trust Company of America required another financial boost to stay afloat, and Morgan furnished it. The stockbrokers still had no credit, and Morgan raised another $10 million to keep the stock exchange open.

At 3 p.m., the weekend finally arrived, and New York had a chance to catch its breath. The stock exchange would only open for a few hours on Saturday, and the banks would not have to open at all. Morgan urged the treasury secretary to return to Washington to signal that the crisis had receded. His associates met with ministers, priests, and rabbis from all over New York City and begged them to tell their congregations to remain calm and keep their money in the bank. Even President Roosevelt belatedly threw his support behind Morgan's efforts, publishing a letter that praised "those conservative and substantial business men who in the crisis have acted with such wisdom and public spirit."

As for Morgan, he went to his country home in the Hudson Valley to show New York that he was at ease. He also needed the rest. After a frantic week of anxiety, illness, late nights, and early mornings, he finally acted like the 70-year-old he was by sleeping through the ride.[83]

NEW YORK, NEW YORK, OCTOBER 28, 1907

Manhattan was quieter on Monday. A rainstorm that flooded gutters overnight gave way to a clammy mist that blotted out New Jersey and Long Island. The weather kept people off the streets and dampened the usual vigor of the Curb. The lines outside the banks and trusts were fewer and shorter. Millions of dollars in gold arrived from England, Paris, Argentina, and Australia to soothe the bankers. The stockbrokers made their way without any more assistance from Morgan.[84]

But someone else needed his help. In the afternoon, Mayor George B. McClellan arrived at Morgan's private library in midtown. Because of the tight credit market, the city government had struggled to borrow money for months. Morgan had already come to its aid in September, underwriting $40 million in municipal bonds. Now the mayor reported that the money was spent and the city could not meet payroll. If he didn't raise another $30 million by the end of the week, it would go bankrupt.

A default by a city the size of New York would have had dangerous repercussions under any conditions. In the midst of a panic, it would be catastrophic. That evening, Morgan conferred with other prominent bankers in his private library, as he had been doing almost every night since the panic began. They all recognized that they had little choice.

On Tuesday, the mayor returned to the library. Morgan sat down at his desk and took out a pen and paper. "With scarcely a hesitation, without even stopping to select a word," one of his aides, George W. Perkins, recalled, "he covered three long sheets of paper..." When he had finished, Morgan read over the pages and handed them to Perkins. It was a term sheet for $30 million in municipal bonds.[85]

NEW YORK, NEW YORK, NOVEMBER 2, 1907

On Saturday morning, Morgan called an emergency conference at his library. A new crisis threatened the uneasy calm that had settled over the city. A large brokerage house, Moore & Schley, owed $30 million to various New York banks and trusts. For collateral, the company relied on its holdings in the Tennessee Coal and Iron Company, but TC&I's share price had fallen during the crisis, and the creditors were getting nervous. If they called in their loans, the brokerage house would fall.

"It is very serious," Morgan warned his guests. "If Moore & Schley go, there is no telling what the effect on Wall Street will be and on the financial institutions of New York, and how many other houses will drop with it, and how many banks might be involved in the consequences."[86]

A lawyer representing TC&I had a bright idea. What if the United States Steel Corporation bought TC&I? US Steel was the largest steel producer in the world, not to mention America's biggest corporation. If it acquired TC&I, no one would have any concerns about the share value, and Moore & Schley's credit would be restored.

Morgan liked the idea. Not only would it save Moore & Schley, it would extend the dominance of US Steel, which already controlled 60 percent of the American market. Unlike Theodore Roosevelt, Morgan appreciated monopolies. They offered economies of scale and avoided the chaos of "ruinous competition." He had made his fortune by gathering small companies into giant trusts, and the consolidation of US Steel in 1901 was one of his signature achievements. The opportunity to expand the trust by swallowing one of its southern competitors was tantalizing. He telephoned Henry Frick of US Steel.

Frick arrived with Elbert Henry Gary, the namesake of Gary, Indiana. The two steel executives did not share Morgan's enthusiasm for the merger. They thought TC&I's share price was too high under the circumstances, and they worried that the acquisition would open up the company to an antitrust lawsuit from the White House. They offered a lower price. Moore & Schley rejected it.[87]

The brokers and industrialists were still negotiating the fate of TC&I when the sun went down. Meanwhile, a stream of well-dressed men in black top hats passed between the sleek marble lionesses guarding the entrance to the library. Few of the visitors knew about Moore & Schley. They had come because the Trust Company of America was in trouble again. This time, Morgan had no intention of using his own resources to bail it out. He installed the ten trust presidents in the East Room and urged them to collect $25 million to save their fellow. Then he left the room.

The presidents hedged. They had already contributed $8.5 million to save the trust. Now Morgan was asking for three times as much. If the panic were to reach their own trusts, they would need every penny in their vaults to survive the storm. They deliberated past midnight among Morgan's books and tapestries but came no closer to an agreement.

With dawn approaching, Morgan delivered his final warning. If they did not act immediately "the walls of their own edifices might come crumbling about their ears." He presented them with a contract for the $25 million loan. The men shifted from one foot to another, but no one stepped forward. Morgan waited a few moments then put his hand on the shoulder of Edward King, president of the Union Trust Company. "There's the place, King," he said, "and here's the pen." He placed a gold pen in the man's fingers. King signed. The rest followed one by one.

Morgan opened the doors to the library, which he had locked to keep anyone from leaving. It was nearly 5 a.m. on Sunday morning.[88]

NEW YORK, NEW YORK, NOVEMBER 3, 1907

There was still one more hole to plug before the stock market opened on Monday. On Sunday evening, Frick and Gary of US Steel and Grant B. Schley of Moore & Schley returned to the library. Morgan finally persuaded them to reach an agreement, but the steel men had a condition.

"Before we go ahead with this," Gary insisted, "we must consult President Roosevelt."

"But what has the President to do with it?" Morgan asked.

"If we do this without consulting the administration," Gary replied, "a bill in equity might stop the sale, and in that case more harm than good would be done. He cannot say that we may or may not purchase, but we ought to know his attitude since he has a general direction of the law department of the United States."

"Can you go at once?" asked Mr. Morgan. He wanted a deal before the stock market opened on Monday.

Gary and Frick left New York at midnight on a special train consisting of a locomotive and a single Pullman sleeping car. The signalmen along the route to Washington received instructions from the chief dispatcher of the Pennsylvania Railroad to expedite the one-car special.[89]

WASHINGTON, DC, NOVEMBER 4, 1907

On Monday morning, Secretary of the Interior James Garfield interrupted Roosevelt's breakfast with an urgent message. Two men from US Steel had come from New York to see him about a matter of great importance. It was essential that they speak to him before the markets opened. Frick and Gary entered Roosevelt's office at 9:55, five minutes before the opening bell of the Stock Exchange. They told him about their plan to acquire TC&I, explaining that they were entertaining the deal at the urging of the New York bankers to "prevent a panic and general industrial smashup at this time." While they did not ask for any explicit commitments from the President, they wanted to make sure that he had no objections.[90]

To expand a vast trust that already dominated the US steel market ran counter to everything Roosevelt had preached for the past six years, but with the minutes ticking by while Wall Street teetered at the edge of a cliff, he felt that he had little choice. Accepting the industrialists' assurances that the acquisition was relatively minor, he told them that he felt no "public duty" to object. "I do not believe that anyone could justly criticize me for saying that I would not feel like objecting to the purchase under the circumstances," he added.[91]

And no one did criticize him, not at the time. Even William Jennings Bryan, already angling for the Democratic nomination, avoided censuring the President. Most Americans were simply relieved to see the crisis pass. Buoyed by the news of the steel merger and the $25 million trust pool, the stock markets rebounded, and the bank runs subsided. Ships laden with European gold steamed into New York harbor to help relieve the currency drought. The papers announced that the crisis had passed and that confidence had returned.[92]

Praise for J. Pierpont Morgan's efforts echoed across the headlines. The *Wall Street Journal* named him "the man of the hour, the undisputed leader who has stood between the business of the country and disaster." The *New York Times* called him a "bank in human form," a "Colossus...carrying the Nation's banks across the troubled waters of shaken confidence."[93]

With Morgan's aid, the Panic of 1907 had indeed come to an end. Moore & Schley restored its credit, and the Trust Company of America survived the bank runs. Even the Knickerbocker Trust reopened after a few weeks. On Wall Street, confidence steadily improved through the month of November.

ALTHOUGH WALL STREET'S TRAUMA WAS OVER, the rest of the country's had just begun. New York's convulsions spooked banks and investors from coast to coast. Rural banks withdrew their deposits from reserve banks in the cities. Many banks suspended withdrawals to protect themselves. Governors in several states declared legal holidays, which had the effect of closing banks entirely. Other states limited withdrawals to $10 increments. Citizens responded by hoarding cash under mattresses and hearthstones. Rentals of safety deposit boxes surged.

As a result, New York's currency shortage went national. People began to trade with cashier's checks instead of cash. Companies paid their employees with certified checks and IOUs. Streetcar companies in Omaha and St. Louis resorted to paying their employees with nickels from the fare boxes and five-cent fare tickets. The currency shortage spawned a credit crunch. Unable to get loans, businesses began to fail. Industrial production slumped. The GNP declined 11 percent. Unemployment jumped from 3 to 8 percent. Deflation set in.[94]

The recession was not long-lived—it would fade the following summer—but it was one of the most severe in American history. The hardship exacerbated the tensions that had been brewing in the West. By the time the economy revived, many Americans no longer sang J. Pierpont Morgan's praises. Though his efforts had spared the country from even greater devastation, people blamed reckless speculation for creating the panic in the first place. Few of them understood much about finance. Woodrow Wilson, president of Princeton College, scoffed, "There seems to be the impression in the public mind that the millionaire keeps his millions in a cash stocking..."[95]

But if most people failed to grasp the intricacies of high finance, they keenly sensed that they had lost control of their own prosperity, and they had definite ideas about who was in control and what those people wanted. Rumors began to circulate that Morgan had provoked the crisis to enrich himself and expand his power.

Meanwhile, President Roosevelt received hostility from the other side. Industrialists and Standpatters blamed the panic on his railroad reforms. At a Chamber of Commerce dinner in Manhattan, former Senator Spooner decried the "the war on corporations" and warned against rule by "philosophers," leaving little doubt about whom he meant. "I think the people of the United States ought to think a long time before they allow the commerce of the United States to be put in a straitjacket," he inveighed, "to be tightened or loosened as someone at Washington may think best." When the toastmaster proposed a toast to President Roosevelt, the guests stood silently. From a corner of the room, one man shouted, "Hip-hip..." But no one answered with a "Hurrah."[96]

In time, Roosevelt would also take criticism from people who had begun to call themselves progressives. In retrospect, his arrangement with the US Steel Corporation would seem naïve rather than decisive. He had accepted at face value the industrialists' assurances that the acquisition of TC&I was insignificant, allowing them to expand their dominance of the steel market at bargain prices.[97]

But that criticism would come a few years later—after another president initiated antitrust proceedings against US Steel, after another congress investigated the banks and forced J. Pierpont Morgan to testify. For the moment, Theodore Roosevelt still sat in the White House, and Nelson Aldrich and Joseph Cannon still ruled the Capitol.

THE MONEY POWER

We used to have a mule... We never could figure out if he was braying because he was kicking or kicking because he was braying. But all we did was to keep out of the barn and let him kick and bray all he wanted. That's all you can do with the kickers—let them alone. They are beyond reasoning with.

—Uncle Joe[1]

WASHINGTON, DC, DECEMBER 18, 1907

Nelson Aldrich sat patiently while Senate Minority Leader Charles Culberson expounded his theories on the panic of 1907. "Various reasons have been assigned for this condition of affairs," the Texas Democrat drawled. "By some it is attributed to a lack of elasticity in our system of currency. By others it is ascribed to mere fright and panic among bankers, which will speedily pass away without legislation." But he insinuated that the actual source of the panic was more sinister. "It is said by others, and among them I believe men high in authority, that it is due to a conspiracy on the part of those who opposed recent Congressional legislation and certain corporate reforms..." He demanded an immediate congressional investigation to determine what or who had provoked the terrible panic and the economic hardship that followed.

Senator Aldrich listened, serene as ever. Culberson's ploy was transparent. The Democrats had no hope of passing the resolution. They only wanted to put the Republicans on the record opposing an investigation. That was simple enough to parry.

"I ask that this resolution may be referred to the Committee on
Finance," Aldrich motioned, "with the view, not of preventing any
inquiry which the Senate should see fit to cause to be made in this matter, but in order that we may proceed in a practical and proper manner
first to ascertain the facts...If it is then the desire of the Senate that
we should undertake to investigate further as to the cause, the committee will cheerfully undertake that task, but at present the time of the
committee..."

Culberson interrupted him and tried to deflect his course, but it was
no use. After a brief debate, the Senate voted to refer the resolution to
the Finance Committee. There would be no investigation, of course, not
while Aldrich chaired the committee. Culberson didn't even get the roll
call he wanted. The Republicans passed the motion with an anonymous
chorus of Yeas.[2]

Aldrich wasn't concerned about Culberson. Even when he was sober,
the Texan was hopelessly outmatched, and everyone knew what the new
minority leader poured in his tea glass. Trust the Democrats to elect an
alcoholic to lead their caucus.[3]

The currency business would be tricky though. The economy
was a shambles, and the public was agitated. Aldrich worried that the
Republicans would suffer terrible congressional losses come November.
Worse, William Jennings Bryan might finally capture the presidency.
Congress would have to pass some kind of currency legislation this ses-
sion—nothing too radical, of course, just enough to placate the voters.[4]

WASHINGTON, DC, JANUARY 7, 1908

Aldrich spent the Christmas holiday in New York meeting with Pierpont
Morgan and the other bankers. He had originally asked them to draft the
Senate currency bill, but after several days delay, they replied that they
couldn't draw one. "We could not even agree among ourselves, and we do
not know how," they told him. He also solicited advice from a few outside
experts, including an enthusiastic German banker named Paul Warburg.
Warburg had an idea for a modified central bank modeled on European
monetary systems, but it was too ambitious for Aldrich's needs. In time,
Warburg's ideas would occupy an important place in his plans, but at that
moment, he only wanted a modest bill to defuse the Democrats' attacks
and pacify the public.[5]

In the end, he opted for a stopgap measure that would enable banks
to issue additional banknotes to expand the currency supply. Ordinarily,
banks had to back their notes with federal bonds. In the event of a currency
shortage, Aldrich's bill permitted them to issue "emergency currency"

with the treasury secretary's approval. In lieu of federal bonds they could back these emergency notes with state, municipal, and corporate railroad bonds.

Before introducing the bill, Aldrich made sure to secure the cooperation of the Republican leadership. The President was an easy sell. Roosevelt was acutely conscious of the public's discontent, and he was eager to add currency reform to his list of accomplishments. Unlike other issues over which he and Aldrich had clashed, he had no particular demands for the legislation. Finance bored him. "I have not the kind of mind that fits me to take the lead in the currency," he confessed. With his advisers offering him conflicting opinions, he was willing to let Aldrich lead the way.[6]

The House was thornier. Charles Fowler, chairman of the House Committee on Banking and Currency, was preparing his own currency bill, which was nothing like the Senate version. Fortunately for Aldrich, Fowler did not pull the strings in the House. Speaker Cannon had finally come around to monetary reform—if only to keep William Jennings Bryan out of the White House. Uncle Joe had no love for Charles Fowler or his asset-currency ideas, so he was happy to accept the Senate bill. He would make sure that Fowler's legislation never made it past the Speaker's desk.

Aldrich introduced his emergency currency bill on January 7. With the President and the Speaker in accord, quick passage seemed assured.[7]

WASHINGTON, DC, JANUARY 31, 1908

The Constitution instructs the President to address Congress "from time to time." Ever since George Washington, most presidents understood the directive to mean one *annual message* each year and occasional *special messages* when the need arose. Roosevelt interpreted "from time to time" more liberally than his predecessors. Over the course of his presidency, he sent hundreds of special messages to Congress—as many as five a week at one point—to the annoyance of the legislators. Roosevelt paid them no heed. "My critics will call this preaching. But I have got such a bully pulpit," he crowed, meaning *bully* in the colloquial sense of first-rate.[8]

On the last day of January, he sent the "hottest message ever sent to Congress." A year of vilification by conservatives and industrialists had strained his instinct for accommodation. No longer content to vent his anger and suspicions in private, Roosevelt itched to retaliate out loud. For the past seven years, he had wobbled along a narrow rail between conservative Standpatters and radical reformers using seesaw rhetoric to denounce each extreme in turn. This time, he abandoned the balancing act and focused squarely on "those most dangerous members of the criminal class—the criminals of great wealth."[9]

Announcing a "campaign against privilege," he demanded legislation to regulate the stock market, expand federal antitrust powers, and require employers to pay for workplace injuries. He also pressed for additional railroad regulation. In order to "protect the individual against unlawful exaction for the use of these public highways," he argued that the Interstate Commerce Commission (ICC) should be able to valuate the railroads and reduce shipping rates on its own initiative—the same proposal he had lambasted La Follette for "screaming" about two years earlier.[10]

As a clerk read the message out to the House of Representatives, a group of Democrats began to answer each paragraph with applause. The clapping spread through the Democratic side of the chamber, and a few progressive Republicans joined in. When the message concluded, pandemonium ensued. Congressmen cheered and pounded their desks. Southern Democrats roared out a rebel yell. Many of the Republican seats were empty by then. In the cloakroom, angry Standpatters declared that the party was being ruined, that the country was going to the dogs, that the President was a fit candidate for hell. Speaker Cannon quipped, "That fellow at the other end of the avenue wants everything, from the birth of Christ to the death of the devil."

The Senate received the message in dignified silence as usual. When it was done, Senator Jefferson Davis of Arkansas, a Democrat known for his populist leanings, jumped up and motioned, "I move that 10,000 extra copies of this message be printed for the use of the Senate. It is the best Democratic doctrine I have ever heard emanate from a Republican source." But most of the Republican senators had already walked out.[11]

The uproar flooded out into the headlines. Progressive papers praised Roosevelt for his courage and patriotism. Conservative papers concluded that he had gone insane. Even the *New York Times*, which often supported political reform, denounced Roosevelt's "unseemly and undignified violence of language" and "delusion of persecution." Predicting that none of the proposed laws would pass Congress, the editor saw the message as a campaign pamphlet designed to rouse the public.[12]

But Roosevelt's special message was nothing like any campaign speech he had ever delivered. On the stump, he always maintained a careful reserve to avoid antagonizing voters. To the contrary, he now expressed himself with such abandon precisely because he was not campaigning. His political career was nearly over—or so he thought at the time. Nor did he have any illusion that the legislators would adopt his recommendations. Congress rarely heeded lame-duck presidents in their final year of office. With no office to seek and no bills to pass, Roosevelt finally escaped his relentless pragmatism. Like Bob La Follette and Albert Beveridge, he allowed himself to lift his gaze beyond the narrow horizon of his presidency, for he no longer had anything to lose.[13]

Not that he had entirely abandoned political expediency. In addition to setting out a vision for the future, his message also served a more immediate purpose. He had timed it to coincide with a major policy address by Governor Charles Evan Hughes of New York, Taft's strongest rival for the presidential nomination. With the press in a frenzy over the President's hot words, the newspapers consigned Hughes's big speech to small typeface.

"If Hughes is going to play the game," Roosevelt boasted afterward, "he must learn the tricks."[14]

KANSAS CITY, MISSOURI, FEBRUARY 10, 1908

Unlike Roosevelt, Bill Taft had reason to be cautious. He *was* campaigning for office, and he had to win Republican support to get the nomination. When Roosevelt showed him a draft of the message, he urged him to tone it down. After it went to Congress, a journalist asked him for a statement. He replied simply, "Secretary Taft declined to comment on the President's message."

The following week, he reconsidered. Critics insisted that if he did not accept the message in its entirety, "he will be shown to have been swept off his feet by his chief supporter." He decided to work Roosevelt's message into his own campaign, though he softened it as much as he could. "The measures he recommends, and the positions that he takes, are in accord with the conservative position of the Republican party," he assured the Young Man's Republican Club of Missouri.[15]

His reserve was not entirely due to political calculation. Though he agreed with Roosevelt on most policy matters, he did not favor his style. Roosevelt was too temperamental and pugnacious to his taste. Taft took no pleasure in political combat. Truth be told, he was not even sure that he wanted to run for president. His ambition had always been to become chief justice of the Supreme Court. But others had laid the path for him to follow so that he might lead, and here he was. There was nothing to be done about it now. The wheels were in motion. A formidable campaign machine had sprung up around him, and his staff was busy collecting delegates by whatever means necessary. Party politics wasn't pretty, and Taft did his best to stay out of it.[16]

WASHINGTON, DC, FEBRUARY 13, 1908

Bob La Follette had none of Taft's reticence. He enjoyed the heat of battle as much as Roosevelt, and unlike Roosevelt, he was not afraid to lose. Indeed, he thrived on lonely crusades that everyone thought hopeless.

He had been waiting for two years to reintroduce the railroad valuation amendment that the Senate had summarily dismissed in 1906, and the panic had increased his resolve. The railroads had a history of watering their stock: misrepresenting their assets and earnings to artificially inflate share value. La Follette believed that the practice contributed to the panic of 1907 by encouraging speculators to drive stock prices too high. In contemporary terms, he believed the corporations' lack of transparency had fueled a market bubble.

So when Roosevelt revived the valuation proposal in his message to Congress, La Follette leaped at the opportunity. Lauding Roosevelt's message as "the ablest state paper the President has ever sent to Congress," he proposed legislation to grant the ICC subpoena power to investigate the railroad corporations' assets. He did not offer the legislation as a stand-alone bill. Instead, he attached an amendment to another bill that was already in the Senate schedule: Aldrich's currency proposal. The Aldrich measure permitted banks to back their emergency currency with railroad bonds. La Follette reasoned that if railroad securities were to serve as a basis for US currency, then surely the government should be able to determine what those companies were worth.[17]

His amendment produced "a flutter of excitement" from the Standpatters. "Disgust and consternation were plainly manifest," he proudly recounted. "For two years they had been able to deny me a vote in the Senate on the valuation of railway property and the reactionary Senators had learned to fear being placed on record with roll calls. And here I was rudely thrusting this troublesome proposition upon them in violation of all the regulations governing 'senatorial courtesy.' "[18]

WASHINGTON, DC, MARCH 16, 1908

The opposition to the currency bill was more intense than Aldrich had anticipated. Critics called the bond provision a boon to the railroad companies because it would create a new market for their bonds. Western banks also objected because the railroad bonds were concentrated in New York. The uproar didn't bother Aldrich, but some of the western senators were anxious about the upcoming elections and the threat of another La Follette roll call campaign. Aldrich tallied the votes. Incredibly, it looked like La Follette's valuation amendment might actually pass. Something would have to be done.[19]

Aldrich reached out to Albert Beveridge. Though Beveridge was tilting toward the radicals, the currency bill was not his chief concern. He was preparing another one of his crusades—tariff reform this time—and he wanted Aldrich to permit a vote on his bill. Aldrich agreed in exchange for Beveridge's support on currency. He could deal with the tariffs later. Besides, Beveridge's bill would have to survive the House, and no one loved tariffs more than old Uncle Joe.[20]

On March 16, the night before La Follette's railroad valuation speech, Aldrich conferred at the White House with Roosevelt, Beveridge, and J. Pierpont Morgan's assistant, George W. Perkins. A deal was struck. The President would call for a tariff commission in the next session of Congress, and Aldrich would remove the railroad bond provision from the currency bill—at least temporarily. Perkins reported back to Morgan that Aldrich would reinsert the provision "when the fight comes in the House and it goes to Committee."[21]

WASHINGTON, DC, MARCH 17, 1908

Belle La Follette and her children arrived early at the Capitol to make sure they had seats. Bob was still working on his speech when they'd left home; they had teased him not to miss his own speech. From the Senate gallery, they looked down on the heads and shoulders of the senators meandering through their morning routine. The chaplain said a prayer. A clerk reported on the proceedings in the House of Representatives. Various senators presented petitions from their constituents. Then Senator Aldrich rose to speak.

Nonchalant as always, he reported that the Finance Committee had made "sundry amendments" to the currency bill. He listed the first two. "The third amendment," he continued, "strikes from the bill all provisions in regard to railroad bonds."

Belle was dumbfounded. She turned to ask if she'd heard correctly and saw thirteen-year-old Bob Jr. rushing out of the gallery. He returned a few minutes later and whispered to her, "I got Daddy on the telephone before he had left the house and told him what happened."[22]

When Senator La Follette arrived at the Capitol a short time later, Aldrich asked for the floor. "The Senator from Wisconsin is now in the Chamber, and he has given notice of his intention to speak to-day," he announced with a hint of smugness. "I do not know whether he desires to speak now or whether he will wait until the appropriation bill is completed."

"I shall be glad to begin whenever the Senate is ready to yield me the time," La Follette replied. The Senate yielded, and he began his speech. Unfazed by Aldrich's last-minute maneuver, he declared that the change only made his comments "more pertinent, if possible." He said little about his obsolete amendment or the railroad corporations. Instead, he talked about banks.

Like other industries, the financial sector had consolidated during the previous decade. By 1908, a few large banking consortiums dominated the industry. As they combined, the biggest banks shifted from commercial banking to investment banking, and they now held substantial equity in the country's industrial corporations. To illustrate the point, La Follette named 62 executives from New York's largest banking consortiums and enumerated the companies on which they held board seats. The list was extensive. Each man directed from 10 to 70 companies spanning every major industry in the country.

When he had finished reading the list, La Follette promised to reveal the banking consortium's influence over the currency bill, but Senator Aldrich interrupted him.

"This measure is opposed not only by the National City Bank of New York, but by all the banks in the city of New York," Aldrich insisted, snapping his jaws with increasing emphasis as he spoke. "I know of no bank or bank man who is in favor of this bill."

La Follette, incredulous, replied, "I will inquire of the chairman of the Finance Committee what is the position of Mr. Morgan upon this proposition?" Giggles bubbled from the galleries.

"I do not know what Mr. Morgan's position is," Aldrich answered, "but I do know that Mr. Morgan is a man of wide experience, a man of patriotism and of wise judgment, and I should feel highly gratified if I thought Mr. Morgan approved this bill in all its features."

La Follette bent forward and peered at Aldrich under low-drawn brows. "Mr. President," he dryly retorted, "perhaps in some indirect way the chairman of the Committee on Finance will be able to find out where Mr. Morgan stands. But his beaming countenance from the galleries of this Chamber while the Senator from Rhode Island was making his speech would rather indicate that Mr. Morgan, the head of one of these great groups, was not entirely adverse to the propositions embraced in this bill."

After the exchange, he returned to his speech. Minority Leader Culberson had made similar points, but La Follette did not resort to innuendo and rhetorical questions. Like a good lawyer, he methodically built his case against the bankers and the currency bill using expert testimony and public records to support his argument. Then he went beyond the evidence. Turning to the panic of 1907, he marshaled the facts that he had presented—the network of interlocking financial interests, the banks' speculative activities, J. Pierpont Morgan's support for the currency bill—and wove them into a fairytale. In his story, the panic was not a tragedy engendered by the economic and political conditions of the era; it was a crime perpetrated by bankers to extend their wealth and power.

"The panic came," he said, "It had been scheduled to arrive. The way had been prepared." The bankers had smashed United Copper on the Curb and then waited patiently for fear to run its course. Depositors panicked, interests rates climbed, the stock market teetered. Then, at the last minute when all seemed lost, Morgan and company rode to the rescue, dispersing money to desperate stock brokers and ailing trusts, capturing the gratitude of the country.

When La Follette finished speaking, the other senators applauded—Democrats mainly. Most of the Republicans had walked out during the speech. A few who remained came up to shake his hand. Beveridge was one of them, notwithstanding his deal with Aldrich.[23]

La Follette wasn't finished though. He carried over his speech into two more days. The emergency currency would not add any elasticity to the currency, he argued. The "Money Power," as he called the bankers, would simply exploit the additional capital to accelerate corporate consolidation and spread their dominion across every sector of American industry. As for the "jack-in-the-box" railroad bond provision, he predicted that they hadn't seen the last of it.

The US monetary system desperately needed reform, he acknowledged, but the Aldrich plan was not the way to do it. Even its proponents admitted that it only was a "makeshift" expedient to mitigate the severity of currency shortages. To address the problem effectively, he proposed to establish a commission of economists, government officials, industry experts, commercial bankers, and consumer representatives that would investigate the monetary system and deliver its recommendations to Congress.[24]

WHILE LA FOLLETTE SPOKE, SENATOR BEVERIDGE had a word with Aldrich. He liked La Follette's commission idea and wanted to know what Aldrich thought about it. Perhaps the opposition to the currency bill would subside if he agreed to such a study, Beveridge suggested.

Aldrich was intrigued. He was under no illusion that his bill would solve the country's monetary troubles. It might temporarily ease currency shortages, but he had mainly offered it as a political expedient for want of a better plan. Given enough time, perhaps a better solution could be devised. Of course, he would have to make sure that right people were on the commission. He told Beveridge that he had no objection.[25]

As soon as La Follette finished speaking, Beveridge took the floor. "I was impressed with what the Senator from Wisconsin said about five minutes ago concerning the necessity for investigation," he said. "I have thought of asking the distinguished Senator from Rhode Island, who is the chairman of the Committee on Finance, what he thinks of the wisdom and expediency, in order that it may not be delayed, of a commission to investigate and to inquire into and give Congress the benefit of its deliberations upon this very grave subject."

Aldrich rose and replied, "Mr. President, the bill before the Senate is a bill to provide an emergency currency for use whenever emergencies arise. It does not undertake to treat the general question of currency or of banking reform...I hope that before the present Congress adjourns legislation will be enacted which will provide for a commission, either a commission of Members of the House and Senate, or a mixed commission, to consider this question, with a view of reporting at an early day in the future."[26]

With that statement, a process went into motion that would have momentous consequences for the future of the United States. The monetary commission proposal did not become part of the emergency currency bill right away; Aldrich wanted time to evaluate it. But as Beveridge predicted, his endorsement of the commission helped to defuse opposition to the currency bill. It passed the Senate two days later by a vote of 42 to 16 with five Republicans voting against it.

Though La Follette failed to stop the bill, his failure belied a significant achievement. The freshman senator from Wisconsin, who two years earlier had been mocked as irrelevant, had stared down the "Boss" of the Senate over the railroad bond provision, and the Boss had blinked.

"SENATE OLIGARCHY FIGHTING FOR LIFE...MET DEFEAT ON CURRENCY," proclaimed the *New York Times*. Headlines and editorials quoted liberally from La Follette's "Money Power" speech. Conservative papers and prominent bankers denounced him as a dangerous demagogue, which only increased his fame. His office received numerous requests for copies of the speech. For previous speeches, 85 percent of such requests had come from the West. This time, half of them came from the East. Fighting Bob had proven himself a national force in American politics.[27]

The emergency currency bill then moved to the House Committee on Banking and Currency chaired by Representative Charles Fowler of New Jersey.

WASHINGTON, DC, MAY 5, 1908

Charles Fowler irritated Uncle Joe. Instead of reporting Aldrich's bill out of committee for the House to vote on it, Fowler spent weeks taking testimony from its critics. Western bankers opposed the Senate plan because New York banks owned most of the bonds required for emergency notes. They also distrusted Wall Street's cozy relationship with Washington and worried that the treasury secretary would approve funds for the Eastern banks only. Fowler called in numerous experts who testified that the Aldrich plan was insufficient to prevent a panic. When the hearings were over, the Banking and Currency Committee tabled the bill.

Cannon was furious. There was barely a month left in the session. After that, Congress would not resume until after the election. If they didn't pass a currency bill right away, the Republicans were in for trouble. With Aldrich's bill mired in committee, he and Roosevelt urgently sought an alternative.

Representative Edward Vreeland of New York provided it. The bill he proposed was very similar to Aldrich's, but in a nod to western bankers, it allowed banks to back emergency notes with "any securities, including commercial paper." Vreeland's bill went to the Committee on Banking and Currency. Fowler tabled it as well.[28]

By May, Uncle Joe had had enough. He called a meeting of the Republican caucus in order to circumvent Fowler's committee. "It is our duty to pass a law," he admonished his colleagues, "so that we can say to the people of the country we have made a panic due to currency stringency such as occurred last fall impossible in the future." He allowed the Republican congressmen five minutes each to speak, but it didn't matter what they said. Everyone appreciated why he wanted a bill. At the end of the conference, they voted 115 to 21 to suspend the House rules and bring the Vreeland bill directly to the floor, bypassing Fowler's committee.[29]

The House vote took place the following week. Cannon gave each congressman ten minutes to talk this time. The Democrats and a few Republicans protested his suspension of the rules, but there was nothing they could do. The Vreeland bill passed 184 to 145, with sixteen Republicans and the entire Democratic caucus voting against.[30]

From there, the bill went into joint conference where Aldrich, Vreeland, and Cannon hashed out a compromise between the Senate and House versions. The final Aldrich-Vreeland bill returned to the House on May 27, and the Republicans once again suspended the House rules. Cannon allowed only one hour of debate this time—thirty minutes for each side. Speaking for the Democrats, Minority Leader John Sharp Williams scoffed, "This bill ought to be called the Aldrich-Cannon Political Emergency bill." When sixty minutes were up, the House passed the Aldrich-Vreeland bill by a vote of 166 to 140.[31]

The bill then moved for final passage in the Senate with only four days remaining in the session.

WASHINGTON, DC, MAY 29, 1908

Bob La Follette visited the House chamber to hear the abridged debate over the currency measure. The final bill was even worse than the original Senate version. By allowing banks to back emergency notes with any securities, it effectively allowed railroad bonds to be used after all, just as he had predicted. The revised bill did include the monetary commission he had requested, but the makeup of the commission looked nothing like his proposal. Instead of experts and private citizens, it would be composed of nine senators and nine congressmen. He could easily guess who would be appointed.

He tried to persuade the Democrats to join him in a filibuster. If they held the floor continuously until the end of the session, they could stop the bill by running out the clock. But Democratic leaders felt that a filibuster would be politically unwise and declined to take part. Only a couple of low-ranking Democrats agreed to participate. Senator William J. Stone was in Missouri when the House passed the bill. When he heard the news, he immediately boarded a train and returned to Washington "bedecked with war paint and feathers" to help La Follette fight the bill in the Senate. Senator Thomas P. Gore of Oklahoma also agreed to assist the filibuster but would not be able to talk very long, for he was blind and had to speak without notes. No one had ever sustained an extended filibuster without the support of one of the major parties. La Follette had just recovered from a long illness, so he was far from peak condition. The papers predicted that he would only hold out two or three hours in the summer heat.[32]

He started speaking at 12:30 in the afternoon. The temperature outside was in the 90s, and the chamber was stifling. "Mr. President," he began, "I should like to have the attention of the Senator from Rhode Island for a moment while I state, in brief, my position with reference to the pending bill. I believe it, sir, to be a very bad bill. I think it ought not to pass." The senators soon discovered that his statement would be anything but brief. While he spoke, they sweated in their wool frock coats and swished themselves with palm-leaf fans. At every opportunity, they fled to the cloakroom and the outdoor balconies for relief from the heat.

La Follette never let them stay long. His secretary kept a count. Whenever the number of senators in the chamber fell below 45, he asked Vice President Fairbanks for a quorum call. The bells would ring through the Capitol until the senators glumly returned to their seats. La Follette did not call them back to torment them. The quorum calls were his only opportunity to sit down and rest.[33]

An intricate parliamentary dance unfolded. There was no cloture rule at that time, so Aldrich could not call a vote to terminate the speech. As long as La Follette kept talking and kept standing, he would hold the floor. But the conservatives employed little-used Senate rules to exhaust him. He was not permitted to ask a clerk to read out documents, which would have given him a respite. When the senators discovered that his secretary was counting heads for quorum calls, they threatened to remove the secretary from the chamber. After Senator Gore briefly spelled him, they ruled that if La Follette gave up the floor again, he would not be allowed to have it back.[34]

So La Follette kept on talking. While he spoke, voters deluged western senators with telegrams urging them to help, but they did not join the filibuster. A few Democrats supported it passively by pretending to be absent during quorum calls so that La Follette would have more time to rest. Senator Jeff Davis, the "Arkansas Cyclone," telegraphed from Little Rock, "Hold the fort, for I am coming. Will be there in the morning."[35]

At the White House, President Roosevelt fumed. "Congress is ending with a pointless and stupid filibuster by La Follette. It is sheer idiocy for the Senate to permit such silly rules as will allow this kind of filibuster."[36]

In the evening, the galleries filled with men and women in formal wear who had come to witness the curiosity. The line for seats extended through the sweltering corridors of the Capitol. The audience energized La Follette. He capered about the floor, shouted and stamped his feet. But he was getting tired. As the night wore on, his eyelids drooped, and his voice fell to a whisper. Not allowed to sit, he folded his arms and rested his weight against the arm of his chair.

The quorum calls offered his only relief. At 1 a.m., Aldrich denied him even those. Calling upon another obscure Senate precedent, he motioned that quorum calls be barred until some new business required one. For the tradition-bound Senate, the motion represented a startling breach of convention, but Vice President Fairbanks sustained it. Many of the senators gratefully left for home. Others removed their coats and collars and curled up on the couches and floor of the cloakroom.[37]

La Follette bided his time for an hour and a half until almost all the other senators were gone. Then he formally appealed the vice president's ruling. That put Aldrich in a bind. There were no longer enough Republicans in the chamber to defeat the appeal. In the end, Aldrich had to call a quorum himself in order to bring back his allies. La Follette gained an hour of relief while the sergeant-at-arms rousted the senators from their beds. They drifted in with missing neckties, shoes untied, and suspenders showing.[38]

Once the senators had tidied themselves and returned to their seats, the roll was taken, and La Follette continued his speech. He carried on until 7:03 a.m., when Senator Stone of Missouri came to relieve him. "Mr. President," La Follette announced, "I am rather reluctant to surrender the floor for the time being, but as others desire to speak and are in waiting, I yield the floor for the present." Once Stone had secured the floor, La Follette finally departed the chamber. He told reporters waiting outside that he felt fine except that his feet were sore. After a shave from the Senate barber, he returned home with his eldest daughter to get some sleep. He had held the floor for 18 hours and 23 minutes, shattering the previous Senate record. The *Boston Daily Globe* calculated that he had uttered 66,600 words.[39]

Senator Stone spoke quietly to conserve his voice. Aldrich complained that he could not hear him, but there was no Senate rule against speaking quietly. Unlike La Follette, who never seemed to run out of words, Stone eventually gave out and resorted to reading a treatise on the Persian monetary system, prompting more complaints. At 1:30, Aldrich moved for a half-hour lunch break. It was another ploy. The Democratic leaders were not keen on one of their own carrying the filibuster, and they gathered around Stone for a talk. After the break, he spoke for only fifteen more minutes and then yielded to Thomas Gore, the blind senator from Oklahoma.[40]

Gore spoke for over two hours, impressing his listeners with a comprehensive recitation of facts and statistics he had memorized. Even Aldrich indulged in a smile of admiration. Gore concluded at 4:27 to a swell of applause.[41]

When the applause subsided, there was a brief silence before Vice President Fairbanks said, "The question is on agreeing to the report of the committee of conference." At that moment, awareness flashed through the Senate chamber. Senator Stone was supposed to relieve Gore, but he wasn't in the room. The blind senator had no way of knowing it.

Aldrich stood up. "I ask the roll be called," he said.

Senator Weldon Heyburn, a moderate Republican from Idaho who had previously declined to participate in the filibuster, leapt to his feet. "Mr. President!" he cried out. But Fairbanks proceeded to call for votes on the bill in alphabetical order, starting with Aldrich.

"Aye," said Aldrich.

"I addressed the Chair before the commencement of the roll call," Heyburn protested, his face red with indignation. Aldrich countered that the roll call could not be suspended once it had begun. Fairbanks wavered for a moment and then sustained the senator from Rhode Island.[42]

La Follette, meanwhile, had already returned to the Capitol. He was in his basement committee room preparing his next speech. He intended to relieve Senator Stone and deliver another marathon speech that would break the Senate record he had just set. The bells clanged, signaling a roll call. He raced upstairs, but it was too late. The filibuster was over; the roll call had proceeded. The Aldrich-Vreeland bill passed 43 to 22.[43]

AT 9 P.M., ROOSEVELT ARRIVED AT THE CAPITOL in evening dress with a white rose in his lapel. Senators and congressmen came to greet him in the President's Room. He pulled Aldrich aside, and they held an earnest conversation in the corner. La Follette came in while they were speaking, and Roosevelt motioned him over. He smiled mischievously while the two senators shook hands.

"I should have been de-e-lighted to have heard your lengthy address," he said to La Follette. "Senator Aldrich has just been telling me how much he and his fellows enjoyed it." He threw back his head and laughed uproariously. Aldrich and La Follette joined in, though a *New York Times* correspondent observed that "their mirth seemed somewhat strained."[44]

Then President Roosevelt signed the Aldrich-Vreeland bill into law. He signed a number of other bills as well but little else of significance. Beveridge had managed to pass a worker's compensation bill for federal employees, but the tariff commission he had negotiated with Aldrich as his price for supporting the currency measure went nowhere. Roosevelt's proposal to expand the President's antitrust authority had also disappeared into a House committee. Nonetheless, he expressed satisfaction to his son, Kermit, writing, "[A]ltho I am chagrined that more has not been done, I am glad that we have gone a little ahead and not a little behind."[45]

THE SENATORS RETURNED TO THEIR CHAMBER at 10:30 the same evening. The Aldrich-Vreeland Act having been enacted, Vice President Fairbanks announced the composition of the new Monetary Commission. Eight of the nine Senate representatives were members of the Finance Committee, including Aldrich, W. B. Allison, and Eugene Hale of Maine, who had replaced John Spooner and Orville Platt in Aldrich's inner circle.[46]

The commission held its first meeting after midnight in the office of the Senate Finance Committee. Nine congressmen appointed by Speaker Cannon joined the senators. Edward Vreeland was one of them. Charles Fowler was not, nor any other congressman who had been disloyal to the Speaker. The commission voted Aldrich chairman and Vreeland vice-chairman. They arranged to meet in secret at the Plaza Hotel in New York later that month. "My idea is, of course, that everything shall be done in the most quiet manner possible, and without any public announcement," Aldrich explained.[47]

On the surface, Aldrich seemed to have won the day. The filibuster was broken, the bill was passed. The Republicans could now boast to the public that they had responded to the panic and stabilized the economy. But their triumph proved shallow, for the public was now less inclined to believe them. La Follette had again turned legislative defeat into political victory. His sensational filibuster made front-page news. It awakened sympathy for his cause and intensified suspicion of Aldrich and the Standpatters. His strategy of "publicity, discussion, and agitation" was bearing fruit. A new political movement was rising. In his "Money Power" speech, La Follette had given it a name that would echo through the ages: the Progressive Movement.[48]

6

THE SMILE

The trouble with Taft is that if he were Pope he would think it necessary to appoint a few Protestant Cardinals.

—Uncle Joe[1]

GREENWICH, CONNECTICUT, JUNE 1, 1908

By the age of 42, Lincoln Steffens had reached the pinnacle of his career. Wealthy and famous, he lived with his wife in a beautiful farmhouse on the Connecticut shore. He and his colleagues Ray Stannard Baker and Ida Tarbell had launched their own monthly, *The American Magazine*, which gave him freedom to write about what he wanted.

Despite his success, a sense of unease gnawed at him. "I simply don't know where I'm at," he confided to his sister. "I know things are all wrong somehow; and fundamentally; but I don't know what the matter is and I don't know what to do." Muckraking had lost its appeal; exposing a few corrupt officials would not fix The System. He compared his exposés to a vigilante mob that lynches individual wrongdoers while doing nothing to improve the conditions that produced them. "I hate this hate and this hunt," he wrote. "I have bayed my bay in it, and I am sick of it."[2]

Restless and lost, Steffens cast about for answers to society's fundamental problems. "I'm listening to all but the ignorant," he explained to his sister. "I'm playing a long, patient game, but before I die, I believe I can help to bring about an essential change in the American mind." He began his quest with an article titled "What the Matter Is in America and What to Do About It," which posed the question to three leaders he respected—Theodore Roosevelt, William Taft, and Robert La Follette.[3]

Steffens found much to admire in Roosevelt's accomplishments. As President, he had drawn attention to the nation's problems and shown that strong government could serve the interests of the people. But breaking up a few "bad" trusts and passing a few regulations would not cure the disease. As long as the flawed political and economic machinery remained in place, Steffens believed that powerful men would find ways to cripple or exploit the new laws. "[Roosevelt's] record of victories is long and splendid, but incomplete," he concluded. "He leaves the enemy in possession of the field."[4]

He worried that Taft would be even less effective. "We don't need any more laws," Taft told him. "If we enforce those that we have, with certain amendments for their practical application, it will be enough." Where Roosevelt had at least located the enemies and raised a public clamor against them, Taft preferred to deal with his opponents in private. Steffens feared that this approach would be counterproductive, for though Taft might achieve some practical results, he would forfeit the popular sentiment that Roosevelt had aroused, leaving the public to return to its apathetic slumber.[5]

In contrast to Roosevelt and Taft, La Follette had an answer to Steffens's question. "Politically, the trouble can be summed up in one phrase, misrepresentative government," he told Steffens. "I mean that our Government is manned by the agents, sometimes honest, often corrupt, of businesses which have, or want to have, what we call 'special privileges,' which really are just plain advantages over other men and other businesses."

"What do you propose to do about it?" Steffens asked.

La Follette described his uncompromising legislative strategy and roll-call campaigns in Wisconsin. "We weren't after 'a bill,'" he explained. "We wanted that bill, and the reason we wanted it was that we proposed to drive out of politics the men who represented the railroads, and leave only those who represented the people."

"Then, Senator, every measure you father has two purposes," Steffens suggested, "one to achieve the end described in the bill; the other to put the senators on record."

"Exactly," La Follette replied. "And my first purpose is to put the senators on record, for, if we could get the Congress and our legislatures generally to be truly representative, the other things would come of themselves. Not one or two mangled bills a session, but all the legislation we need."

"And what if that doesn't solve all our problems?" Steffens pressed him.

"Oh, well," La Follette said with a laugh, "that's as far as we shall get in my time. But, with a government that has made and survived that test, we shall have the power and the intelligence and the character to solve any problems that arise; and we will solve them—all."[6]

WASHINGTON, DC, JUNE 5, 1908

Theodore Roosevelt was accustomed to Steffens's backhanded compliments and sly barbs. He used to appreciate his friend's provocations and to enjoy their repartee, but Steffens seemed to have changed lately. His criticisms were more earnest, and he was dabbling with dangerous ideas.

When Steffens published "What the Matter Is in America," Roosevelt responded with as much subtlety as he could muster. "It is a little difficult for me to express myself clearly without seeming to be slightly uncomplimentary," he wrote to him. Then he proceeded to denounce Steffens's position as "erroneous," "childish," "silly," "foolish," "simply nonsense," and "not much above the average long-haired and wild-eyed socialist type."

"It is only the quack who will tell you that he has a cure for everything," he added, leaving no doubt who the quack was. "[La Follette] talks about the railroads; but as far as action goes, he has not helped at all, since he came to the Senate, in the great work we have actually done towards getting control over the railroads. He has rather hindered this work. The men who have done good in the twenty-five years I have been in politics are those who have had ideals but who have tried to realize them in plain, practical fashion, and who have tried to do each his duty as the day came, and to fight each evil as they found it arise without bothering their heads as to the 'ultimate' evil. I believe in the men who take the next step; not those who theorize about the 200th step."[7]

GREENWICH, CONNECTICUT, JUNE 9, 1908

"No, I don't think representative government will correct all evils," Steffens fired back. "I do think, however, that fighting for it, consciously, will uncover not only the principal evils, but their common source...It is privilege. Trace every case of corruption you know to its source, and you will see, I believe, that somebody was trying to get out of Government some special right; to keep a saloon open after hours; a protective tariff; a ship subsidy; a public-service franchise."

Steffens ended the letter on a warmer note. "I think we see things differently, fight them differently; express ourselves differently, and that your patience with me has been founded, like my very great respect and my very quiet but very genuine affection for you, upon the sense that, at bottom, I in my humble way and you in your whole splendid career are working toward the same end."[8]

But the truth was that they were drifting apart. While Roosevelt sidestepped tentatively toward progressive ideas, Steffens raced faster and farther than Roosevelt would ever venture. A few months later, he would write that he had "given up reading Steffens." It was not the first of Roosevelt's many and varied friendships to tear under the strain of widening political fault lines. Nor would it be the last.[9]

CHICAGO, ILLINOIS, JUNE 17, 1908

Senator Henry Cabot Lodge of Massachusetts stood at the other end of the spectrum from Steffens. He and Roosevelt had been close friends since the 1880s, fellow aristocrats who condescended to dirty themselves in the vulgar business of politics. Though the conservative Lodge had cast his lot with Aldrich and the Standpatters, his long friendship with Roosevelt remained solid.

On June 17, Lodge stood on the semicircular stage at the Chicago Coliseum surveying the delegates to the Republican National Convention. They were much too quiet, even more subdued than the crowd that had attended Roosevelt's nomination four years earlier. Senator Julius Caesar Burrows of Michigan had been a poor choice for convention chairman. His stilted, inaudible speeches put people to sleep—literally. The press reported that the Chinese minister had tipped forward his black silk hat and nodded off. The delegates were not much livelier. This would not do.[10]

Lodge was determined to rouse the convention. He began by lambasting the Democrats, a certain crowd-pleaser. His ringing tones infused the hall with nervous energy. The fire primed, he lit the spark. "The President has fearlessly enforced the laws as he found them upon the statute books," he cried. The crowd applauded, modestly. "[T]he President is the best abused and most popular man in the United States today," he continued. The applause intensified, and the fire caught. Some delegates from the territories jumped onto their chairs. Colorado, West Virginia, Texas, and North Carolina followed suit. A roar rolled through the Coliseum. Up in the gallery, men waved star-spangled umbrellas over the railing. A Louisiana delegate pulled off his coat and swung it over his head as he hollered. Another roar swept the hall. The cheers crested and ebbed in succession like crashing waves. Lodge tried to continue his speech but could not make himself heard. Finally, he gave up and paced on the stage with a satisfied smile.

A collective cry broke from the galleries, "Four-four-four years more!" They stamped their feet in unison at each beat of the chant. The Texas delegates took it up. Colorado echoed them, and the cheer bounced back and forth between the two delegations. Lodge pounded his gavel. "Teddy, Teddy, we want Teddy!" yelled the crowd. "Roosevelt, Roosevelt! Rah for Roosevelt!" Someone dragged an enormous teddy bear up to the press gallery and hurled it into the Illinois delegation. Illinois pitched it to Iowa, which whirled it through the air to California. The bear tumbled across the states and territories until it landed in Oklahoma and disappeared.

Half an hour later, Senator Lodge finally restored order. The *New York Times* clocked the ovation at 46 minutes, 55 seconds, a magnificent display of Republican fervor. The only problem was that it was for the wrong man.[11]

WASHINGTON, DC, JUNE 18, 1908

Roosevelt fussed nervously in his office. Down the hall, the stutter of the telegraph machine announced the progress of the third and final day of the convention. The previous day's four-years-more demonstration had gratified and troubled him at the same time. He knew that Taft had the most delegates; he had made sure of it by pressuring the Credentials Committee to recognize pro-Taft delegates in the disputed caucuses. His only concern was that Taft's opponents would engineer a Roosevelt stampede to nominate him for a third term. Of course, everyone would think that he had planned it himself.[12]

ACROSS THE STREET AT THE WAR DEPARTMENT, Nellie Taft was even more anxious. She neither liked nor trusted Roosevelt, and she worried that he had set up her husband in order to finagle a third term for himself. On the final day of the convention, the Tafts gathered with a few friends in his office. Nellie fidgeted in her husband's desk chair while he sat to the side with some friends. Ten-year-old Charlie scurried back and forth from the telegraph office delivering telegrams to his mother. She read them aloud to the group.[13]

Speaker Cannon's nomination came first. His ovation was modest and brief; the cheers lasted less than two minutes. Vice President Fairbanks's reception was no better. Governor Hughes received no ovation at all. When Taft's turn finally came, it was almost four o'clock in Washington. A telegram reported that the cheering had begun. Nellie prayed that it would endure. "I only want it to last more than forty-nine minutes," she blurted out. "I want to get even for the scare that Roosevelt cheer of forty-nine minutes gave me yesterday."

Her husband smiled patronizingly. "Oh, my dear, my dear!" he chided her.[14]

The applause lasted 25 minutes—longer than any of the other candidates' receptions but not even close to Roosevelt's.

More bulletins came in as the remaining candidates were nominated. Senator Foraker garnered thirty seconds of applause. Senator Knox of Pennsylvania had a more respectable showing. Then the crowd surprised everyone by offering Senator La Follette a long vigorous demonstration second only to Taft's.[15]

No sooner had the nominations concluded than little Charlie rushed in with a new telegram. Nellie opened it and froze. "A large portrait of Roosevelt has been displayed on the platform and the convention has exploded," she read. The room went silent. Taft drummed his fingers on the arm of his chair and whistled softly. Charlie returned a couple minutes later with another report. Nellie read it impassively, her face a mask. "A huge American flag with a Roosevelt portrait upon it is being carried about the hall; and the uproar continues with increased fury."

The silence returned. After what seemed an eternity, Charlie came in with the next bulletin. Nellie all but leaped out of her chair when she read it. "Massachusetts gives 26 votes for Taft!" The Roosevelt demonstration was over; the voting had begun.

Everyone stood up, excited and confused. How had Massachusetts, in the middle of the alphabet, already voted? They learned the next day that Senator Lodge had pulled it off. At the height of the frenzy, he had ordered the roll call starting with his home state and thereby averted the threat of a Roosevelt stampede.[16]

The bulletins came in quickly after that. State after state declared for William Howard Taft. The fateful message arrived at 5:57. Nellie glanced at the slip of paper and dropped it to the floor. "Oh, Will!" she cried, grasping her husband by the hand.

The sound of cheering erupted outside the office. The door burst open, and a crush of people surged in to congratulate the new Republican nominee. Reporters followed on their heels, demanding a statement.

"Words don't frame themselves for me now," Taft replied, "but I don't deny that I am very happy. Later tonight I may have something to say."[17]

As the Tafts celebrated, the telegraph machine rattled off the final tally: Taft, 702; Knox, 68; Hughes, 67; Cannon, 58; Fairbanks, 40; La Follette, 25; Foraker, 16. News of the vice-presidential nomination also came in over the wire. Taft had wanted Albert Beveridge of Indiana or

Jonathan Dolliver of Iowa "or some western senator who has shown himself conservative and at the same time represents the progressive movement." But the Standpatters gave Taft no more deference than they had given Roosevelt four years earlier. They chose one of Cannon's allies, Representative James Sherman of New York. With the presidential nomination concluded, Uncle Joe came to the Coliseum and set the delegates laughing and cheering as he praised Sherman's courage and integrity. "Sunny Jim" won easily with 816 delegates.[18]

DENVER, COLORADO, JULY 10, 1908

The Democrats met in Denver, the first time a major party ventured so far west for a national convention. Eastern visitors who expected to find gun-toting cowboys galloping down dusty streets were disappointed. Electric lights illuminated Denver's paved avenues, which conveyed as many automobiles as horses. The mounted policemen looked a bit like cowboys, but instead of shooting outlaws, they guarded a huge pile of snow that the city had carted down from the mountains to entertain the visitors. The cops periodically ordered revelers to "stop stealing that snow," but they seemed unsure how to handle a gang of misbehaving New Yorkers who told them to "chase themselves."[19]

Denver did display one cultural idiosyncrasy that astonished the easterners. The automobiles were familiar enough, but the drivers were unusual. Many of them were *women*. Women also rode *astride* horses on public streets, and they jumped onto trolley cars without waiting for the vehicles to stop. Ladies "of good standing" ate and drank alone at fashionable restaurants, some of which employed "girl waiters." Even more extraordinary, Colorado accorded full voting rights to women and had elected the convention's only female delegate.[20]

In 1908, only three other states allowed women to vote—Idaho, Utah, and Wyoming—but Americans were beginning to see women's suffrage as possible if not quite imminent. "I believe that women's suffrage will come eventually," Secretary Taft conceded, though he insisted that the moment had not arrived because "most women do not want suffrage." Roosevelt was slightly less supportive. "Personally, I believe in woman's suffrage," he affirmed, "but I am not an enthusiastic advocate of it, because I do not regard it as a very important matter." Bob and Belle La Follette would eventually become prominent advocates of women's suffrage, but as of 1908, neither had publicly endorsed the cause. Most male politicians shared Uncle Joe's opinion that "man must always sustain the family; women bear and rear the children. It is the law of God, or nature, whichever we choose to call it, and will be maintained to the end."[21]

At the Democratic convention, party leaders ignored suffragists' demands for a plank in the platform. They also refused to consider a resolution on race equality. They did, however, agree to a resolution to bar "Asiatic immigrants who can not be amalgamated with our population" from entering the United States. "The Democratic party is the champion of equal rights and opportunities to all," the platform proudly concluded, meaning all white men.[22]

William Jennings Bryan had endorsed the race equality plank but abandoned it in the face of southern opposition. On most other questions, he got his way. Newspapers reported that the conservative Bourbon Democrats had surrendered unconditionally to the western radicals. They insinuated that Bryan had choreographed the entire convention by telephone from Lincoln, Nebraska. "The humble commoner of twelve years past is now the domineering overlord," the *Washington Post* warned. "He has become [the party's] dictator, its supreme master, and, like a haughty Caesar, has but to crook his finger to make it bend the knee."[23]

Not everyone agreed with this assessment. "Bah! Bryan doesn't rule here," Lincoln Steffens wrote from Denver. "[T]he delegates who sit down there in those little pens, are not delegates at all, but the creatures of the State bosses who rise when their State is called and vote them." Their enthusiasm for Bryan had nothing to do with progressive ideals, he argued. They voted for him because their bosses hoped to exploit Bryan's popularity. "Fear of the people dominates this convention," he concluded, "not love and not respect, but fear; the dread of you and me."[24]

There were elements of truth to both accounts. Many of the bosses were wary of the growing progressive movement but eager to conquer Washington no matter who carried the Democratic standard. On the other hand, Bryan was hardly a naïve victim of their machinations. In his third and final race for the White House, he too yearned for victory, and he welcomed the whole motley Democratic caucus into his coalition—southern racists, urban bosses, conservative Bourbons, and all. He pushed his allies to embrace progressive policies but shied away from divisive issues like railroad nationalization and race equality.[25]

The compromise platform that emerged from the Democrats' diverse alliance looked oddly familiar. It included almost everything President Roosevelt had asked for in his various messages to Congress—railroad valuation, antitrust legislation, income taxes, campaign finance laws, and forest conservation. In an attempt to capitalize on Roosevelt's popularity, the Democrats hoped to "out-Roosevelt the Republicans" by adopting the platform that the President had failed to persuade his own party to endorse. So began a peculiar campaign strategy in which the Democrats tried to promote their nominee as the true political heir to the Republican incumbent.[26]

As for the Democratic rank-and-file, they were happy to cheer for whoever needed cheering. They cheered for the convention chairman every other sentence. They cheered for Judge Parker, for the late President Cleveland, and for "Dixie." They even cheered for President Roosevelt, the new Democratic hero. Most of all, they cheered for their nominee, the "Great Commoner," the "Peerless Leader," William Jennings Bryan. When Thomas Gore, the blind senator from Oklahoma, invoked Bryan's name on the second day of the convention, the crowd shouted and stomped and hurled their hats for an hour and a half without interruption.[27]

HOT SPRINGS, VIRGINIA, JULY 11, 1908

William Howard Taft was not a complete neophyte. As a high-level administrator and adviser, he'd had plenty of secondhand political experience. But, he had never run for office himself. His career was a long series of political appointments: county assistant prosecutor, district tax collector, Ohio state judge, US solicitor general, federal judge, governor-general of the Philippines, and finally, secretary of war. At every juncture, some powerful politician had rewarded his talents by hauling him up to the next level. Now, Theodore Roosevelt had all but appointed him the Republican nominee.

But not even Roosevelt could appoint a president. For the first time in his life, Taft had to fight for the job he wanted... or thought he wanted. It did not take him long to discover that he hated politics. He hated the prying reporters. He hated the media attacks. He hated issuing denials and explanations and partial-denials-partial-explanations. Some days, he regretted ever leaving the quiet comfort of the courtroom. "The next four months are going to be a kind of nightmare for me," he moaned.

"Poor old boy!" Roosevelt wrote to him. "Of course, you are not enjoying the campaign. I wish you had some of my bad temper! It is at times a real aid to enjoyment."[28]

While his presidential campaign rolled into motion, Taft retreated to a remote Appalachian resort in western Virginia, ostensibly to work on his acceptance speech for the notification ceremony. He wrote from 9 a.m. to 3 p.m. each day and then relaxed with 18 holes of golf in the misty mountain air. "I am fond of the sport," he told reporters, "and it always puts me in excellent condition." After a few days on the rugged green, his weight dipped below 300 pounds. "Oh, I am becoming Apollo-like," he joked.[29]

OYSTER BAY, NEW YORK, JULY 23, 1908

The respite could not last. On July 22, Taft took an overnight train to Long Island for a meeting with Roosevelt. While his train paused in Philadelphia, a group of railroad men asked him to come out and shake hands. When he hesitated, one called out, "You're not a little bit like Teddy or you would have been out here long ago getting busy." Taft laughed and went out to a greet them. "There goes the next President of the United States!" one of them shouted as he returned to his car.[30]

Taft reached Roosevelt's summer estate in Oyster Bay the following afternoon. After lunch, the two men adjourned to the library to discuss Taft's upcoming acceptance speech. Roosevelt never hesitated to shower his protégé with advice. "My own voice is always for aggressive warfare, and in your position I should go hard at Bryan," he had recommended in a letter. "I believe you will be elected *if we can keep things as they are*," he added, "so be *very* careful to say nothing, not one sentence, that can be misconstrued." He also discouraged Taft from discussing his judicial record, "for the moment you begin to cite decisions people…promptly begin to nod."[31]

When Taft showed him a draft of his acceptance speech, Roosevelt advised him, "I think that the number of times my name is used should be cut down. You are now the leader, and there must be nothing that looks like self-depreciation or undue subordination of yourself."[32]

CINCINNATI, OHIO, JULY 28, 1908

Two days later, Taft stepped off the train in Cincinnati. His brother Charles was there to meet him. So were several hundred cheering supporters, each of whom wanted to shake his hand. As he left the station, Taft looked up to see a large portrait of himself draped with an American flag and inscribed with the words *No place like home*. "That's a true sentiment," he told the onlookers, though he hadn't lived in Cincinnati for eight years.[33]

His long absence did not stop the city from claiming him. Unlike Roosevelt's modest notification ceremony in the little village of Oyster Bay, Cincinnati could barely contain its excitement at the prospect of a homegrown president. City officials had organized a "Taft Day" extravaganza that dwarfed the recent Fourth of July. American flags fluttered from the windows of every building as a parade of 10,000 marched through the city. Cannon-fire echoed through the hills, and daylight fireworks exploded overhead.

The ceremony took place at Charles Taft's sprawling Colonial-style mansion downtown. Modern skyscrapers towered over the old white frame house, which dated to the early days of the Republic. Faces peered out from the high windows of the buildings, straining for a glimpse of the future president. At ground level, thousands gathered in street. Hurrahs periodically wafted up from the crowd, "Bill's all right!" "Taft's all right!" Inside the house, Taft conferred with Republican officials, ignoring the spectators outside until Nellie dragged him to the doorway to greet them. "Go to it, Bill!" shouted a man through a megaphone from a nearby rooftop. The crowd took up the refrain, "Go to it, Bill! Go to it, Bill!"[34]

At noon, the Republican delegation assembled on a platform in front of the house while the crowd cheered. After the officials formally notified Taft of his nomination, he stepped up to the podium to deliver his acceptance speech. When he emerged from beneath the awning, the summer sun struck his face and the bald spot on top of his head. He began to sweat. He removed his pince-nez and put on spectacles that would not slide off his nose while he spoke. He opened his manuscript and drew a breath.

"Go to it, Bill!" yelled the man with the megaphone again. Taft looked up at him and smiled. It was not a big smile, nothing like Roosevelt's toothy grin. The corners of his mouth disappeared into his bushy handlebar mustache so that only his lower lip peeked out below the bristles. But Taft's smile was not confined to his mouth. Every feature joined in the pleasure of it. His eyes narrowed to slits, his cheeks expanded, his chin doubled up, and his whole face went round with infectious delight.

America was in love with Taft's smile. People sang songs about it, stamped its likeness on buttons and posters, published essays on its many virtues. To a country ravaged by recession and ruptured by class conflict, the Taft smile promised harmony, prosperity, and hope. It lodged in the popular imagination and ballooned in size until it all but obscured Taft himself—so that it didn't matter what he said or did so long as he kept smiling.

When Taft smiled at the man with the megaphone, another great cheer burst from the crowd. It swept up and down the street where it was taken up by distant figures who could neither see nor hear the proceedings. When they finally quieted, Taft asked that the gates be opened so that some of the spectators could come closer. Then he began to speak. His words carried easily, undecorated by rhetorical flourishes or dramatic pauses. He spoke matter-of-factly with the muted cadence of a mid-century public service announcement.[35]

"Gentlemen of the Committee, I am deeply sensible of the honor which the Republican National Convention has conferred on me in the nomination which you formally tender," he began. "I accept it with full appreciation of the responsibility it imposes."

The sun bore down. His starched collar wilted, his shirt wrinkled, and his cuffs clung to his wrists. Perspiration trickled into his eyes and drenched his hair and clothes. He soaked through handkerchief after handkerchief trying to staunch the flow while he slogged along through the heat. The speech lasted more than hour—he had not heeded Roosevelt's advice to keep it short—but he persevered though all 12,000 ponderous words. Some of the corseted ladies in the audience were not so durable; ambulances carted off the ones who fainted. When it was over, Taft rushed off to the bathroom without waiting for the applause and doused himself in cold water.[36]

THE NEXT DAY, THE NEWSPAPERS DELIVERED their verdict on Taft's acceptance speech: "dignified and temperate," "frank and sincere," "straightforward and incisive," "progressively conservative," and "conservatively progressive." He addressed all the major issues of the day with subtlety and intelligence. His words were clear; his voice was loud. His unqualified endorsement of Roosevelt's policies encouraged progressives; his cautious style and calm demeanor impressed conservatives. It was a perfectly competent campaign speech.[37]

It was also perfectly forgettable. The opinions Taft expressed were nearly indistinguishable from those Roosevelt had already advocated in many messages to Congress, and his bland promise to "complete and perfect the machinery" that his predecessor had initiated added nothing new to the mix. Nor did his views differ much from those of his rival, William Jennings Bryan. His efforts to distinguish his own proposals from Bryan's slightly more ambitious variations collapsed in a mire of jurisprudence.

But Taft did not have to shake up the political establishment to win the election. For conservatives, it was enough that his name was not Bryan. For many progressives, he had only to promise to carry on Roosevelt's agenda. For most everyone else, he simply had to keep smiling.

The day after his speech, Taft returned to Hot Springs, Virginia, and played eighteen holes to unwind from the ordeal of the notification. He planned to rest up at the resort for another month before beginning the campaign.[38]

SOUTHAMPTON, ENGLAND, AUGUST 11, 1908

Grim news greeted Aldrich when he landed on the English coast in August. He came with several members of the Monetary Commission to study the European banking systems, but Senator W. B. Allison had stayed behind in Iowa, too ill to travel. When Aldrich's ship reached port, he learned that he would never see his old friend and colleague again. Allison had died of kidney failure the day they left New York.[39]

The loss was devastating, personally and politically. Among the Big Four, the venerable Iowan had been second in authority to Aldrich, a partner, not a subordinate. Allison's geniality and talent for conciliation had smoothed the way for their legislative schemes. He was "the compromiser, the weather prophet, the man who brings irreconcilable things together." Aldrich still controlled the committees, but without Allison's charm, he would have to resort to more forceful methods.[40]

Allison's death also created a second problem for Aldrich, a problem named Albert Cummins. Governor Cummins of Iowa was almost as radical as La Follette, and he spearheaded a militant antitariff movement. After Allison died, Cummins gave his compatriot a warm eulogy—and then vowed to take his place in the Senate.[41]

That was not the only bad news to greet Aldrich upon his arrival. Kansas had held its first direct primary while he was at sea. The incumbent senator, Chester Long, had received President Roosevelt's endorsement, but he faced a stiff challenge from a crusading reformer named Joseph Bristow. Aldrich had little love for Long ever since he sided with Roosevelt in the railroad fight, but Bristow was far worse—a La Follette man. Before the Kansas primary, La Follette canvased the state on Bristow's behalf. Bristow won handily.[42]

Two more radical senators did not threaten Aldrich's majority in the Republican caucus, but with Beveridge, Dolliver, and other westerners on the fence, his control of the Senate was in jeopardy. If the Democrats picked up a few more seats and the radical Republicans voted with them, they could make real trouble.

LINCOLN, NEBRASKA, AUGUST 12, 1908

William Jennings Bryan did not look like a wild-eyed radical. He was tall, clean-cut, and square-jawed with a wide grin that stretched from ear to ear. When he spoke, he did not bellow or shriek or froth at the mouth. His words were simple and straightforward; he peppered them with jokes, anecdotes, and biblical allusions. His leisurely baritone filled auditoriums with a singsong cadence that penetrated his listeners' skins and gently drew them toward him.[43]

Back in 1896, Bryan's famous Cross of Gold speech stunned the rowdy Democrats into silence at the Chicago Coliseum. As he issued the final defiant line, "You shall not crucify mankind upon a cross of gold!" he stretched out his arms Christ-like and stood motionless for several seconds. The audience leaned forward, waiting for some word to follow. When they realized it was over, murmurs of admiration began to buzz on all sides. The murmurs changed to applause, the applause changed to cheers, and suddenly the Coliseum exploded with a "tumultuous, deafening, ear-cracking noise" that "thundered forth like the tearing asunder of the foundations of the earth." Shrieking men and women stood on their chairs and hurled hats, coats, flags, paper, and "everything moveable" into the air. Young ladies danced like "savages." Old men wept into their beards. A farmer who had called Bryan a "crazy Populist" before the speech banged his coat against a chair and screamed, "My God! My God! My God!" That speech catapulted Bryan into his first Democratic nomination.[44]

His 1908 acceptance speech in Lincoln, Nebraska, did not meet the same standard. It was not a bad speech, far better than the one Taft delivered in Cincinnati, but it lacked the stirring call to arms for which he was famous. Echoing Theodore Roosevelt's cautious rhetoric, he promised "reformation not revolution," and he drew a fine distinction between "legitimate corporations" and "lawless combinations." Even conservative Republican papers marveled at his mildness. The *New York Times* remarked that his "soothing" speech was actually less militant than President Roosevelt's recent messages.[45]

After two failed campaigns as a passionate young firebrand, Bryan now sought to present himself as a mature statesman who would continue Roosevelt's moderately progressive policies with the sensibility and gravitas that Americans expected from a president. There was some wisdom to this strategy. Many voters were weary of the political warfare in Washington, and even Roosevelt's supporters longed for a gentler proponent of his policies.

But Bryan's ambition to rebrand himself as a moderate progressive statesman suffered from a critical flaw: His opponent had beaten him to it. When it came to mildness, he could not compete with Taft's harmonious smile and judicial temperament. To critics, Bryan's transformation looked like shameless calculation, while his supporters complained about his diminished zeal. Nor could he persuade voters to accept him as Roosevelt's true political heir when Roosevelt had made it quite clear whom *he* believed his heir to be.

OYSTER BAY, NEW YORK, SEPTEMBER 5, 1908

Nonetheless, Roosevelt worried. "Taft does not arouse the enthusiasm which his record and personality warranted us in believing he ought to arouse," he fretted. Nor did Taft seem to be doing anything about it. Instead of campaigning, he spent the month of August playing golf in Hot Springs followed by a weeklong fishing vacation on an island in Lake

Erie. Roosevelt knew that he should not interfere—there were already enough rumors that Taft was his puppet—but he could not bear to sit idle while his protégé frittered away the election.[46]

When Taft returned from his fishing trip, Roosevelt sent him a blunt letter marked *strictly private*. "Dear Will," he began, "I do not want this letter to be seen by anyone but you and Mrs. Taft." He warned him that his recreational activities were not playing well in the press and implored him to attend to the election. "You should put yourself prominently and emphatically into this campaign," he wrote. "[F]rom now on, I hope your people will do everything they can to prevent one word being sent out about either your fishing or your playing golf. The American people regard the campaign as a very serious business…"[47]

But Taft no longer obeyed Roosevelt so readily. He said nothing to suggest any disloyalty to his old boss, but he did not seek his counsel or invite Roosevelt's confidants to his strategy meetings. The silent treatment drove Roosevelt crazy. He compensated by bombarding the nominee with unsolicited advice. He urged him to smile more, fight harder, and cooperate with the Standpatters—except for Senator Foraker, whom he should "smash." He should avoid talking about his Unitarian faith, and he should certainly not play any more golf.[48]

When Taft didn't respond, Roosevelt invited Nellie to come see him in Washington, knowing how much influence she had over her husband, but he found her to be no more pliable.

"I can't imagine what Teddy wants," Nellie wrote to her husband when she received the invitation, "but probably only to complain about something."[49]

CINCINNATI, OHIO, SEPTEMBER 23, 1908

Taft was on the road by then. He had originally hoped to restrict his campaign to his brother's front porch in Cincinnati, but upon the advice of his staff, he finally agreed to a full speaking tour. The four-car "Taft Special" rumbled out of Cincinnati at 8 a.m. on September 23 and raced across the dusty, drought-stricken prairie lands at a top speed of 82 miles an hour. It paused long enough for Taft to deliver one speech in Brook, Indiana and two in Chicago, then continued west and parked next to a cornfield so that the passengers could catch a few hours sleep without jostling.[50]

Taft was up at 6:30 the next morning. He dressed quickly so that he could speak to the citizens of Caledonia, Illinois, from the rear of the train. But when he tried to talk, his voice was so hoarse that he could barely get the words out. A throat specialist who accompanied the train applied several treatments while they chugged into Wisconsin, but Taft's voice continued to rasp at every stop.[51]

He reached Madison at 11 a.m. Senator La Follette met him at the station and escorted him to the University of Wisconsin's gymnasium, crammed tight with 5,000 people. It was a critical moment. Ever since the convention, rumors had circulated that La Follette would bolt the presidential ticket because of his admiration for Bryan and his disappointment with the Republican platform. Even if he offered Taft a tepid endorsement, his equivocation might signal disapproval and prompt Wisconsin voters to break for Bryan.

But La Follette came through. Putting aside his skepticism, he stood by his party's candidate and introduced William Taft as a leader of "poise, judicial temperament, great force of character, and tenacity of purpose." Then he uttered the word that everyone was waiting for. "From a somewhat intimate acquaintance with him for twenty years," he continued, "I say today that he is progressive in principle."[52]

The word *progressive* rang out through the gym. The pressmen wrote it down and sent it hurtling west into Iowa, Nebraska, Kansas, and Minnesota. That odd, awkward adjective packed a wallop. "The followers of La Follette and Cummins have made this the password," explained the *Chicago Daily Tribune*, "without which no one can secure entrance to their political holy of holies." When La Follette named Taft a progressive, he signaled to western voters that Taft was on their side. "All fears of a La Follette rebellion disappeared," the *Tribune* continued, "and in place of them the insiders in Wisconsin politics have substituted declarations of unquestioning loyalty to Taft and the republican ticket."[53]

After La Follette's endorsement, Taft embarked for Milwaukee, delivering several hoarse speeches along the way. He reached the Milwaukee Hippodrome after 9 p.m. The building was packed with 6,000 people and nearly 100 degrees inside. This was the second critical event of the day, for Taft had an announcement to make. The crowd could barely hear him, but the press correspondents dutifully recorded the message. If elected president, he promised to call a special session of Congress the day after his inauguration. The entire session would be dedicated to achieving a single purpose—"a genuine and honest revision of the tariff."[54]

It was a bold promise. After a century of backroom deals, the tariff schedules had grown so rotten with corporate favors that the phrase "genuine and honest revision" seemed oxymoronic. The Standpatters were adamant to preserve the institution and all its perks; the progressives were just as adamant to overhaul it. Theodore Roosevelt had avoided the issue for seven years because he feared a confrontation would shatter the Republican Party. He counseled his successor to proceed cautiously, but Taft shrugged off his warnings. "I don't propose to be involved in a bunko game with the public," he replied. "My strong impression is that the people are [so] insistent, as they ought to be, on a real revision, that we are not going to encounter the difficulties that we would have encountered in the last Congress had such a revision been proposed."[55]

After the Milwaukee speech, he returned to Chicago for the night. Early the next morning, the Taft Special embarked for Iowa as the sun rose over the ripening cornfields and the word *progressive* echoed through the morning papers.

NEW YORK, NEW YORK, OCTOBER 20, 1908

Europe changed Aldrich's point of view. After two months of discussions with the top bankers of Britain, France, and Germany, America's glaring economic deficiencies struck him with new force. He saw advantages and drawbacks to the other nations' monetary systems, but he could not even begin to compare them to America's, for the United States had no monetary system at all.[56]

Before he went to Europe, Aldrich believed that a few legislative tweaks would be sufficient to help Pierpont Morgan and the other bankers manage the next financial panic, but now he saw the folly of relying on a 71-year-old man to save the country. He'd had dinner with Morgan in London and listened to him describe his plans to bequeath his art collection to New York's Metropolitan Museum of Art after his death. "Something has got to be done," Aldrich was forced to admit. "We may not always have Pierpont Morgan with us to meet a banking crisis."[57]

Aldrich had also begun to contemplate his own mortality. At 67, he was not much younger than Morgan. His dear colleagues Orville Platt and W. B. Allison were dead, the foundations of his beloved Senate were crumbling, and he was weary of fending off the barbarians pounding on the gates. He decided to retire when his term ended in 1911. That left him only two-and-a-half years to secure his legacy.

Money was no longer an object. After selling the United Traction & Electric Company, he had invested the profits shrewdly—some of it in King Leopold II's notorious rubber operation in the Belgian Congo. The entire fortune had passed through the panic of 1907 unscathed. Soon he would begin construction of his long-awaited mansion in Rhode Island, a granite monument to his success.[58]

When he returned from Europe in fall 1908, he had another monument in mind, not a building but an institution. Though he had been a member of the Finance Committee for 27 years and had served as its chairman for a decade, he had spent most of his time blocking legislation, not passing it. Few of his legislative accomplishments would be long remembered. An opportunity now presented itself to leave a more endur-ing mark on American history. He would find a solution to the periodic currency crises that wreaked havoc on the economy every decade or so. He would build an American monetary system.[59]

CINCINNATI, OHIO, NOVEMBER 2, 1908

The Taft Special rolled counterclockwise in a wide half-circle through the Middle West, looping north from Iowa into Minnesota and the Dakotas then southwest into Nebraska, Colorado, and Kansas. At each stop, Taft rasped out competent but unremarkable speeches detailing his judicial record and his political differences with Bryan.[60]

Bryan's train curled in the opposite direction through Missouri, Illinois, Indiana, Kentucky, Ohio, and West Virginia—as if tracing a yin to complement Taft's yang. He delivered as many as 24 speeches each day, always eloquent but never as inspiring as he had been in his younger days. "Shall the people rule?" he asked over and over in cities and towns across the West. At each stop, he pleaded for contributions as small as 30 cents to finance his cash-strapped campaign. By the end of October, the Democrats had netted $600,000, almost all of it from donations less than $100.[61]

Republicans relied on big donors as usual. Bankers and industrialists flocked to Taft's aid despite their unhappiness with Roosevelt's policies, concluding that he could not be worse than Bryan. Taft was not always receptive to their generosity, however. As a former judge, he was sensitive to conflicts of interest—"oversensitive," Roosevelt chided him—and he refused contributions from anyone identified with the railroads or the big trusts. "If all these avenues are to be closed," his campaign treasurer complained, "will you please tell me, Mr. Secretary, where I am going to get the money?" But Taft stayed firm. When Bryan accused him of serving the interests of John D. Rockefeller, he was able to honestly respond that he had not taken "one cent" from Standard Oil or any of its executives. And in the end, his campaign treasurer was able to find plenty of money without Rockefeller's help. The Republicans raised twice as much as the Democrats.[62]

Both candidates delivered speeches right up until the eve of the elec-tion and finished their campaign tours in their respective hometowns. Both confidently predicted victory.[63]

CINCINNATI, OHIO, NOVEMBER 3, 1908

William Taft waited with family and friends in the music room of his brother's house. A campaign aid shuttled in and out of the office where

Charles had installed new telegraph and telephone lines. The news from New York came first—not definite but very favorable for Taft. More good news followed on its heels from Massachusetts, New Jersey, Connecticut, Michigan, Tennessee, Wisconsin, and California. It looked as if he might even win Maryland.[64]

Congratulatory telegrams began to arrive, a trickle, then a stream, then a flood.

"I need hardly say how heartily I congratulate you, and the country even more," Roosevelt transmitted.

"No man ever had a greater opportunity than you," wired Senator La Follette. "The country confides in your constructive leadership for the progressive legislation needed to secure equal opportunity for all in our industrial development."

"The people do rule," quipped Speaker Cannon. "Congratulations over your great victory and the victory of the Republican Party."

As midnight approached, music and cheering could be heard from the street. Taft stepped out onto the porch. A crowd of revelers with banners and torches filled the avenue. The Citizen's Taft Club band struck up "Hail to the Chief," and the people cried "Speech! Speech!"

Taft thanked them briefly and promised to make his administration "a worthy successor of that of Theodore Roosevelt, and beyond that I claim nothing higher."[65]

The reporters wanted a statement, but he was too tired to indulge them. "Please say that I am perfectly healthy but exhausted," he told them, adding that he would depart for Hot Springs the next day. "It is to be a period of as near absolute rest and quiet as I can make it."[66]

OYSTER BAY, NEW YORK, NOVEMBER 4, 1908

Roosevelt was *dee-lighted*. Taft had won with 321 electoral votes to Bryan's 162, a landslide almost as large as his own election in 1904. In the House, Republicans lost five seats but retained a large majority. In the Senate, it appeared that they would only lose one. The stage was set for four, perhaps even eight, more years of his policies.

When the press asked him for a statement the day after the election, he called Taft's victory a triumph over both "reactionary conservatism" and "improper radicalism." That was slightly more dignified than his first public response to the election, "We've got 'em beaten to a frazzle!" He also assured the journalists that he was looking forward to retirement, though he confessed that he had loved the job. His friend "Big Bill" would not enjoy the White House nearly as much, he predicted.[67]

HOT SPRINGS, VIRGINIA, DECEMBER 2, 1908

Big Bill did not dispute Roosevelt's prediction. He was uneasy about his new responsibilities and tried to defer them as long as he could. Though he could not avoid meeting with Washington officials who came to see him in Hot Springs, the remoteness of the resort offered him some breathing space—and plenty of golf. He extended his two-week trip to a month.

"I pinch myself every little while to make myself realize that it is all true," he wrote to a friend. "If I were now presiding in the Supreme Court of the United States as chief justice, I should feel entirely at home, but with the troubles of selecting a Cabinet and the difficulties in respect to the revision of the tariff, I feel just a bit like a fish out of water. However, as my wife is the politician and she will be able to meet all these issues, perhaps we can keep a stiff upper lip and overcome the obstacles that just at present seem formidable."[68]

NEW YORK, NEW YORK, DECEMBER 29, 1908

The Metropolitan Club was an odd place for government commissioners to meet. The soaring central hall flaunted marble walls, stained-glass windows, scarlet carpets, and a magnificent double staircase to the second-story loggia. Newspapers called it the "Millionaire's Club" and joked that the gilded M on the iron balustrades stood for Morgan.[69]

Paul Warburg came to the club at Senator Aldrich's request. Warburg had been raised and educated in Germany, and Aldrich wanted his opinion of the European bankers who had met with the Monetary Commission. At least that was the ostensible reason for the invitation. After Warburg gave his testimony to the commission, Aldrich pulled him aside.

"Mr. Warburg," he said quietly, "I like your ideas. I have only one fault to find with them."

Warburg was stunned. It had been a year since he'd last met Aldrich. At the time, the senator had dismissed his idea for a modified central bank. He tried to maintain his composure and asked what the fault was.

"You are too timid about it," Aldrich answered.

That surprised Warburg even more. He protested that he was the only one in the banking community with the courage to press for such radical changes.

"Yes," Aldrich replied, "but you say we cannot have a central bank, and I say we can."

With a jolt, Warburg suddenly realized that their positions had reversed. Aldrich was no longer determined to limit the scope of the commission's recommendation. On the contrary, he now envisioned more ambitious changes than even Warburg thought possible.[70]

7

THE TARIFF

Whence comes this so-called demand for tariff tinkering? Look at the latest balance sheets of the Treasury. Don't they show everything is all right? Is there need for revenue legislation? Who says there is? Aren't all of our fellows happy?

—Uncle Joe[1]

NEW YORK, NEW YORK, APRIL 8, 1789

James Madison was impatient for his colleagues to arrive. The First Congress of the United States officially commenced on March 4, 1789, but only 13 legislators showed up at Federal Hall on Wall Street that day, not nearly enough for a quorum. Muddy roads and swollen rivers delayed many of the southerners for weeks. Every lost day sent the new government deeper into debt. After eight years of war and over a decade without consistent revenue, the United States owed more than fifty million dollars, not including the individual states' debts.[2]

When the House of Representatives finally obtained a quorum at the beginning of April, Madison took up the budget matter immediately. "The deficiency in our Treasury has been too notorious to make it necessary for me to animadvert upon that subject," he announced. "[A] national revenue must be obtained; but the system must be such a one, that, while it secures the object of revenue, it shall not be oppressive to our constituents. Happy it is for us that such a system is within our power, for I apprehend that both these objects may be obtained from an impost on articles imported into the United States."[3]

The other congressmen welcomed Madison's proposal as the most sensible way for the government to collect revenue. The Constitution clearly granted federal authority to tax imports, and since almost all foreign goods entered through a handful of ports, the duties would be straightforward to collect. The only constitutional alternatives—property and poll taxes—were difficult to enforce and prone to abuse.

Import tariffs also appealed to the congressmen for another reason. America's primitive industries had trouble competing with established European manufacturers. In England, water-powered cotton mills took advantage of new technology and abundant labor to produce fabric that was better and cheaper than American cloth. High tariffs would help American manufacturers compete with Europe by raising the price of imports until the US was able to grow its population and develop its own industries.

Thomas Fitzsimons of Pennsylvania was particularly enthusiastic about protective tariffs to "encourage the productions of our country, and protect our infant manufactures." He proposed import duties on a long list of products from beer and butter to boots and buttons. The other congressmen added more products to the list; every state had local industries to protect. Maryland proposed a 10 percent duty on window glass. Massachusetts asked for 7.5 percent on anchors. Virginia requested 3 cents a bushel for coal. Pennsylvania added 2 cents per pound of candle tallow.[4]

Conflicts soon emerged. To encourage hemp production in its western territory, Virginia proposed a duty of 75 cents per 112 pounds of hemp. New York worried that a hemp tariff would bankrupt its rope makers and insisted that the rope tariff be increased in proportion. But Massachusetts complained that high rope prices would harm the shipbuilders and so objected to tariffs on rope or hemp. South Carolina, which had little industry and relied on imports, objected to all the protective tariffs on manufactures and called for a straight 5 percent revenue tariff across the board.[5]

As the quarrels and deliberations extended into summer, the spring import season passed without new revenue, and the government sank deeper into debt. At last, on July 4, 1789, Congress passed "an Act for laying a Duty on Goods, Wares, and Merchandises imported into the United States." It included duties on 76 items, beginning with rum and ending with horse carriages, each taxed according to its importance to the congressmen and senators who assembled at Federal Hall that summer. Everything else was taxed at 5 percent.[6]

MADISON HAD ORIGINALLY CONCEIVED THE TARIFF proposal as a temporary measure to furnish the government with immediate, short-term revenue. It proved anything but. As the young nation spread across the continent, the population swelled and splintered, the economy bubbled and stratified, and the federal government stretched to accommodate the changes. Meanwhile, like a dark shadow of the expanding nation, the tariff schedules grew ever longer and more convoluted. By the end of the nineteenth century, they filled 70 pages and enumerated 705 categories of merchandise, from aluminum and peppermint to feather dusters and "toothpicks of wood or other vegetable substance." The average duty was nearly 50 percent of the import price, but it varied by product, quality, and country of origin. Raw sugar, for example, was taxed at 0.95 cents per pound, but the duty increased at a rate of 0.035 cents for each degree of refinement greater than 75 percent. By that scale, sugar refined to 100 percent would have been taxed at 1.825 cents, but an additional clause taxed fully refined sugar at 1.95 cents. Hawaiian sugar was exempted by treaty.[7]

Though devised as a revenue mechanism and a tool for protecting America's fledgling industries from European competition, the tariff became something far more monstrous. Most American industries no longer needed protection, and the duties had little correlation to the relative production costs of American versus foreign manufacturers. Rather, they tended to reflect the political influence of well-connected businessmen who lobbied or bribed their way into legislators' graces in order to gain tariff schedules that would maximize their profits.[8]

The Sugar Refineries Company of New York, popularly known as the Sugar Trust, was a master of the game. In the 1880s, the company's officers enlisted a young senator from Rhode Island, Nelson Aldrich, to help consolidate its supremacy over the US refining market. In a feat of parliamentary deal-making, Aldrich delivered a tariff schedule exquisitely designed to benefit the Sugar Refineries Company. He raised the tariff on refined sugar, which protected the trust from foreign competition. He lowered the tariff on unprocessed sugar, which enabled the trust to import raw Caribbean sugar more cheaply. And to ice the cake, he raised the tariff on partially refined sugar. The last modification pressed hard on the country's remaining independent refiners, which lacked the technology to process raw sugar. By 1892, the American Sugar Refining Company—which had incorporated under a new name in New Jersey to evade New York's antitrust laws—controlled 98 percent of the nation's sugar refining capacity. One year later, the trust's officers invested in the United Traction and Electric Company of Providence, Rhode Island, and Nelson Aldrich became a multimillionaire.[9]

Similar manipulations by other large trusts encouraged the consolidation trend. Independent producers lacked the resources to lobby powerful legislators. When the trusts negotiated favorable tariffs for themselves, smaller companies often had to merge with their larger competitors to avoid bankruptcy. Sugar magnate Henry O. Havermeyer called tariff laws "the mother of all trusts...inasmuch as they provide for an inordinate protection to all the interests of the country—sugar refining excepted." By the time he made this statement, Havermeyer could afford to criticize the tariffs. He had already wiped out or acquired his East Coast competitors. The remaining West Coast competition benefited from tariff-free Hawaiian sugar, so Havermeyer wanted to eliminate the tariff on raw Caribbean sugar.[10]

The biggest losers in the arrangement were American consumers. The tariffs directly inflated import prices and indirectly inflated prices for domestic products by suppressing foreign competition. In essence, the tariff was a regressive consumption tax, and the burden fell heaviest on poor farmers and laborers who had to spend the majority of their incomes on food and clothing. When tariff-supported monopolies took over the market, the lack of competition drove prices even higher.

In those days, few Americans disputed the principle of protectionism. Free trade was considered heresy, and no one wanted to eliminate tariffs entirely. Instead, reformers pressed for lower, fairer duties based on actual production costs rather than the influence of powerful interests. Bob La Follette and Albert Beveridge advocated a federal commission of experts who would determine tariff rates "scientifically." William Jennings Bryan called for a constitutional amendment to supplement lower tariffs with income taxes. Other reformers advocated corporate and inheritance taxes to compensate for lower tariffs.

Such proposals went nowhere, blocked year after year by Standpatters who dismissed taxes as socialist and warned that tariff reductions would wreck the economy. They saw no contradiction in championing protectionism in the name of capitalism. Their objective was not to create a pure free market in the modern sense but to protect US manufacturers from interference, both foreign and domestic. They opposed tariff reductions for the same reason they opposed labor laws and antitrust regulations—because they believed the legislation would harm American industry.

Economic principle was not the Standpatters' only motive, though. The tariff was the lifeblood of the Gilded Age political order they represented. Since small differences in the tariff schedule could bring considerable profits to the companies concerned, corporations spent lavishly to secure favorable treatment from Congress. Their campaign contributions fueled the political machines that the Republican Standpatters and Bourbon Democrats controlled, ensuring conservative dominance of Congress and effectively encasing the government in a cocoon of corporate influence.

In essence, the tariff debate epitomized the rupture between two different conceptions of federal government: one, an elitist view that entrusted national leadership to political bosses and captains of industry; the other, a populist view that sought to eliminate corporate privilege and empower the masses.

WASHINGTON, DC, DECEMBER 9, 1908

President-elect William Taft did not think in such grandiose terms. He was an administrator and a judge, not a visionary. When he looked at the tariff, he saw a flawed tax code that needed correction, and he sought the most expedient means to repair it. He did not care whether conservatives or progressives passed the legislation as long as they did it honestly and efficiently.

The Standpatters controlled Congress, so it seemed logical to work with them to secure new legislation as Roosevelt had done. Taft was pleased to collaborate with Senator Aldrich, whom he admired, but he thought Uncle Joe was vulgar and conniving. The Speaker's flippant comments on tariff revision after the election particularly disturbed him. "Cannon's speech at Cleveland was of a character that ought to disgust everybody who believed in honesty in politics in dealing with the people squarely," he wrote to Senator-elect Elihu Root, "and just because he has a nest of standpatters in his House and is so ensconced there that we may not be able to move him is no reason why I should pursue the policy of harmony."[11]

But Root and Roosevelt urged him to meet with Cannon for the sake of Republican unity, and he reluctantly consented. When they finally met, he was pleasantly surprised by Cannon's attitude. "I had a most satisfactory talk with him," he wrote afterward, "in which he said that he was entirely in sympathy with my effort to carry out the pledges of the Chicago platform, and that he would assist me as loyally as possible."[12]

After the meeting, some papers rhapsodized about new friendship between the Speaker and president-elect. "When the tariff lovefeast…was over tonight, great gobs of harmony decorated the landscape," gushed the *Los Angeles Times*. "And back of it all shone the beaming smile of William H. Taft."

But the *Wall Street Journal* wasn't so sure. All that smiling reminded its editor of a popular limerick:

> *There was a young lady of Niger*
> *Who smiled as she rode on the tiger.*
> *They returned from the ride with the lady inside,*
> *And the smile on the face of the tiger.*[13]

WASHINGTON, DC, DECEMBER 11, 1908

At 75, William Peters Hepburn was in excellent health. He would have kept working if the voters had let him, but after 22 years in the House of Representatives, they voted him out of office in November. Iowa had little patience for Standpatters anymore.[14]

Hepburn had enjoyed a long illustrious career crowned by the Hepburn Act of 1906—the railroad bill that had provoked such a furor—but one goal had always eluded him: to check the power of the Speaker. He held no personal animus against Uncle Joe. They were much alike, both old-fashioned prairie conservatives, and Cannon had always treated him well. It was the Speaker's authority he opposed. For almost two decades, long before Cannon assumed the office, Hepburn had been fighting a lonely battle to change the House rules to give more power to the rank-and-file. At the beginning of each new congress, he steadfastly introduced his resolution. He lost every time.[15]

He would not be able to vote when the new Congress opened in March, but he hoped to see his colleagues realize his goal at last. The House was more restive than it had been in decades. Many Republicans chafed under Cannon's dominance—young radicals, mostly, but also a few veterans like Charles Fowler. The Democrats showed signs of life as well. They had selected a new minority leader, James Beauchamp Clark of Missouri. "Champ" Clark was a big, friendly-looking lawyer, white-haired, clean-shaven, and dapper, but his mild appearance belied a ferocious temperament. "He crunches 'em, and hunches 'em, and munches 'em," wrote one awed correspondent. "Fierce? Geminy! he is so fierce he is scared of himself."[16]

Hepburn also hoped for assistance from the White House. There were rumors that Taft had no love for the Speaker. Hepburn neither wanted nor believed it was possible to remove Cannon from office, but if all three forces united, they could force a parliamentary rule change to reduce his power.

On December 11, 25 Republican insurgents met after hours in Hepburn's committee room to plot their offensive. They crafted a resolution to eliminate the Speaker's arbitrary control of committee membership, require him to recognize anyone who requested the floor, and allow committees to introduce legislation without his approval.[17]

The next day, one of the insurgents sent the resolution to Taft, who responded skeptically. "I am glad that you think it likely that the rules will be changed," he replied. "I doubt however whether the speaker would consent to it."[18]

AUGUSTA, GEORGIA, DECEMBER 18, 1908

After only two weeks in Washington, Taft departed for the mild weather and fabled golf links of Augusta, Georgia, where he and his family wintered in a friend's cottage. He charmed the Georgians by requesting "possum and taters" at a dinner in his honor and appeased them by defending voter literacy tests, which southern states used to disenfranchise blacks. Newspapers cheerfully predicted that the Democratic South might finally reconcile itself to a Republican president. Toymakers saw an opportunity and introduced a stuffed animal named Billy Possum to succeed the Teddy Bear.[19]

Between speeches and golf, Taft worked on his cabinet. Matching the right combination of skills, personalities, and constituencies was like putting together a "picture puzzle," as he put it. He had originally promised Roosevelt to reappoint most of the current cabinet members, but that idea no longer seemed prudent. Roosevelt's team didn't fit the puzzle.[20]

WASHINGTON, DC, JANUARY 4, 1909

Senator Henry Cabot Lodge returned from Augusta in a huff. Taft had kept him waiting for two days, he complained to Roosevelt, refusing to meet him without his wife or brother present. When he finally saw him, Lodge learned that Taft planned to replace anyone who was closely connected to the old administration, including almost all the cabinet members.[21]

The news was depressing if not completely surprising to Roosevelt. After the Republican convention, Taft had asked him to let "the boys" know that he wanted to keep them all on, and Roosevelt cheerfully passed on the message to his cabinet members. But that was before Taft began to drift. After the election, he hinted that he might replace some members of the cabinet. Now it seemed that he would replace almost all of them.[22]

Though disappointed, Roosevelt no longer tried to second-guess him as he had during the campaign. Taft was duly elected now and would make his own way. To give him space, Roosevelt arranged to remove himself from the continent after the inauguration. "Ha ha! *you* are making up your Cabinet," he wrote to Taft at the end of December. "*I* in a lighthearted way have spent the morning testing the rifles for my African trip. Life has compensations!"[23]

Still, the information from Lodge rankled him, especially since he had told his cabinet members that they would stay on. He dictated a letter to Taft. "I think it would be well for you to write them all at once that you do not intend to reappoint them," he urged with a hint of reproach, "They will be making their plans, and less than two months remain, and I do not think they ought to be left in doubt."[24]

When Taft complied by sending bland excuses to the rejected cabinet members, Roosevelt felt obliged to follow up with them personally. "Something has come over Will," he told Secretary of the Interior James Garfield. "He is changed, he is not the same man." To Luke Wright, Taft's successor as secretary of war, he apologized, "I am distressed, General, that you will not continue to be Secretary of War, but unfortunately you have been too close to me, I fear."[25]

Despite the disappointment, Roosevelt's sense of loyalty ran strong. He defended Taft's decisions from a growing chorus of critics, insisting that he would have done the same in his place. Yet, he was uneasy. Years later, he would recall, "The first friction came in the matter of his cabinet."[26]

MADISON, WISCONSIN, JANUARY 23, 1909

In January 1909, Bob La Follette rolled out a new weapon. His Senate speeches and Chautauqua lectures could only reach limited audiences. To propagate his ideas and expand the new progressive movement, he decided to start a magazine. His friends and family worried about the physical and financial strain. "You mustn't let Bob take on this terrible load," Lincoln Steffens warned Belle. "It will kill him." But she just laughed and replied that he knew Bob well enough not to expect her or anyone else to stop him once he'd made up his mind.[27]

La Follette christened his new publication with the straightforward if unimaginative title, *La Follette's Weekly Magazine*.[28] It balanced modern home-making and child-rearing advice for women with hard-hitting political articles by many of the progressive leaders of the era, including senators, congressmen, governors, and journalists like Lincoln Steffens and William Allen White.

In the third issue, John Nelson of Minnesota, one of the insurgent congressmen, described the looming battle with the Speaker. He argued that there was only one hope to end Uncle Joe's tyranny. "Mr. Taft must play the part of King David," he wrote. "He has the sling, which is the message to Congress. He has plenty of pebbles, which are the great legislative propositions of his predecessor. Will he play the part of David? Has he the courage? Has he the skill? Two armies are waiting with bated breath and anxious hearts to witness the result of this fateful contest."[29]

WASHINGTON, DC, MARCH 4, 1909

Washington bubbled with excitement. The papers predicted that the inaugural ceremonies would be the most magnificent in American history. As the day approached, 200,000 visitors streamed into the swollen city, nearly doubling its population. The hotels and boarding houses were so jammed that railroad companies parked passenger cars around the city and rented out the sleeping berths at exorbitant rates. Restaurants doubled their prices, and barbershops charged a stiff 25 cents for a shave. Peddlers hawked peanuts, sandwiches, lemonade, and souvenir buttons that said, "Smile, Smile, Smile."[30]

The newspapers prattled merrily about America's future under President Taft. The *Baltimore Sun* printed a paragraph-length paean to his "honest, simple, genuine and generous smile" and predicted that he would "restore the mental, business and political equilibrium of the country." The *New York Times* published a stream of glowing predictions by "great captains of capital and industry," who enthused one after another that Taft's inauguration would usher in a new era of harmony and prosperity. Even the United States Weather Bureau joined in the spirit of optimism, cheerfully predicting fair weather for the ceremonies—right up to the moment the snow came down.[31]

The storm struck from the north at 8:30 p.m. on the eve of the inauguration. All through the night, it hurled ten inches of thick, wet snow over the brick row houses huddled shoulder-to-shoulder in the wind, the austere federal buildings leaning stoically on their marble columns, the matronly White House crouching protectively over her gardens, and the gold-crowned Capitol poised imperiously on her hill. In the morning, tree limbs encased in icy skins cracked and moaned while gusts yanked at the red, white, and blue bunting that lined Pennsylvania Avenue. The snow-entombed train tracks and the telegraph wires sprawling limply in the icy streets revealed that Washington was virtually cut off from the rest of the country.[32]

Under heavy skies, thousands of tenacious visitors braved the bitter wind and wet flakes to witness the inauguration ceremony and the grand parade. The snow turned to a yellow mush under their feet and oozed into their shoes. The lucky ones wore tall rubber boots, but the shoe stores sold out of them by 7 a.m. For everything else, prices dropped rapidly. Seats for the parade fell from five dollars to one, sandwiches from a quarter to pennies. Washington's street cleaning department mobilized 6,000 men to shovel, but the snow kept coming. By late morning, inauguration officials decided to move the ceremony indoors.

Taft was disappointed but tried to make the best of it. In the White House, he bantered with Roosevelt over breakfast.

"Mr. President," he quipped, "even the elements protest."

"Mr. President-elect," Roosevelt rejoined, "I knew there would be a blizzard clear up to the minute I went out of office."

Taft countered, "I always knew it would be a cold day when I was made President of the United States."[33]

UNCLE JOE WAS IN A SOUR MOOD THAT MORNING. He'd expected the new minority leader to thank him for his "impartial" leadership, as John Sharp Williams had always done at the end of each session. But Champ Clark lacked his predecessor's manners. When the time came for the Democrats to offer a traditional motion of thanks to the Speaker, he just sat there silent and smug.

Cannon mounted the podium and glared across the chamber. "After all is said and done in the affairs of parties and of men, what is needed in the public service is virile men," he bristled. "Strong men, in public life as well as in private life, strike above the belt and tell the truth." Then he wished them health and prosperity without much feeling and declared the 60th Congress adjourned.

At the rap of his gavel, the galleries applauded, and the congressmen filed toward the door. Cannon took his place at the front of the line, as the boys sang out, "My country, 'tis of thee, sweet land of liberty." Then he led his congressional chorus down the hall to the Senate chamber for the inaugural ceremony, a red carnation in his coat and a defiant spring in his step.[34]

In the dull sunlight that had forced its way through gray clouds and snow-veiled skylights, the Senate chamber was a mass of black and gray coats. Due to the weather, even the women in the gallery dressed soberly, leaving only the glittering foreign ambassadors to brighten the room. The senators and other dignitaries were packed tightly into small cane chairs on one side of the chamber. Aldrich sat next to the elegant Elihu Root, former secretary of state and now senator from New York. There were rumors that Aldrich was grooming him for his inner circle.[35]

At a quarter past twelve, the sound of cheers from the corridor signaled the arrival of Roosevelt and Taft. The two men strode arm-in-arm to their seats in front while the onlookers rose and cheered. Roosevelt offered the crowd a big toothy grin. Taft maintained a solemn expression until seated, then flashed a brief Taft-smile at his wife and children in the gallery.[36]

Vice President Fairbanks had the first speech. Alarmed by the rising sentiment for direct election of US senators, he directed his valedictory remarks at the muckrakers who had savaged Aldrich and other prominent senators. "In these latter days, much severe criticism is heard of the Senate of the United States," he began. "The Senate, it is sometimes said, is not always responsive to the popular will. Such assumption is erroneous, judging by the record of legislation accomplished. The will of the people finds utterance in the public law in due course; not that will which is the unreasoning passionate expression of the moment, but that will which is the fruit of deliberate, intelligent reflection." He concluded his speech with a warning that direct election of senators risked overturning "one of the strongest safeguards of our political fabric."

Incoming Vice President James Sherman spoke next. Unlike Fairbanks, his prior experience was in the House, not the Senate, but he immediately dispelled any idea that he would use his role as presiding officer of the Senate to challenge its aristocratic character. "A hundred years has demonstrated the far-sightedness and wisdom of the framers of that instrument which has furnished the foundation of our legislative action," he declared.[37]

Yet, for all the powers of conservatism arrayed about the Senate chamber that day, there remained the imposing figure of William Howard Taft. He had won the presidential election by repeatedly promising to fulfill Roosevelt's progressive agenda, and his moment had finally arrived. A hush fell over the crowd as he approached the rostrum, and the frail 78-year-old chief justice faintly intoned the oath of office. Taft, towering over him, repeated the words in a booming voice that rolled over the politicians in dark coats and ambassadors in florid costumes, then veered upward to meet the families and guests watching from the upper galleries.[38]

"So help me, God," he concluded, kissing the right-side page of the large open Bible where he had laid his hand. The chamber burst into applause. Then Taft turned to the audience, held up his hand to quiet the ovation, and began reading from a typewritten manuscript.

He opened his inaugural address with another promise to make Roosevelt's reforms "a most important feature of my administration." The original draft of the speech had read "the *chief* feature of my administration." Roosevelt had previewed the earlier draft, but if he noticed the last-minute amendment, he gave no sign.[39]

Taft's smile made no appearance during the speech. He was a statesman now, not a candidate, and he conducted himself with the gravity expected of a president. He carefully laid out the issues he intended to tackle during his presidency: construction of the Panama Canal, conservation of the nation's forests and waterways, monetary reform, expansion of the military, increased trade to "the Orient," and education of "the Negro."

He singled out one particular issue as "a matter of most pressing importance." Though it had been twelve years since the last tariff bill, Taft insisted that unstable business conditions required Congress to act immediately to reduce import duties, and he called for new rates that honestly reflected "the difference between the cost of production abroad and the cost of production here." Should revenues fall short of the government's needs, he recommended alternative taxes, such as an inheritance tax. But he was careful not to overstep the jurisdiction of the executive branch. "I venture this as a suggestion only," he concluded, "for the course to be taken by Congress, upon the call of the Executive, is wholly within its discretion."[40]

As soon as he'd finished, Theodore Roosevelt bounded to the platform and grasped him by the shoulder. "God bless you, old man," he said. "It is a great state document." With that, he bid Taft good luck and promptly departed the Capitol, galoshes and all, to catch the first train home to Long Island, leaving his successor to his fate.[41]

The galleries buzzed with suppressed conversation as the Supreme Court justices and various ceremonial officers filed sedately out of the chamber. Taft followed arm-in-arm with his selection for secretary of state, Philander Knox, and the occupants of the chamber applauded loud and hard. Next went the ambassadors in their finery. Then Fairbanks departed amid fond cheers from the senators, followed by Vice President Sherman, whose former House colleagues offered him a standing ovation. Finally, the governors, congressmen, senators, and assorted honorees departed. Uncle Joe slipped out a side door and was seen heading back to the House chamber, furiously puffing a big black cigar.[42]

Outside, the snow had finally stopped, and the sun strained to break free from the clouds. President Taft climbed aboard the inaugural horse-carriage and paraded down Pennsylvania Avenue, tipping his hat to the cheering spectators as the wind blew his hair awry. Nellie sat conspicuously beside him, much to the chagrin of traditionalists who objected to such a prominent display of the first lady. The flags along the route waved brightly as if to make up for their bedraggled appearance in the morning. The glistening snow that clung to trees accentuated the colors and added to the beauty of the scene.[43]

In the evening, an estimated 10,000 distinguished guests joined the Tafts at the inaugural ball. The *Chicago Tribune* pronounced it the most beautiful inaugural ball since "the first president led Lady Washington through the mazes of the stately minuette," a somewhat dubious assertion since Martha Washington had not attended her husband's inauguration or the unofficial ball that took place a week later. Without pausing for a breath, the *Tribune* writer went on to compare the setting to "Alhambra or some Byzantine palace, en fête, brilliant with countless lights and sweet perfume of rare blossoms." Other serious newspapers scrutinized and extolled the fair young ladies in their elaborate gowns like modern-day tabloids. Though the superlatives varied, the papers all agreed that the men were distinguished, the women were beautiful, the decorations were magnificent, and the President enjoyed himself immensely.[44]

Meanwhile, fireworks dazzled some 200,000 uncelebrated visitors standing outside at the foot of the Washington Monument. The ice that coated the trees reflected the radiant colors exploding overhead, and the low-hanging clouds held the illuminations "as though the heavens were afire." The white marble Peace Monument glowed vividly in the icy sheen produced by sleet and the spray of its own fountain. The climax of the presentation was a futuristic set piece called Magic City. Stationary fireworks fastened to mobile steel scaffolds presented a colorful mini-drama in which two airships floated ominously over a shining city and began to bombard it with explosives. The simulated buildings caught fire, blew up, and crumbled away. An aerial fleet belatedly emerged to defend the burning city, and the two opposing forces engaged in pyrotechnic combat until they had thoroughly incinerated one another. After the airships burned away and the last fireworks melted into the sky, darkness fell over Washington. The marble goddess of Peace, presiding silently over her memorial pool, slipped softly into shadow as she contemplated the Capitol and clutched her olive branch.[45]

WASHINGTON, DC, MARCH 5, 1909

The next day, President Taft met with the Republican representatives of the House Ways and Means Committee. In the afterglow of the inaugural festivities, the mood was upbeat. The congressmen expressed their earnest desire for harmony with the President and pledged to provide him a tariff law by June 1. Taft, delighted by their goodwill, promised to be as harmonious as the best of them and entrusted the details of the bill to their capable hands.[46]

But he soon learned that harmony had a price. Three days later, Aldrich and Cannon came to see him. They warned him about a hitch in the plan for prompt tariff legislation. If Republican insurgents succeeded in reducing the Speaker's power, the change would throw the Ways and Means Committee into chaos and delay tariff revision indefinitely. If he wanted a tariff bill, they suggested, Taft should keep out of the rules fight.[47]

The next day, three representatives from the insurgent faction came to seek Taft's help in their fight against the Speaker. He told them that he sympathized with their objectives but that the time was not right. Because of the disturbed business conditions, the country could not afford to delay tariff legislation. He urged them to postpone their endeavor for a more suitable moment.

The insurgents protested. The House could only adopt new rules at the beginning of the session, so the next opportunity would not come for two years. They promised not to interfere with the Ways and Means Committee or the tariff bill. But they made no headway with the President; he had made up his mind.

"I am here to get legislation through," he explained. "The question with me is practical and not theoretical, and I ask you how a man of sense, looking at the situation as it is, can do otherwise than to support the regular organization in the House. I should have been glad to beat Cannon and to have changed the rules within the party, but I must rely on the party and party discipline to pass the measures that I am recommending."[48]

He had only been in office for a week, but Taft already sensed that things were going badly. In a poignant farewell letter to Roosevelt, he gloomily predicted, "I have no doubt that when you return you will find me very much under suspicion by our friends in the West." Nonetheless, he stood by his decision, explaining that he could not afford to alienate the only men capable of passing legislation. "Cannon and Aldrich have promised to stand by the party platform and to follow my lead," he assured his predecessor. "They did so, I believe, for you in the first Congress of your administration and this is the first Congress of mine."

Of course, Taft was no Roosevelt, which he readily acknowledged. "I have not the facility for educating the public as you had through talks with correspondents," he continued, "and so I fear that a large part of the public will feel as if I had fallen away from your ideals; but you know me better and will understand that I am still working away on the same old plan…"[49]

Without question, Taft lacked Roosevelt's talent for publicity, but in blaming his problems on poor public relations, he avoided taking responsibility for the consequences of his decision to work with the Standpatters. Roosevelt had indeed deferred to Aldrich and Cannon during his first term, but the United States had been a different country then—before muckrakers and progressives and Roosevelt himself upended American politics. Taft did not have the luxury of straddling the middle ground between Standpatters and reformers. He had to choose a side, and the choice he made in his first week of office set the course of his presidency.

ROOSEVELT'S SHIP WAS ALREADY STEAMING through New York Harbor when he received Taft's letter accompanied by a parting gift of an extendable gold ruler. He scribbled out a telegram and sent it ashore for transmission. "Am deeply touched by your gift and even more by your letter. Greatly appreciate it. Everything will turn out all right, old man. Give my love to Mrs. Taft."

But Taft never received the cable, and his resentment at Roosevelt's perceived indifference would simmer quietly for the next fifteen months.[50]

WASHINGTON, DC, MARCH 15, 1909

Uncle Joe wasn't worried about his reelection chances. There was no one who could beat him, and the insurgents knew it. They would fall into line. The rules fight was another matter. If the Democrats and insurgents united, they had enough votes to strip the Speaker's power of recognition and control over the committees. To forestall the crisis, he offered the insurgents a concession. One day each week, he would allow committees to introduce legislation directly to the House, bypassing his authority. Calendar Tuesday, he called it. But the insurgents didn't take the bait.

So Cannon looked elsewhere. He knew some Democrats who might be open to persuasion. John J. Fitzgerald of Brooklyn was irked because Minority Leader Champ Clark hadn't offered him a Democratic seat on the Rules Committee. A few others wanted favors in the upcoming tariff bill. Uncle Joe was in a position to help.

The battle opened on the first day of the new session. Cannon easily won reelection, as expected. Then the real fight began. The insurgents took the first round. In a close vote, they joined the Democrats to prevent the House from automatically adopting the existing rules. Celebratory shouts erupted from the Democrats and insurgents. They stood on their chairs howling and applauding with delight.

When the room was quiet, Minority Leader Champ Clark asked for the floor. He offered an amendment to the rules of the previous Congress. It included all the changes that the Republican insurgents had devised to restrict the Speaker's power. Another roll call began. Then came Cannon's surprise. Fitzgerald of Brooklyn voted against Clark's resolution. So did a number of other Democrats from New York and Georgia. The motion failed, 203 to 180. Now it was the Standpatters' turn to cheer.[51]

After the vote, Fitzgerald asked for the floor. He proposed an amendment that placed only one restriction on the Speaker's power. It allowed one day each week for committees to introduce legislation directly to the House—Calendar *Wednesday*. Otherwise, it preserved rules of the previous Congress.

Clark and the Republican insurgents were livid. They sparred with Fitzgerald, trying to threaten or cajole him into altering his amendment. He refused, and the roll call began. The Standpatters lined up for Fitzgerald's plan. The insurgents and most Democrats voted against it—but not enough of them. The amendment passed 211 to 173. The battle was over. For all the sound and fury, the insurgents achieved only one small change, Calendar Wednesday, which Cannon had already conceded to them.[52]

Uncle Joe was in a pugnacious mood when journalists interviewed him the next day. "All this talk about my being a czar is tommyrot, tommyrot and rubbish," he told them, flicking ash from his cigar and sawing his hand through the air. "What the insurgents and the Democrats wanted yesterday was to put fifteen czars in power—fifteen czars led by Champ Clark and La Follette." He deliberately mispronounced La Follette like "laugh-o-let." "That La Follette is a fake," he added. "You can say I say so."[53]

WASHINGTON, DC, MARCH 16, 1909

The special congressional session for consideration of the tariff convened at noon on March 16. In the Senate, La Follette eagerly awaited the President's message to Congress. He hoped for some strong words on the tariff to compensate for the previous day's disappointment in the House.

The President's secretary arrived and passed Taft's typewritten message to Vice President Sherman. Sherman relayed it to the Senate clerk and directed him to read it out. "To the Senate and House of Representatives," the clerk began, "I have convened the Congress in this extra session in order to enable it to give immediate consideration to the revision of the Dingley tariff act." In his message, Taft briefly addressed the changed economic conditions that required "readjustment and revision of the import duties." To balance the budget, he also called for "at least one new source of revenue" to supplement tariff income. Finally, he urged Congress to act as quickly as possible to alleviate uncertainty in the business community. Then the clerk stopped reading.

La Follette waited for him to continue. The Senate was silent. When people realized that the message was over, a smattering of applause tricked down from the galleries. One of the Standpatters clapped his hands slowly. Another called out, "That's bully!"—a jab at Roosevelt and his bellicose messages. Aldrich laughed.

La Follette was appalled. The two-minute message was nearly devoid of content. There was nothing about a tariff commission or an income tax, or even mention of a tariff *reduction*. He and Beveridge exchanged glances. This did not bode well.[54]

AS USUAL, THE CONGRESSMEN DOWN THE HALL responded vigorously to the President's message. After years of Roosevelt's browbeating, they did not try to conceal their delight at Taft's innocuous first message.[55]

Once they had settled down, Cannon announced the committee assignments. Traditionally, the Speaker allowed the minority leader to select the committee assignments for his own party. Cannon had always granted this privilege to John Sharp Williams, but he did not honor Champ Clark with the same authority. Defying tradition, he chose the Democratic assignments himself and doled out desirable positions to those who had supported him in the rules fight.

The House did not take it well. When Cannon announced that Fitzgerald of Brooklyn would sit on the Rules Committee, hisses and groans issued from the galleries as well as from a few Democrats below. Uncle Joe scowled and beat his gavel on the marble edge of his desk. "The galleries will observe the proprieties of the occasion and not hiss," he admonished them. But they did it again a few minutes later when he assigned more Democratic allies to the Ways and Means Committee. He banged his gavel and repeated, "The galleries will again refrain."

Then he threw them a defiant smile. All the hisses in America couldn't change the rules. He was still the undisputed master of the House.[56]

WASHINGTON, DC, MARCH 22, 1909

La Follette had been after Senator Jonathan Dolliver of Iowa ever since the election. "[B]reak away from Aldrich," he coaxed. "These fellows are not serving the public; they are betraying the public and you are following them. Your place is at the head of a movement here in the Senate and in the country for the public interest."

But Dolliver laughed him off. "Bob, your liver is all out of order," he replied. "You're jaundiced. You see things awry: cheer up."

Jokes aside, he was sympathetic to La Follette's overtures. Like his friend Albert Beveridge, he had begun to question the conservative principles he once took for granted, but he kept these doubts to himself. Other than bucking Aldrich on the railroad bill three years earlier, he had kept faith with the Standpatters in deference to his old mentor, W. B. Allison. "Jonathan, don't do it; don't do it now," Allison had implored him, "wait until I am gone."[57]

Allison was gone now, but Dolliver still wasn't ready to join La Follette's insurgents. He had spent years "carrying water to the elephant," as he put it, and he did not intend to throw away that political capital by poking Aldrich in the eye. The start of the next session was particularly important. There were five open spots on the Finance Committee, and Senate tradition dictated that he should receive Allison's place. Finance was one of the most prestigious committees in the Senate. With tariff revision on the schedule and currency reform on deck, a seat on the committee was an opportunity to make history.[58]

Dolliver submitted his committee requests to Aldrich in early March, stressing his tariff experience as a congressman in the 1890s and his long distinguished record in the Senate. Under the impression that Aldrich would honor his request, he withdrew from the Interstate Commerce Committee to make room for Albert Cummins, the new junior senator from Iowa.

But when Aldrich announced the Finance Committee assignments, Dolliver's name was not on the list. Instead, Aldrich selected two first-term senators who were less experienced but more faithfully conservative. Compounding the indignity, he also honored Dolliver's request to withdraw from Interstate Commerce and relegated him to less significant committees.[59]

Dolliver was furious. The next day, he bumped into La Follette in the corridor.

"Jonathan, are you pretty nearly ready to have that conference with me?" La Follette asked him.

"Yes, I am coming over to see you," he replied.[60]

With Dolliver on board, La Follette's band of insurgents acquired new strength. There were six of them now: La Follette, Beveridge, Dolliver, Albert Cummins of Iowa, Joseph Bristow of Kansas, and Moses Clapp of Minnesota. Six was not nearly enough to challenge the Republicans' 60-32 hegemony, but it was a big step up from La Follette's days as the "lonely man of the Senate." If they could peel off a few more votes, they could create real trouble for the Standpatters. They began plotting their strategy on the tariff bill.

WASHINGTON, DC, APRIL 9, 1909

Sereno Payne, chairman of the House Ways and Means Committee, reported out the promised tariff legislation on March 17. President Taft was pleased. The bill slightly reduced overall import duties and added a new inheritance tax. He objected to a few favors for certain manufacturers, such as the exorbitant duties on gloves and hosiery, but on balance, he thought it a major improvement over the existing law. "I am hopeful that we shall get through the tariff bill not very different from the bill as proposed to the House," he wrote to a journalist.[61]

Not everyone was happy about it. Westerners complained about reduced protection for lumber and hides. Women's groups protested that the glove and hosiery duties would fall disproportionately on women. And the insurgent Republicans objected that the bill didn't go far enough.[62]

But Uncle Joe fulfilled his commitment to Taft and moved the bill swiftly through the House with minimal changes. In a rare act of defiance, the western Republicans forced him to restore lumber tariffs and to remove a controversial duty on oil, but after that was done, they fell into line and voted for the bill, little changed from the original. When it passed on April 9, the Republicans cheered long and hard.

Then the battle moved to the Senate.

WASHINGTON, DC, APRIL 11, 1909

Nelson Aldrich excelled at tariff-making. All day long, representatives from various industries waited in the corridor to plead their cases before his Finance Committee. Senators begged him to look out for the industries of their respective states. Congressman Payne and President Taft presented their demands during long drives in the evenings. Letters poured in with more entreaties.

All these interests had to be weighed and balanced. Stubborn men had to be coaxed and soothed. The proper equilibrium between industry, agriculture, and mining had to be sustained—with high tariffs on manufactured goods and low tariffs on raw materials. And then there were a few pet interests like rubber, in which he was heavily invested, and elimination of art duties so that Pierpont Morgan could bring home his European collection tax-free.[63]

To fuse these conflicting demands into a coherent whole was an awesome endeavor, but Aldrich had been making tariffs for nearly 40 years. Like the veteran conductor of an immense orchestra, he smoothly wove the cacophony into harmony. Two days after the House passed the Payne bill, he presented his masterpiece to the Senate. Gone was any notion of a downward revision. He had increased the duties specified by the Payne bill on 847 items. There was no need for an inheritance tax or any other new taxes, he assured his colleagues. The Payne-Aldrich bill would supply plenty of revenue.[64]

In Aldrich's experience, this was the end of the story. The Republican majority would swiftly approve the Finance Committee's creation. There would be some haggling when the bill went to conference. He would get together with Payne and Cannon to smooth out the differences, and that would be that.

But it was not the same Senate that met in March 1909. The three men he had relied on to break down barriers with conciliatory words and penetrating arguments were gone. In their places sat new headstrong opponents, immune to persuasion and intimidation. Aldrich still commanded raw firepower. The senators who did his bidding far exceeded those who resisted him. But their votes were blunt weapons. They overwhelmed the opposition rather than quietly disarming it, which bred more opposition.

An admiring article in the *Providence Tribune* portrayed Aldrich as a human colossus who forced his will on lesser men. "The House, the Senate, the Administration, the Republican party itself, sink into comparative inconsequence beside him as he stands towering above the whole aggregation," the awed journalist wrote, "looking down almost compassionately on the smaller men around him, steadily, unswervingly and successfully pursuing day by day his purpose of giving the American people precisely the tariff which in his confident self-sufficiency and his almost untrammelled power he has decided they must have."[65]

But this depiction precisely captured the attributes that most Americans abhorred in Nelson Aldrich of Rhode Island. The harder he crushed his opponents, the higher he elevated them, and the lower his reputation sank.

WASHINGTON, DC, APRIL 22, 1909

La Follette's little band of insurgents worked long days and late nights. When not occupied by Senate duties, they researched the arcane tariff system, divvying up responsibilities by industry. They plotted strategy in the evenings, taking turns to host at their homes. They had never worked closely together, and their strong personalities often clashed under the pressure of fatigue, but humor and a ready supply of beer helped soothe the quarrels. Gradually, their fractious band became a cohesive team.[66]

They launched their assault on April 22. As soon as the Senate convened, Aldrich asked the clerk to begin reading out the text of the 300-page tariff bill. When the clerk reached "earthenware and china" on page 21, La Follette requested the floor. "I merely wish to ask the

Senator from Rhode Island at this point," he inquired, "if he will state to the Senate what portion of the duty provided in this paragraph measures the difference in the cost of production in this and in other countries, and what portion of duty is fixed as the measure of the reasonable profit, which he states was guaranteed by the Republican platform?"

Titters sounded from the galleries. The other senators smiled.

Aldrich brushed him off. "I shall be glad to furnish the Senate later with those precise facts. I have not them before me now," he replied, "but they have been submitted to the committee."

After a brief debate, the clerk continued reading. When he reached "glass bottles, decanters, or other vessels or articles of glass" on page 24, Jonathan Dolliver spoke up. He questioned whether the thriving glass industry required so much protection from foreign competitors.

Senator Nathan Scott of West Virginia, a glass factory owner, replied that the tariffs safeguarded American glassmakers against "rascally importers" and protected American jobs.

But Dolliver wanted evidence. "I do not propose to swallow without inquiry and without criticism these schedules that have been built up during the last twenty years," he protested, "and have grown so complex that nobody in Congress or out can tell what the duties actually laid by the bill are to be."

As he elaborated, using his experience with cotton schedules as an example, Beveridge jumped in, playing innocent. "May I ask the Senator who prepared the phraseology about the density and number of threads and so forth? Where did it come from?"

Dolliver dryly answered, "I understand that it has been customary, and a very proper custom, for the tariff committees to consult the manufacturers."

Now Aldrich interjected, "If the Senator will permit me just there upon that point, no manufacturer has been before the Committee on Finance in regard to this schedule. Every change that was made in it was made upon the recommendation of the government experts and nobody else."

Beveridge replied slyly, "I sincerely hope so, and of course I believe that that is true." But how, he wondered, did the experts get their information? "Have they examined any witnesses? Have they put them under oath? Have they opened books? How do they know and how does the committee know what the facts are?"[67]

And so it continued. Day after day, the insurgents harassed Aldrich and the other Finance Committee members, contesting each point on the schedule to expose the tainted mechanisms behind tariff legislation.

They alternated between well-researched challenges to specific duties, discourses on corruption, and withering sarcasm, playing off one another as they confronted their opponents.

Other western Republicans and numerous Democrats joined their rebellion against Aldrich. There were almost enough senators to amend the bill—but not quite. They needed fifteen Republicans and every Democrat to outvote the Standpatters. The defectors helped them force a few changes, but the support was inconsistent. On big votes, they invariably lost a few crucial senators.

Lacking a majority to substantially alter the bill on their own, they put their hopes on the only man with enough influence to unite the wavering opposition: President William H. Taft.[68]

WASHINGTON, DC, MAY 5, 1909

President William H. Taft was doing his best to stay of out of it. "I don't much believe in a President's interfering with the legislative department while it is doing its work," he told La Follette. He encouraged the insurgents to do what they could to reduce Aldrich's tariff increases and, with a slam of his fist, vowed to veto the bill if it did not meet his expectations. But he declined to send a message to Congress or engage in any other public agitation. He had made his position known in his inaugural address and did not deign to repeat himself after that.[69]

Though he refused to publicly comment on the tariff fight, Taft was willing to mediate behind the scenes. When congressmen and cabinet members joined him on afternoon horseback rides through Rock Creek Park or evening jaunts in his steam-driven motorcar, he often dropped casual threats to veto the tariff bill, knowing that his remarks would get back to Aldrich.[70]

But in truth, he lacked the nerve to follow through on the threat. To veto the bill would alienate the congressional leaders and indefinitely delay any changes to the tariff system. He acknowledged that a veto might bring him some "cheap popularity," but it would leave the Republican Party in shambles and prevent him from accomplishing any further reforms. He would not think of actually vetoing the bill unless the Standpatters deliberately double-crossed him.[71]

ALEXANDRIA, VIRGINIA, MAY 17, 1909

The President's yacht crawled down the Potomac toward Mount Vernon on a muggy May afternoon. Attorney General George Wickersham lounged on the deck with Nellie Taft. He spoke to her and was puzzled when she didn't respond. He repeated himself, but she still said nothing. Then he looked closely at her. She was very pale and very still.

"Mrs. Taft has fainted," he cried out. "See if there is any brandy aboard." The ship's captain found some rye whiskey and poured it down her throat while the President's military aide, Archie Butt, applied ice to her temples. She seemed to revive but did not say a word. When she tried to stand up, she staggered. Butt carried her to the saloon and called for the President. When Taft saw her, he blanched. He went into the room with her and shut the door. The yacht raced back to Washington at full speed.

It was a stroke. Nellie lost control of her right arm, right leg, and vocal chords. She recovered her motor skills quickly, but it took her months to relearn how to talk, and she spoke with an impediment for the rest of her life.

Taft was devastated. In Nellie's room, he laughed and tried to amuse her, but when he left, he sat by himself staring off into the distance. She had been his closest confidante and most trusted political adviser. Without her companionship and counsel, he was more alone than ever. He snapped at the White House servants and put on weight. Depression set in. With depression came anger.[72]

Archie Butt wrote, "Mr. Roosevelt once said that Mr. Taft was one of the best haters he had ever known, and I have found this to be true." Taft never raged in public like Roosevelt. He was cordial, even friendly, with people he couldn't stand. He held his hate to his chest and never let it go.[73]

After Nellie's stroke, he directed the brunt of his anger at La Follette's insurgents. He had tried to arrange compromises to expedite the tariff bill, but they rejected them. "[W]henever I give them an opportunity to carry out those reforms, or to make real progress," he complained, "they turn and oppose that because they say they will not accept anything which comes as a gift from Aldrich."

His frustration turned personal. Like Roosevelt, he found the radical reformers to be sanctimonious and intractable, but his reaction was more venomous. "I have better use for my time than spending it with such a blatant demagogue as either Dolliver or Cummins," he wrote to one correspondent. "Mr. Clapp is a light-weight," he told another, "and has shown himself to be so in so many regards that I have no confidence in him." He complained to Nellie about having to listen to a speech by La Follette "and somebody else equally objectionable." Beveridge "tires me awfully," he added. "He attitudinizes so much, and is so self-centered and so self-absorbed."[74]

As he backed away from the insurgents, Taft inched closer to the Standpatters. "I am not afraid to refer to Senator Aldrich as a friend of mine," he wrote, "and as one of the most useful men in the Senate." The tariff rate increases worried him, but Aldrich explained that he'd done it to appease certain senators and that he expected to remove them when the bill went to conference. Taft accepted this explanation at face value. "I have not found Aldrich or Cannon in any way deceptive in the dealings that I have had with them," he wrote to his brother, "and I believe they are acting in good faith."[75]

WASHINGTON, DC, MAY 20, 1909

One day in late May, Dolliver stomped up to Beveridge in the Senate chamber. Trembling with excitement and anger, he asked him to come outside. They stepped out to the terrace. Dolliver, pacing back and forth, told Beveridge what he'd heard: President Taft had turned against the insurgents. He had said that he "would not have anything to do with such an irresponsible set of fellows."

Beveridge couldn't believe it. Taft had been meeting with them regularly and had encouraged them to "insurge." He decided to test Dolliver's revelation. That evening, he assembled a list of quotes from Taft's campaign speeches promising to reduce the tariff duties. He read them in the Senate the next day. "The President has perhaps expressed it with a nice precision it has not yet received from any other interpreter within twenty years," he concluded.

The day after that, he called on Taft at the White House. The reception was chilly—"The coldest atmosphere I ever encountered in the White House." He knew nothing about Nellie Taft's stroke; the papers had announced that she'd had a nervous breakdown and was nearly recovered. From the President's demeanor, Beveridge concluded that Dolliver was right; the insurgents were on their own.[76]

Nonetheless, they carried on their struggle. La Follette delivered an epic five-hour speech during which he nearly fainted in the heat, then followed it the next day with a sensational clash with Aldrich. "La Follette tore the cotton schedule to pieces," Beveridge reported jubilantly to his wife. "Aldrich utterly lost his composure." The next day, Dolliver gave the speech of his life against the cotton schedule; Aldrich walked out. The day after that, Beveridge and Aldrich tangled so fiercely the other senators feared they might hit each other.[77]

But the amendment to increase cotton duties passed all the same. The insurgents did not have the votes. Without Taft, their only hope of achieving any positive outcome was to attach some progressive amendment to the bill.

Beveridge tried to revive his tariff commission proposal by offering it as an amendment, but Aldrich easily absorbed the attack. He made a public show of embracing the idea and then emasculated the amendment by eliminating the commission's subpoena power. A crippled advisory commission became part of the Payne-Aldrich bill.[78]

That left only one arrow in the insurgents' quiver. Early in the spring, Albert Cummins had proposed an amendment to establish a national income tax to supplement the tariff revenue. The idea was popular in the West, and a number of western Republicans were inclined to support it. For once, it seemed like they might have the votes to pass it.

WASHINGTON, DC, JUNE 8, 1909

Aldrich had never been comfortable on the Senate floor. In the old days, he would sit quietly in his seat while Allison, Spooner, and Platt shepherded his legislation through the Senate. This time was different. He still had plenty of allies but none with the skill or authority to manage the tariff debate, so he had to do it himself. He tried to ignore the barbs and hurry the process along, but his composure often slipped under the strain.

In order to expedite the bill, he extended the daily Senate hours until 11 p.m. Everyone was worn out. Senator Elihu Root quipped that if the debate lasted much longer "we will be saved from being torn limb from limb by an outraged public by the fact that death from exhaustion will supervene."[79]

The worst part was the heat. The muggy spring had become a scorching summer. Most senators spent hours on the terrace or near the electric fans in the cloakroom, but Aldrich had to remain on the floor to supervise the process.[80]

Through it all, he successfully managed to fend off unwanted amendments and hold the majority together. Balance was the key. No single item in the tariff bill commanded majority support, but every senator had pet interests. The wool men supported cotton so that the cotton men would support wool. *Logrolling*, people called it, a reference to pioneers who helped each other cut logs for cabins. That was how tariff bills had always been passed, and that was how this one would pass.

One last issue confounded him. He calculated nineteen Republicans likely to vote for Cummins's income tax amendment, enough to pass it. The whole idea appalled him. "[T]he income tax is supported by the Socialist party, by the Populist party, and by the Democratic party," he declared in 1894, "as a means for the redistribution of wealth." Even worse, to his mind, an income tax would generate so much revenue that it would eventually render the tariff system obsolete.[81]

But he could not see how to stop it. For once, he didn't have the votes. So, like the insurgents, he turned to the one man who could influence the wavering senators. On June 8, he terminated the session early and surreptitiously took a closed carriage to the White House with two of his allies. Instead of entering at the executive offices where journalists often skulked, he had the carriage drop them at the residential entrance.

Once inside, they sat down with Taft and explained the situation. The President was sympathetic. Though he supported an income tax in principle, he did not want it in the tariff bill. In 1895, the Supreme Court had ruled income taxes unconstitutional, and he was not one to defy the courts.

Aldrich was ready with an alternative. Suppose he were to introduce a constitutional amendment to authorize the federal government to tax personal income? A constitutional amendment required two-thirds approval from the House and Senate and three-fourths approval from the states. With most state governments still controlled by bosses, state approval seemed unlikely anytime soon. Aldrich liked the odds. It took years for the states to ratify constitutional amendments. He expected the momentary progressive mania in the West to recede before it did any lasting damage.

Taft liked the idea for a different reason: A constitutional amendment would avoid any trouble with the Supreme Court. But there was still the immediate problem of the budget deficit. He agreed to support Aldrich's plan on one condition. In place of an income tax, he wanted a new corporate tax added to the tariff bill.

Aldrich hedged. He preferred corporate taxes to income taxes, but he wasn't keen on either. He suggested that the new corporate tax be limited to two years, but Taft wouldn't budge, insisting that he could not sway the wavering Republicans with such a constraint. So Aldrich reluctantly agreed.[82]

WASHINGTON, DC, JUNE 18, 1909

Ten days later, Taft submitted a message to Congress calling for a 2 percent tax on corporate profits and a constitutional amendment to authorize a federal income tax. The insurgents were shocked. For months, Taft had resisted their entreaties to send a message opposing Aldrich's tariff increases, but now he had plunged into the fray with a message on Aldrich's behalf. *La Follette's Weekly* roared, "This message came to Congress at a most opportune time to serve the fixed determination of

Senator Aldrich to defeat the income tax, and to aid him in passing the tariff bill with its excessively high duties just as he wanted it."[83]

Aldrich did not deny the accusation. "I shall vote for the corporation tax as a means of defeating the income tax," he bluntly acknowledged, adding that he thought it should be repealed within two years. The gambit worked as he'd intended; the insurgents' fragile coalition broke. On July 2, the Senate voted to substitute a corporate tax for the original income tax proposal by a vote of 45 to 31.

Three days later, Aldrich introduced a constitutional amendment granting Congress "the power to lay and collect taxes on income." The Senate unanimously voted to submit it to the states. The consequences of Aldrich's maneuver were poetic. It would take only four years for the states to ratify the amendment and seal his destiny as the father of the Sixteenth Amendment, which he had only introduced to avoid passing an income tax in the first place.

Finally, there was nothing left but to vote on the tariff bill. It passed on July 8, 45 to 34. Ten Republicans voted against it. Their long hot fight was over. The bill moved into joint conference.

WASHINGTON, DC, JULY 9, 1909

The day after the Senate passed the tariff bill, Aldrich brought a lumber executive to see Taft. They wanted him to sanction a $1.50 lumber duty in the conference negotiations. Taft was alarmed. Aldrich had assured him that he would reduce the rates when the bill went to conference, but here he was at the White House lobbying for a higher lumber tariff.

"Aldrich said to me during this interview that he expected to follow my lead in Conference," he wrote to Nellie after the meeting. "But I don't know how much that means. I asked him where he would put that in writing, and he said, with the emphasis on the word 'expect,' that he expected to follow me."

For the first time, Taft began to question Aldrich's sincerity. "I do not know whether I am going to succeed in winning this tariff fight or not," he brooded. "I am dealing with very acute and expert politicians, and I am trusting a great many of them and I may be deceived." The complexity of the legislation also confounded him. "If I had more technical knowledge I should feel more confident," he wrote to Nellie. "However, I shall have to struggle along with the assistance of such experts as I can find."[84]

Unfortunately for Taft, most of Washington's tariff experts were loyal to Aldrich, Cannon, or the various industrial interests. That left only one alternative pool of expertise—the six insurgents he had so recently scorned. When Bob La Follette called on the White House a few days later, Taft urged him to come in and sit down with him. "I want to talk with you about the tariff," he said, "What am I to do with this bill?"

La Follette told him to veto it.

"Well," he replied, "suppose I find that I can't do that. What changes ought I to insist upon in conference?"

He took notes while La Follette enumerated excessive import duties from the Payne-Aldrich bill. When he'd filled up a sheet of a paper, he put down his pen and asked La Follette to send him a comprehensive list. La Follette did so the next day.[85]

After La Follette, Taft brought the other insurgents back to the White House one by one. He listened to their views and then tried to apply pressure to Aldrich and Cannon in a way that he had avoided since taking office. On July 16, he told a conference of congressional Standpatters that he was "committed to the principle of a downward revision." The papers applauded him for putting "his foot down" and wielding the "big stick." Many declared that he had won the tariff fight. Taft, pleased, boasted to Nellie that he had the "whip hand."[86]

But in truth, Taft's only whip was a presidential veto that he dared not use. Had he made his speech while the flames of insurgency licked at Aldrich's heels, it might have had some effect. Now it was too late. Aldrich and Cannon appointed a slate of loyal Standpatters to the joint conference committee, and the insurgents were powerless to amend the bill. Taft had lost his leverage.

Unable to significantly alter the legislation, Taft chose a few battles that he thought he could win. In the end, his belated engagement with the Standpatters hinged over whether lumber was taxed at $1.25 or $1.50 per thousand feet and whether Uncle Joe got to keep his exorbitant glove tariffs. On these two issues, Taft refused to budge. "They have my last word," he declared on July 29, "and now I want to show my scorn for further negotiations by spending the afternoon on the golf links." He was not on the green ten minutes when the message come that the conferees had agreed to his terms. Taft's features gathered into a smile. "Well, good friends, this makes me very happy," he said.[87]

WASHINGTON, DC, AUGUST 5, 1909

The tariff bill came up for a vote one week later. On the Senate floor, Aldrich expressed relief at having reached the end and lauded his bill as "the most important and comprehensive measure ever enacted by the American Congress."

Jonathan Dolliver disagreed. "[T]he Republican party...did not arise merely to meet or solve problems of economy and finance," he declared. "It must stand guard over the American marketplace to prevent capital, massed in great corporations, from exercising the evil influences which follow monopoly and the injurious restraint of trade. It must see to it that prejudices based on race and color are not permitted to degrade American labor, as slavery once degraded it. The Republican party is face to face, as in the days of its youth, with the elementary questions which concern justice and liberty."[88]

The roll call came quickly. All six insurgents voted against the bill. Senator Knute Nelson of Minnesota was the only other Republican to join them. The Senate passed the Payne-Aldrich Act 47 to 31. The House affirmed with it a voice vote.

President Taft signed it the same evening. His praise was somewhat fainter than Aldrich's. "This is not a perfect tariff bill," he acknowledged after scrawling "William H. Taft" on the top sheet of the towering stack. Nonetheless, he insisted that it represented "a substantial downward revision and a reduction of excessive rates."[89]

Politicians and historians would debate that particular assessment for years afterward. The Payne-Aldrich Act reduced some rates and increased others. Where the balance lay depended on the method of calculation. But whether the rates turned slightly up or slightly down was beside the point. Even under the most charitable assessment, the Payne-Aldrich Act was as convoluted and arbitrary as its predecessors, a product of industry lobbying and political horse-trading, not sound policymaking. It was, in short, an extension of the status quo, just as the Standpatters had intended.[90]

MACKINAC ISLAND, MICHIGAN, AUGUST 23, 1909

Uncle Joe was on vacation in Michigan when the *Chicago Tribune* correspondent reached him. The journalist wanted Cannon's statement on an angry letter that Representative Charles Fowler of New Jersey had just released to the papers in which he accused Cannon of exercising "brutal power like Nero."

"Why in hell should I notice Fowler?" Cannon growled. At the end of the session, he had demoted Fowler and other insurgents from their committee positions. If they chose to defy the party, he saw no reason to sustain their authority, no matter how much seniority they had. He certainly didn't want Fowler mucking up the currency bill that Aldrich was working on.

"Will you speak specifically of any of the items in Fowler's arraignments?" the journalist pressed.

"Why in hell should I answer him?" Cannon retorted. "He is a damned joke. All of Congress knows he is a joke."

With that, he terminated the official interview. The unofficial interview continued for some time, however, during which Uncle Joe called Fowler a "lowbrow," a "four flusher," and a number of other words the journalist deemed unfit for publication.[91]

MOUNT KENYA, BRITISH EAST AFRICA, SEPTEMBER 10, 1909

While Washington boiled in the wet heat of August and the fury of Republican discord, Theodore Roosevelt killed elephants on the cool, dry slopes of Mount Kenya. When Senator Lodge wrote him with news of the tariff fight, he replied cheerfully, "Apparently you have come out as well as we could hope on the tariff question...If, as I am confident, business steadily improves, the grumbling will have no permanent effect—unless indeed the spirit of unrest in the West grows strong."[92]

WINONA, MINNESOTA, SEPTEMBER 17, 1909

The spirit of unrest in the West grew strong. Politicians and journalists from the Ohio River to the Pacific Ocean assailed the President, the Speaker, the senator from Rhode Island, and the new tariff law. Taft, failing to grasp the magnitude of the fury, once again attributed the discontent to poor public relations. He accused the press of exaggerating the rate increases and lamented that he lacked Roosevelt's facility with journalists. In September, he embarked on a nationwide speaking tour to rectify the PR problem. He planned to "get out and see the people and jolly them."[93]

But it would take more than smiles this time. During the election campaign, Taft had promised voters "a genuine and honest revision of the tariff." Most understood him to mean that he would reform the country's tariff policy, which was neither genuine nor honest. But what he delivered was at best a minor rate adjustment, and his labored argument that the average duty was slightly lower than before missed the point. Worst of all for westerners, most of those rate reductions came from raw materials, which tilted the balance even further in favor of the industrialized East.

Nor did Taft improve the public's mood when he praised Aldrich as "one of the ablest statesmen in financial matters in either House" at a speech in Boston, or when he made half a dozen speeches in Wisconsin without uttering the name "La Follette." But these were mere warm-ups to the disastrous address he delivered in Winona, Minnesota.[94]

Winona was in Representative James Tawney's district. The antitariff movement was strong in Minnesota, and Tawney had risked his seat by voting for the tariff act. Taft hoped to help him out with a forceful speech that would finally persuade skeptical westerners to see the bill's merits. Though he had planned the speech since August, he'd had no time to work on it and ended up dictating it to a stenographer between stations as he hurtled toward Winona. "Speech hastily prepared, but I hope it may do some good," he telegraphed Nellie on the day of the speech.[95]

That evening, he stood on the stage of Winona's elegant opera house and delivered a long defense of the Payne-Aldrich Act. "Now the promise of the Republican platform was not to revise everything downward," he argued. "What I promised was that there should be many decreases." Chiding the insurgents who voted against the bill—including both Minnesota senators—he described in detail which rates had gone up, which had gone down, and how the aggregate result fulfilled his campaign promises. "On the whole," he concluded momentously. "I am bound to say that I think Payne bill is the best bill that the Republican party ever passed."[96]

The correspondents who accompanied the tour took down his words and wired them to their editors back home. They provoked a national sensation the next day but not the one Taft had intended. The details of the speech faded into obscurity behind the explosive headlines: "BEST TARIFF BILL WE HAVE EVER HAD," PRESIDENT TELLS "INSURGENTS."[97]

On the editorial pages, western journalists reacted with renewed fury. Many papers that had supported his election turned on him angrily. "Shades of Theodore Roosevelt," cried the *Des Moines News*, "may the ghosts of the wild animals he has killed in Africa ever haunt him for having foisted on the country this man Taft." Among the gentler critiques, one word echoed through editorial after editorial: *disappointment*.[98]

Taft still didn't get it. "I can not myself see that I have done anything to call for such severe criticism," he complained. "I meant every word of my Winona speech." But that was precisely the problem. In the speech, he stated publicly what he had been saying privately for months—that he was proud of this bill, that he was pleased with Aldrich for preparing it, and that he resented the insurgents for attacking it. In Winona, he conspicuously abandoned the middle position between "radicals" and "reactionaries" that Roosevelt had long maintained. His vigorous praise for the bill and his public criticism of the insurgents placed him squarely on the side of the Standpatters. When journalists began to divvy up politicians as *progressive* or *conservative*, Taft's name dropped neatly into the conservative basket.[99]

SPOKANE, WASHINGTON, OCTOBER 20, 1909

"Poor Taft made a sad mess of it at Winona," Dolliver wrote to La Follette. "I knew he was good natured but I never dreamed he was so dull...Is he ignorant of the fact that Aldrich himself organized the proceedings around the textile schedules, every paragraph drawn by the parties in interest?" He worried about the consequences of alienating the President along with the Republican establishment but declared that he'd rather go back to his farm than renounce the fight. "I feel that my life has been enriched and strengthened by the new light in which I have had a glimpse of your motives and purposes in American public life," he gushed.[100]

Meanwhile, La Follette charged along as heedless as ever. He was not shocked by the revelations from Minnesota. He'd been skeptical of Taft from the start. By the time the tariff bill passed, his skepticism had turned to contempt. While Taft traveled the country defending the Payne-Aldrich Act, La Follette traveled even farther denouncing it. From Minneapolis to Los Angeles, he went to the districts of the men who had voted for the bill and read out the roll. Old friends and new allies met him at every station. The crowds were larger than ever.

When La Follette returned to Washington, DC, a journalist asked him if he thought the progressive movement was receding. "Those who are seeking to stem the tide of the progressive movement...are preparing for a flood," he answered. From Washington "to the Pacific Coast the masses are aroused."[101]

THE INSURGENCY

Adam and Eve were insurgents and ate of the forbidden fruit expecting to become gods. They only learned to see their own nakedness. Judas was an insurgent and sold his master for 30 pieces of silver; I have no doubt he would have been applauded by the newspapers of Jerusalem had there been any in that day.

—Uncle Joe[1]

WASHINGTON, DC, MARCH 2, 1907

Gifford Pinchot worried about the future. The forests that once blanketed the continent had nearly vanished from the East and were rapidly receding from the West. The coalfields and iron mines were petering out. The topsoil was washing into the sea. "When the natural resources of any nation become exhausted," he warned, "disaster and decay in every department of national life follow as a matter of course."[2]

Most Americans were oblivious to the catastrophe. Like Pinchot's grandfather, who had made a fortune stripping timber from Pennsylvania's green mountains, they treated wilderness as a boundless resource to be exploited and discarded at will. As Pinchot recalled in his autobiography, "What talk there was about forest protection was no more to the average American than the buzzing of a mosquito, and just about as irritating."[3]

But one man understood very well. The first time Pinchot met Theodore Roosevelt, the irrepressible governor of New York challenged the lanky forester to a wrestling match. Roosevelt won, but when they boxed, Pinchot's long arms knocked him "off his very solid pins." They were much alike. Born into money and educated at the best schools, they rejected the "ignoble ease" of the New York social scene for what Roosevelt called "the strenuous life." Roosevelt hiked and hunted, raised cattle, and ran for public office. Pinchot climbed mountains and slept outside on a wooden pillow to toughen himself. Instead of becoming a socialite or a businessman like his father, he studied forestry in France and took a job at the Department of Agriculture.

When Roosevelt moved to Washington, he and Pinchot grew close. They hiked together through Rock Creek Park, swam in the Potomac, and swatted tennis balls on the White House court. Pinchot became a privileged member of Roosevelt's "Tennis Cabinet," an informal group of friends who advised him during post-match lunches. Not that Roosevelt required any convincing. As an avid outdoorsman, he had championed forest conservation since his days as governor. At White House strategy sessions, he and Pinchot prepared to revolutionize the nation's environmental policies.[4]

At the time, the General Land Office in the Department of the Interior managed the bulk of federal property. Throughout the nineteenth century, the office operated as a farm distribution machine, dangling cheap land as bait to draw settlers westward. By the twentieth century, there wasn't much land left. The remaining mountains and deserts held little appeal to pioneer farmers. But others were interested. Lumber companies, mining corporations, railroads, and speculators conspired to acquire cheap land from "settlers" who applied for homesteads with no intention of farming them. One notorious speculator in Oregon described how he would visit a saloon, buy the patrons a few rounds, and distribute land applications for them to sign. To facilitate his scams, he paid off Oregon's Republican bosses, including a senator, a congressman, and the commissioner of the General Land Office.[5]

Thus, the first step to conserve America's remaining forests was to withdraw them from the Land Office's tainted purview. Soon after the Oregon land scandal broke, Roosevelt promoted a bill to transfer forest reserves to Pinchot's agency, the United States Forest Service. Congress, reeling from the scandal and conviction of an eminent senator, passed the law with little dissent.

The congressmen did not expect what happened next. With Roosevelt's blessing, Pinchot directed his staff to review the public lands and designate any woodland a national forest reserve, effectively transferring it from the Land Office to the Forest Service. By 1907, he had added 21 million acres to his jurisdiction. The new commissioner of the

General Land Office, Richard A. Ballinger of Washington State, tried to stop the reclassifications, but Roosevelt overruled him.[6]

In 1907, Congress acted to reign in the wayward chief forester. Senator Charles Fulton of Oregon scorned Pinchot's conservation efforts. "While these chiefs of the Bureau of Forestry sit within their marble halls," he protested from the Senate floor, "the lowly pioneer is climbing the mountain side where he will erect his humble cabin, and within the shadow of the whispering pines and the lofty firs of the western forest engage in the laborious work of carving out for himself and his loved ones a home and a dwelling place." Fulton did not explain what the lowly pioneer was supposed to grow amid the lofty firs on the mountainside. Nor did he mention his own attempt to quash an investigation into the scandal that had rendered this myth so ludicrous. Instead, he proposed an amendment to an agricultural appropriations bill. His measure required congressional approval for the President to create new forest reserves in six Far West states. It passed easily.[7]

Roosevelt opposed Fulton's amendment, but he couldn't afford to veto the whole appropriations bill, so he let it sit on his desk. For the next seven days, he and Pinchot pressed the Forest Service staff to work 48-hour shifts pouring over maps from the six affected states and assigning every last patch of woodlands to a national reserve while they still had the power. By the end of the week, they'd created 16 million acres of new forest reserves. Only then did Roosevelt sign the bill. "The opponents of the Forest Service turned handsprings in their wrath," he chuckled.[8]

BEVERLY, MASSACHUSETTS, AUGUST 18, 1909

William Taft did not approve of Roosevelt's methods. Though he supported forest conservation, the judge in him recoiled whenever Roosevelt played too fast and loose with the law. He also frowned on the way Roosevelt's friendship with Pinchot had twisted the chain of command by elevating the chief of the Forest Service above the cabinet secretaries.[9]

When he became president, Taft set about correcting what he saw as the deficiencies of the previous administration. First he replaced Secretary of the Interior James Garfield, who had exercised authority "far beyond legal limitation." In his place, he appointed Richard Ballinger, the former commissioner of the General Land Office who had resisted Pinchot's land transfers. Ballinger's commitment to conservation was questionable, but he was a trained lawyer and shared Taft's deference to legal constraint. One of his first acts as secretary of the interior was to reverse some of Roosevelt's land transfers on legal grounds. Taft approved. "Congress has the power to dispose of lands," he declared, "not the President."[10]

During the cabinet selection process, Taft had ignored a warning from Gifford Pinchot that he and Ballinger "might clash." It was not the place of a bureau chief to question a president's choice for secretary. To Taft, this was yet another instance of the insubordination that Roosevelt had fostered. He had mixed feelings about Pinchot in general. On one hand, he recognized his talent and appreciated what he had accomplished. On the other, he regarded him "as a good deal of a radical and a good deal of a crank" and complained that he was "quite willing to camp outside the law to accomplish his beneficent purposes." Despite these misgivings, he determined to keep him on as chief forester. To lose such a prominent member of Roosevelt's inner circle would signal to the country that he was not committed to his predecessor's reform program—a signal that would be heard as far away as Africa.

Pinchot was not making it easy, however. In the summer of 1909, his feud with Ballinger increased in intensity and spilled out into the press. Taft worried about their quarrel as he vacationed on the coast of Massachusetts. "I am sorry about this Pinchot-Ballinger business," he wrote. "I shall have to knock some heads together when I get back to Washington, after my trip."[11]

But the conflict came to a head before he got there. On August 18, a young civil servant named Louis Glavis came to see him in Massachusetts, bearing a letter of introduction from Pinchot. Glavis worked for the Department of the Interior. He had uncovered information, he told Taft, that Ballinger had facilitated fraudulent coal land deals in Alaska on behalf of a former client.[12]

Taft was dubious. Glavis seemed overzealous, and his charges were speculative. Nonetheless, he carefully reviewed the documents Glavis provided and sought counsel from a few cabinet members. They all shared his skepticism. Then he invited Secretary Ballinger to come to Massachusetts to defend himself. After they met, Taft concluded that Ballinger was innocent of all charges. He officially exonerated him and authorized him to dismiss Glavis "for disloyalty to his superior officers in making a false charge against them."[13]

Next he turned his attention to Pinchot. He was disturbed by the chief forester's involvement in the matter and thought Pinchot's ideas were "of a lunar character," but to lose such a prominent conservation advocate would be public relations disaster. It would further provoke his progressive critics and even risk a rupture with Roosevelt himself. To make sure that Pinchot did not resign, Taft composed a friendly letter. "I write this to urge upon you that you do not make Glavis's cause yours," he wrote. "I should consider it one of the greatest losses that my administration could sustain if you were to leave it…"[14]

WASHINGTON, DC, NOVEMBER 10, 1909

When Taft returned to Washington after his publicity tour to promote the tariff bill, he found his staff despondent over the Ballinger affair. "One member of the Cabinet tells me that there is a cabal of the Roosevelts' friends to force an issue between us and another that Pinchot has got to be dismissed," he told Archie Butt, his military aide. "Still another tells me that the reformers don't believe that I intend to push any of the reform measures instituted by Roosevelt and that hell is to pay everywhere."

Despite the pervasive gloom in the White House, he was optimistic that Congress would vindicate him. The congressmen were still on vacation, but there was talk of an investigation into Glavis's accusations. Taft welcomed it, confident that the evidence would show how lenient he had been toward Pinchot. "Of course, Roosevelt would have come back at those preferring the charges and would by now have them on the run," he acknowledged, "but I cannot do things that way. I will let them go on, and by and by the people will see who is right and who is wrong. There is no use trying to be William Howard Taft with Roosevelt's ways."[15]

NEW YORK, NEW YORK, DECEMBER 27, 1909

Gifford Pinchot had promised Taft not to comment on the Ballinger affair, but that did not prohibit him from speaking generally about conservation. He traveled the country defending Roosevelt's conservation policies wherever he went. Two days after Christmas, he slogged through Manhattan's snow-choked streets to the University Club in order to present the most forceful address he'd ever delivered. Because of the blizzard, few people attended, but he gave out copies of the speech to the press, which broadcast his words to the country.[16]

This speech was not about the importance of conservation. By 1909, most Americans understood that the country's natural resources required careful stewardship. Pinchot raised a different question. "For whose benefit shall they be conserved?" he asked. In contrast to radical environmentalists like John Muir, he did not endorse conservation for its own sake. He believed that the nation's natural resources should benefit its people. But which people?

Employing the epic language of the progressives, he spoke of a "great conflict… between special interest and equal opportunity, between the privileges of the few and the rights of the many, between government by men for human welfare and government by money for profit, between the men who stand for the Roosevelt policies and the men who stand against them." The objective of the conservationist, he argued, must be to preserve natural resources for the people by protecting them from corporate exploitation.

"This is the heart of the conservation problem to-day," he concluded. "The conservation issue is a moral issue."[17]

By framing his environmental crusade as the peoples' fight against the corporations, Pinchot embedded it in the great wave of reform that was sweeping out of the West. In the past, there had been Standpatters who supported conservation and reformers who ignored it. Henceforth, conservationism and environmentalism would be regarded as progressive issues. Conversely, the people who began to think of themselves as conservatives increasingly opposed it.

More immediately, Pinchot's speech represented an implicit challenge to President Taft. There were only two sides, he implied, and the President was on the wrong one. A few days later, he made this challenge explicit in a letter to Theodore Roosevelt. "We have fallen back down the hill you led us up," he lamented to his friend. He did not accuse Taft of deliberately surrendering to the Standpatters but argued that his "weakness and indecision" and "desire to act as a judge" had allowed Senator Aldrich and Speaker Cannon to manipulate him. "Unless Mr. Taft turns squarely about and promptly abandons his present direction and tendencies," he warned, "I foresee a clear-cut division between the Administration and the Reactionaries on the one side, and the Progressives and the great mass of the people on the other. The coming investigation must inevitably tend to make that division sharp and clear."[18]

WASHINGTON, DC, JANUARY 6, 1910

If Pinchot refrained from discussing the Ballinger affair in public, his staff was less discreet. When he returned to Washington, he learned that two forestry officials had leaked information to the press and had assisted Louis Glavis with a sensational article about the case for one of the muckraking magazines. He did not try to conceal his pride in their insubordination.

Nonetheless, they had deliberately flouted the President's directive. Action would have to be taken. He instructed them to send him a letter confessing what they had done. Upon receiving it, he formally reprimanded them. From his point of view, that was the end of the story. But there was one complication—the impending congressional investigation. With the Standpatters in control of the proceedings, Pinchot expected no leniency. His valiant foresters would be "hauled over the coals" and dismissed from the service.

With typical audacity, he decided to preempt the investigation by coming clean "and so give no one a chance to uncover anything that could be held against us." In order to engage Congress on his own terms, he enlisted the help of his friend, Jonathan Dolliver. At the beginning of January, he sent him a letter explaining what had happened. With his permission, Dolliver read it out to the Senate on the same day that Taft transmitted his report to Congress.

Pinchot's letter acknowledged that the two agents had "violated a rule of propriety," but he insisted that they broke no laws, and he commended them for endangering their careers to prevent a loss of public property. "A public officer is bound first to obey the law and keep within it," he concluded. "But he is also bound, at any personal risk, to do everything the law will let him do for the public good." The words were offered on behalf of his staff, but he may as well have presented them in his own defense.[19]

WASHINGTON, DC, JANUARY 7, 1910

Taft received the news of Pinchot's letter with grim dismay. "The trouble has come to a head sooner than I expected," he sighed to Archie Butt. Pinchot's deliberate insubordination left him little choice; the entire cabinet agreed that he should be dismissed. But the man whose opinion mattered most was now shooting rhinoceroses in the Belgian Congo. Taft had promised Roosevelt that he would make no decision without considering "what his predecessor would have done under the same circumstances," but that was difficult when his decision determined the fate of Roosevelt's close friend and trusted adviser. To fire Pinchot was unquestionably the correct thing to do, but Taft was not sure that Roosevelt would agree.[20]

By the end of the day, his rectitude had conquered his fidelity. "When the people of the United States elected me President," he wrote to Pinchot, "they placed me in an office of the highest dignity, and charged me with the duty of maintaining that dignity and proper respect for the office on the part of my subordinates... [I]t therefore now becomes my duty to direct the Secretary of Agriculture to remove you from your office as the Forester."[21]

Few historians question Taft's decision. Glavis's charges were unsubstantiated, and Pinchot had openly defied the President. Most argue that he should have done it sooner. But however correct the choice, in backing Ballinger and firing Pinchot, President Taft had once again chosen a side.

And this time, he did so in direct opposition to the man he had pledged
to emulate.

LADO ENCLAVE, BELGIAN CONGO, JANUARY 17, 1910

On the savannas of central Africa, Theodore Roosevelt slumbered
through hot nights beneath a canvas tent wearing nothing but netting.
There were scarcely any human inhabitants in the equatorial grasslands,
but the game was plentiful—except for the northern white rhinoceros. All
but extinct today, they were scarce even in Roosevelt's time. Theodore
and his son Kermit shot nine of them, eight of which would end up on
display in American museums.[22]

One day in the middle of January, a naked runner jogged into camp
with news from a faraway land. He carried a telegram from the Press
Agency. President Taft had fired Gifford Pinchot, the cable reported.
The press wanted Roosevelt's statement.

Shocked and bewildered, he did not answer the press but sent the
courier back with a private letter. "Dear Gifford," he wrote, "We have
just heard by special runner that you have been removed. I cannot believe
it. I do not know any man in public life who has rendered quite the service
you have rendered; and it seems to me absolutely impossible that there
can be any truth in this statement. But of course it makes me very uneasy.
Do write me, care of the American embassy at Paris, just what the real
situation is. I have only been able to follow things very imperfectly while
out here."[23]

WASHINGTON, DC, MARCH 7, 1910

Taft was weary and bitter. He had endured Pinchot's insubordination
for months and had finally dismissed him only when the forester's open
defiance of his authority left him no choice. "I would not have removed
Pinchot if I could have helped it," he lamented. But in the eyes of the
"progressives," he could do nothing right. Despite his forbearance of
Pinchot, the radical papers protested his decision and attacked him for
violating Roosevelt's principles.[24]

Taft consoled himself that the congressional investigation would
prove how lenient he'd been, but the hearings weren't going very well.
Collier's, the muckraking magazine that published Glavis's allegations,
had hired a sharp Boston lawyer named Louis Brandeis—another progressive type. Brandeis flayed Ballinger and other government witnesses
in withering cross-examinations. In the evenings, he dined at the La
Follettes' home.[25]

Taft's legislative agenda wasn't going much better. In accordance with his promise to "complete and perfect" Roosevelt's reforms, he hoped to pass a railroad bill to rectify some flaws in the Hepburn Act. The railroads had challenged a number of the Interstate Commerce Commission's (ICC) rulings in court, and the lawsuits had become mired in the overloaded legal system. In order to expedite the proceedings, Taft proposed a five-judge Commerce Court with jurisdiction over the ICC. He reasoned that swift decisions by a panel of expert judges would benefit both the railroads and the shipping companies. Aldrich and Cannon agreed to shepherd the bill through the Senate without amendment, but the insurgents again made trouble. La Follette, Cummins, Dolliver, and Bristow complained that the Commerce Court would usurp the authority of the ICC in favor of the railroads. Setting railroad rates was a policy question, they argued, not a legal matter."[26]

Taft couldn't understand their objections. With his faith in the legal system, he could see no flaw in such a reasonable and moderate solution, so, like Roosevelt, he assumed that the insurgents must have ulterior reasons for opposing it. "The situation in Congress is uncertain," he wrote to his brother, "but with the assistance of my wicked partners, Cannon and Aldrich, I am hopeful that I can pull off the legislation that I have most at heart. Cummins, La Follette, Dolliver, Clapp and Bristow are five senators who are determined to be as bitter as they can against the administration, and to defeat anything that the administration seeks."[27]

Months of vilification over his handling of the tariff bill, Pinchot, and the railroad legislation had convinced Taft that the progressives were deliberately persecuting him. He was not like Aldrich, who ignored the barbs, or Cannon, who furiously returned fire. Taft wanted to be liked and appreciated; the daily criticisms tormented him. Sometimes he wallowed in fatalism, predicting that "radicals" would dominate the next election. "Sooner or later I fear we have got to turn the government over to this element," he told Senator Jonathan Bourne of Oregon, "and let it demonstrate its incapacity to govern the country." Other days, he brimmed with defiance. "I don't propose to have my administration a failure because of the hostility of Dolliver and Cummins," he blustered to Archie Butt.[28]

It was the latter spirit that gripped him one muddy March afternoon when he directed his driver to the Arlington Hotel, two blocks from the White House. Finding Aldrich at home in his suite, Taft invited him for a ride in his steam car. Instead of the usual route through Rock Creek Park, they chugged down secluded side streets where they would be less conspicuous. The cold wind chilled the aging senator, so Archie Butt fished out one of Taft's sweaters, which fit Aldrich like a tent.

As they drove, Taft laid out his plan. He had spoken with former Congressman Hepburn and other Standpatters in Iowa, who promised to make trouble for Dolliver and Cummins at the next election. They just needed a little financial assistance. Taft hoped that Aldrich might be able to help in this matter.

Aldrich agreed to raise the money from certain friends of his and promised to donate some of his own money to the cause. He also urged Taft to withhold patronage authority from Dolliver, Cummins, and Beveridge, which would prevent them from rewarding supporters with government jobs.

Taft agreed and offered to contribute his share to the Iowa fund. He delivered Aldrich back to the Arlington and returned to the White House. "Well, Archie," he said to his aide as they pulled in, "I had to descend into politics this afternoon. I believe in fighting the devil with fire."[29]

The next day, Taft took another drive, this time to the Capitol, where he picked up the Speaker of the House. Uncle Joe, dismayed by the cold gusts of wind, asked if they might take a closed car, but Taft just laughed and called him a mollycoddle. He took off his sweater, the same one Aldrich had worn, and gave it to Uncle Joe, who found it even roomier.

Taft did not speak to Cannon about his Iowa scheme. Instead, they discussed the legislation pending in Congress.

"I am getting so damned tired, Mr. President," Cannon complained, "of this everlasting yielding to popular outcry against wealth that unless we put a check on it somewhere there is no telling where it will lead."

"Exactly," Taft agreed, "but those fellows in the Senate who are opposing this bill are not doing it for any reasons which you have given, but merely to make trouble or else to freight it down with heavier populistic burdens."

"I believe that," replied the Speaker, "and that is why I have such a contempt for those who are fighting you and am willing to give you my support."[30]

And so the battle lines were drawn. Taft had finally come to see politics as the progressives did: a war with only two sides. But he chose the other side.

WASHINGTON, DC, MARCH 16, 1910

Congressman Adolph Sabath of Chicago was an insignificant little Democrat with an insignificant little bill. He proposed to amend the census act to classify immigrants by their mother tongues in addition to their nationalities. "Lots of people were classed as citizens of Austria-Hungary when they were really Bohemians and Poles," he explained.[31]

Uncle Joe didn't give a hoot about Sabath or his amendment, but he saw an opportunity. He told Edgar Crumpacker of Indiana, chairman of the Census Committee, to introduce the bill on March 16—Calendar Wednesday, the day committee members were permitted to introduce bills to the floor without the Speaker's approval. The rules dictated that the committees present in a specific order, but Cannon recognized Crumpacker without waiting for the Census Committee's turn. When some of the congressmen objected, he declared that the legislation was exempt from the usual order because it concerned a constitutional mandate: Article I, Section 2 required the government to conduct a national census every ten years. Consequently, he argued, the legislation was "made privileged by the Constitution" and exempt from ordinary House rules. This rationale offered Cannon a clever way to undermine Calendar Wednesday. Using the census bill as a precedent, he could invoke "constitutional privilege" for many other bills.

But then something unexpected happened. John Fitzgerald of Brooklyn, who had supported Cannon during the previous rules fight, appealed his ruling. A spirited debate ensued. As the congressmen argued, Cannon silently counted heads and came to a shocking realization. With an election looming in November, the unpopular tariff act had turned wavering Republicans and Democrats against him. He didn't have the votes.

In an evasive maneuver to avoid humiliation, he and Crumpacker tried to postpone the measure to another day, but the House voted against postponement, and the roll call on constitutional privilege proceeded. The Democrats were nearly unanimous this time, and 42 insurgent Republicans joined them, far more than had voted to establish Calendar Wednesday in the first place. Cannon lost badly—163 to 111, the worst legislative defeat of his career. "The decision of the Chair does not stand as the decision of the House," he ruefully acknowledged when it was over.[32]

The loss sparked the usual round of press pronouncements that his leadership was in jeopardy, but Cannon ignored them. He was still the Speaker with same authority that he'd had before the vote. Technically, he'd lost nothing except a modicum of pride. Or so he thought.

WASHINGTON, DC, MARCH 17, 1910

George Norris from McCook, Nebraska, fingered a piece of paper in his pocket, so tattered that it barely held together. He'd been carrying it for a long time. Few Americans outside his district were familiar with his name. He was just another small-town congressman, soft-spoken and smartly dressed with a tidy silver mustache. He was not a member of any important committees. He had never sponsored any important bills.

But people who paid attention to goings-on in Washington had seen his name in the news. When Speaker Cannon tried to appoint conservative committee members to investigate the Ballinger-Pinchot affair, Norris proposed and passed an amendment to select the committee members by House vote. When President Taft announced that he would not distribute patronage jobs to insurgent Republicans, Norris coolly warned him that he was making "a grave mistake by aiding Cannon." He never indulged in histrionics or mockery in his dogged pursuit of Uncle Joe. As he calmly explained on the pages of *La Follette's Weekly*, his fight was not against Joseph Cannon the man but the extraordinary power that he had amassed.[33]

Norris did not participate in the census battle. In his opinion, Calendar Wednesday was nothing but "a comic parliamentary joke... a homoeopathic dose of nothingness." The only way to reign in the Speaker, he believed, was to take away his control of the Rules Committee. So he kept his head down while the other congressmen quarreled about constitutional privilege. During the debate, he spoke only once. After Marlin Olmsted of Pennsylvania defended the Speaker's position, Norris put a question to him. "Would it not follow logically, from the gentleman's theory," he asked, "that any Member of the House tomorrow could present here a bill touching the census without ever having it referred to a committee, as a question of the highest privilege under the Constitution and the law, and would it not be the duty of the Speaker to say that that was privileged?" Olmsted agreed that the Speaker was obliged to recognize any congressman who raised a matter of constitutional privilege. That was all Norris needed to hear. He yielded the floor.

The next day, the House began its business amicably. Now that it was no longer Calendar Wednesday, the congressmen were more charitable toward the census bill. They declared the resolution "privileged under the Constitution" and approved it by a wide margin.

Then Norris spoke up. "Mr. Speaker, I present a resolution made privileged by the Constitution," he said.

Cannon awarded him with a good-natured smile. "If it is a resolution made privileged by the Constitution," he said, "the gentleman will present it." Laughter flickered around the chamber.

Norris drew the crumpled paper from his pocket and passed it to the House clerk. As the clerk silently read it, an odd smile passed across his face. He handed the paper to the Speaker. Cannon looked at it and frowned.

Impatient cries erupted from the Democratic side of the chamber, "Read it! Read the resolution!"

Cannon hesitantly passed the paper back to the clerk, who read it out to the House: "*Resolved*, That the rules of the House be amended as follows: 'The Committee on Rules shall consist of 15 members, 9 of whom shall be members of the majority party and 6 of whom shall be members of the minority party...'" The members were to be elected by the House, not appointed by the Speaker. And the Speaker would not be eligible for membership.

The congressmen were out of their seats and in the aisles by the time the clerk finished reading. Cannon remained silent while his lieutenants spoke in his defense, insisting that the resolution was not privileged under the Constitution.

But Norris responded calmly, "Article I, section 5, paragraph 2, of the Constitution reads as follows: Each House may determine the rules of its proceedings. I submit, Mr. Speaker, if the action of the House just had makes a census bill privileged because of the Constitution, then any proposition to amend the rules must be privileged by virtue of that same instrument."

His logic was compelling. If the Constitution privileged an insignificant amendment to the census act, then surely it must also privilege an amendment to the House rules. Cannon was caught in a trap of his own making. In trying to open a way for the Speaker to bypass the rules on Calendar Wednesday, he had inadvertently opened a way for any congressman to bypass the Speaker on any other day. Norris simply walked through the door that Cannon had opened.

Of course, parliamentary logic was not the deciding factor in the House of Representatives. Cannon could certainly find a way to rule Norris's resolution out of order. But the House could then appeal the decision, and the previous day's vote had demonstrated that the congressmen no longer feared their Speaker. If he ruled against the resolution, the majority would almost certainly countermand him.

He stood at the podium, nervously tearing up bits of paper until the rostrum looked like a snow bank. There was only one path open to him. The House could overrule his decision, but it could not force him to decide. So he chose not to. As congressmen swirled about the chamber in chaos, he kept insisting that he needed more time to consider the matter. While he delayed, taxis went forth into the city to drag back absent Standpatters from their sickbeds. Telegrams whisked down the wires, begging distant allies to return posthaste. But the Democrats and insurgents reached out to their own absentees, and congressmen from both sides scurried to reach the Capitol before their opponents.[34]

The stalemate lasted all night. Uncle Joe retired to his office, smoked a long black cigar, and went to sleep on his couch. Back in the chamber, congressmen dozed in their chairs or entertained themselves with song. The temporary presiding officer rapped his gavel and chastised them for impropriety, but the chorus ignored him and sang a round of "There'll Be a Hot Time in the Old Town Tonight," which was duly recorded in the *Congressional Record*. Some congressmen briefly escaped to their apartments and hotels until the sergeant-at-arms went out to fetch them. They soon returned disheveled and indignant to the Capitol.[35]

The next day, Cannon's allies proposed a compromise to end the standoff. They agreed to expand the Rules Committee and elect the members but insisted that the Speaker be permitted to retain his seat on the committee. The insurgents refused, confident that they had the upper hand. "We will beat them," Norris predicted. "There is no doubt of the result unless there is some legerdemain."[36]

The negotiations collapsed in the afternoon. At 4 p.m., after 26 hours of continuous session, the congressmen finally voted themselves a recess so they could get some sleep.[37]

WASHINGTON, DC, MARCH 19, 1910

The next day, every congressman who could reach the Capitol crowded into the House chamber. Senators, diplomats, government officials, and a few lucky members of the public overflowed the galleries. Less fortunate visitors jammed the stairways in hopes of hearing proceedings they could not see.

At noon, the Republican side of the chamber applauded as Uncle Joe, looking vigorous as ever with a fresh carnation in his lapel, entered the chamber and ran lightly up to the Speaker's desk. The cheers echoed through the galleries until he pounded the podium and called the House to order. He had to thump the ivory gavel again and again while the excited congressmen muddled through the morning routine.[38]

At last, the Speaker began his long-awaited ruling. Reading slowly and deliberately from a typewritten document, he parsed the principle of "constitutional privilege" so as to include the census amendment while excluding Norris's resolution. To no one's surprise, he ruled, "[T]he resolution is not in order."

George Norris was on his feet even before the Republicans broke into applause. "Mr. Speaker," he shouted over the din, "I appeal from the decision…" He demanded a floor vote to overturn the Speaker's ruling.

Amid the chaos, it took the clerk more than half an hour to complete the count. When he handed a slip of paper to the Speaker, the congressmen finally went quiet.

"On this vote," Cannon somberly announced, "the yeas are 164 and the nays are 181." The cheers from the Democratic side drowned him out as he added, "The decision of the Chair does not stand as the judgment of the House."[39]

There would be several more hours of chaos before the final vote on Norris's resolution. La Follette and the other insurgent senators circulated on the floor, plotting strategy with their House counterparts. Cannon waited impassively behind his desk, his sharp features silhouetted by the American flag draped behind his back.

When the speeches had concluded, Norris asked for the floor. "Mr. Speaker," he said, "I move the previous question on the substitute and resolution to the final passage."

Shouts and cheers roared through the chamber. The crowds in the stairwells pressed so hard that they cracked the glass on the gallery doors. On the main floor, the surging mob in the hallway pushed the women in front through the doors and onto the floor of the chamber. Uncle Joe crashed his ivory gavel over and over against the marble rostrum until the chamber finally quieted. Then he handed it to one of his lieutenants and sauntered out of the chamber.

The final roll call was even more chaotic than its predecessors. The members were on their feet, and everyone was talking. One by one, the "Yeas" and "Nays" bubbled up from the roiling mass. Then it was done. The vote was 193 to 153. Every Democrat voted "Yea." Republican congressmen who had never before defied their leader joined the insurgency and voted to change the rules. Norris's resolution was sustained; the Speaker's power was broken. The chamber exploded with frantic shouts of excitement.[40]

Amid the tumult, Cannon strolled back into the chamber and casually resumed his place. When the room finally quieted, George Norris took the floor. "Mr. Speaker," he said, "I move that the House do now adjourn."

"One moment," Uncle Joe replied in an imploring tone. "The Speaker asks the indulgence of the House for not exceeding three minutes to make a statement."

"Mr. Speaker, I am willing to withhold the motion," Norris answered.

Cannon put on his glasses. He peered down at a few sheets of paper in one hand while the other toyed with the gavel. "Gentlemen of the House of Representatives," he said, "Actions, not words, determine the conduct and the sincerity of men in the affairs of life." For once, the House was silent. Congressmen and visitors listened intently to find out whether old Uncle Joe would resign.

"In the judgment of the present Speaker," he continued, "a resignation is in and of itself a confession of weakness or mistake or an apology for past actions. The Speaker is not conscious of having done any political wrong." The silence broke as the Standpatters roared their assent. Instead of resigning, Uncle Joe dared the Democrats and insurgents to depose him. "[T]he real majority ought to have the courage of its convictions," he goaded them, "and logically meet the situation that confronts it."[41]

It was a trick. The Republican insurgents didn't have the votes to elect one of their own, and they didn't dare elect a Democrat. Cannon hoped to save face and humiliate the opposition by instigating a failed attempt to unseat him. When he finished speaking, jubilant Standpatters flooded into the aisles, hollering and waving their handkerchiefs in the air. The insurgents, taken by surprise, begged for a recess. One Democrat, Albert Burleson of Texas, stood up and waved a piece of paper over his head. "Mr. Speaker, I offer the following resolution," he yelled over the din.

The insurgents turned on him. "It is untimely!" they shouted. "It is suicidal!" Edmund Hinshaw of Nebraska grasped the Texan by the arm and cried into his ear, "Don't offer this now, don't do it this evening. Wait till we have had time to think it over!" But Burleson pulled himself free, marched up to the Speaker's desk, and delivered his resolution.

"Read! Read!" shouted the Standpatters.

Cannon banged away at the rostrum. "The House will be in order," he demanded. "Gentlemen will be seated." He passed the resolution to the clerk, who read it out: "Resolved, That the office of Speaker of the House of Representatives is hereby declared to be vacant, and the House of Representatives shall at once proceed to the election of a Speaker."

The tumult continued. Cannon ordered the sergeant-at-arms to clear the aisles and force the congressmen back to their seats. The roll call on Burleson's resolution commenced. Most of the Democrats voted to depose the Speaker. The insurgents split. Some voted for the resolution. Others against. The latter were heckled by Democrats and mocked by Republicans. When George Norris's turn came, he said, "Nay." A murmur passed through the chamber.[42]

In the end, the motion to depose the Speaker was handily defeated. Though Cannon had lost control of the Rules Committee, he was still the leader of the House. He tossed aside his gavel and stepped down into the mass of supporters who rushed up to congratulate him. As he exited the chamber, a joyful chorus of "For He's a Jolly Good Fellow" filled the air.

In his office, Cannon lit a fresh cigar and settled into his desk chair while reporters gathered round. "We tried to make a little news for you today," he joked. Boasting of his victory, he insisted that the rules fight was a positive development, for it had reaffirmed his leadership and debunked the "bugaboo of Cannonism." One of the journalists asked him if the "newly elected Speaker" had any comment on his future policy. Cannon laughed. "I'll just keep on, speaking and praying," he replied.[43]

Later that evening, he amplified his bravado at a political banquet, calling the insurgents "feeble minded, abnormal, insane, or, to use a shorter and more common word, they are cranks…And the Sunday papers will be out in the morning with stories about the end of Cannonism and Czarism," he continued. "You in Washington know differently. But the people in the country apparently believe the uplift magazines and the cowardly members of Congress who wrought such havoc today."[44]

So said Uncle Joe, the embodiment of homespun sensibility who had spent his career extolling the wisdom of country folk. Even his boasts betrayed him—tacitly admitting that he had lost the trust of western voters whose interests he had always claimed to represent. He remained Speaker, for the moment, by virtue of eastern congressmen and a few remnants from the old political machines. It could not last. The insurgents' victory in the rules fight had revealed that he was coasting on the fumes of a dying order. The enormous power that he had wielded for six years would never return—not to him or to any of his successors.

Cannon was not the only leader who failed to appreciate the enormity of the vote. President Taft offered no public opinion on the rules fight. In private, he worried about its impact on his legislative agenda. "I don't know what may happen in respect to the organization of the House, and whether we can keep a Republican majority sufficiently loyal and disciplined to pass the legislation which we promised," he wrote to Nellie.[45]

Such sentiments could not have been more different from those of La Follette and the insurgents, who believed that breaking Cannon's choke hold was the *only* way to pass meaningful legislation. But Taft, like Roosevelt, never looked beyond the next session of Congress. Even worse, he looked backward. Staring in the face of the Standpatters' collapse, he behaved as if they still controlled the legislature. "What I am laboring to do is to do something," he explained. "And the idea that I am to stop and make an enemy of Cannon and make an enemy of Aldrich and make an enemy of those who in the present Congress have power to bring about the reforms which I am advocating, does not strike me with favor."[46]

In fact, Taft's blind rush to "do something" would doom him to accomplishing almost nothing. Had he hitched himself to the rising progressive faction instead of the crumbling Standpatters, he might have passed a mountain of reforms in the latter half of his first term and possibly propelled himself into a second. Instead, the productive days of his presidency were already over, and posterity would remember him as one of the least effective presidents in American history.

WASHINGTON, DC, MAY 13, 1910

Amid the cheers that followed Cannon's defeat in the House, someone shouted, "On to Aldrich!" There was no mechanism for such a fight in the Senate, but there was little need. Aldrich already had one foot out the door. With only one year left before his retirement, he had little interest in sparring with the insurgents over legislative details, and he mounted only a halfhearted defense as they riddled the President's railroad bill with amendments. By the end, it looked more like a La Follette measure than a Taft measure.

As Aldrich's grip relaxed, his underlings began to abandon him. Senators who had long feared the power of the Big Four now looked nervously over their shoulders at the rising progressives. "Smooth Steve" Elkins was the first to go. In February, he publicly broke with Aldrich on the Senate floor. "I could not get off the reservation during the consideration of the tariff," he confessed to his colleagues with a rueful grin. "I was afraid to try. The distinguished Senator from Rhode Island knows why. The Senate knows why. But now I have a little more sea room." Aldrich sat next to him during the speech, laughing whenever Elkins mentioned his name as if it were all a terrific joke.[47]

Later, Reed Smoot of Utah, who had received Dolliver's place on the Finance Committee, agreed to put through one of the progressive amendments that Aldrich opposed—a mandate requiring railroads to maintain consistent mileage pricing regardless of the length of the trip. Aldrich discovered him on the Senate floor, cutting up copies of various amendments and rearranging them as if he were making an art project. When Smoot caught Aldrich's penetrating stare and enigmatic half-smile, his hands began to tremble, and he struggled to operate the scissors. Aldrich walked over and casually inspected Smoot's handiwork. Then he reached out his hand to steady the quivering paper and pointed out some minor textual corrections that Smoot had overlooked. The amendment passed easily.[48]

Aldrich had successfully fended off that particular proposal for 24 years, but now he accepted its passage with equanimity. He simply didn't care anymore. With the tariff bill out of the way, he poured all his passion and energy into a single goal—monetary reform. The opportunity to craft historic legislation was a new and exciting experience for him.

After the tariff bill passed in August, he vacationed in Europe, where he held "unofficial talks" with Winston Churchill, the head of the British Board of Trade, and other European finance experts. When he returned to the United States, he embarked on a western speaking tour to generate popular support for his plans, the first time in many years that he had put himself in front of the public. With seven colleagues accompanying him in a private car, Aldrich played the genial host in a roaming house-party that took them deep into enemy territory—Michigan, Illinois, Wisconsin, Iowa, and Indiana.

The publicity tour was not a runaway success. Aldrich impressed westerners with his unwavering courtesy, but his vague speeches failed to inspire much excitement for the National Monetary Commission. "I have a plan the details of which I cannot work out to-night; but it is one that will make the United States the financial center of the world," he announced. "Are you willing to help me and help this commission make it that?"

A hotel clerk in Des Moines quipped, "[T]he Senator's meeting beat anything that had happened since the school-marms' convention."[49]

Nonetheless, he persevered with his mysterious plans to the make the United States the financial center of the world. As the spring session of 1910 wound down, he prepared for the final push to devise an American version of a central bank. Despite the insurgency raging in the Senate, Aldrich was confident that the tactics he had employed for two decades would serve him one last time.

WASHINGTON, DC, MAY 14, 1910

Louis Brandeis noticed something odd about the dates. When Ballinger had met with Taft in Massachusetts, he brought along a mountain of documents to defend himself from Glavis's charges—661 pages in small type. Five days later, Attorney General George Wickersham filed an 87-page report on the subject. Two days after that, Taft sent a letter to Ballinger absolving him of all charges.

It was physically impossible. Brandeis had spent weeks poring over the material. There was no way that Wickersham could have produced his report in five days and no way that Taft could have digested it all two days later. When he asked Wickersham for a copy of the report, the attorney general answered with an angry letter that denied wrongdoing and asserted executive privilege over communications with the President.[50]

At the congressional hearings in May, Brandeis put Ballinger on the stand. He asked him about documents that he had shared with the President. In particular, he wanted to know about a certain memorandum written by Assistant Secretary of the Interior Oscar Lawler. Ballinger was evasive. "I could not definitely define just what he had in his port-folio or what he took with him," he hedged. But Brandeis kept press-ing until Ballinger finally exploded, "I appeal to this committee for protection against the insolence of this man who is attempting to cross-examine me."[51]

Brandeis was sure that the administration was covering up something. He suspected that Lawler's "memorandum" was really a letter of exon-eration—the same letter that Taft claimed to have written to Ballinger after reading the 87-page Wickersham report. But he still didn't have a smoking gun, and he dared not accuse a president of lying without hard evidence.[52]

It arrived the day after Ballinger concluded his testimony. On May 14, Frederick M. Kerby, stenographer for the Department of the Interior, went public. He told the press that Lawler had dictated the suspicious memorandum to him in Ballinger's private office while Ballinger looked on approvingly. It had the form of a letter expressed in the first person from the President to the secretary of the interior. Ballinger, it seemed, had been exonerated by his own assistant.[53]

Taft's first reaction was to deny. He released a press statement declar-ing that there was "absolutely no foundation" for Kerby's charges. "The President dictated his letter personally as the result of his own investiga-tion of the record," the statement asserted.[54]

But even before the presses rolled, Wickersham "found" the missing Lawler memorandum. He sent it to the investigation committee the same afternoon without checking with the President. The memorandum was not identical to the letter Taft had sent to Ballinger, but there were far too many similarities.[55]

As the country reacted with incredulity to Taft's denial, he finally came clean. In a letter to the investigation committee, he explained that he had been pressed for time, so he had asked Lawler to prepare an opin-ion "as if he were the President." Taft and Wickersham then reviewed Lawler's memorandum and made substantial changes before using it as the basis for the Ballinger letter. They also agreed that Wickersham would write a full report and backdate it "to show that my decision was fortified by his summary of the evidence and his conclusions therefrom."[56]

On the scale of political scandal, Taft's improprieties were minor. Glavis's accusations were never substantiated, and historians concluded that Ballinger was only guilty of poor judgment. The congressional committee completed its investigation without taking action, and the furor died away. Nonetheless, the administration's attempt to conceal its maneuvers took another bite from Taft's dwindling popularity. Through all the bombardment in his first year, he had held onto his reputation for honesty. Now, even that was tainted. The investigation that he hoped would vindicate his conduct toward Pinchot instead brought him lower than ever.

"It was the lying that did it," Brandeis concluded. "If they had brazenly admitted everything, and justified it on the ground that Ballinger was at least doing what he thought best, we should not have had a chance. Refusal to speak the truth is the history of many a downfall."[57]

BROCKENHURST, ENGLAND, JUNE 9, 1910

Theodore Roosevelt spent the final hours of his fifteen-month voyage wandering the English countryside with Sir Edward Grey, the British foreign secretary. They followed a brook as it twisted through the reeds beneath the shade of gnarled trees and sleepy cottages. Roosevelt pursued no quarry this time, only birdsong. Sir Grey delighted him by pointing out blackbirds, larks, warblers, and other English species that Roosevelt only knew from books and poetry.[58]

But the valley's charms could not hold his attention indefinitely. His thoughts drifted back to a sad letter he'd just received from an old friend.

"It is now a year and three months since I assumed office and I have had a hard time," Taft had written. "I do not know that I have had a harder time than other Presidents, but I do know that thus far I have succeeded far less than have others. I have been conscientiously trying to carry out your policies, but my method of doing so has not worked smoothly." He counted out his troubles: Nellie's collapse, the "hostile press," the Republican insurgents who "have done all in their power to defeat us," and the Ballinger-Pinchot controversy, which "has given me a great deal of personal pain and suffering."[59]

The letter troubled Roosevelt. He sympathized with Taft's misery but felt terribly disappointed in his protégé. He had learned much since he left Africa. Henry Cabot Lodge kept up a frequent correspondence, and Gifford Pinchot came to see him in Italy. In addition to his own tale of betrayal, Pinchot brought letters from Dolliver and Beveridge. Proudly describing their insurgency, they accused Taft of surrendering Roosevelt's legacy to Aldrich and Cannon.[60]

The disturbing letters and Pinchot's stories prompted Roosevelt to reevaluate his opinion of Taft. "For a year after Taft took office," he confided to Lodge, "I would not let myself think ill of anything he did. I finally had to admit that he had gone wrong on certain points; and I then also had to admit to myself that deep down underneath I had all along known he was wrong, on points as to which I had tried to deceive myself, by loudly proclaiming to myself, that he was right."[61]

As he roamed the English meadows and woodlands, Roosevelt described his dilemma to Lord Grey. He loved Taft dearly and had done everything in his power to get him elected. How could he turn against him now? On the other hand, how could he stand by while Taft undid his accomplishments and subverted the policies he believed in?

He came to no conclusion that day, but he intended to abide by the promise that he had made to Taft in reply to his mournful letter. "I am of course much concerned about some of the things I see and am told," he'd written to his old friend, "but what I have felt it best to do was to say absolutely nothing—and indeed to keep my mind as open as I kept my mouth shut!"[62]

NEW YORK, NEW YORK, JUNE 18, 1910

White foam kissed the towering hull of the USS *South Carolina* as she surged into New York harbor, bristling with heavy cannon. An array of lesser battleships and destroyers flanked the big dreadnought. Two straggly columns of tugs, yachts, mail boats, and merchant craft trailed behind like ducklings. At the head of the line, just behind the dreadnought, a wood-hulled cutter bedecked with flags steamed toward the city. Theodore Roosevelt perched on the roof of the pilothouse. His top hat cut a silhouette against the blue sky as he swung it in greeting to the eager little boats that jostled close on every side.

When the cutter closed in on the southern tip of Manhattan, the horns of every boat in the bay began to shriek and bellow in a joyful cacophony of pressurized steam. On the island, factory whistles and automobile horns added their voices to the din. The masses of people who lined the piers on both banks of the Hudson shouted and waved. The sound of their cheers rose and fell with the shifting wind.

When Roosevelt finally came down from the pilothouse, there were tears on his cheeks. Stern-faced, he followed his escorts down the gangplank to the pier and along a covered walk to a small wooden stage in Battery Park. A sea of spectators waited in nervous expectation. Emerging from the shadows, he held up his hat to shield the sun from his eyes. Someone shouted, "There he is!" Cameras crackled, and cheers exploded from every side. The roar echoed up Broadway, where spectators lined both sides of the road for blocks. Roosevelt broke into a toothy grin and waved his hat wildly. "Howdy-do!" he cried out to old friends that he spotted in the stands. A tall, gaunt man called to him. Roosevelt clasped his left wrist above his head and yelled back, "Hello Pinchot!"

The speech he gave was brief and diplomatic. "I am more glad than I can say to get home, to be back in my own country, back among the people I love," he enthused. Addressing the political turmoil that had erupted in his absence, he vaguely promised "to do my part, so far as I am able, in helping solve problems which must be solved if we of this, the greatest democratic Republic upon which the sun has ever shone, are to see its destinies rise to the high level of our hopes and its opportunities."

With that, he climbed into a carriage and paraded up Broadway under an avalanche of ticker tape. The Rough Riders led the way past thousands of cheering spectators who cried out, "Teddy, Teddy, Bully for you, Teddy! Eat 'em alive, good boy, Teddy!" The store windows exhibited teddy bears and stuffed lions, lithograph portraits of the former president, and placards that read "Welcome Home, Teddy," and "We Want You in 1912." At Bleeker Street, a man with a megaphone demanded, "Who'll be our next president?" The crowd replied in unison, "Teddy!"[63]

The skies were still clear when Roosevelt reached Central Park. The thunderstorm brewing to the west waited for the parade to disband before it unleashed its fury on the city, uprooting trees, hurling street signs, capsizing boats, and tearing the decorations to shreds. Eight people drowned at sea. The storm pounded Roosevelt's train with furious raindrops all the way to Oyster Bay and then vanished before the train pulled into the station.

Amid the welcoming festivities in town, a reporter pushed forward to ask Roosevelt for an interview. "There is nothing more that I can say," he replied. "One thing I want now is absolute privacy. I want to close up like a native oyster...I hope you representatives of the press will not come up to Sagamore Hill, because I have nothing to say."[64]

OYSTER BAY, NEW YORK, JUNE 27, 1910

Bob La Follette arrived in Oyster Bay nine days later. He pulled a straw hat down over his eyes so the newspapermen wouldn't recognize him and climbed into the car that Roosevelt had sent. At the house, a servant showed him to the library and, using Roosevelt's preferred title, announced that "the Colonel" would join him presently.

Colonel Roosevelt breezed in a few minutes later. He had been pitching hay, bits of which were still stuck to his knickerbockers. They discussed the events of the past fifteen months. La Follette described the gathering strength of the progressive movement and Taft's ineptitude. "[N]othing short of a miracle could save the administration," he predicted. He hoped that the Colonel would finally commit himself fully to the progressive cause.[65]

But he found Roosevelt as cautious as ever. "He is not greatly changed," he wrote to a friend afterward. "He will help some reactionaries on the one hand and some Progressives on the other, being cautious not to aid men who are regarded as ultra and extreme on either side."

He also noticed something else. It was nothing that Roosevelt had said, just an impression. "I will venture to guess that he very much wants to be President again," he conjectured. He had "all the symptoms of a man who is ready and willing."

At that moment, La Follette was particularly sensitive to concealed presidential aspirations; he too had the symptoms.[66]

BEVERLY, MASSACHUSETTS, JULY 6, 1910

Secretary Ballinger looked like "death's head" when he arrived at Taft's summer residence on the Massachusetts coast, but he put on a brave face for the journalists who hovered at the depot. "I am not a quitter and never have been," he told them. "I did not bring a resignation with me and will not leave one behind."

Taft had no intention of asking for Ballinger's immediate resignation, but he could not deny that the secretary of the interior had become a drag on his administration. His staff was working on a plan to ease Ballinger out by promoting him for an open Senate seat in Washington State.[67]

But the next day, a news release from Oyster Bay complicated these plans. According to the report, Roosevelt had endorsed an insurgent congressman, Miles Poindexter, in the Washington Senate race. Taft was taken aback. "Poindexter is one of the most bitter political opponents," he fumed to Archie Butt. "Mr. Roosevelt's support of him seems most gratuitous and unnecessary." His old friend had called on him only once since returning to the country, an awkward social encounter at which they avoided discussing the Republican rift. Meanwhile, a steady stream of insurgents had gone to see Roosevelt at Sagamore Hill. "[H]e sees no one but my enemies," Taft brooded. "I confess it wounds me very deeply. I hardly think the prophet of the square deal is playing it exactly square with me now."

Nellie Taft's assessment of the Poindexter endorsement was blunter. "Well, I suppose you will have to fight Mr. Roosevelt for the nomination," she told her husband matter-of-factly, "and if you get it he will defeat you. But it can't be helped. If possible you must not allow him to defeat you for the renomination. It does not make much difference about the reelection."

Archie Butt was incredulous when Taft told him what Nellie said. Did he really imagine that Roosevelt would mount a third-party challenge?

"I do not know," Taft answered pensively. "I have thought sometimes he did, and then I don't see how he can. In his mind, however, it may be the only logical way of reaching a third term."

The next day, Roosevelt denied the Poindexter story, partially. He acknowledged that he had met with Poindexter and approved of his conservation record but insisted that he had not endorsed him for the Senate.

Taft was skeptical. He knew his former boss well enough to appreciate his dealings with the press. Roosevelt clearly did not want to see any such commitment in the papers, but his conspicuous silence and the long line of progressives marching through Oyster Bay persuaded him that Roosevelt had chosen. A confrontation with his old friend was imminent.[68]

OSAWATOMIE, KANSAS, AUGUST 31, 1910

Roosevelt did not yet realize it, however. In his mind, he remained neutral. On one hand, he thought the Taft was "utterly helpless as a leader." On the other hand, he despised the "narrow fanatics, wild visionaries and self-seeking demagogues" who led the progressive movement. And though he believed that the country desperately needed a "legitimate" reform leader, he denied any interest in a third term, telling friends that he would not even consider running for president "unless it was practically universally demanded."[69]

But as Lincoln Steffens had observed, Roosevelt's *mind* did not make the decisions. His *hips* were on the move. While his mind dithered, they charged into battle. First, Roosevelt threw himself hip-first into New York State politics by running for chairman of the Republican state convention. "I could not help myself," he tried to explain, even though he admitted that the position was unsuitable for a former president. Then he embarked on a western speaking tour, ostensibly to unify his fractured party. "The greatest service I can render to Taft," his mind rationalized, "is to try to help the Republican Party to win at the polls this Fall, and that I am trying to do."[70]

As he set off through Ohio, Roosevelt settled instinctively into his old seesaw rhetoric. "I am against the corporation when it does wrong and I am against the mob when it resorts to violence," he hollered at Cleveland, banging his fist in the air. And even though he still insisted— still believed—that he did not intend to run for president, he could not help adding, "And whenever I have power I will keep order on the one hand and I will insist upon justice from the rich man and the corporation on the other."[71]

Roosevelt had always had innate sense for popular opinion. As his private car rolled through Illinois and Iowa—accompanied by Senator Cummins and other insurgents—his body seemed to absorb the western ethos, and his speeches began to evolve. The old standbys, the "violent mobs" and the "wild-eyed fanatics," slipped into the background. Instead of railing against miscreants and thugs, he blamed wrongdoing on "the effects of a false social system"—words that evoked the writings of his old friend Lincoln Steffens. By the time he reached Denver and Cheyenne, Roosevelt was attacking reactionary judges and proclaiming, "I stand for progress, as all men must stand who are progressive."[72]

But he saved the biggest speech for Osawatomie. There was a grassy old battlefield at the edge of the otherwise insignificant little town on the Kansas border. Half a century earlier, the militant abolitionist John Brown battled pro-slavery militias from Missouri on that field. On August 31, 1910, thousands stood on the wet grass to hear Colonel Roosevelt memorialize the battleground as a new state park. Senator Joseph Bristow was there. So was the progressive governor of Kansas, W. R. Stubbs. Gifford Pinchot came with former secretary of the interior, James Garfield. Kansas's acclaimed progressive journalist, William Allen White, attended as well.

At 2:15, Roosevelt climbed onto a kitchen table on a stage in the middle of the field and looked down on the sea of faces that radiated a hundred feet in every direction. He began his speech with an homage to John Brown's violent insurgency—"one of the epochmaking events of the long struggle for the rights of man." Tracing the history of the fight for equal opportunity from the American Revolution to the Civil War, he announced that the country had arrived at a new stage in the long struggle.

"Exactly as the special interests of cotton and slavery threatened our political integrity before the Civil War," he proclaimed, "so now the great special business interests too often control and corrupt the men and methods of government for their own profit. We must drive the special interests out of politics."

With these words, Roosevelt turned a corner. In one rhetorical stroke, he eliminated the middle ground on which he had balanced for his entire political career. By framing the political conflict as a historic conflict between privilege and democracy, he left no place for conservative-progressives, rendering them as improbable as royalist-patriots or pro-slavery-abolitionists. And by praising John Brown—the wild-eyed fanatic of an earlier era—he implicitly made common cause with the "demagogues" and "agitators" whom he had so long condemned.

With the rhetorical foundations in place, Roosevelt hurtled through a list of policy proposals more radical than any he had previously recommended. They poured out like a gusher: tariff overhaul, workmen's compensation, child labor laws, direct Senate elections, voter referendums and recalls, minimum wages, maximum workweeks, workplace safety regulations, physical valuation of *all* corporations, graduated income and inheritance taxes, environmental conservation, and public disclosure of campaign donations.

"[W]e must have progress," Roosevelt concluded in his clipped, high-pitched patois, "and our public men must be genuinely progressive."

It was the greatest speech he ever delivered. None of the ideas he presented on the battlefield that day were novel. Reformers had promoted them in the states for years. Progressives like La Follette and Beveridge had advanced many of them individually in Congress. Yet by assembling them altogether, elevating them to national scope, and vesting them with the epic drama of two celebrated wars, Roosevelt presented a whole that was much greater than its parts: a soaring vision of a large, muscular national government that fought for social and economic equality and safeguarded the welfare of all its citizens.

This concept of broad federal authority and obligation to the people, so familiar to modern Americans, was revolutionary in 1910—a *new nationalism*, Roosevelt called it. "This New Nationalism regards the executive power as the steward of the public welfare," he declared. "It demands of the judiciary that it shall be interested primarily in human welfare rather than in property, just as it demands that the representative body shall represent all the people rather than any one class or section of the people."

Presented so eloquently by a leader of his stature and popularity, his words and his vision carried momentous force. They radiated through the telegraph lines from the center of the country to the furthest coasts, bursting from the wires onto the front pages of every newspaper in every city in the United States.[73]

When the tremendous ovation finally subsided, Governor Stubbs leaped onto the table and declared, "My friends, we have just heard one of the greatest pronouncements for human welfare ever made."

Gifford Pinchot likewise proclaimed, "This is one of the biggest moments in the history of the United States."[74]

The next day, progressive papers echoed the praise, while conservative papers derided Roosevelt's speech as "rank socialism" or worse. "His speech yesterday outstrips not only the most extreme utterance that he himself ever made previously, but that of any of the most radical men of our time," editorialized the *New York Post*. But the papers on both sides could agree on two points: one, Roosevelt had joined the insurgents; two, Roosevelt would run for president in 1912.[75]

Reading the press reaction to his speech, Roosevelt's mind regretted what his hips had done in Osawatomie. "I had no business to take that position in the fashion I did," he wrote to his conservative friend, Henry Cabot Lodge. At the end of the speaking tour, he retreated back to the comfortable middle ground. Ray Stannard Baker visited him in Oyster Bay and noted with some disappointment that Roosevelt was "trying to be both radical and conservative." Baker asked him straight out if he planned to run for president.

"I will answer your question as plainly as you have asked it," Roosevelt replied. Leaning forward for emphasis, he said, "I don't know."[76]

THE PROGRESSIVE

Men who are too obstinate or vain to yield are the martyrs who burn at the stake and go to torture on the rack.

—Uncle Joe[1]

TRENTON, NEW JERSEY, SEPTEMBER 15, 1910

Jim Smith, the boss of Newark, sat calmly in his seat at the New Jersey Democratic convention. Bedlam exploded all around him. Half the room was applauding; the other half screamed epithets. A gang of Princeton boys was shouting, "Sis boom bah!" Old Judge John Crandall was flailing his cane at a crowd of delegates and smacked one across the head. Politics as usual in New Jersey.

Smith rose from his seat. Six feet tall, dignified and handsome, the former senator commanded respect. The opera house quieted at the sound of his booming voice. He had never met Woodrow Wilson, he said, and would have preferred a party insider, but they needed a man who would appeal to all the voters in the state. Wilson was that man. He seconded Wilson's nomination for governor.

The machine went into motion. Party regulars worked the crowd, cajoling and threatening. The opposition was stiff. Labor men detested Wilson because of his criticism of the unions. Reformers objected to a candidate they regarded as a stooge of the bosses. The Irish Catholics distrusted an intellectual Presbyterian from Virginia. Even the regulars questioned the wisdom of nominating an unfamiliar college president with no political experience. But Smith wasn't worried. He had the machine well in hand.

Two hours later, Wilson won with twice the votes of his nearest rival. Embittered opponents made for the doors, but Smith and his allies were ready with a piece of stagecraft. "Wait a few moments," urged the convention chairman, "and you will hear what Dr. Wilson has to say about it." Curiosity got the better of the disaffected delegates. They lingered in the hall.

A few minutes later, Woodrow Wilson appeared on the stage, still in his golf clothes. He was calm and smiling, a thin man with a long rectangular face, high cheekbones, and silver hair. His thoughtful blue-gray eyes surveyed the crowd through rimless glasses. When he spoke, his voice seemed to carry effortlessly. He eschewed the grand oratorical flourishes popular in those days. His words were sincere, direct, and penetrating.

The speech itself was vague on specifics and full of Roosevelt-esque caveats. Reform should be undertaken "only when we have done some careful thinking." Corporations should be regulated but not treated like "public enemies." The tax system should be reformed but not "suddenly or too radically."

Despite the caveats, Wilson's emphasis on reform pleased the skeptics, particularly when he declared his absolute independence from the party machine that had arranged his nomination. And his stirring climax moved even his staunchest opponents. "We are witnessing a renaissance of public spirit," he proclaimed, "a re-awakening of sober public opinion, a revival of the power of the people..."

His final words provoked unbridled cheers all through the hall. Men wept and shouted, "Thank God, at last, a leader has come!" Old Judge Crandall waved his deadly cane in the air and cried, "I am sixty-five-years old, and still a damn fool!" Excited delegates mobbed Wilson and tried to lift him onto their shoulders.[2]

Boss Smith was pleased with his handiwork. He wasn't concerned about Wilson's remarks on political reform. A certain amount of reform talk was required to win elections these days. Wilson's backers were good Bourbon Democrats. They had convinced Smith that the Princeton president was a reliable conservative who supported small government, respected the party organization, and most importantly, would finally win back New Jersey for the Democrats.

Winning New Jersey was the key, for then Smith would finally be able to return to the Senate. He had left office in 1899 amid accusations of bribery by the Sugar Trust, and he looked forward to rehabilitating his legacy. Getting elected would be a little more complicated than it had been in the old days. New Jersey had a direct primary now. Another man had won it; Smith hadn't even entered the primary race. But that was a minor complication. Who was to say that the state legislators had to abide by their own primary law? Not when Smith owned the governor. This was New Jersey, after all.[3]

INDIANAPOLIS, INDIANA, OCTOBER 18, 1910

With the arrival of election season, political warfare swept the states like a wave of tornadoes. Progressive insurgencies erupted at Republican conventions from California to New York. Standpatters counterattacked progressive strongholds in Iowa and Kansas, pinning the insurgents between conservative Republicans and populist Democrats.[4]

Senators Cummins, Bristow, and La Follette fended off the onslaughts, but Beveridge was in trouble. Though he was popular among the voters, he could only be reelected if the Republicans retained control of the Indiana state legislature, which looked unlikely. Standpatters resisted his efforts to make the state party more progressive; Democrats attacked the Taft administration and the much-hated tariff.

Theodore Roosevelt and Beveridge's fellow insurgents tried to help by speaking on his behalf, but La Follette was ill with gallstones, and Dolliver was suffering from heart trouble. "It is with deep regret that I dictate this to you," Dolliver wrote to him in early October, "For three weeks I have been confined to my house, unable to eat my meals, and just barely able to get my breath... The probability is that it will be a long time before I am able to make a speech of any sort. I regret the situation, but I am up against the real thing."

That was the last Beveridge heard from his friend and ally. Eight days later, Dolliver was dead.

Stricken, Beveridge wanted to desert his campaign to attend the funeral, but Cummins talked him out of it. "Your first duty is at home," Cummins telegraphed. "It would be an irretrievable disaster if, after losing Dolliver by death, we should lose you by defeat."[5]

PITTSBURGH, PENNSYLVANIA, NOVEMBER 8, 1910

The news got worse at every stop. Taft was en route to Washington after casting his vote in Cincinnati. In Columbus, he learned that the Democrats had won the governor's race in Massachusetts. In Dennison, Ohio, telegrams announced that governors' seats in New York, Connecticut, and his home state had fallen too. In Pittsburgh, reports of legislative casualties poured in. The House would become Democratic for the first time in

16 years, and Republicans faced severe losses in the Senate. Standpatters lost everywhere. The Indiana statehouse went to the Democrats, which put an end to Beveridge. In New Jersey, Woodrow Wilson won the governor's election by a landslide.

The President's travel companions unanimously blamed Colonel Roosevelt for the drubbing, but Taft demurred. "I fear Roosevelt did not help the ticket very much," he said, "but I am inclined to think that even had he remained in Africa the result would have been just the same."

Secretary of State Knox soberly acknowledged, "It seems to be a landslide, doesn't it?"

"I should say it was not only a landslide," Taft replied, "but a tidal wave and holocaust all rolled into one general cataclysm."[6]

JEKYLL ISLAND, GEORGIA, NOVEMBER 30, 1910

Late one November night, a southbound train idled in Jersey City, across the river from glittering Manhattan. In addition to the usual line of Pullman sleepers, a luxurious private car was attached to the end. Its occupants had shuttered the blinds, revealing only slender threads of amber light. They had come by ferry from New York but arrived separately to avoid attention. If anyone asked, they said that they were going duck hunting.

Even in the privacy of the car, the passengers referred to one another by first names or aliases so that railroad staff wouldn't recognize them. Frank Vanderlip of National City Bank went by "Orville." Henry Davison of J. P. Morgan & Co. was "Wilbur." "Paul" was Paul Warburg from Kuhn, Loeb & Co., "Abe" was A. Piatt Andrew Jr., assistant secretary of the treasury. "Nelson" was the owner of the car and the leader of the expedition, Senator Nelson Aldrich.

The men set to work as soon as the train left the station. Aldrich had assigned them an awesome task: to design a central bank for the United States. Vanderlip was all business. He set the agenda and recorded the proceedings in shorthand. Warburg, the German banker whom Aldrich had met in New York, provided the intellectual vision. Though brilliant, his stubborn intensity clashed with the other egos in the car. The genial Davison soothed their quarrels. By the time they reached the Georgia coast, they had come together on the broad outline of the idea.

They took a ferry to a slender strip of land that lined the coast, fringed by white sand on the east and marshland on the west. At the center of the island, a paradise of immaculate lawns and moss-bearded oaks surrounded a magnificent beige clubhouse. Long verandas and broad bay windows graced the exterior. A conical turret, double-ringed by balconies, anchored one end of the structure like a rocket embedded in the lawn.

The Jekyl Island Club[7] was the "the richest, the most exclusive, the most inaccessible" hunting club in the world. Its bylaws permitted no more than a hundred members. To be rich was a prerequisite, not a qualification. To join, you had to be *someone*—a Morgan, a Rockefeller, a Vanderbilt, or a Pulitzer. Among the rich and powerful men who arrived in secret at the end of November, only Nelson Aldrich was someone enough to belong to the club.

They had little time to savor its charms, however. A couple of them rose at dawn for a swim or a ride, but breakfast to midnight was reserved for business. On Thanksgiving Day, they ate wild turkey with oyster stuffing and went right back to work. Other than Aldrich, they were all relatively young men in their late 30s and early 40s—a new generation of Wall Street bankers, not the old guard fixed in its ways. The task Aldrich had assigned them was the most extraordinary thing they had ever attempted, and they tore into with vigor. "I enjoyed that period as I never have enjoyed anything else," Vanderlip later recalled. "I lived during those days on Jekyl Island at the highest pitch of intellectual awareness that I have ever experienced. It was entirely thrilling."[8]

The institution they devised had the core features of European central banks. It would issue paper currency, lend money to banks at discounted rates, clear bank checks, and serve as the fiscal agent of the Treasury. But it differed in two crucial respects. First, it was not a single bank but a voluntary consortium made up of the largest banks in the country—a *National Reserve Association*. As a result, it would be less centralized than its European counterparts.

Second, the government did not control it. There would be federal representatives on the board of directors, but the private member banks would control the majority of the votes. Warburg strongly objected to this feature of the proposal. As he scornfully observed years later, the plan "followed the Republican doctrine of 'keeping the government out of business.'"[9]

Ten days later, the men returned to New York as quietly as they'd left. Aldrich carried their report with him. He planned to introduce the proposal to Congress in January and pass it before the end of the session in March—his final crowning achievement in the United States Senate. There would be no mention of the Jekyll Island group, of course. If word got out that a gang of Wall Street bankers had written the plan, popular outrage would doom the bill. He would present the Aldrich Plan as the findings of the National Monetary Commission.

As he outlined his strategy to the bankers, they noticed an odd blind spot in his otherwise acute political vision. His primary concern was whether the business community would accept the plan. That was the only constituency that mattered to him. If business backed the bill, he seemed to have no doubt that he would be able to push it through Congress. The insurgents were "negligible," and the recent Republican defeat, a "passing vagary of the electorate." He seemed not to appreciate his loss of control in the Senate and the widespread animus against him, nor to realize that most Americans would see the "Aldrich Plan" as another name for the "Wall Street Plan" even if Jekyll Island remained a secret.[10]

TRENTON, NEW JERSEY, JANUARY 24, 1911

A few days after Woodrow Wilson's election, Boss Smith went to see the governor-elect in Princeton to claim his reward for engineering the Democratic nomination. To his dismay, Wilson refused to support his Senate bid. He reminded Smith that primary voters had elected another man, James Martine.

"The primary was a joke," Smith retorted.

Wilson disagreed. "[T]he way to save it from being a joke hereafter is to take it seriously now," he replied. "It is going to be taken seriously, and there will be no more jokes."[11]

Smith left Princeton promising a fight. He got one. During the next two months, New Jersey's Democratic civil war splashed into national newspapers. The governor-elect's fierce battle against the party boss offered readers a vivid minidrama of the ideological divisions that had engulfed both parties. Even though he had never governed anything larger than a college of 1,400 students, the press treated Wilson as a national Democratic figure and potential presidential candidate in 1912. He was smart, eloquent, and popular, raised in the South and established in the North. He seemed to represent a new kind of Democrat, a serious statesman who combined the progressive ideas of the Bryanites with the rationality and sobriety of the Bourbons.[12]

It seemed unlikely that a political neophyte would be able to live up to such high expectations against a seasoned boss like Smith, yet Wilson surpassed them. His tactics were deft and ferocious. In the press, he regaled readers with the details of their Princeton meeting and hurled accusations of false dealing. Behind the scenes, he worked New Jersey's legislators to round up votes for James Martine. In a stirring public address, he portrayed the conflict as a moral crusade in which there were only two sides. "These are our terms," he proclaimed. "War, if you are allied with the enemy. Peace if you are on the other side of justice."

Smith returned fire in the press and employed all the weapons of the party machine. The evening before the Senate election in the New Jersey legislature, thousands of his supporters marched on Trenton in a show of force. At 11 p.m., Smith reviewed his army from the steps of his hotel as a brass band led the cheering parade of Democratic regulars down the street.

But it was the legislators who mattered. Martine, an indifferent politician, was not in Trenton for the vote, but Governor Wilson was. As Martine pulled ahead in the initial voting, Wilson turned one last county boss and secured his election. A broken Smith conceded the race and disappeared into obscurity.[13]

After only one week in office, with a political base barely three months old, Wilson had transformed himself from a cautious college president into a mighty general in the tremendous new movement that was about to sweep the country.

MADISON, WISCONSIN, JANUARY 25, 1911

The next day, Wisconsin legislators formally notified another leader in the progressive movement that they had reelected him to another six years in the Senate. When La Follette strode to the podium of the packed state assembly chamber, "a roar of applause went up that shook the walls," according to the *Milwaukee Sentinel*, the old Stalwart paper that used to attack him at every turn.[14]

By 1910, the once indomitable Stalwarts were irrelevant. La Follette easily routed their well-financed primary challenger, despite a shoestring budget and a gallstone operation that had prevented him from giving a single speech. At the state convention, the Republican Party adopted the most progressive platform in the nation. In the general election, La Follette and his slate of progressive candidates swept the state with nearly 80 percent of the votes.[15]

But his greatest triumphs occurred out of state. The direct primary that he pioneered in Wisconsin had spread rapidly across the country. With a touch of pride, the *Milwaukee Sentinel* noted that 18 states had adopted comprehensive direct primary laws. The new laws opened channels for the great wave of antitariff hostility to pour into state conventions, washing away deep-rooted party machines from coast to coast. In Washington State, the progressive Miles Poindexter defeated Secretary of the Interior Richard Ballinger for the Republican senate nomination. In Michigan, another progressive Republican knocked out Senator Julius Burrows, the Aldrich loyalist who had put the 1908 convention to sleep. Insurgents shredded the Republican machine in California, electing a governor and senator who proudly identified "with that nationwide movement led by La Follette, Cummins, Bristow, and other brave progressives." A string of retirements and Democratic victories further depleted the Standpatters' ranks, all but eliminating Aldrich's ruling clique. Uncle Joe won reelection in his district, but the new Democratic majority ended his eight-year reign as Speaker once and for all.[16]

La Follette was not discouraged by the Democratic victories. A few days before the election, he had urged voters to cast out "any candidate of any party" who served the corporations, and he was delighted when progressive Democrats defeated Republican Standpatters. Beveridge's defeat had been a heavy blow, but no other prominent insurgents lost their seats, and many of the new Democratic leaders shared his ideals. *The Outlook* described Woodrow Wilson's campaign as a "Western Insurgent Republican platform."[17]

As the Standpatters and Bourbon Democrats fell into decline, people all over the country spoke of a new era in American politics. From California to Massachusetts, Democrats as well as Republicans began to speak enthusiastically about "the progressive movement," a phrase La Follette had been using since 1906. Ray Stannard Baker forwarded him an editorial that described him as "the pioneer in the movement" and "the most conspicuous figure in the Senate." He added, "It expresses a feeling that I have heard quite generally here—that your prestige in the East is growing greatly, that you are coming into your own after all these years of fighting. I was at luncheon at Oyster Bay yesterday, and was surprised and greatly pleased at the warm words in regard to you spoken by Col. Roosevelt."[18]

Such sentiments convinced La Follette that the moment he had dreamed about since his lonely days as a Wisconsin Half-Breed had nearly arrived. In his acceptance speech at Madison, he proudly declared, "In the beginning, our program of legislation was viewed with alarm and denounced as visionary, extreme, radical, and a menace to capital and to business interests. Today, the justice, the wisdom, the economic soundness of every Wisconsin law to which the progressive movement gave being, has conquered opposition and compelled approval in every enlightened commonwealth in America, and even in some portions of New England."

The heart of the movement, La Follette maintained, was not its policies but its democracy. Given a truly representative government, he had faith that the American people would choose wise progressive policies, but they "have been betrayed by their representatives again and again" due to "the corrupting influence of powerful business organizations." The solution, he argued, was to break the grip of the machines once and for all with true democracy. To this end, he and his allies had founded a new organization called the National Progressive Republican League (NPRL) to challenge

President Taft and the Standpatters for control of the Republican Party. In a meeting at La Follette's Washington residence the week before, they had settled on a platform with just five planks: direct election of US senators, not only in the primaries but in the November general elections as well; direct election of delegates to presidential conventions; direct election of all state officials; ballot initiatives and judicial recalls; and a comprehensive anticorruption act. If the entire country established these reforms, La Follette was certain that the rest would follow.[19]

He listed the names of the men who had committed themselves to the NPRL, including almost every prominent progressive in the country—Cummins, Beveridge, Bristow, Steffens, Baker, Brandeis, Pinchot, and numerous other politicians and journalists. But one name was conspicuously absent.

La Follette harbored mixed feelings about inviting Theodore Roosevelt. On one hand, his famous name would elevate the prestige of the organization and put Roosevelt on record as a true progressive. On the other hand, he mistrusted the Colonel's post-Africa conversion, remembering all too well how Roosevelt had abandoned him during the coal lands fight in the Senate.

There was something else, though, that he did not admit to anyone, perhaps not even to himself. Theodore Roosevelt tended to dominate whatever he participated in. His children joked that when he went to a wedding, he thought he was the bride, and when he went to a funeral, he thought he was the corpse. La Follette feared that if Roosevelt joined the league, his outsized personality would eclipse the other members. The NPRL was La Follette's brainchild, and he could not bear to see it become Roosevelt's organization.[20]

In the end, he put his concerns aside and agreed to invite Roosevelt, but his heart wasn't in it. After a brusque invitation that he neglected to sign, he delegated further correspondence to other members of the league. Roosevelt repeatedly invited him to discuss the NPRL in person, but La Follette declined first on an account of illness and then injury. These excuses looked flimsy, however, when he visited New York without informing Roosevelt.[21]

Eventually, Roosevelt gave up and responded by letter. "I rather question the wisdom of at this time going into the proposed Progressive Republican League," he wrote. He worried that some of the planks, particularly the ballot initiatives, were too radical for voters in most states, adding "I want to try to lead the people and not drive them." In his capacity as editor of *The Outlook*, he offered to write a supportive editorial, but he declined to join the league. "I do wish I could see you and talk this over," he wistfully concluded.[22]

The letter confirmed La Follette's fears. Roosevelt was not content to simply join the league. He wanted to dictate the platform according to his own terms, and those terms were decidedly more cautious than La Follette's.

"My dear Colonel," he replied, "I am really very sorry that you do not see your way to come in with us." In answer to Roosevelt's objection, he argued that a "campaign of education" would convince voters all over the country to embrace the NPRL's platform. "If we wait for them all to be ready," he wrote, "it will be a generation before we get very far with our legislative program."[23]

Once again, Roosevelt and La Follette's discordant strategies for achieving political change prevented them from working together. Roosevelt sought legislation that could be achieved in the current political environment. La Follette intended to change the political environment by promoting legislation that would be achieved in the future.

There was one other unstated element to the disagreement. As in 1904, when Roosevelt worried that Wisconsin "bolters" would endanger his election, political ambition complicated their relationship. This time the situation was reversed. La Follette felt sure that Roosevelt intended to run for president at the head of the progressive faction. That would create a direct conflict with his own political plans, which he and his supporters had already put in motion.

WASHINGTON, DC, MARCH 4, 1911

Uncle Joe was not one to go out quietly. During his eight-year tenure, he had prided himself on running the House as smoothly and efficiently as possible. In his last three months, he strove to create the opposite effect. Like a retreating general who burns the fields behind him, he turned the House into a circus. The new rules adopted by the insurgents on the Rules Committee opened loopholes that invited obstructionism, and Cannon encouraged his allies to exploit them, ruling in their favor as they clogged the House with filibusters. When the Rules Committee allowed committees to "discharge" their bills to the floor without a report, James Mann of Illinois filled the calendar with 107 discharge petitions. In response, chagrined insurgents tried to modify the rules to prevent such abuses, but vindictive Standpatters and amused Democrats blocked the changes.[24]

The chaos reached its climax on the last day of the session. Democrats, jubilant at the prospect of becoming the majority for the first time in sixteen years, determined to halt any more Republican legislation. They poured into the aisles, shouting to be recognized while Cannon banged away at the podium. Amid the bedlam, he ordered the sergeant at arms to bring out the mace. A white-haired little man struggled onto the floor bearing a heavy mahogany club lined with silver ribbons and topped with a large silver eagle. As he staggered to and fro with his burden, the clumps of congressmen gradually quieted.

At issue was an administration-backed bill that would strengthen the tariff commission established by the Payne-Aldrich Act, the one that Beveridge had proposed and Aldrich had emasculated. Taft had promoted the legislation to try to appease the public after the unpopular tariff act. Senate Standpatters, chastened by election losses, yielded to his wishes and joined the insurgents in moving the bill through the Senate in a rare display of Republican harmony.

But Uncle Joe was less accommodating. The low-tariff men that Taft had appointed to the commission did not please him. While he did not openly oppose the bill, he put up little fight when House Democrats led by the ubiquitous John Fitzgerald filibustered it on the last day of the session. Cannon allowed repeated interruptions and multiple roll calls to sidetrack the vote until it was almost noon, leaving no time to pass the bill. Its supporters surrendered, and "one of the dearest requests of President Taft" expired to the sound of Democrats cheering.

Even so, the clock had to be set back half an hour before the House finished its business. It was nearly 12:30 when Cannon delivered his final valediction. As he stood at the podium, shoulders squared and chin thrust forward, his voice carried a faint tremor. After years of rancor, the bitterness seemed to drain from the room. The man standing at the Speaker's rostrum was once again dear old Uncle Joe.

"I leave this place, but not with regret," he said. "I do not leave the House with malice in my heart toward any colleague, toward any Member with whom I have served…And now nothing remains for me but to wish each and every one of you health, strength, courage, and having said the last word as Speaker, having signed the last bill, sustained or overruled the last point of order, rapped vigorously for the last time with the gavel, the hour of 12 o'clock noon having arrived, I declare the House of Representatives of the Sixty-first Congress adjourned without day [, *sine day*]."

When he lay down the gavel, congressmen rushed up the aisles to grasp his hand—Republicans, Democrats, and even a number of visitors who pushed their way onto the floor. While Uncle Joe shook the hands of his colleagues, someone started singing, and the voices of some two hundred congressmen filled the chamber with the sweet sad words of "Auld Lang Syne."[25]

NELSON ALDRICH WAS NOT IN WASHINGTON when his Senate career ended. He had returned to Jekyll Island—for relaxation this time. Seventy years old and suffering from a sleep disorder, the doctors had ordered him to put aside his work to avert a "nervous break." While he rested in quiet luxury beside the ocean, President Taft inquired anxiously after his health. "I long for your presence," he wrote. "I feel about you as Scott said of Rhoderick Dhu. A blast upon your bugle horn were worth a thousand men."

But Taft was on his own, for Aldrich was no longer a senator. His political career was not quite over, though. He was still chairman of the National Monetary Commission. Before he retired, Aldrich was determined to establish the National Reserve Association that he and the bankers had devised. His chief concern was the western bankers who had opposed his previous currency bills. If he could convince the entire banking community to endorse his greatest initiative, he was confident that his remaining allies in Congress would implement it. He gave little thought to the Democrats and insurgents who now dominated Congress or to the so-called progressive movement. He and Taft made plans to pass the currency bill after the inevitable Republican comeback in 1912.[26]

Beveridge's metaphor about the old men with bad watches waiting for a train that had left the station never seemed more apt.

WASHINGTON, DC, MAY 15, 1911

On May 15, the Supreme Court put an end to the Standard Oil Company. Following Theodore Roosevelt's example, President Taft had sued Standard Oil in 1909 under the Sherman Antitrust Act. After two years of legal proceedings and appeals, the Supreme Court ruled in the administration's favor, ordering Standard Oil to dissolve within six months.

Bob La Follette listened from the crowded gallery as the Chief Justice read out the decision. He was appalled. Though he welcomed Standard Oil's dissolution, he deplored the court's reasoning. By penalizing Standard Oil for creating an "unreasonable and undue restraint of trade," the justices opened the door for other monopolies to circumvent the Sherman Act by arguing that they did not impede competition.

"Every trust will now come into court and claim . . . it is not restraining trade unreasonably," La Follette told a reporter. "I fear that the court has done just what the trusts wanted it to do and what Congress has steadfastly refused to do."[27]

The next day, he sent a telegram to Louis Brandeis in Boston, "We need you to consider next important step in view of decision yesterday. Come immediately if possible." Brandeis hurried to Washington to meet with La Follette and a few other progressive congressmen. They agreed to draft a new antitrust bill that would unambiguously prohibit all corporate monopolies.

Their first attempt did not pass Congress, but their trust strategy would play a key role in the looming elections of 1912.[28]

WASHINGTON, DC, JUNE 11, 1911

When the Senate reconvened in April, the old guard had been nearly wiped clean. Aldrich, Hale, Elkins, Kean, and several other senior Republicans were gone. A younger generation of Standpatters struggled to consolidate power. They managed to exclude most of the insurgents from important committees, but the presence of La Follette's famous pompadour in the office of the Finance Committee testified that times were changing.

More significantly, the Standpatters no longer controlled a majority in the Senate. The 13 insurgents and 41 Democrats could easily out-vote the remaining 37 Standpatters. Soon it would be 36. La Follette had opened an investigation into the election of Senator William Lorimer, the "Blond Boss" of Chicago, which determined that he had bribed his way into office.[29]

In the wake of the Lorimer scandal, the progressives pressed for a constitutional amendment to establish direct elections of US senators. Elihu Root of New York, the rising conservative luminary, protested that popularizing the Senate would imperil the country. "The framers of the Constitution realized that the weakness of democracy is the liability to continual change," he argued, "they realized that there needed to be some guardian of the sober second thought, and so they created the Senate to fulfill that high and vitally important duty."

But his arguments held no weight with La Follette and his allies. They championed direct election precisely because the conservative Senate had bottled up popular reform bills for decades. They had a majority at last, and they were determined to prevent the Senate from ever again becoming an impediment to the popular will. On June 11, 1911, the Senate narrowly passed a constitutional amendment declaring, "The Senate of the United States shall be composed of two Senators from each State, elected by the people thereof, for six years."[30]

WASHINGTON, DC, JUNE 17, 1911

In the spring of 1911, La Follette deliberated over whether to run for president. He believed that a progressive should challenge Taft for the nomination, and he believed that he was the one to do it, but he had two reservations. The first was financial. Campaigns were expensive, and as it was, La Follette could barely support his family and fund the magazine.

His second reservation was Theodore Roosevelt. In private, the Colonel continued to deny any interest in a third term, but his refusal to make any definitive public statement aroused La Follette's suspicions.

Unwilling to meet with Roosevelt himself, he struggled to make sense of the thirdhand reports he received from friends. Pinchot assured him that Roosevelt was dead-set against running for president and, though he refused to endorse anyone, had promised to "quietly" support La Follette's candidacy.[31]

La Follette remained skeptical. He could not shake his suspicion that Roosevelt still coveted the White House and was just using him as a stalking horse. "He is willing to have some one do the Light Brigade Act, stop Taft, and get shot about the right time," he confided to a friend. Nonetheless, he declared that he was ready "to go to the front" if he could raise enough money. "The progressive cause is the only hope of the country," he continued. "It should not be permitted to foozle because no one has the courage to go up against the Administration forces and the solid South."[32]

In April, Roosevelt embarked on a speaking tour in Wisconsin, praising La Follette at every stop. "Roosevelt has now definitely and irrevocably placed himself on the progressive side," one Wisconsin supporter wrote him. "He is with the progressives on both feet."

A few weeks later, Roosevelt published a glowing editorial in *The Outlook*. "After my visit I felt like congratulating Wisconsin upon what it had done and was doing," he wrote, "and I felt much more like congratulating the country as a whole because it has in the State of Wisconsin a pioneer blazing the way along which we Americans must make our civic and industrial advance during the next few decades."[33]

Meanwhile, La Follette received more thirdhand reports that Roosevelt would support his candidacy, and the campaign funds poured in, much of it from Gifford Pinchot. Mollified, he let down his guard. On June 17, he pledged himself to run for president.[34]

OYSTER BAY, NEW YORK, OCTOBER 27, 1911

"Suppose the House should be Democratic, and then imagine what would be done," Uncle Joe had warned in 1906. "We should have a long period of investigations, not to cure evils, if any exist, but to create scandals and party capital." In 1911, his prophecy came true. No sooner had the Democrats recaptured the House than two separate committees launched investigations into the panic of 1907.[35]

"Wall Street brought on the 1907 panic and got the people to demand currency reform," charged Representative Charles Lindbergh Sr., father of the future aviator, "and, if it dares, will produce another panic to pass the Aldrich central bank plan." Other prominent Democrats echoed his accusations, including Governor Wilson, who declared, "The great monopoly in this country is the money monopoly." This was a far cry from his assessment two years earlier, when he had dismissed the outcry against Wall Street as "a farce" and praised J. Pierpont Morgan as "a man of brains" who "would make a good leader."[36]

The papers followed the hearings with fascination as the House hauled the country's prominent capitalists to Washington and demanded explanations. In June, one committee issued an even more sensational subpoena—to Colonel Theodore Roosevelt. The congressmen wanted to interrogate him about US Steel's acquisition of the Tennessee Coal and Iron Company during the panic. Taft urged him to refuse, but Roosevelt relished the opportunity to publicly defend himself.[37]

In August, he marched into New York City Hall, where the committee was then meeting. At the hearing, he bridled at Democrats' insinuations that J. Pierpont Morgan and US Steel executives had duped him into allowing them to expand their monopoly at bargain prices. "The word 'panic' means fear, unreasoning fear," he argued. "To stop a panic it is necessary to restore confidence; and at the moment the so-called Morgan interests were the only interests which retained a full hold on the confidence of the people of New York..."[38]

Afterward, the papers concluded that he had conducted himself admirably. The hearings continued, but Roosevelt considered the matter closed and returned to the quiet seclusion of Oyster Bay. He read voraciously, wrote articles about wildlife, and sent letter after letter denying his interest in the presidency. In September, he devoured the first magazine installment of La Follette's new autobiography, co-written by Ray Stannard Baker.

"Dear Senator La Follette," he wrote. "I must send you just a line to say how greatly interested I have been in your first article in the *American*. It is capital!" Roosevelt identified with La Follette as a young man, fresh from school and full of passion but lacking clear political ideas. He had been the same once. His opinion of the Wisconsin senator had much improved now that he longer had to worry about La Follette interfering with his legislation.[39]

"I like La Follette," he wrote to Governor Hiram Johnson of California, "He has done well in Wisconsin, and he is constantly doing better in National affairs." His only complaint was La Follette's obsession with majority rule. Roosevelt did not necessarily trust the public to support wise polices; he worried that socialists and radical labor unions might seduce the voters into supporting dangerous ideas. "[I]t is our duty to stand against the evil men of both sides," he insisted. Nonetheless, he resisted Johnson's pleas for him to seek the nomination himself. He doubted that La Follette could win the presidency, but he wasn't confident that he could either. "My honest judgment is that I should be a weak candidate," he wrote. "I have no cause to think that at the moment there is any very real or widely extended liking for or trust in me among the mass of the people."[40]

And so he might have remained, immersed in his reading and wild-life, blissfully removed from the political hullabaloo while La Follette, Taft, and the Democrats battled it out. Except that the steel business was not quite over after all. On October 26, on the eve of Roosevelt's fifty-third birthday, Taft sent him a most unwelcome present.

"U.S. BEGINS SUIT TO SMASH THE STEEL TRUST," the *New York Evening World* blasted across its front page.[41]

Roosevelt's presidency had overshadowed Taft's in every respect save one: trust-busting. Legal action suited Taft's judicial nature, and he prosecuted antitrust suits far more aggressively than Roosevelt had ever dared. In October 1911, with the Democratic hearings still raging, Taft targeted the one trust guaranteed to enrage his predecessor. For if US Steel's acquisition of TC&I was illegal, it followed that the man who had approved the deal was, in Roosevelt's own words, "a fool or a knave." He could not leave such charges—even implicit—unanswered.[42]

The next day, he behaved as if nothing had changed. He sent off more letters exhorting supporters not to "sacrifice" him by trying to press him into a campaign that he could not win. But inside, the machinery was clicking, and his dormant hips revved into motion. Nothing moved Roosevelt like an assault on his reputation.[43]

Three weeks later, he delivered his answer in the form of an *Outlook* editorial. It did not mention Taft by name, but his strident defense of the US Steel merger—"I was not misled" and his impassioned critique of "destructive litigation" left no doubt who the target was. He blasted Taft's policy of breaking up trusts "merely because they are large and successful" in contrast to his own stated practice of punishing only corporate "wrong-doing." More sensationally, he called for an entirely new approach to dealing with the trusts, which emphasized regulation over litigation.[44]

The charge against Taft was certainly unfair. Though he did not dress his antitrust suits in moralistic rhetoric like Roosevelt, there was little substantive difference between their respective trust policies. Rather, they disagreed about one trust in particular. Roosevelt had anointed US Steel a "good trust," while Taft accused it of deceptive and monopolistic practices. Moreover, even this difference of opinion would hardly have aroused Roosevelt's indignation if the issue had not been personal. His real grievance was not Taft's trust policy but the fact that Taft had called his judgment into question.

The details of their disagreement were not nearly as important as its effect. Roosevelt's broadside detonated like a grenade in the middle of the presidential race. Not only did the newsmen treat his editorial as a public repudiation of Taft, many interpreted it to be a *de facto* statement of his candidacy. In response to feverish speculation, Roosevelt issued another public denial, insisting that he was "not a candidate, nor has been at any time" and urging everyone to "drop this once for all." But for all the denials, he did not say that he would never be a candidate, nor that he would refuse the nomination if it were offered to him.[45]

NEW YORK, NEW YORK, JANUARY 22, 1912

Two weeks later, La Follette received a letter from Ray Stannard Baker about a recent conversation he'd had with Roosevelt. "I am not a candidate and I don't want the nomination," the Colonel had told Baker, "but I can see that things might so shape themselves that it might be my duty to accept a nomination—provided there was an unmistakable call from the country." In his letter, Baker concluded "that if the demand is loud and long enough, and if the prospects seem right, that he [Roosevelt] will certainly jump into the game. He thinks Taft's prospects are gone, he evidently thinks you cannot command enough strength to be nominated—therefore—!!"[46]

La Follette was deeply disturbed but not wholly surprised by Baker's assessment. He had already begun to question the loyalty of some of his supporters. They seemed hesitant to fully commit to his candidacy, as if they were waiting for something...or someone. James Garfield, the secretary of the interior under Roosevelt, was one of them. At a conference of progressives in Chicago, he had tried unsuccessfully to persuade the participants not to endorse La Follette, arguing that they should back a platform, not an individual. Afterward, he quibbled that the endorsement was actually a "recommendation," not a pledge. Garfield was close to Roosevelt, and La Follette suspected that some intrigue was in the works.[47]

Pinchot was also behaving strangely. At a banquet in New York, he publicly reiterated his commitment to La Follette's candidacy, but the endorsement was somewhat backhanded. "La Follette has courage to that degree which makes him perfectly willing to be beaten," he declared, as if willingness to be beaten were a desirable trait in a presidential candidate. Questioned by reporters, he elaborated, "I mean that since Col. Roosevelt had eliminated himself Senator La Follette is his logical successor." The word *since* said it all: La Follette was the second choice.

A few weeks later, the *since* changed to *if.* At a strategy meeting in Washington, Pinchot proposed that La Follette write Roosevelt a letter asking him to declare once and for all whether he would accept the nomination under any circumstances. But there was a catch. Pinchot insisted that the letter include a quid pro quo that would commit La Follette to supporting Roosevelt if he chose to run.[48]

Smelling a trick, La Follette refused. He suspected Roosevelt was trying to manipulate him—through Pinchot—into holding his place until he was ready to join the race. But even if the suggestion were innocent, he still would never commit to supporting him. Despite the "New Nationalism" rhetoric, he remained convinced that Roosevelt was an inveterate compromiser who would ultimately betray the progressive movement by settling for half-a-loaf legislation. Better to lose to the Democrats or even Taft than to elect a faux-progressive, he reasoned.

"I know Roosevelt's strength, and I know his weakness," he told Pinchot. "His whole course on the tariff during the seven years he was President proves him to have been as much a standpatter as Aldrich or Cannon. Now, I am not seeking any break with Roosevelt. I have no doubt he could take a large Progressive following with him because he is accepted by many people unacquainted with the details of his record, as a Progressive. He is probably in a position to divide the Progressives and destroy all chance of success in this campaign." Nonetheless, he refused to quit the race. As always, opposition hardened his resolve. "[T]here is no other way for me than to go on making the best fight I can for the nomination," he vowed.[49]

And so La Follette kept fighting. Telling reporters that he would not quit "until the gavel falls" at the Republican convention, he raced through Illinois, Indiana, Ohio, and Michigan, firing off blistering speeches at every stop. Speaking to crowds so large they overflowed the capacity of the halls, he tore off his collar and laid into the tariff, the trusts, "Aldrich's banking scheme," and the fourteen capitalists he accused of running the country. He championed labor laws and direct election of US senators, as well as two new issues: judicial recall and women's suffrage. Disavowing partisanship, he praised the progressive work of Governor Wilson but insisted that he and other Democrats were chained to the conservative South. Of Roosevelt, he said little except to laud his conservation efforts and denounce his approval of the US Steel merger.[50]

After the western tour, he made his first foray east of the Hudson. People had warned him that no-nonsense New Yorkers would have no patience for long speeches and radical ideas, but when he arrived in Manhattan in late January, he found Seventh Avenue jammed for blocks with thousands who had failed to get seats for his address. They refused to let him pass until he gave them an impromptu speech from his automobile.

Inside Carnegie Hall, tier after tier of well-dressed men and women stretched from the footlights to the last row in the top balcony. Gifford Pinchot delivered the introduction. He described how he had first met La Follette—"a solitary man in the Capitol, feared and disliked by the old leaders, for he represented a point of view that had fewer followers in the Senate than is the case today." He had been skeptical at first, but La Follette's brave stand against the establishment had won his admiration.

In this, he spoke for many. The quixotic bills, "pointless" filibusters, and relentless speaking tours had shaken the Republican Party to its core and helped to inspire the greatest political transformation since the Civil War. At the 1904 Republican National Convention, only one lonely voice had objected when the party leaders summarily dismissed La Follette's Wisconsin delegates. Eight years later, he rode at the head of a mighty national movement and, as Pinchot put it, "has a good chance to capture the fortress."

La Follette took the stage to a standing ovation and a flutter of handkerchiefs, touching Pinchot's arm as he passed. "I come to you in a bad voice," he said hoarsely, "because I have been trying to talk to the thousands outside who were unable to get into this hall. I have been admonished that the audience I address tonight is different from any other audience that I ever faced."

"Don't worry," a man shouted from the balcony, "this audience means business!"

"Yes, and I mean business, too," La Follette rejoined. "That's why I am regarded as a very dangerous man." Another ovation filled the hall.

He spoke nostalgically of the early years of the Republic, before corporate trusts and party machines. "In those days, they legislated not for the Standard Oil, the Steel Trust, or any other corporation, but for the people," he said, "a pure, a representative government. Is it such a government this January 22, 1912?"

A torrent of "Nos" gushed from the tiers of well-dressed New Yorkers.

"I say my friends," he responded, "that this is either a representative government, or it is but a shell, a husk, nothing at all." Then he presented his remedies—direct elections, ballot initiatives, judicial recalls, women's suffrage. He promised that genuine democracy would neutralize corporate power and at last restore a government that served the interests of the people.

"You have been told that I am the most dangerous man in the world," he concluded two hours later. "I am here to tell you that I am the safest."

An hour after the end of the speech, he was still shaking hands with admirers. The *New York Times*, one of the papers that had ridiculed La Follette years earlier, reported that Carnegie Hall had never held "a bigger nor a more enthusiastic audience."[51]

THEODORE ROOSEVELT DID NOT ATTEND La Follette's speech. Earlier the same day, he had met with a few confidantes at *The Outlook* headquarters. Pinchot was present, but Roosevelt sent him away before revealing the purpose of the meeting. After he left, he told the others, "I have had all the honor the American public can give me. If I should be elected I would go back not so young as I once was, with all the first fine flavor gone, and take up the horrible task of going in and out, in and out, of the same hole over and over again. But I cannot decline the call."[52]

A few weeks later, he made the point more colorfully to a supporter who saw him at his office. Banging his fist on his desk, he declared, "Well, the fight is on; I am stripped to the buff."[53]

PHILADELPHIA, PENNSYLVANIA, FEBRUARY 2, 1912

However brightly La Follette's star burned, it would never outshine the supernova that was Theodore Roosevelt. Though Roosevelt had made no public announcement of his candidacy, a series of coordinated endorsements abruptly siphoned off the enthusiasm that La Follette had spent months gathering. At the end of January, six progressive Republican governors declared themselves for Roosevelt. The governor of Michigan, purporting to speak on La Follette's behalf, launched a surprise attack and called for him to drop out of the race. Pinchot defected one week after his Carnegie Hall tribute. Senator Cummins of Iowa abruptly announced his own presidential campaign. Even La Follette's own campaign manager began quietly working to undermine him.[54]

February arrived cold and bleak. On top of Pinchot's exodus, thirteen-year-old Mary La Follette developed a tubercular abscess on her neck. Her surgery was scheduled for February 3, the day after an important banquet at which La Follette was to speak. He wanted to cancel but worried that the press would interpret it as capitulation. Anxious, sleep deprived, ill prepared, and sick to his stomach, he took a train to Philadelphia on February 2.

Six hundred leading magazine publishers, writers, and newspaper correspondents attended the Periodical Publisher's Association banquet at the luxurious Bellevue-Stratford Hotel. It was supposed to be a lighthearted affair, an opportunity for the journalists to tease the politicians. Governor Woodrow Wilson spoke just before La Follette. The banquet had run late, so he put aside his prepared remarks and delivered a brief impromptu speech that charmed and captivated his audience.

It was well past 11 p.m. by the time La Follette's turn came. The toastmaster's eyes went wide when he saw the stack of papers under his arm. La Follette explained, "For fear there may be some here who will not report what I say correctly, and because I am going to say some things I consider important, I want to have a record of them." This belligerent opening did not endear him to the audience members, who had little appetite for a long serious speech so late in the evening.

His topic was perfectly germane. Since effective democracy depended on well-informed voters, he urged the magazines to take responsibility for educating the public on progressive issues. It was a fine speech on paper, but the guests were in no mood to hear him read it to them past midnight. As they shifted in their chairs and murmured to each other, La Follette saw that he was losing his audience. He responded angrily, "I have the floor; those who don't care to listen had better get out." Many took him up on the offer.

The atmosphere deteriorated. His anger boiled up. The bitterness of betrayal, the fear for his daughter and his campaign, and the helpless frustration while Roosevelt swooped up his supporters churned and seethed inside him. As always, the opposition aroused his stubborn streak. As he recalled afterward, "I felt that the crowd was against me & threw down my manuscript determined to compel them and master them."

La Follette was adept at improvisation. On a good day, he could spellbind an audience for hours without looking at his notes. But this was not a good day. Suffering from exhaustion, nausea, anxiety, and resentment, he stumbled badly. He meandered, lost his train of thought, shook his fist at the crowd and accused them of trying to sabotage him. He tried to return to his notes, but they were jumbled, and he read the same passage over and over. After an hour, many of the journalists began shouting for him to sit down and clapping ironically to drown him out. When La Follette asked rhetorically, "Is there a way out?" someone yelled, "We hope so!"

The tenacity that had always enabled him to persevere against overwhelming odds finally betrayed him. In defiance of the catcalls, he carried on for nearly two hours, compounding the humiliation. At the finale, he launched into a diatribe against the newspapers, castigating them for becoming tools of the "money power," which served only to alienate the journalists. Finally, at 1:30 in the morning, he ceased talking, collapsed in his chair, and cradled his forehead in his palm with one elbow on the table. Governor Wilson sat next to him, his face impassive. He had listened courteously to the entire speech, barely moving a muscle while La Follette self-destructed.

In the nervous silence that followed, the toastmaster stood to address the audience. "I want to apologize to the newspaper press," he said slowly, "for the foolish, wicked and untruthful attack that has just been made upon it." Then he introduced the next speaker, who was still waiting his turn.

At 2 a.m., the banquet concluded. La Follette returned to his room without a word, went into the bathroom and vomited. Lincoln Steffens and a few other close friends joined him, but he said nothing. He caught a late night train to Washington and met Belle at the hospital before their daughter's surgery.

Mary recovered. The campaign did not. After the speech, the papers gleefully recounted his debacle, speculating that he had suffered a nervous breakdown and would have to go to the Mediterranean for treatment. President Taft, without naming him, warned that progressive "extremists" were like deranged anarchists. "Such extremists are not Progressives," he continued, "they are political emotionalists or neurotics…"

La Follette contested the reports that he was ill, but the damage was done. The political establishment concluded that he was, if not insane, certainly unfit for the presidency. Many of his remaining supporters fled like "a scattering of rats from the sinking ship." Whatever slim chance he'd had to capture the nomination was gone. Nonetheless, he stayed in the race, defiant to the end.[55]

10

THE BULL MOOSE

I haven't much patience with these men who are wiser than all the other fel-
lows put together, and whose views are unchangeable . . . If he can't fight it out
in party ranks and yield if he is beaten, then he had better go out and join the
enemy or, better still, form an organization of his own.

—Uncle Joe[1]

COLUMBUS, OHIO, FEBRUARY 21, 1912

"Poor La Follette!" Roosevelt wrote to Governor Walter Stubbs of Kansas. "As you say, that was a pitiable tragedy." He didn't waste much time on sympathy, though. One sentence later, he was assessing the political opportunity that La Follette's implosion had produced. "[T]he tremendous public sentiment which is unquestionably against Taft must be crystallized into delegates if anything has to come from it," he continued.[2]

Though he had not publicly declared his candidacy, Roosevelt immediately began peeling off La Follette's supporters. The Republican governors of Nebraska and California, previously pledged to La Follette, switched to Roosevelt. So did the editors of the *Kansas City Star*, *Philadelphia North American*, and *Pittsburgh Leader*. The staff of La Follette's Chicago headquarters defected en masse. A number of leading progressives hesitated, still unsure of the former president's dedication to the cause, so Roosevelt sent a letter to the editor of the *Leader* promising, "You can say to the progressives that I will not desert the cause, and they will find me fighting side by side with them to the finish."[3]

Still more was required for Roosevelt to establish his progressive bona fides. Ever since the 1910 election, he had studiously avoided controversy, but as he prepared to launch a new presidential campaign, he charged into the thick of it. There was no more seesaw to his rhetoric. The words he used and the positions that he advocated sounded very much like those of a certain senator from Wisconsin. First he endorsed woman's suffrage in an *Outlook* editorial, a sharp turnabout from his insistence one year earlier that "[w]omen do not really need the suffrage." But that was just a warm-up for his next bombshell.[4]

La Follette's most controversial campaign issue was judicial recall. Since reactionary federal judges had frequently nullified progressive legislation, La Follette championed recall laws that would allow citizens to vote them out of office. The Standpatters abhorred the idea. "Judicial recall!" Taft snorted. "The words are so inconsistent that I hate to utter them. Are we going to make our constitution a liquid thing, so that a majority can...override with popular passion and prejudice every principle of this government, the greatest God ever made?"[5]

At first, Roosevelt kept to the comfortable middle. He objected to the decisions of certain conservative judges, including some that he had appointed, but worried that popular recall went too far. "The more I see of it, read of it, and think of it, the less I care for it," he wrote in 1911. "So far I have simply refrained from committing myself in favor of it, but it may be I will have to be outright against it." As late as February 5, 1912, he assured a concerned conservative, "I do not myself believe in the recall of the judiciary as the best or indeed as a normal remedy." But his ideas were evolving rapidly these days. Two weeks later, he said something quite different in a speech in Columbus, Ohio. "When a Judge decides a Constitutional question," he declared, "when he decides what the people as a whole can or can not do, the people should have the right to recall that decision if they think it wrong."[6]

The words thundered across the political landscape. "[T]he Colonel's speech makes Senator La Follette look like a reactionary," gasped the *New York Times*, for even La Follette had not proposed recall of judicial *decisions*. Progressives were euphoric. When Roosevelt announced, "My hat is in the ring," on his way home from Columbus, wavering La Follette supporters like Albert Beveridge, Moses Clapp, and George Norris jumped into his campaign with both feet. By the beginning of March, he was the undisputed progressive candidate for the Republican nomination.[7]

What he did not expect was the backlash. Conservatives launched a fusillade of obloquy—"fanatical," "deplorable," "radical," "despicable," "monstrous," "dangerous in the extreme," "the end of our government," and "the death knell of our prosperity." Judges, journalists, and

Republican politicians united in mutual contempt for the man who had been their president.[8]

Roosevelt was used to criticism, but he did not anticipate the reaction from his old allies. In public, his dear friend Henry Cabot Lodge said only, "[T]he Colonel and I have long since agreed to disagree on a number of points." Senator Lodge had always been more conservative than Roosevelt, but they were both practical men. In the past, they had never permitted minor political differences to interfere with their friendship. That was no longer possible. By 1912, the gap between progressives and conservatives yawned wide. When Roosevelt made that speech in Columbus, Ohio, he threw himself once and for all onto the progressive side of the gorge, alienating those who had once supported him. Lodge now stood far across the chasm with so many other old friends and colleagues, such as Roosevelt's former attorney general Philander Knox, his former secretary of state Elihu Root; and, of course, his former secretary of war William Howard Taft. These three senators and the President were now the leaders of the conservative faction of the Republican Party. When Roosevelt became the leader of the progressive faction, he became their enemy.[9]

NORTH DAKOTA, MARCH 20, 1912

Truth be told, La Follette preferred to be on his own. Free of intrigues and tepid praise from lukewarm supporters, he was once again the lonely long-shot radical, and he relished the role. Belle noticed that "he seems to gather strength and power" from the adversity. "He feels better always when things are straightened out and the decks seem cleared for action," she added, "no matter how big a fight he has on his hands."[10]

North Dakota held the first primary that year. Defying critics who declared his campaign defunct, La Follette put on his "fighting clothes" and plunged into the race. "He is tense, vigorous and full of fighting ire," remarked a *Minneapolis Tribune* correspondent. "Picture this 'little giant' with the bushy head of hair, tramping up and down the platform, face, hands and figure in nervous action as he drives home his points... There is an indominitable [sic] something in this little fighting man that evokes admiration whether willing or unwilling."[11]

Pinchot was there too, campaigning for Roosevelt. He praised La Follette but compared him to a disabled steam engine. "[A]nother human engine, Roosevelt, must take the progressive train to the terminal," he said.

La Follette rejoined, "[M]y fire box is all right, my drive wheels strong, and my sand box isn't empty."[12]

North Dakotans emphatically agreed. On March 20, nearly 29,000 voters braved a blizzard to nominate La Follette, compared with 19,000 for Roosevelt and a mere 1,500 for Taft. "That's better even than I expected," La Follette crowed. "My friends in that State can't be fooled by mere talk, and North Dakota can't be shaken from its progressive trend."[13]

"La Follette is a wonder," admitted a rueful Roosevelt supporter. "What other man on earth could collapse as he did, not only physically but politically, and 'come back' so soon as he has done?"[14]

But it could not last. Roosevelt was too popular, and if many admired La Follette's pluck, few believed he could win. He had far fewer financial resources than Roosevelt, who had enlisted George W. Perkins of J. P. Morgan & Co. and newspaper tycoon Frank Munsey to raise money. Meanwhile, the pro-Roosevelt governors worked hard to deliver their states to the Colonel, creating fierce headwinds in progressive states. La Follette raced across the country making speeches from New Jersey to California, but Roosevelt, equally vigorous, raced right along with him and rolled up victory after victory.

La Follette's loss in progressive Oregon, where Roosevelt did not campaign, was particularly devastating. The Colonel was rolling through the backwoods of Arkansas when he heard the news. He was lounging on the rear platform of his train, basking in the southern sun. His throat ached from speaking, but his victory over that "half zealot and half self-seeking demagogue" tasted like honey. A journalist from the *New York Sun* joined him. He wanted a comment for the paper. Roosevelt declined to discuss the election but declared that he was "feeling like a bull moose."

Roosevelt's subsequent biographers never discovered the origin of this quote. The words, however, would go down in history.[15]

BOSTON, MASSACHUSETTS, APRIL 25, 1912

President Taft had no hope of winning direct primaries. He was wildly unpopular in the progressive states that had adopted them, and even conservative supporters were annoyed by his trust busting. But many states still lacked direct primaries, and Taft's backers helped dissuade other legislatures from adopting them before the convention. In the south and northeast, his staff invoked the power of patronage to ensure that anyone holding federal office was committed to reelecting the President, and he quickly racked up delegates.[16]

Taft found the whole business unbearably depressing. He became irritable and seldom smiled. His weight ballooned to 332 pounds. His attitude was fatalistic. "I have to set my teeth and go through with it as best I can," he vowed. "But after it is all over I shall be glad to retire and let another take the burden…It seems to me that intelligent men have lost their heads and are leaning toward fool, radical views in a way I never thought possible. Perhaps we'll have to get worse before we get better. The day of the demagogue, the liar and the silly is on."[17]

The worst part was Theodore Roosevelt. His old friend had become almost unrecognizable—"violent," "desperate," and "temperamentally irresponsible." Despite their strained relations, Taft was determined to avoid a public quarrel. He avoided mentioning Roosevelt in speeches and exhorted his supporters to do the same. But the Colonel had not shown him the same courtesy and was viciously attacking him all along the campaign trail. "It is very hard to take all the slaps Roosevelt is handing me at this time, Archie," Taft complained to Butt. "I don't know what he is driving at except to make my way more difficult." He added poignantly, "[I]t is hard, very hard, Archie, to see a devoted friendship going to pieces like a rope of sand."[18]

At the end of March, Taft won his first direct primary—in Roosevelt's home state of New York—but there were reports of fraud at the hands of New York City bosses. An embittered Roosevelt publicly accused the Taft campaign of stealing the election. Taft was indignant. The "hypocrisy of such attacks" particularly galled him. Roosevelt had employed the same tactics and associated with the same machine bosses when he was president. "It is only when they support me that bosses are wicked," he fumed.[19]

In April, he went to Massachusetts to campaign in the primary. Speaking to packed halls and from the back of the train, he declared, "This wrenches my soul…I am here to reply to an old and dear friend of mine, Theodore Roosevelt, who has made many charges against me. I deny those charges. I deny all of them. I do not want to fight Theodore Roosevelt, but then sometimes a man in a corner fights. I am going to fight."

He launched his counterattack before a crowd of 9,000 in the Boston Arena. He accused Roosevelt of misrepresenting his record and exaggerating the voting flaws. Presenting old letters as evidence, he argued that his predecessor had exploited the same patronage powers and relied on the same political bosses that he now accused Taft of misusing. He revealed that it had been Roosevelt who encouraged him to work with Cannon and Aldrich in the first place. "In all Mr. Roosevelt's history he never failed to use as instruments for his purpose those whom he found in power," he continued. "I have merely followed his example…" In not so many words, he accused his old friend and mentor of shameless hypocrisy.

After it was over, he returned to his train and slumped into a lounge chair with his head in his hands. A reporter came in to speak to him. "Roosevelt was my closest friend," he said, his voice breaking. Then he began to weep.[20]

For once, the loyal Archie Butt was not there to comfort him. At Taft's insistence, he had taken a vacation in Europe. He was supposed to return a week before the Boston trip, but he never arrived. On April 15, his ship struck an iceberg off the coast of Newfoundland. He perished with 1,500 fellow passengers aboard the RMS *Titanic*.[21]

"It is hard to believe that he is gone," Taft lamented, "I expect to see him walk in at any moment."

He sorely missed Butt's soothing presence in the weeks to come, for the quarrel with the Colonel became an all-out war. He called Roosevelt a "dangerous egotist," a "demagogue," and a "flatterer of the people." Roosevelt called him a "puzzlewit" and a "fathead" with the intellect of a guinea pig. The epithets escalated—"honeyfugler," "hypocrite," "apostate," "Jacobin," "brawler." By the time the convention finally arrived, they loathed each other.[22]

PRINCETON, NEW JERSEY, JUNE 9, 1912

Like Roosevelt, Woodrow Wilson was a man who rode the wave of popular sentiment, but he was more deliberate about it—all head, no hips. While Roosevelt did not even notice that his political ideas had evolved, Wilson was fully conscious of what he was doing. "My idea of a progressive man is one who keeps up with the world," he told his audience. "A stand-pat is one who stands still, with eyes shut and ears stuffed with cotton, and refuses to concede that the world is moving on." Wilson was a progressive man; he kept up with the world.[23]

His conversion had been even sharper than Roosevelt's. Two years earlier, he had been a steadfast Bourbon Democrat, hand-picked by the bosses to rescue the party from the clutches of William Jennings Bryan. Now he hoped to position himself as Bryan's heir. The trick was to bury his past.

Ever since his gubernatorial victory, Wilson had assiduously courted Bryan in hopes of winning his endorsement for the presidential nomination. He invited him to dinner in Princeton and praised him effusively in speeches. When Bryan returned the praise, it seemed as if the effort was paying off. But then Wilson hit a snag. In January 1912, the *New York Sun* published a letter that he'd written a few years earlier. Commenting on a speech that excoriated Bryan, Wilson wrote, "I have read it with relish and entire agreement. Would that we could do something at once dignified and effective to knock Mr. Bryan into a cocked hat!"[24]

There was no way to justify the letter or explain it away, and Wilson didn't try. They were both scheduled to speak at a fund-raising dinner the next day. To his relief, Bryan greeted him with a warm handshake. When it was Wilson's turn to speak, he acknowledged that he'd had differences with Bryan in the past but now praised him for having had "the steadfast vision all along of what it was that was the matter." Turning to the man that he had once threatened to knock into a cocked hat, he said, "Let us apologize to each other that we ever suspected or antagonized one another; let us join hands once more...which will show us at the last to have been indeed the friends of our country and the friends of mankind."

Bryan rose and put his hand on Wilson's shoulder. "That was splendid, splendid!" he murmured.

The next day, friendly newspapers cheered the reconciliation. Even the *New York Sun*, which had instigated the rift, had to admit that the evening "fairly dripped harmony." The magnanimity of Wilson and Bryan contrasted sharply with the personal enmities that divided the Republican leaders, La Follette and Roosevelt, Roosevelt and Taft.[25]

Wilson was pleased. "The great Jackson Day banquet came off—and was a great triumph for me," he wrote to Mary Allen Hulbert Peck, an intimate friend,[26] "and the effect of it all (for it was a national affair) seems to have been to strengthen the probabilities of my nomination manyfold."[27]

Wilson's past was not quite finished with him, however. In February, one of his opponents publicized excerpts from an American history book he'd written in 1902. The book denigrated nearly every constituency in his new progressive coalition, including labor organizers, western populists, and immigrants—"men of the lowest class from the south of Italy and men of the meaner sort out of Hungary and Poland." There was no single leader to conciliate this time, so Wilson issued a series of tortured excuses and exculpations to representatives of the groups he had offended, alternately praising the "the great people of Italy" and expressing his "admiration of the Polish character." It wasn't enough. At last, a Polish-American group suggested that he insert erratum slips into unsold copies of the book and rewrite the offensive passages in the next edition. Wilson, after some hesitation, agreed to literally rewrite his past.[28]

Despite these efforts, his campaign was foundering. He had counted on his Virginian roots to help him win the south, but conservative voters in Virginia and Georgia delivered their delegates to Representative Oscar Underwood of Alabama. Governor Judson Harmon of Ohio, another conservative, won his populous home state. Meanwhile, Champ Clark of Missouri, who had succeeded Cannon as the Speaker of the House, dominated the western primaries.

Nor did Wilson have much hope for the no-primary states. The Democratic bosses had little love for the man they regarded as a double-crossing radical. Three weeks before the convention in Baltimore, Wilson wrote Mary Peck, "Just between you and me, I have not the least idea of being nominated...the outcome is in the hands of the professional, case-hardened politicians who serve only their own interests and who know that I will not serve them..." Feigning indifference, he added, "I am well and in the best of spirits. I have no deep stakes involved in this game."[29]

CHICAGO, ILLINOIS, JUNE 15, 1912

In June, the Republicans returned once more to the Chicago Coliseum to choose their presidential nominee. The circumstances were entirely different from Roosevelt's nomination eight years earlier. In 1904, the party was united and confident of victory. The Standpatters reigned supreme, and the party bosses were firmly in control of every state save Wisconsin. There were no questions about the platform or the nominee. Everything had already been decided.

In 1912, the party was bitterly divided and stumbling toward defeat. Nothing was determined, and the battle lines were sharp. On one side, Roosevelt stood for popular elections, big government, and a host of progressive reforms. On the other, Taft represented machine politics, corporate power, and the narrow government that the country had always known.

The race was tight going into the convention. Roosevelt had won more than three-fourths of the delegates in primary states, but Taft dominated the rest. Some papers estimated a slight lead for Roosevelt, others for Taft. Their guesswork was complicated by numerous contested delegates. Like Wisconsin in 1904, rival factions in many states had held their own conventions and sent competing delegations to Chicago. There were 254 disputed seats, almost a quarter of the total delegate count. The Republican National Committee would have to settle the disputes before the convention just as it had settled the Wisconsin delegate fight eight years earlier.

Unfortunately for Roosevelt, Taft men controlled the committee. Ignoring the hisses and occasional fistfights, they proceeded to "steam-roll" the hearings, awarding delegate after delegate to Taft. From Oyster Bay, Roosevelt howled that his opponents were "deliberately conspiring to steal the victory from the people." That was somewhat overstated, for a large number of his delegate challenges had been spurious. Nonetheless, the committee members certainly erred on Taft's side, and the lopsided results gave credence to the allegations: 235 disputed seats went to Taft, only 19 to Roosevelt.[30]

FOUR DAYS LATER, COLONEL ROOSEVELT BOUNDED out of a passenger car in Chicago. He was not supposed to be there, brazenly campaigning for his own nomination, but righteous fury had buried his deference to political decorum. Emerging from the station, he looked out over a sea of screaming supporters in straw hats all along the avenue. "Thank you! Thank you!" he shouted. He took off his new hat, a big buckskin sombrero with a five-inch brim, and waved it vigorously. When he came down the stairs, the surging crowd smashed through the police lines and eagerly stretched out their arms. He grasped every hand within reach, grinning and clicking his teeth with pleasure as he squeezed past.

A brass band led his car down Michigan Avenue to the tune of "There'll Be a Hot Time in the Old Town Tonight." He waved his big hat at the onlookers choking the sidewalks. The Congress Plaza Hotel was also jammed with people. The band tried to lead him into the lobby, but the bass drummer got knocked over, and the other musicians were scattered. His escorts had to shove their way through a swarm of delegates and a phalanx of suffragists who wanted to petition him. "Stand back, stand back, stop crowding!" he shouted.

When he finally reached his suite, he went to the window and waved his hat once more at the mob outside. Thrusting his jaw forward, he yelled, "Chicago is a mighty poor place in which to try and steal anything!"

The crowd roared back, "Hurrah for Teddy! Soak them! Go to it Teddy!"

"The people have spoken," he continued, "and the politicians, dead or alive, will be made to understand that they are the servants and not the masters..."

"Give it to them, Teddy! That's the way to talk!"

Leaning out over the edge of the parapet, he bellowed, "It is a fight against theft, the thieves will not win!"[31]

CHICAGO, ILLINOIS, JUNE 17, 1912

The day before the convention, Roosevelt addressed an audience of 5,000 at the Chicago Auditorium; 10,000 more waited outside in roped off streets. It was not a campaign speech in the traditional sense, not like any campaign speech that he had ever given. He did not discuss his policies or political vision. The speech resembled a cross between a prosecutor's opening statement and a Christian jeremiad. Roosevelt spent most of the time detailing the crimes of the men who had "stolen" the people's votes from him, but he veered regularly into righteous lamentation.

"Tonight we come together to protest against a crime which strikes straight at the heart of every principle of political decency and honesty," he proclaimed, "a crime which represents treason to the people, and the usurpation of the sovereignty of the people by irresponsible political bosses, inspired by the sinister influences of moneyed privilege."

And so it continued for 9,000 words until he reached the religious finale: "We fight in honorable fashion for the good of mankind; fearless of the future; unheeding of our individual fates; with unflinching hearts and undimmed eyes; we stand at Armageddon."[32]

This was a new Roosevelt. He had always preached to his audiences, but his lectures usually resembled the scoldings of a stern schoolmaster. On that warm Chicago evening, he took the form of an evangelical preacher thundering about the devil. The old Roosevelt—the one who had regarded party machines as defective institutions that should be gradually reformed—would have called the new Roosevelt a demagogue, an agitator, and a wild-eyed fanatic.

But it wasn't just Roosevelt who had changed. This was a new America. The Standpatters hung back in the old America, scrabbling desperately to staunch the flow of progress. La Follette raced ahead, breaking down dams and cutting new channels. Roosevelt rode the crest of the wave. The people had no more patience for the old ways, so neither did he. The people demanded a leader who would change the world, so he became one. His mind and his hips, united at last, charged into the future.

There was only one problem. His party was not with him.

WASHINGTON, DC, JUNE 18, 1912

While the Colonel was leading his crusade in Chicago, La Follette remained in Washington, observing the proprieties that Roosevelt had defied. The morning before the convention, he received a phone call from his delegates. Roosevelt's people had asked for their assistance in electing a progressive convention chairman. To defeat the conservative favorite, they needed Wisconsin's 13 votes. To sweeten the deal, they dangled a tempting candidate, Francis McGovern, governor of Wisconsin.[33]

La Follette was familiar with Roosevelt's interest in the matter. The Colonel wanted a favorable chairman who would assist him in challenging Taft's disputed delegates on the convention floor. Many of La Follette's allies, including McGovern himself, had urged him to accept the olive branch, put aside his differences, and unite with Roosevelt against the conservatives.

But that was not his nature. For nearly two decades, he had doggedly rejected any compromise of his principles regardless of the consequences. He was not about to abandon that policy for the sake of a man who embodied its antithesis—the proud pragmatist and eager compromiser who had repeatedly betrayed and undermined him. He refused to sully his progressive principles by making any deals with Taft *or* Roosevelt. One of the delegates on the call warned him that this decision would likely split the Wisconsin delegation. "Let the split come then," he answered. As always, he would hold his course to the bitter end.[34]

CHICAGO, ILLINOIS, JUNE 18, 1912

On the surface, the Chicago Coliseum looked much as it had in 1904 and 1908. The usual profusion of red, white, and blue swathed every wall, railing, and post. But hidden beneath the bunting that girded the grandstand, barbed wire waited for anyone who dared to rush the stage. The basement held a temporary police headquarters and an emergency hospital. Two hundred bluecoats manned the aisles while a reserve force waited downstairs, and another hundred plainclothes cops lurked in the stands.[35]

The delegates who started filing in at 10 a.m. were subdued at first. As the hall filled up, they began to let loose. "Rah, rah, rah, who are we?" sang the New Jerseyans, "We are the delegates from New Jers-ee. Are we in it? Just you wait. Till we give Teddy 28 straight!" The other states countered with their own cheers. Soon, defiant shouts of "Teddy!" and "Taft!" punctuated the air. Roosevelt's supporters cried "Toot! Toot!" to mock the national committee's steamroller.

At noon, the temporary presiding officer rapped his gavel. The first order of business was the election of a convention chairman. One of Taft's supporters nominated Senator Elihu Root of New York. It was an inspired choice. Root was a distinguished statesman, brilliant, poised, and widely respected. He had been a member of Roosevelt's inner circle. The Colonel could hardly object to someone he had once called "the ablest man I have known in our government service."[36]

Then a Wisconsin delegate asked for the floor. "I present the name of the brilliant, the able, the impartial and the fearless governor of my commonwealth, Hon. Francis E. McGovern, of Wisconsin," he called out. The Roosevelt delegates erupted in cheers and enthusiastically seconded the nomination.

Their celebration did not last long. A few minutes later, La Follette's campaign manager repudiated McGovern's nomination. "Men have spoken from this platform today," he said, "claiming to represent the interests of Senator La Follette. I am here to say to you that they have neither the authority, nor do they represent him in this direction...he refuses now to be forced into such an alliance." The nomination stood, but Wisconsin did not stand behind it.

After the speeches, a chaotic roll call proceeded. Whenever the disputed delegates voted for Root, the Roosevelt men protested angrily. "You are a pack of thieves!" shouted William Flinn of Pennsylvania. But they couldn't stop the tide. When Wisconsin's turn came, the delegation split; loyal La Follette delegates voted for other candidates. It would not have made a difference in any case. Root won, 558 to 501.

When Senator Root mounted the podium to give his speech, someone shouted, "Receiver of stolen goods!" He ignored the barb and began speaking. Hundreds of Roosevelt supporters walked out. By the time he finished, entire sections of seats were empty.[37]

CHICAGO, ILLINOIS, JUNE 19, 1912

The next day, the Coliseum was full again, and the delegates were even rowdier. Shouts, cheers, hisses, fistfights, and endless toot-toots roiled the hall. Elihu Root stood serenely at the podium, silver haired and impeccably dressed, sweeping his eyes across the storm that thundered around him. He let the police handle the fights; his gavel did the rest. William Allen White recalled, "Root seemed to us like a diabolical sphinx. He pushed the program of the convention through steadily, and as swiftly as possible...When he clicked the gavel on the marble block that topped the speaker's table, order ensued almost hypnotically."

It was time for the convention to approve the national committee's decisions on the disputed delegates. Roosevelt's supporters planned to challenge 72 of those decisions. It was their last chance. If they failed to unseat those delegates, Taft would win the nomination easily. But there was a catch. In order to overturn the committee's decisions, they needed a majority. Because of the disputed delegates, they didn't have one; the "thieves" would judge their own cases.

On the convention floor, Governor Herbert Hadley of Missouri argued that the 72 disputed delegates should be prohibited from voting on any credentials decisions. The Taft people were prepared for this. They moved that Hadley's motion be referred to the Committee on Credentials, which they controlled. The roll was called. It proceeded along the same lines as the previous day. The disputed Taft delegates naturally voted for referral.

When Wisconsin's turn came, the room went quiet with anticipation. Governor McGovern stepped nimbly into the aisle. "Wisconsin is solid this time," he announced proudly. "It votes 26 votes No." Pandemonium broke out anew. Roosevelt supporters leaped onto their chairs and cheered.

But even with Wisconsin, it was not enough. Their only hope was to discount the votes of the 72 delegates on the referral motion. In desperation, Hadley appealed for a ruling from the chairman. This was the pivotal moment.

Amid the uproar, Elihu Root's soft voice did not carry more than ten feet. "No man can be permitted to vote upon the question of his own right to a seat in the Convention," he said slowly, "but the rule does not disqualify any delegate whose name is upon the roll from voting upon the contest of any other."

The Taft supporters roared with delight. Roosevelt's people got up to leave. For all intents and purposes, the convention was over: Roosevelt could not win.[38]

THAT NIGHT, A CROWD OF HIGH-LEVEL SUPPORTERS gathered in Roosevelt's hotel suite. Few had any illusions about winning the nomination. The question was what to do next. Governor Hiram Johnson of California urged his colleagues to bolt the convention and found a new party. Governor Walter Stubbs of Kansas counseled patience. Senator William Borah of Idaho argued vehemently against abandoning the party.

Roosevelt circulated among the fray, deliberating. He had spent his career in the Republican Party, alternately battling and negotiating with the old guard while he gradually prodded his colleagues toward reform. He'd never had any patience for "bolters" like La Follette at the 1904 convention. But it was different this time, or at least seemed different to him now. In a fair election, he knew that he would have won easily. He believed that the party had committed fraud at the highest level to thwart the will of the people. This was not about a man named Theodore Roosevelt. It was about justice and democracy. It was about the men all around him—good men, loyal Republicans—who believed in his cause enough to abandon their own party and embark on an uncertain future.

After midnight, Senator Borah was still trying dissuade him from bolting when a representative from the Credentials Committee burst into the room. He announced that Roosevelt's supporters had walked out of the committee meeting en masse. They had assembled in a ballroom downstairs with the other delegates.[39]

"You see," Roosevelt said to Borah, "I can't desert my friends now."

He left the suite, hat in hand, and descended to the ballroom. Squeezing his way through the crowd, he climbed up on a table and stood over them, his head framed by Renaissance-style murals that adorned the arched ceiling. "So far as I am concerned, I am through," he announced. "If you are voted down I hope that you, the real and lawful majority of the convention, will organize as such, and you will do it if you have the courage and loyalty of your conviction." When he finished, Governor Johnson took his place and described the progressive Republicans' plans to found a new political party.

Roosevelt left the delegates to their organizing and returned to his suite. Many of his supporters were still there, but it was late, and the crowd was thinning. Soon there were only three left: journalist Henry Stoddard and Roosevelt's financial backers, George Perkins and Frank Munsey. They sat on the bed until dawn discussing their plans while Roosevelt leaned wearily against the headboard. Perkins and Munsey promised to fund the new party. "My fortune, my magazines and my newspapers are with you," Munsey pledged. It was decided. They would abandon the Republican Party to its fate. A new progressive party would hold its own convention and nominate its own candidate for president.[40]

TAFT RECEIVED THE NEWS WITH EQUANIMITY. "If I win the nomination and Roosevelt bolts, it means a long, hard fight with probable defeat," he predicted. "But I can stand defeat if we retain the regular Republican Party as a nucleus for future conservative action."[41]

Many Taft supporters in Chicago were less sanguine. Desperate to preserve Republican unity, they reached out to Roosevelt, offering to change their votes to some other candidate who would be acceptable to him. But Roosevelt's compromising days were behind him. Channeling La Follette, he stood on principle and refused to negotiate until the disputed delegates were disqualified. "No! No! No! I won't hear it! I won't have it!" he retorted to one of the negotiators. "[T]his is a crooked convention, I won't touch it with a forty-rod pole."[42]

And so, the fate of the Republican Party was sealed. Three days later, it nominated William H. Taft for president on the first ballot. The Wisconsin delegation remained at the convention and proudly voted for Robert M. La Follette; 107 Roosevelt delegates registered their votes for the Colonel. Others answered, "present but not voting." The rest left behind empty seats, silent testimony that the progressives were leaving the party. Henceforth, the Republican Party, whose members had founded the progressive movement, would be known as the conservative party of the United States.

SEA GIRT, NEW JERSEY, JUNE 25, 1912

Wilson waited out the Democratic convention at the governor's summer cottage on the Jersey shore. The fifteen-room colonial-style mansion was a replica of George Washington's Revolutionary War headquarters, constructed for the 1904 World's Fair in St. Louis. After the exhibition, the state reassembled it next to a National Guard rifle range in Sea Girt. The pop pop pop of distant gunfire drifted in on the wind now and then. The reporters, photographers, and "moving-picture" men made much more racket, snapping photos, and begging for comments every time Wilson left the house. He teased them with small talk and funny anecdotes but refused to discuss politics.[43]

Despite the public show of disinterest, Wilson followed the convention closely. His campaign manager called him regularly from Baltimore, and his staff relayed news bulletins from a makeshift telegraph office under a tent on the lawn. The convention was rancorous even by Democratic standards. Bryan had launched an all-out war on Tammany Hall, the bastion of New York's Democratic machine. He proposed to disqualify every delegate who was "under obligation to J. Pierpont Morgan . . . or any other member of the privilege-hunting and favor-seeking class," which meant all of New York City's delegates. The Tammany bosses fought back furiously, and it seemed as if the Democrats might split like the Republicans before Bryan finally relented.[44]

The quarreling delayed the nominations until midnight of the third day. The usual demonstrations of Democratic fervor accompanied them, slightly tempered by exhaustion. Underwood received 30 minutes of cheers; Clark got 65. Wilson's supporters, not to be outdone, lasted 75 minutes. The nominations were still coming in at dawn. Finally, at 7 a.m., the Democrats voted: Speaker Champ Clark of Missouri, 440½; New Jersey Governor Woodrow Wilson, 324; Ohio Governor Judson Harmon, 148; Alabama Congressman Oscar Underwood, 117½; the rest, 56. Clark had a big lead, but he needed a two-thirds majority to win the nomination.[45]

The delegates recessed to get some much-needed sleep. When they returned in the afternoon, they voted again with little change. And again. And again. And again. The weaker candidates dropped out, and a few delegates trickled into the Wilson camp but not enough to make a difference.

BACK AT SEA GIRT, WILSON BEHAVED AS IF nothing unusual were happening except for the swarm of reporters and photographers camping on his lawn. He played with his daughters, joked with his wife, took long walks, and refused to discuss politics. After the eighth ballot, he broke his silence to predict, "This is to be a ten-inning game, and I fear several more than that."

Before midnight, he called for a glass of buttermilk, declaring that things were too interesting for him to sleep, but no further information came in, and he retired to bed. Looking out his bedroom window, he spotted one of his campaign advisers leaving for home. "Tumulty, is there any news from Baltimore?" he called.

"Nothing new, governor," Tumulty replied.

But Wilson could see from his long face that something had happened.[46]

SEA GIRT, NEW JERSEY, JUNE 29, 1912

In the morning, Wilson received a phone call from his campaign manager in Baltimore, William McCombs. The bombshell had landed just after midnight. On the tenth ballot, Tammany Hall withdrew its support from Governor Harmon and sent 81 delegates into the Clark camp. Clark now had a majority of the delegates—556 to Wilson's 350½. Though Clark remained shy of the two-thirds threshold, the attainment of a majority was normally the signal for a stampede to the frontrunner. McCombs told Wilson that the situation was hopeless and advised him to send a telegram authorizing his delegates to vote for other candidates.

Wilson hung up the phone and put on a cheerful expression. "Well dear," he said to his wife, "Do you realize that now we can see our beloved Rydal again?" referring to their favorite vacation spot in England's Lake District. He asked for a pen and paper to draft the telegram for his delegates. But before he'd had a chance to send it, he received a call from another high-level adviser in Baltimore who vehemently disagreed with McCombs. "Your nomination is inevitable," he promised, "your delegates will stick, if it takes all summer." Wilson put aside the telegram. Sure enough, his delegates stuck; the anticipated stampede never materialized.[47]

In the afternoon, another bomb exploded. For the first thirteen ballots, William Jennings Bryan had observed the wishes of Nebraska's primary voters and cast his vote for Clark. But after New York switched to Clark, his disgust for Tammany Hall's bosses overcame his fealty to the voters. Declaring that he would not vote for Clark "as long as New York's vote is recorded for him," he voted for Wilson. Pandemonium broke loose in the hall. Bryan and a few Nebraska delegates who joined him added only five votes to Wilson's count, but the Great Commoner's vote meant far more than its direct contribution to the total. The tide began to turn.[48]

At 5 p.m., news reached Sea Girt that delegates were "breaking for Wilson all along the line." A swarm of reporters rushed over to the house to alert the governor.

"Is that so?" he replied. "Marvels will never cease."

The ballots kept coming. By the end of the night, Wilson trailed Clark by only 56 votes.

"I find that if I continue to gain strength at the exact ratio," Wilson teased the reporters, "I will land the nomination just after the 175th ballot is cast."[49]

SEA GIRT, NEW JERSEY, JULY 2, 1912

It only took 46 ballots. On the seventh day of the marathon convention, Wilson received a phone call from Baltimore. The connection was bad, and he couldn't make out who it was. The caller said something about Underwood withdrawing and a motion to unanimously nominate Wilson, then hung up.

Wilson quietly put down the phone and walked upstairs to see his wife. "Well, dear," he said, "I guess we won't go to Mount Rydal this summer after all."[50]

CHICAGO, ILLINOIS, AUGUST 5, 1912

The Chicago Coliseum was red, white, and blue again. Except for the stuffed moose head standing guard on one wall and the oil painting of Theodore Roosevelt watching from the other, a careless visitor might not have noticed that the scenery had changed. But a glance at the people who streamed into the hall on August 5 revealed that this was no ordinary party convention. Career politicians and party henchmen were scarce. Instead, the delegates included lawyers, journalists, teachers, farmers, laborers, and other middle-class professionals—a well-mannered, clean-cut crowd "like a convention of Sunday School Superintendents," quipped the New York Times.

At the Republican convention, purple and gold sashes had cordoned off a special section for the millionaires' wives. Young women in shirtwaists now occupied these seats, and the trim was no different from any other row. Many of the delegates on the floor were women, including Jane Addams, the eminent philosopher, social activist, and proponent of women's suffrage, who was treated with reverence second only to Theodore Roosevelt.

The conduct of the delegates was even more striking than the demographics. Instead of jingoistic rhymes, the delegates sang hymns, parading through the hall to the tune of "Onward, Christian Soldiers" and "The Battle Hymn of the Republic." The religious overtones recalled the spiritual atmosphere that Roosevelt had evoked in his Armageddon speech. "It was not a convention at all," the *Times* concluded. "It was an assemblage of religious enthusiasts."[51]

Albert Beveridge, who was running for governor of Indiana, chaired the convention. Even in the Senate, his speeches had been sentimental. At the Chicago Coliseum, he inaugurated the National Progressive Party with an operatic homily that moved many of the delegates to tears. "We stand for a nobler America," he began. "We battle for the actual rights of men." He catalogued the failures of the Democratic and Republican parties—bosses, tariffs, corporate interests, child labor, and hyperpartisanship. To heal the country's ills, he heralded the formation of a new party "from the grass roots." He concluded his speech with a line from "The Battle Hymn of the Republic"—"Oh, be swift our souls to answer Him! Be jubilant our feet! Our God is marching on!" That was supposed to be the cue for the band to play the song, but it started up with "Rally 'Round the Flag, Boys" by mistake. The delegates knew better, and they shook the hall as they sang, "Glory, Glory, Hallelujah! His Truth is Marching On."[52]

Other than Beveridge and other speakers that day, few referred to the new party by its official name. In the press, in mouths of politicians and voters alike, it was simply the Bull Moose Party. The nickname belied one element of Beveridge's speech. The Progressive Party was not exactly the spontaneous grassroots organization that he made it out to be. It owed its existence to the charisma, vitality, and ambition of one man.

Theodore Roosevelt did not regard the Bull Moose Party as his personal fief. To the contrary, he saw himself as its instrument. But as La Follette had feared, the man who thought he was the bride at every wedding could not avoid dominating his own political party. When prohibitionists and other "radical" elements tried to substitute several planks in the platform, Roosevelt threatened, "Each one of those planks will go back, or I am not a candidate." When Jane Addams, among others, protested the exclusion of black delegates from southern delegations, he insisted that southern blacks were not enlightened enough to lead the progressive movement. "I earnestly believe that by appealing to the best white men in the South," he rationalized, "we shall create a situation by which the colored men of the South will ultimately get justice..." Consequently, the few black delegates at the convention came only from northern states.[53]

Given Roosevelt's dominance of the party, it seemed almost natural that he should break a century of tradition by speaking at his own convention. The National Progressive Party was his church, and he was its messiah. He titled his speech, appropriately, "My Confession of Faith." Despite the title, it was mostly a dry recitation of his proposed policies: corporate regulation, minimum wages, workman's compensation, child labor laws, tariff reductions, women's suffrage, conservation, currency reform, direct primaries, judicial recall, and ballot initiatives. The litany lasted two hours with delegates cheering all the way through. At the finale, Roosevelt returned to the heroic biblical imagery that had served him so well. "Our cause is based on the eternal principles of righteousness," he proclaimed, "and even though we who now lead may for the time fail, in the end the cause itself shall triumph."

La Follette could not have put it better. Roosevelt had come a long way from the man who once told Lincoln Steffens that he believed in fighting one evil at a time, that he trusted those "who take the next step; not those who theorize about the 200th step." Shorn of his former power, alienated from his old allies, facing long odds and an uncertain future, he dared to look above the horizon. "Now to you men, who, in your turn, have come together to spend and be spent in the endless crusade against wrong," he continued, "to you who gird yourselves for this great new fight in the neverending warfare for the good of humankind, I say in closing...We stand at Armageddon, and we battle for the Lord."

He left his crusaders cheering and waving red bandannas. "Thy gleaming sword shall never rust, Roosevelt O Roosevelt," they sang as he strode from the stage. "In thee we hail a leader just...to crush the powers of greed and lust, Roosevelt, O Roosevelt."[54]

BUFFALO, NEW YORK, SEPTEMBER 2, 1912

Wilson wasn't worried about Taft. The President didn't stand a chance. Roosevelt was the competition. In a popularity contest, the Colonel would win easily. "He appeals to their imagination; I do not," Wilson admitted to Mary Peck, "He is a real, vivid person, whom they have seen and shouted themselves hoarse over and voted for, millions strong; I am a vague, conjectural personality, more made up of opinions and academic prepossessions than of human traits and red corpuscles." To beat the beloved Colonel, he would have to emphasize policy over personality. But it was not obvious how to differentiate his policies from Roosevelt's. "When I sit down and compare my views with those of a Progressive Republican, I can't see what the difference is," he confessed.[55]

Three days later, Louis Brandeis brought him the answer. Brandeis had campaigned for La Follette during the primaries, but he was not keen on the new Bull Moose Party or its benefactor, George Perkins. As an expert in antitrust law, he found the party's trust regulation plank, which Perkins had helped draft, particularly suspect. Roosevelt and Perkins believed that effective federal oversight could reform the "bad" trusts. Brandeis thought their plan was futile and dangerous. The closer the government was to the trusts, the more likely the trusts were to corrupt it, raising the specter of a tyrannical government-industrial partnership that would oppress workers and small businesses alike. Outlining the anti-trust legislation that he and La Follette had prepared after the Supreme Court's Standard Oil decision, he argued that Congress shoud outlaw all monopolies, regardless of whether government officials deemed them "good" or "bad," because monopolies were inherently anti-competitive.

Wilson's understanding of trust policy was limited, but Brandeis's ideas resonated with his skepticism of Roosevelt's paternalistic approach to government. During their three-hour lunch meeting, they agreed on the broad outline of an alternative antitrust policy, which Brandeis would help him to formulate in detail. In juxtaposition to Roosevelt's "New Nationalism," he would call it the "New Freedom".[56]

A few days later, he introduced the idea to the public in a Labor Day speech for 10,000 workers in Buffalo. "My kind of leading will not be tell-ing other people what they have got to do," he told the workers. "What I fear is a government of experts...What are we for if we are to be scien-tifically taken care of by a small number of gentlemen who are the only men who understand the job?"

He continued, "As to the monopolies, which Mr. Roosevelt pro-poses to legalize and to welcome, I know that they are so many cars of juggernaut, and I do not look forward with pleasure to the time when the juggernauts are licensed and driven by commissioners of the United States."

A century later, modern conservatives would erroneously castigate Wilson as a paternalistic "statist." In fact, he pioneered an alternative strain of progressivism, suspicious of big government and big business alike. He did not believe that a nation's government should manage the business of its corporations or the lives of its citizens. Rather, he appealed to a Jeffersonian ideal of individualism. He differed from the Standpatters in that he believed government must actively protect the freedom of the individual. He differed from the Bull Moosers in that he believed the government should go no further than that. "Ours is a programme of liberty," he concluded, "theirs is a programme of regulation."[57]

The New Freedom theme enabled Wilson to differentiate his policies in a way that appealed to the individualistic westerners at the core of the progressive movement. It also exposed the flaw in the Colonel's magnetism. Roosevelt had always been a moralizer. In his new role as progressive evangelist, he was insufferably sanctimonious. He not only preached paternalism, he embodied it.

WARWICK, RHODE ISLAND, SEPTEMBER 10, 1912

Nelson Aldrich paid little attention to politics these days. The press had circulated rumors that he would return to the Senate in 1913, but he denied them. He was enjoying his retirement. His new mansion was magnificent—a great stone palace reigning majestically over a kingdom of manicured lawns and rocky shores. Stonemasons and carpenters from France and Italy had labored for two years to build the 70-room structure according to Aldrich's exacting standards. Intricate murals graced the lofty ceilings. Flemish masterpieces adorned the walls. Streaked marble and ornate woodcarving framed the fireplaces. It was the house of a king.[58]

But Aldrich wasn't a king, not anymore. He still held out hope that the progressive hysteria would fade, but no one else did. Though he'd succeeded in persuading the bankers to embrace his National Reserve Association, his allies in the Senate kept postponing the bill. They knew it could not pass. In the House, Democratic leaders did not even discuss it. They were busy preparing another investigation that would soon drag old Pierpont Morgan before its tribunal. Even the Republican Party avoided mentioning the Aldrich Plan in its convention platform.

On September 10, the American Bankers' Association, which had twice endorsed the plan, declined to extend its support. The bankers' opinions of the plan had not changed, but the political world had. They recognized that no proposal with Aldrich's name on it would pass Congress in the foreseeable future. New leaders were destined for Washington, and the practical bankers prepared themselves to work with them. The Aldrich Plan was dead.[59]

It would not be forgotten, however. Its memory would live on in the establishment of the Federal Reserve.

NEW YORK, NEW YORK, SEPTEMBER 12, 1912

John F. Schrank did not receive many visitors at his dingy tenement on the Lower East Side of Manhattan. Unemployed and reclusive, he stayed in his room writing poetry. But the man—or whatever it was—who tapped his shoulder at 1:30 in the morning was no ordinary visitor. "Let not a murderer take the presidential chair," it whispered. "Avenge my death."

Schrank had seen that face before, in a dream eleven years earlier on the day the man died. He recognized him from the pictures that filled the newspapers—President William McKinley. In the original dream, McKinley rose from his coffin dressed like a monk. "This is my murderer," he had said, "avenge my death." He pointed a cold finger at another man Schrank knew from the papers: Vice President Theodore Roosevelt.

Inspired by the second ghostly visit, Schrank scribbled a poem into his notebook:

> But when night draws near
> And you hear a knock
> And a voice should whisper your
> Time is up; Refuse to answer
> As long as you can
> Then face it and be a man.

A week later, Schrank borrowed $350, bought a .38 caliber Colt revolver, and boarded a southbound steamship.[60]

BEVERLY, MASSACHUSETTS, SEPTEMBER 29, 1912

President Taft had no illusions about his chances. "Sometimes I think I might as well give up so far as being a candidate is concerned," he sighed. "There are so many people in the country who don't like me." He consoled himself that he had at least stopped Roosevelt from taking over the Republican Party and, hopefully, the presidency. His disgust with the Colonel had grown so toxic that he preferred Wilson. "As the campaign goes on and the unscrupulousness of Roosevelt develops," he wrote to Nellie, "it is hard to realize that we are talking about the same man whom we knew in the presidency…it is impossible to conceive of him as the fakir, the juggler, the green goods man, the gold-brick man that he has come to be."

While the other candidates gave speeches and gobbled up headlines, Taft relaxed on the Massachusetts coast and focused on his golf game. When a campaign adviser complained to him about all the golf pictures in the press, Taft shrugged him off. "I seem to have heard that before," he wrote. "It always makes me impatient, as if I were running a P. T. Barnum show, with two or three shows across the street, and as if I ought to have as much advertising as the rest."[61]

At the end of September, he ventured as far as the veranda of his cottage to address the Republican clubs of Essex County, Massachusetts. "A third party has split off from the Republican Party," he declared, "not for any one principle, or indeed on any principle at all, but merely to gratify personal ambition and vengeance…This new party is not united on any cohesive principles, and is only kept together by the remarkable personality of its leader. Were he to die the party would go to pieces…" He dismissed the Bull Moose platform as a "crazy-quilt" of "preposterous," "impracticable," and "Socialistic" doctrines, then eloquently articulated the Republican credo: "A National Government cannot create good times. It cannot make the rain to fall, the sun to shine, or the crops to grow, but it can, by pursuing a meddlesome policy…halt enterprise, paralyze investment, and throw out of employment hundreds of thousands of working men."[62]

Then he returned to his golf and waited out the inevitable.

MADISON, WISCONSIN, OCTOBER 12, 1912

Bob La Follette shared Taft's enmity of the Colonel but for a different reason. While Taft thought Roosevelt had gone crazy, La Follette believed he hadn't changed in the slightest. After the Bull Moose convention, he authored a scathing editorial in his magazine. "It is characteristic of Roosevelt," he wrote, "that while he seizes upon issues that make good propaganda and gives them publicity, he has not the patience nor stability nor depth of conviction to prevent his sacrificing essential principles and permanent results to personal considerations and temporary advantage." Privately, he was even harsher. "[E]verything should be done to prevent true progressive republicans from joining the Roosevelt party," he wrote to a friend. "His success means disaster to the progressive cause and to the country."[63]

La Follette had always maintained a principled policy of avoiding personal attacks. Even in his roll-call campaigns, he had named names only during the recitation of the roll. But when it came to Roosevelt, his resentment and fear of losing control of the progressive movement got the better of him. Defeating the Bull Moose became his crusade, and he pursued it on every front. *La Follette's Weekly* printed article after article lambasting Roosevelt and his party, including one by Brandeis that assailed the antitrust policies of the "Roosevelt-Perkins-Steel-Trust-Party." In the Senate, La Follette launched one investigation into Roosevelt's 1904 campaign, to which the trusts had contributed heavily, and another into the Bull Moose Party's financing in 1912. In Wisconsin, he campaigned against the Colonel. Though he did not endorse any candidate, his speeches clearly favored Wilson.[64]

La Follette's most trenchant attacks arrived in the final installments of his autobiography. First, he criticized Roosevelt's progressive record, describing his failure to enact substantive legislation during his presidency and his refusal to support La Follette's Wisconsin delegation in the 1904 credentials fight—a charge that was particularly damning in light of Roosevelt's complaints about delegate theft. Then he moved on to the 1912 campaign. He expounded his theory that Roosevelt had used him as a stalking horse, deliberately manipulating his supporters to set him up for a fall. Nor did he spare his erstwhile advocates—Pinchot, Cummins, Johnson, and other progressives who deserted him when Roosevelt joined the field.

La Follette's anti-Roosevelt vendetta was effective, but it cost him his reputation. The vindictiveness of the accusations belied his claims to be above personal feuds, and the unsubstantiated allegations made him look paranoid. By naming the people he considered traitors to the cause, he further alienated his old allies and splintered the progressive faction of the Republican Party. He would always be recognized as a pioneer of the progressive movement, but he forever sacrificed his place as its leader.

MILWAUKEE, WISCONSIN, OCTOBER 14, 1912

Roosevelt raced across the country at even more breathtaking pace than during his primary campaign six months earlier. In September, he traveled a 9,000-mile circuit around the nation. At every stop, thousands of ecstatic supporters greeted him with cheers and hymns, crowding close enough to touch his feet. Roosevelt seldom indulged them with soaring oratory, however. On the stump, he exchanged religious-themed rhetoric for more conventional campaign speeches that focused on his policies and, more often, his opponents.[65]

He wasted little time on Taft. "I never discuss dead issues," he shrugged. In North Dakota, he took a shot at La Follette. "Look out for the man who is going about attacking the Progressive party," he warned. "Any man claiming to be a Progressive that does not heartily support the Progressive party is merely a tool." For the most part, he concentrated his fire on Woodrow Wilson. He had trouble drawing a bead on him though. First he dismissed him as a stooge of the bosses, then a fusty academic wedded to outmoded doctrines, then a naïve rookie.[66]

By contrast, Wilson was proving a disciplined campaigner who always hit his mark. In speech after speech, he charged that Roosevelt was too paternalistic and too close to the trusts. Pro-Wilson papers assisted with the first charge, caricaturing Roosevelt as Caesar and Napoleon, and

La Follette's Senate investigations underscored the second. Even Eugene Debs, the perennial Socialist candidate, laid into the Colonel for belatedly embracing a cause "that four years ago he denounced as anarchistic" In less reputable papers, slanderous and unfounded rumors of alcoholism dogged him.

Roosevelt fell onto the defensive, spending much of the time rebutting the charges against him. He had trouble articulating why a large federal government—an unattractive idea in the abstract—was necessary for progressive reform and why people should put their trust in "government by experts," as Wilson put it. In Atlanta, he all but called Wilson a liar, which did not play well in the Democratic South where Wilson had grown up. When the crowd heckled him, Roosevelt jumped onto the speaker's table and yelled, "I'll get up here so that you'll all have a chance to see me," momentarily silencing the stunned hecklers.[67]

One man had traveled all the way from New York to see the Colonel in Atlanta, but he did not get the opportunity. After missing Roosevelt's speech, John Schrank left town by train, hoping to catch his quarry in another city.[68]

BY THE TIME ROOSEVELT RETURNED TO OYSTER BAY, his voice had given out, and he was thoroughly exhausted. "I am hoarse and dirty and filled with a bored loathing of myself whenever I get up to speak," he wrote to his son Kermit on the way home. But he wasn't finished. A week later, his campaign manager sent him west to hit a few cities that he'd missed on the first lap. That was how he ended up in Milwaukee on October 14.

At his speech that evening, he intended to refute La Follette's charges that he had rebuffed the Wisconsin Half-Breeds at the 1904 convention. He planned to read a letter proving that he had endorsed their cause—after the Wisconsin Supreme Court decided in La Follette's favor. Naturally, he would not read from the letters he'd written before the convention.[69]

He left his hotel at 8 p.m. A throng of people had gathered around the automobile that was to take him to the auditorium. His escorts cleared a path, and he climbed into the rear seat. The crowd edged closer. A short, plump man pushed his way to the front. The Colonel stood up in the car and tipped his hat to the crowd.

Bang. Roosevelt's knees bent and he clutched the car door. His stenographer, a six-foot tall former football player, hurtled through the air and landed on John Schrank's shoulder. Schrank went down. The stenographer seized the revolver and wrapped his arm around the man's neck. The enraged crowd was shouting, "Lynch him! Kill him!"

Roosevelt straightened up and raised his hand. "Don't hurt him," he said. "Bring him here. I want to see him." He reached down and took

Shrank's head in both hands. "What did you do it for?" he asked. "Oh, what's the use? Turn him over to the police."

He gave another reassuring tip of the hat to the crowd, and his car roared off. As they rode, one of Roosevelt's secretaries examined his overcoat. "Why, Colonel, you have a hole in your overcoat," he exclaimed. "He has shot you."

"I know it," Roosevelt replied, and opened up his coat. His shirt was drenched with blood.

The other men insisted on taking him to the hospital, but Roosevelt refused. He felt the way he did when he charged up San Juan Hill so many years ago—that if he were hit he must keep straight on as long as he could. "I know I am good now," he said. "I don't know how long I may be. This may be my last talk in this cause to our people, and while I am good I am going to drive to the hall and deliver my speech."

When they reached the auditorium, he finally consented to let a doctor examine the bloody hole that gaped below his right nipple, but he still refused to go to the hospital. After covering the wound with a handkerchief, he buttoned up his coat. "Now, gentlemen, let's go in," he said and strode onto the stage.

When the introductory speaker described the assassination attempt, not everyone believed him. "Fake!" someone shouted.

Roosevelt stepped forward and opened his coat, revealing the red stain. Gasps rippled through the crowd. He grinned and boasted, "It takes more than one bullet to kill a Bull Moose." But when he took his speech out from his right breast pocket, he flinched. There was a bullet hole straight through it. Fifty pages of thick paper folded in half plus one steel spectacles case had saved his life. He held up the perforated pages to the crowd.

"The bullet is in me now," he told them, "so that I can not make a very long speech, but I will try my best." He swore that he did not "care a rap" about what happened to him. "I am ahead of the game, anyway. No man has had a happier life than I have led." His only concern was for the progressive cause. "I never in my life had any movement in which I was able to serve with such wholehearted devotion as in this."

"And now, friends," he continued, "I want to take advantage of this incident and say a word of a solemn warning...it is a very natural thing that weak and vicious minds should be inflamed to acts of violence by the kind of awful mendacity and abuse that have been heaped upon me for the last three months by the papers...they cannot month in and month out and year in and year out make the kind of untruthful, of bitter assaults that they have made and not expect that brutal violent natures...will be unaffected by it."

As he spoke, his friends kept trying to persuade him to stop talking, but Roosevelt waved them off. He turned to his prepared speech and doggedly worked his way through in spite of the bullet-sized gaps in the text. When he mentioned La Follette's name, the crowd cheered so much that he could not make himself heard, but he persevered and said his piece.[70]

After an hour and twenty minutes, Roosevelt finally concluded the address and agreed to go to the hospital.

"Oh, gosh! Shot again!" he said to the press photographers as he climbed into the ambulance.

The X-rays located the bullet next to one of his ribs, which had cracked on impact. The surgeons decided not to remove it. They inoculated Roosevelt for tetanus, monitored him for infection, and ordered him to rest. One of the doctors assured him, "Mr. President, you were elected last night. It was the turning of the tide in your favor."

The next day, telegrams arrived from all over the world. The king of England, the kaiser of Germany, and the emperor of Japan expressed their concern. Closer to home, the President of the United States was particularly agitated. "I am greatly shocked to hear of the outrageous and deplorable assault made upon you," Taft wired, "and I earnestly hope and pray that your recovery may be speedy and without suffering."

Governor Wilson sent his "warmest sympathy" and offered to suspend his campaign. "Bully," Roosevelt said when he read the telegram. "Wilson is of the right American blood, notwithstanding the fact that he and I are opposed in a political sense."

Senator La Follette expressed "profound regret that your life should have been in peril" and wished him a speedy recovery. "Let me see that again," Roosevelt said. He immediately dictated a thank you reply, as he had for Taft and Wilson. A few days later, *La Follette's Weekly* praised Roosevelt for "the spirit with which he met the ordeal."[71]

These expressions of goodwill did not end the feuds or change the course of history. Roosevelt, Taft, and La Follette still despised one another. Roosevelt and Wilson were still hostile. But for a moment, at least, the malice of the bitter campaign gave way to a breath of humanity. A madman's bullet had finally compelled these resentful men to unbutton their overcoats and reveal the better angels of their natures.

NOVEMBER 5, 1912

A chastened nation drifted quietly through the final weeks of the campaign. When Roosevelt rose from his sick bed and spoke to a rapturous crowd of 17,000 at Madison Square Garden—with many thousands more waiting outside—most Americans could not help but cheer with them.[72]

The outpouring of affection did not save his candidacy, however. His new party was too disorganized, his political base too fractured, his opponent too strong. Roosevelt won 6 states, 88 electoral delegates, and 27 percent of the popular vote—the best third-party showing in American history. It was not nearly enough. Wilson soared above him with 42 percent of the popular vote and a landslide 435 electoral votes. Roosevelt took some consolation in beating his successor to a frazzle—Taft won only Utah and New Hampshire, a mere eight electoral votes, the worst defeat of any presidential incumbent.

The Progressive Party fared worse than its presidential nominee. Albert Beveridge lost his race for governor of Indiana, as did every other Bull Moose gubernatorial candidate except Hiram Johnson of California. In Congress, the new party won only ten House races and not a single Senate race. "Well, we have gone down in a smashing defeat," Roosevelt admitted to Kermit, "whether it is a Waterloo or a Bull Run, only time will tell." In public, he blustered, "The Progressive Party has come to stay...So far from being over, the battle has just begun." In private, he raged against those he blamed for his defeat—Elihu Root, William Taft, and "that vindictive and unscrupulous faker" Bob La Follette.[73]

The Standpatters could not take much pleasure in the Bull Moose losses, for their own thrashing was even worse. The once unsinkable Republican battleship, which had ruled the seas for 16 years, lay torn and broken on the shoals. The new Democratic dreadnought glided up and blasted it to shreds. When the smoke cleared, the Democrats led the Senate 51 to 44 and the House 290 to 164.

In addition to becoming a minority party, the Republican congressional leaders had been decimated. At the head of the pack, Uncle Joe lost the seat he had held for a record 38 years. "Let me tell you something," he told a reporter, chewing his cigar and staring at the ceiling. "The Republican party is still a great, big patriotic party. It is not dead, and it never will die...The Progressive movement and its effect on the old party will not be everlasting."[74]

Bob La Follette disagreed. "The country is progressive," he told his magazine readers. "The rank and file of the Republican party are progressive." Now that the false prophets and bumbling patsies were out of the way, he was sure that his rising movement would overwhelm the remaining Standpatters. "Freed from the leadership of both Roosevelt and Taft," he predicted, "progressive leadership in the Republican party will now assert itself and the next National Republican Convention will be overwhelmingly progressive."[75]

Amid the bluster and recriminations that followed the election, few Republican and Progressive leaders appreciated the enormity of what had just happened. After eight years of political strife, the wall of obstruction that had blocked progress for half a century lay in ruins. The Standpatters were overthrown, the Bourbons and bosses were marginalized, and the progressives were ascendant. On the long trail of history, it mattered little whether the President was a Democratic progressive, Republican progressive, or Bull Moose progressive. He was progressive. The majority of the Senate was progressive. The majority of the House was progressive. Under President Woodrow Wilson, the government was about to embark on the greatest political revolution since the Civil War, which would set America's course for the next hundred years.

"A great cause has triumphed," Wilson declared the night of his election. "Every Democrat, every true progressive, of whatever alliance, must now lend his full force and enthusiasm to the fulfillment of the people's hope—the establishment of the people's right—so that justice and progress may go hand in hand."[76]

EPILOGUE

It is a damned outrage to put me into the "venerable statesman" class, and I don't like it.

—Uncle Joe[1]

WASHINGTON, DC, MARCH 4, 1913

The midday sun peeked through the clouds as if to catch a glimpse of this new president. He stood on the East Portico of the Capitol looking out over a patchwork of humanity that stretched out in every direction. Mounted soldiers maintained a perimeter around the staircase.

"Let them come up as close as they please," Wilson ordered. "I am going to talk to them and want them to hear me." With a whoop, thousands of people rushed forward into the empty space, shouting "Good boy, Woodrow!" "Oh, you Woodrow!" "What's the matter with Woodrow!" "He's all right!"[2]

Even with the audience standing close, his voice had little hope of reaching more than a fraction of the crowd. It was a vague, uncertain speech that gave little hint of the dramatic changes to come. In tones of wonder and humility, he described the progressive awakening of the nation. He spoke not as one who woke the people but as one had woken with them. "Some old things with which we had grown familiar," he reflected, "have altered their aspect as we have latterly looked critically upon them, with fresh, awakened eyes; have dropped their disguises and shown themselves alien and sinister..." He argued that the nation had a duty "to cleanse, to reconsider, to restore, to correct the evil" that it had recently discovered, a moral obligation that transcended partisan divisions and personal rivalries. "Men's hearts wait upon us," he exhorted, "men's lives hang in the balance; men's hopes call upon us to say what we will do. Who shall live up to the great trust? Who dares fail to try? I summon all honest men, all patriotic, all forward-looking men, to my side. God helping me, I will not fail them, if they will but counsel and sustain me!"[3]

Congress answered his call. Over the next four years, a bipartisan coalition of progressive legislators enacted the most comprehensive political and institutional reforms since the nation's founding. It began as the First Congress had begun—with revenue. By the time Wilson took office, three-quarters of the states had ratified Aldrich's income tax amendment, enshrining it in the Constitution as the Sixteenth Amendment. Congress immediately began work on a new revenue bill. In contrast to Taft, Wilson worked aggressively to prevent legislators from hiking up tariff rates for favored industries. The resulting bill slashed tariffs by a third and created a new federal income tax with a top marginal rate of 7 percent.[4]

The Federal Reserve Act of 1913 superseded the feeble Aldrich-Vreeland emergency currency act. It created a central banking system with the power to issue currency and set interest rates. In many ways, the new Federal Reserve resembled the blueprints from Jekyll Island, but to Aldrich's dismay, Wilson insisted that the government, rather than private bankers, dominate the Federal Reserve Board of Governors. The Federal Reserve eased the cyclical currency shortages and financial panics, though it did not always act aggressively enough to stop them—most notoriously in 1929. Its covert origins as the brainchild of New York bankers at a millionaires' island resort have provided fodder for conspiracy theorists ever since.[5]

In accordance with Wilson's New Freedom campaign, the Clayton Anti-Trust Act of 1914 outlawed price discrimination and gave the President more power to block corporate mergers. Though weaker than the antitrust legislation drafted by Brandeis and La Follette, the Clayton Act remains the cornerstone of American antitrust law to this day.[6]

Not all of the progressives' aspirations were realized during Wilson's presidency. The courts, still dominated by Gilded Age judges, impeded labor reform. Like Albert Beveridge's child labor bill, the Keating-Owen Act of 1916 prohibited interstate transportation of goods produced by children, but the Supreme Court overthrew it. Child labor would remain legal in many states until FDR's New Deal. The Adamson Act of 1916 that established eight-hour workdays and overtime rates for railroad employees avoided the same fate because it was limited to workers engaged in interstate commerce, while the Workingmen's Compensation Act of 1916 applied only to federal employees.[7]

In other cases, Congress passed Constitutional amendments to override the courts. In 1913, the states ratified the Seventeenth Amendment mandating direct election of US senators. In 1920, the final year of Wilson's presidency, the Eighteenth Amendment prohibited the manufacture, sale, and transportation of alcohol—over the president's objections. The Nineteenth Amendment gave women the right to vote a few months later.

By that point, American involvement in World War I had broken the progressive alliance and stalled Wilson's unprecedented string of domestic achievements. The most prominent opponent of the war effort was a certain short Wisconsin senator with a large pompadour. When La Follette led a small band of progressive senators in a sensational filibuster to try to keep America out of the war, Wilson denounced him and his allies as "a little group of willful men representing no opinion but their own."[8]

Theodore Roosevelt naturally agreed. Vilifying La Follette as "the most sinister foe of democracy" and a "skunk" who "ought to be hung," he proposed sending him to the Reichstag. "There he would be in entirely appropriate surroundings," he sneered, "whereas in the senate of the United States he is a cause for shame and humiliation for every worthy American."[9]

The outbreak of war made Roosevelt sick with envy. He repeatedly petitioned Wilson for permission to lead a volunteer cavalry division into Belgium's trench-slashed fields—where machine guns would have mown down his Rough Riders in a flash. The War Department laughed him off.[10]

Roosevelt had reconciled with the Republican leaders by then. A progressive crusader no longer, he struck a deal to bring the limping Progressive Party back into the Republican fold during the 1916 presidential campaign.

His icy relations with Taft took somewhat longer to thaw. Six years after the divisive Republican convention, their paths crossed at a Chicago hotel a few blocks from the Coliseum. Roosevelt, eating alone in the dining room, noticed that the room had gone still. He looked up. There was William H. Taft standing over him. Roosevelt threw down his napkin and took his old friend's hand. As they grasped each other by the shoulder, the other guests cheered. Roosevelt invited Taft to sit, and they spoke for half an hour, bonding over their mutual contempt for Woodrow Wilson. They soon resumed their old correspondence but never saw each other again. On January 5, 1920, Roosevelt died in his sleep from a blood clot.[11]

Taft's dream of becoming chief justice came true the following year. Despite a conservative voting record, his deft leadership earned the respect of his colleague Justice Louis Brandeis, who marveled, "It's very difficult for me to understand why a man who is so good as Chief Justice . . . could have been so bad as President."[12]

Uncle Joe returned to Congress in 1914. He served another eight years and supported the President's war effort—even though Wilson was a Democrat. When Cannon retired at age 86, a new magazine called *Time* featured his wizened face on the cover of its first issue. The Cannon House Office Building is named in his honor.

Nelson Aldrich died of a stroke in 1915. He lived just long enough to see the fulfillment of his greatest legislative accomplishments: the federal income tax (which he regarded as socialistic and unconstitutional) and the Federal Reserve (which he also regarded as socialistic and unconstitutional). In addition to his unintended legislative legacy, Aldrich is the forefather of a progressive political dynasty that includes West Virginia Senator Jay Rockefeller, a Democrat, and former vice president Nelson Aldrich Rockefeller, who led the left wing of the Republican Party in the mid-twentieth century. The Rockefeller Republicans, as the liberal faction was known, remained a potent force in the GOP until the late 1970s. At that point, a conservative insurgency employing La Follette-style grassroots tactics purged the remaining progressives from the party.[13]

The golden era of muckraking was over by the time Wilson became president. The new doctrine of *journalistic objectivity* gradually supplanted it, though modern investigative journalism still honors its pioneers— Steffens, Baker, and Tarbell. Baker supported Wilson in 1912 and later wrote an eight-volume Pulitzer-winning biography of his life. Steffens's quest to defeat the System took him farther afield. In 1919, he visited Russia, fresh from its revolution, and interviewed Chairman Vladimir Lenin. "I have seen the future," Steffens reported optimistically, "and it works."[14]

After Wilson, a backlash against the progressive movement caused both parties to retreat into conservatism. In 1924, La Follette grew so frustrated with the two major parties that he finally broke from the Republicans and ran for president as an independent. Once again, he played the valiant, hopeless underdog, sprinting across the country with little money or national organization. He captured 17 percent of the popular vote but won only Wisconsin's 13 electoral votes. Undeterred, he insisted that the loss was just a "skirmish" and began laying plans for the next election. "The Progressives will close ranks for the next battle," he promised.

Lincoln Steffens sighed, "His plans and his party make me tired, but he, the incurable, unreformable Bob, is wonderful."[15]

But it was to be Fighting Bob's last battle. He died of heart failure on June 18, 1925. Belle held his hand as he slipped away, "pouring out the love and devotion of a lifetime in the last long farewell...telling him her vision of the nobility and beauty of his life and work." His daughter Fola remarked, "His passing was mysteriously peaceful for one who had stood so long on the battle line."[16]

ACKNOWLEDGMENTS

I COULD NEVER CREATE SUCH A BOOK BY MYSELF. THANK YOU TO EVERYONE WHO HELPED ME turn a hazy and uncertain idea into words and sentences, pages and chapters. To Tanya, for loving me and listening to every word. To Mom, Dad, Shnave, and Laura, for your love and counsel. To Jerry, my brilliant adviser on all things book-related. To Colin, for your shrewd commentary and for conceiving the title. To my fellow writers from the Polish beer garden, my colleagues at dagblog.com, and my wonderful friends for your support and fellowship. To Jane, for championing me. To Karen, Katie, Lauren, and the Palgrave Macmillan team for making this book happen. And finally, to the good folks of Cafe Pick Me who have given me safe harbor these many months. Thank you.

NOTES

CHAPTER 1: THE BOLT

1. "Let Tariff Alone!," *Washington Post*, Nov. 17, 1905.
2. "The Old Red Gym: Gateway to the Future," accessed Oct. 14, 2013, http://hum.lss.wisc.edu/uwhist/redgym.html; "Madison Landmarks;" accessed Oct. 14, 2013, http://cityofmadison.com/planning/landmark/Madison%20Landmarks.htm.
3. "Blows Are Struck in Convention Hall," *Milwaukee Journal*, May 18, 1904; Albert O. Barton, *La Follette's Winning of Wisconsin (1894–1904)* (Des Moines, IA: Homestead Co., 1922), 346–350.
4. La Follette pronounced his name with a short *o* and an emphasis on the first syllable so that it sounded like "wallet."
5. Barton, *La Follette's Winning of Wisconsin*, 351–355.
6. Ibid., 355–360.
7. "Bolt in Wisconsin," *New York Times*, May 19, 1904; "Bolt in Wisconsin," *Arizona Republican*, May 19, 1904; "Political Gossip," *Washington Post*, May 20, 1904.
8. "Nicholas Murray Butler to TR," May 19, 1904, Nicholas Murray Butler Papers, Rare Books and Manuscript Library, Columbia University.
9. "TR to Nicholas Murray Butler," May 21, 1904, Nicholas Murray Butler Papers; Fred Greenbaum, *Robert Marion La Follette* (Boston: Twayne Publishers, 1975), 69.
10. "TR to To Lemuel Ely Quigg," Feb. 21, 1900, in Theodore Roosevelt, *Letters* (Cambridge, MA: Harvard Univ. Press, 1951–1954), 2:1200.
11. Ray Stannard Baker, *American Chronicle: The Autobiography of Ray Stannard Baker* (New York: C. Scribner's Sons, 1945), 192.
12. Lewis L. Gould, *The Presidency of Theodore Roosevelt*, 2nd ed. (Lawrence: Univ. Press of Kansas, 2011), 31–32, 45–50, 205–210; Gabriel Kolko, *The Triumph of Conservatism: A Re-Interpretation of American History, 1900–1916*, Kindle ed. (New York: The Free Press, 1963), 70, 74.
13. George Edwin Mowry, *Theodore Roosevelt and the Progressive Movement* (New York: Hill & Wang, 1946), 16–17; Gould, *The Presidency of Theodore Roosevelt*, 23–38; Kolko, *The Triumph of Conservatism*, 70–73, 83–88; Nathaniel Wright Stephenson, *Nelson W. Aldrich, a Leader in American Politics* (New York: C. Scribner's Sons, 1930), 193–199; L. White Busbey, *Uncle Joe Cannon: The Story of a Pioneer American* (New York: H. Holt & Co., 1927), 208–214.

14. TR to John Hay, Mar. 12, 1903, in Roosevelt, *Letters*, 4:445; TR to John C. Spooner, Jan. 25, 1904, in Dorothy Ganfield Fowler, *John Coit Spooner, Defender of Presidents* (New York: University Publishers, 1961), 282; TR to O. H. Platt, Dec. 9, 1903, in Roosevelt, *Letters*, 4:272.

15. TR to William Edward Cramer, May 27, 1904, in Roosevelt, *Letters*, 4:805; Fowler, *John Coit Spooner*, 305–307; Barton, *La Follette's Winning of Wisconsin*, 379–380.

16. "White Girl and Negro Head March of States for the Rough Rider," *Atlanta Constitution*, June 24, 1904; James Creelman, "America at Flood Tide," *Pearson's Magazine*, July 1906, 3; "Personality of Uncle Joe, Late Czar of the House," *Atlanta Constitution*, March 20, 1910; "Speaker Cannon on Panics and Other Things," *New York Times*, Dec. 1, 1907.

17. *2 Cong. Rec.*, H1609 (1874).

18. "House Machine Works as the Speaker Wills," *New York Times*, May 28, 1906.

19. Creelman, "America at Flood Tide," 9; Blair Bolles, *Tyrant from Illinois: Uncle Joe Cannon's Experiment with Personal Power* (Westport, CT: Greenwood Press, 1974), 11.

20. "The Republican Convention," *Wall Street Journal*, June 24, 1904.

21. "National Drama Reaches Climax," *Chicago Daily Tribune*, June 24, 1904.

22. "Nominating Roosevelt," *New York Tribune*, June 24, 1904.

23. "Convention Meets," *Washington Post*, June 22, 1904; "Tame Convention; Anxiety to End It," *New York Times*, June 22, 1904; "Cannon's Ruse Keeps Convention," *New York Times*, June 23, 1904.

24. Henry Kanegsberg, ed., *Addresses at the Republican National Convention, 1904: Nominating for President, Hon. Theodore Roosevelt of New York, for Vice-President Hon. Charles Warren Fairbanks of Indiana* (I. H. Blanchard Co., 1904), 85; "Convention Side-Lights," *Baltimore Sun*, June 23, 1904.

25. William Hard, "'Uncle Joe' Cannon," *Collier's*, May 30, 1908.

26. "'Stand Pat'-Hanna," *Baltimore Sun*, Sept. 28, 1902; Busbey, *Uncle Joe Cannon*, 214. The term "standpatter" originally applied only to opponents of tariff reform but eventually took on a broader connotation as well.

27. Busbey, *Uncle Joe Cannon*, 208; Edmund Morris, *Theodore Rex* (New York: Random House, 2001), 208–209.

28. "Day of Speeches in Convention," *Chicago Daily Tribune*, June 24, 1904.

29. Mark O. Hatfield, *Vice Presidents of the United States, 1789–1993* (US Government Printing Office, 1997), 316.

30. "Fairbanks Shuns the Convention," *Chicago Daily Tribune*, June 24, 1904.

31. "Slap at Roosevelt," *Baltimore Sun*, June 18, 1904; Belle Case La Follette and Fola La Follette, *Robert M. La Follette, June 14, 1855–June 18, 1925* (New York: Macmillan, 1953), 180.

32. "Committee Accused," *Washington Post*, June 22, 1904; *Chicago Record-Herald*, June 19, 1904, quoted in "How It Was Done," *Atlanta Constitution*, June 24, 1904.

33. "Ready for Ticket," *Washington Post*, June 23, 1904.

34. Lincoln Steffens, *The Autobiography of Lincoln Steffens* (Berkeley, CA: Heyday Books, 1931), 257–263.

35. Ibid., 344–346.

36. Ibid., 453.

37. Ibid., 454–456.

38. Ibid., 456.
39. La Follette and La Follette, *Robert M. La Follette*, 182; Lincoln Steffens, "Enemies of the Republic: Wisconsin," *McClure's Magazine*, Oct. 1904, 457.
40. Nancy C. Unger, *Fighting Bob La Follette: The Righteous Reformer*, Kindle ed. (Chapel Hill: Univ. of North Carolina Press, 2000), 56–57, 93.
41. Joe Sonderman and Mike Truax, *St. Louis: The 1904 World's Fair* (Charleston, SC: Arcadia Publishing, 2008), 9; Major J. Lowenstein, *Official Guide to the Louisiana Purchase Exposition at the City of St. Louis, State of Missouri, April 30th to December 1st, 1904* (St. Louis: Official Guide Co., 1904), 61, 92, 134–135; John Brisben Walker, *The World's Fair* (Cosmopolitan Pub. Co., 1904), 509, 522, 571.
42. Steffens, *Autobiography*, 458–459.
43. Steffens, "Enemies of the Republic," 566. Historian David Thelen has challenged La Follette's account, suggesting that Phil Spooner "probably offered only token resistance." La Follette often embellished his own history, and the details should be treated with skepticism, but Steffens corroborated Phil Spooner's hostility in an interview, and Thelen's claim in this particular is speculative. See David P. Thelen, "The Boss and the Upstart: Keyes and La Follette, 1880–1884," *Wisconsin Magazine of History* 47, no. 2, Dec. 1, 1963, 113.
44. Richard Barry, "A Radical in Power: A Study of La Follette," *The Outlook*, Nov. 29, 1922, 567.
45. La Follette and La Follette, *Robert M. La Follette*, 65, 78–79, 86; Unger, *Fighting Bob La Follette*, 85, 94.
46. Steffens, "Enemies of the Republic," 566–567; Unger, *Fighting Bob La Follette*, 90–91.
47. Steffens, "Enemies of the Republic," 571; Robert Marion La Follette, *La Follette's Autobiography: A Personal Narrative of Political Experiences* (Madison: The Robert M. La Follette Co., 1913), 139–149.
48. La Follette, *Autobiography*, 164; Steffens, "Enemies of the Republic," 571.
49. Kenneth Acrea, "The Wisconsin Reform Coalition, 1892 to 1900: La Follette's Rise to Power," *Wisconsin Magazine of History* 52, no. 2 (Dec. 1, 1968): 132–157; David P. Thelen, *Robert M. La Follette and the Insurgent Spirit* (Madison: Univ. of Wisconsin Press, 1986), 19–31; Unger, *Fighting Bob La Follette*, 105–119.
50. La Follette, *Autobiography*, 268, 388; Unger, *Fighting Bob La Follette*, 123–124.
51. Allen Fraser Lovejoy, *La Follette and the Establishment of the Direct Primary in Wisconsin, 1890–1904* (New Haven: Yale Univ. Press, 1941), 79–83; Greenbaum, *Robert Marion La Follette*, 57–58.
52. John C. Spooner to S. M. Booth, Mar. 28, 1903, in Fowler, *John Coit Spooner*, 299.
53. Steffens, *Autobiography*, 459; *Milwaukee Sentinel*, June 28, 1904, quoted in Carroll Pollock Lahman, *Robert Marion La Follette as Public Speaker and Political Leader (1855–1905)* (Madison: Univ. of Wisconsin, 1939), 769.
54. "Loudest Cheers for Cleveland," *Chicago Daily Tribune*, July 7, 1904; "Convention Wild Over Cleveland," *New York Times*, July 7, 1904; C. H. Patton, "All Night at the Democratic Convention: Some Impressions of a Minister in the Gallery," *Congregationalist and Christian World (1901–1906)*, July 23, 1904.
55. "Parker at Close Range," *Baltimore Sun*, April 4, 1904; "It Would Be an Interesting Race," *New York Sun*, March 9, 1904.

56. "The Democratic Convention," *New York Tribune*, July 7, 1904; "How Hill Planned Parker's Nomination," *Los Angeles Times*, July 14, 1904; "Judge Parker's Presidential Room, " *Baltimore Sun*, March 31, 1904.

57. "Parker Bathing When Notified," *Atlanta Constitution*, July 10, 1904. Parker allowed only one exception to his vow of silence. The day of his nomination, he sent a terse telegram to the convention leaders in St. Louis insisting that the Democratic Party repudiate Bryan's anti-gold-standard campaign— thereby antagonizing the populists after all.

58. "The Notification," *New York Tribune*, July 28, 1904; "Roosevelt Receives Formal Notification," *New York Times*, July 28, 1904.

59. Ibid.

60. Ibid.

61. Ibid.

62. "President Is Notified," *Baltimore Sun*, July 28, 1904; Theodore Roosevelt, *The Right of the People to Rule* (New York, 1912), http://memory.loc.gov/ammem/collections/troosevelt_film/trfsnd.html.

63. "President Is Notified," *Baltimore Sun*; "The Roosevelt Notification," *Atlanta Constitution*, July 28, 1904.

64. "Pen Portrait of a Possible President," *New York Times*, April 3, 1904; "Judge Parker Takes Up Collection in Church," *New York Times*, July 11, 1904.

65. "Notified by Clark," *Washington Post*, Aug. 11, 1904; "Parker Accepts for Single Term," *New York Times*, Aug. 11, 1904.

66. Democratic National Committee, *Campaign Text Book of the Democratic Party of the United States, 1904* (New York: Metropolitan Printing, 1904), 32; "Enthusiasm Dampened," *New York Tribune*, Aug. 11, 1904.

67. "Enthusiasm Dampened." *New York Tribune*; "Judge Parker's Speech of Acceptance," *Current Literature*, Sept. 1904, 204; "Parker Has Spoken," *Gunton's Magazine*, Sept. 1904, 257–261.

68. "No Stumping Tour for Judge Parker," *New York Times*, Aug. 23, 1904.

69. "Parker a Disappointment," *New York Tribune*, Oct. 31, 1904; "The Contest of 1904," *Los Angeles Times*, Sept. 25, 1904. "The Progress of the World," *American Monthly Review of Reviews*, Nov. 1904, 522.

70. La Follette and La Follette, *Robert M. La Follette*, 184; "Governor Uses His Auto," *Milwaukee Journal*, Sept. 3, 1904; "The Winton 1904 Touring Car," *Dun's Review*, March 1904, 64.

71. Barton, *La Follette's Winning of Wisconsin*, 425–426, 432–436; La Follette and La Follette, *Robert M. La Follette*, 336–337.

72. Agnews, "Senatorial Characters"; Parker Payson, *Great American Speeches: 80 Years of Political Oratory*, VHS, vol. 1 (New York: Pieri & Spring Productions, 1997).

73. La Follette, *Autobiography*, 338–339; La Follette and La Follette, *Robert M. La Follette*, 172.

74. La Follette and La Follette, *Robert M. La Follette*, 185.

75. Steffens, "Enemies of the Republic," 579.

76. La Follette and La Follette, *Robert M. La Follette*, 185.

77. "Spooner Denies Seat Was Bought," *Chicago Daily Tribune*, Oct. 3, 1904.

78. "Steffens' Story Angers Quarles," *Chicago Daily Tribune*, Sept. 29, 1904.

79. La Follette and La Follette, *Robert M. La Follette*, 185.

80. TR to Henry Cabot Lodge, Oct. 2, 1904, in Roosevelt, *Letters*, 4:965.

81. TR to George Bruce Cortelyou, Oct. 6, 1904, in Roosevelt, *Letters*, 4:973.

82. "Government Controlled by Trusts, Says Parker," *New York Times*, Oct. 25, 1904.

83. TR to Kermit Roosevelt, Oct. 26, 1904, in Roosevelt, *Letters*, 4:993.

84. TR to George Bruce Cortelyou, Oct. 26, 1904, in Roosevelt, *Letters*, 4:995; Gould, *The Presidency of Theodore Roosevelt*, 138.

85. Morris, *Theodore Rex*, 358–360.

86. "Parker, the Orator, Cheered by Throngs," *New York Times*, Nov. 3, 1904.

87. "Thunder of Cheers Greets Judge Parker," *New York Times*, Nov. 1, 1904.

88. "Roosevelt Speaks," *New York Times*, Nov. 5, 1904.

89. "How President Voted," *New York Tribune*, Nov. 9, 1904.

90. Gould, *The Presidency of Theodore Roosevelt*, 121; Isabella Hagner, "Memoirs of Isabella Hagner 1901–1905," *White House History*, accessed Aug. 1, 2012, http://www.whitehousehistory.org/whha_publications/publications_white-househistory-articles.html.

91. "Parker to Roosevelt," *New York Times*, Nov. 9, 1904.

92. "Enjoys His Triumph," *New York Times*, Nov. 9, 1904; "Joy at the White House," *New York Tribune*, Nov. 9, 1904.

93. Barton, *La Follette's Winning of Wisconsin*, 446.

94. "How La Follette Won," *New York Tribune*, Nov. 13, 1904.

95. "Mr. Roosevelt's Great Victory," *New York Times*, Nov. 9, 1904; "A Sin to Laugh, Says Knox," *New York Times*, Nov. 9, 1904; "Roosevelt Was the Sole Issue," *Chicago Daily Tribune*, Nov. 10, 1904; "What the Papers Say," *Baltimore Sun*, Nov. 10, 1904; "La Follette for Senate," *Milwaukee Journal*, Dec. 3, 1904.

96. "The Beginning of a New Era," *Chicago Daily Tribune*, Nov. 9, 1904.

CHAPTER 2: THE RAILROAD

1. James Creelman, "America at Flood Tide," *Pearson's Magazine*, July 1906, 16.

2. *Baltimore American*, July 7, 1828, quoted in John G. Davidson, "Fourth of July–Foundation of the Railroad," *Niles' Weekly Register*, July 12, 1828, 316; John F. Stover, *History of the Baltimore and Ohio Railroad* (W. Lafayette, IN: Purdue Univ. Press, 1987), 25–27, 95.

3. James L. Roark et al., *The American Promise: A History of the United States* (Macmillan, 2008), 438.

4. Howard Zinn, *A People's History of the United States* (New York: HarperCollins, 2010), 256; Ray Stannard Baker, "The Great 'Northern Pacific Deal'," *Collier's Weekly*, Nov. 30, 1901, 15.

5. *Hearings Before the Committee on Interstate and Foreign Commerce of the House of Representatives on Bills to Amend the Interstate Commerce Act*, 58th Cong., 3rd Sess., 35 (1905); Gabriel Kolko, *Railroads and Regulation, 1877–1916* (Westport, CT: Greenwood Press, 1976), 97, 198.

6. "Theodore Roosevelt: Fourth Annual Message," accessed Aug. 20, 2012, http://www.presidency.ucsb.edu/ws/index.php?pid=29545.

7. "Do Nothing Plan Hit by Roosevelt," *Chicago Daily Tribune*, Jan. 7, 1905; "President Advised," *Washington Post*, Jan. 8, 1905; "Weather Conditions.," *Washington Post*, Jan. 7, 1906.

8. Horace Samuel Merrill and Marion Merrill, *The Republican Command, 1897–1913* (Lexington: Univ. Press of Kentucky, 1971), 18; Stephenson, *Nelson W. Aldrich*, 134–137, 202, 204, fn. 443; Claude Gernade Bowers, *Beveridge and the Progressive Era* (Cambridge, MA: The Literary Guild, 1932), 136; "'The Big Five' Who Run the U.S. Senate," *New York Times*, Mar. 19, 1905. *New York Times* correspondent C. W. Thompson included Eugene Hale of Maine to make five, but historians with the benefit of private letters later concluded that Hale remained peripheral until the four began to disintegrate after Platt's death.

9. "President Advised," *Washington Post*.

10. Roosevelt, *Letters* 4:450.

11. Ibid., 4:1100.

12. Ibid., 4:1101; "To Call Extra Session for Rebate Question," Jan. 12, 1905. See also John Morton Blum, "Appendix 1: Theodore Roosevelt and the Legislative Process: Tariff Revision and Railroad Regulation, 1904–1906," in Roosevelt, *Letters*, 4:1138–1139; John Morton Blum, "Appendix 2: Theodore Roosevelt and the Hepburn Act: Toward an Orderly System of Control," in Roosevelt, *Letters*, 6:1561–1563.

13. Robert Harrison, *Congress, Progressive Reform, and the New American State*, Kindle ed. (Cambridge, UK: Cambridge Univ. Press, 2004), 59.

14. Jos Ohl, "Attitude of Railroads as to Rate Legislation," *Atlanta Constitution*, Jan. 23, 1905.

15. "The World's Diary: Day by Day," *The Search-Light*, Jan. 28, 1905, 46; William K. Howard, "Twenty-five United States Senators Estimated to Be Worth $171,000,000," *Washington Post*, May 27, 1906.

16. Ralph Ketcham, ed., *The Anti-Federalist Papers and the Constitutional Convention Debates* (New York: Penguin, 2003), 55.

17. Ibid., 54.

18. Harrison, *Congress, Progressive Reform, and the New American State*, 30–31.

19. Unger, *Fighting Bob La Follette*, 133–135; Herbert F. Margulies, "Robert M. La Follette Goes to the Senate, 1905," *Wisconsin Magazine of History* 59, no. 3 (April 1, 1976): 214–216; "La Follette Will Accept," *Washington Post*, Jan. 22, 1905.

20. "The Significance of La Follette's Election to the Senate," *Baltimore Sun*, Jan. 27, 1905.

21. Lincoln Steffens, "Rhode Island: A State for Sale," *McClure's Magazine*, Feb. 1905, 337.

22. "Aldrich as a Leader," *Baltimore Sun*, Dec. 29, 1901; "'The Big Five' Who Run the U.S. Senate," *New York Times*.

23. Matthew Josephson, *The Politicos, 1865–1896* (New York: Harcourt, Brace & World, 1966); Jerome L. Sternstein, "King Leopold II, Senator Nelson W. Aldrich, and the Strange Beginnings of American Economic Penetration of the Congo," *African Historical Studies* 2, no. 2 (Jan. 1, 1969): 193.

24. Steffens, "Rhode Island," 337.

25. Bernice Kert, *Abby Aldrich Rockefeller: The Woman in the Family* (New York: Random House, 1993), 12.

26. Steffens, "Rhode Island," 342.

27. "Ambrose Everett Burnside," *Encyclopedia Britannica Online* (Encyclopedia Britannica, 2012).

28. James Anthony Rosmond, "Nelson Aldrich, Theodore Roosevelt and the Tariff: A Study to 1905" (PhD diss., Univ. of North Carolina at Chapel Hill, 1974), 35–38; Steffens, *Autobiography*, 506; Nelson W. Aldrich Jr., *Old Money: The Mythology of Wealth in America*, exp. ed. (New York: Allworth Press, 1996), 20.

29. Steffens, "Rhode Island," 36–37; Jerome L. Sternstein, "Corruption in the Gilded Age Senate: Nelson W. Aldrich and the Sugar Trust," *Capitol Studies* 6, no. 1 (Spring 1978): 15–21.

30. "Largest in Rhode Island," *Boston Daily Globe*, Oct. 6, 1901; "A Notable Wedding," *Baltimore Sun*, Oct. 9, 1901; "Senator Aldrich Has a Charming Country Place Near Providence and Will Soon Erect a New House on It," *New York Tribune*, Jan. 4, 1903.

31. Martha Smith, "Hollywood Calls on Aldrich," *Providence Journal-Bulletin*, June 8, 1997; Richard Salit, "Rhode Island's Forgotten Mansion," *Providence Journal-Bulletin*, May 22, 1996; Aldrich, *Old Money*, 26; "Senator Aldrich Has a Charming Country Place..."

32. TR to Ray Stannard Baker, Nov. 13, 1905, in Roosevelt, *Letters*, 5:25.

33. *Ray Stannard Baker, Half-Length Portrait*, George Grantham Bain Collection, Library of Congress Prints and Photographs Division, accessed Oct. 30, 2013, http://www.loc.gov/pictures/item/2005690096/.

34. Ray Stannard Baker, "Theodore Roosevelt: A Character Sketch," *McClure's Magazine*, Nov. 1898; Baker, *American Chronicle*, 191.

35. Baker, *American Chronicle*, 192–193.

36. "Dissent from Pennsylvania," *Washington Post*, Feb. 4, 1905.

37. "Despite a Revolt," *Washington Post*, Feb. 4, 1905.

38. "To Pass H.R. 18588, the Railroad Rate Bill. (p. 2205)," *GovTrack.us*, accessed Aug. 22, 2012, http://www.govtrack.us/congress/votes/58-3/h75.

39. Jason Strykowski, "Santa Fe Ring," *Santa Fe New Mexican*, June 6, 2010; Simeon H. Newman, "The Santa Fe Ring: A Letter to the 'New York Sun'," *Arizona and the West* 12, no. 3 (Oct. 1, 1970): 269–288; Dave Townsend, "Chapter 2," *Alamogordo Daily News*, Jan. 18, 2012; John Alexander Williams, "Davis and Elkins of West Virginia: Businessmen in Politics" (PhD diss., Yale University, 1967), 137–159.

40. Harrison, *Congress, Progressive Reform, and the New American State*, 176.

41. "Elkins Blocks Way," *Baltimore Sun*, Feb. 22, 1905.

42. Morris, *Theodore Rex*, 454–483; "Oath and Address," *Washington Post*, Mar. 5, 1905; "Crowds See Oath of Office Taken," *Chicago Daily Tribune*, Mar. 5, 1905.

43. "Crowds See Oath of Office Taken," *Chicago Daily Tribune*; "President Takes Oath," *New York Times*, Mar. 5, 1905.

44. "President Takes Oath" *New York Times*.

45. Theodore Roosevelt, *The Roosevelt Policy: Speeches, Letters and State Papers, Relating to Corporate Wealth and Closely Allied Topics, of Theodore Roosevelt, President of the United States*, vol. 1 (New York: Current Literature Publishing, 1908), 247–248; "Crowds See Oath of Office Taken," *Chicago Daily Tribune*.

46. Roosevelt, *Letters*, 4:1156.

47. "Elkins Ready to Act," *Washington Post*, Mar. 8, 1905.

48. "Rate Hearings Begin," *New York Tribune*, April 18, 1905.

49. Stephenson, *Nelson W. Aldrich*, 262–265; "Senator Platt Dies," *Washington Post*, April 22, 1905; "Senator Beveridge Back," *New York Times*, June 7, 1905;

"Some Characteristic Anecdotes of Senators Aldrich and Hale," *New York Tribune*, May 1, 1910.

50. "La Follette Wins in Railway Bill," *Chicago Daily Tribune*, May 6, 1905; "La Follette May Not Accept Senatorship," May 15, 1905; "Wisconsin Gets Rate Bill," *Chicago Daily Tribune*, May 19, 1905; John R. Commons, "The La Follette Railroad Law in Wisconsin," *American Monthly Review of Reviews*, July 1905, 76–79. For a more critical analysis of La Follette's work, see Stanley Caine, "Why Railroads Supported Regulation: The Case of Wisconsin, 1905–1910," *The Business History Review* 44, no. 2 (July 1, 1970): 175–189.

51. "La Follette's Bill Passes," *New York Times*, June 2, 1905; "Anti-Lobby Bill Is Passed," *Chicago Daily Tribune*, June 10, 1905.

52. Baker, *American Chronicle*, 262–263.

53. Ray Stannard Baker, "The Railroad Rate: A Study in Commercial Autocracy," *McClure's Magazine*, Nov. 1905, 59.

54. Roosevelt, *Letters*, 5:25.

55. Baker, *American Chronicle*, 197.

56. Baker, "The Railroad Rate: A Study in Commercial Autocracy," 59.

57. Ibid., 47.

58. "Coming to Senate," *Washington Post*, Dec. 6, 1905; "The 'Wisconsin Idea' in the Senate," *Current Literature*, March 1905.

59. "Put La Follette in Cold Storage," *Chicago Daily Tribune*, Dec. 24, 1905; "La Follette Is Coming."

60. Jeffrey K. Tulis, *The Rhetorical Presidency* (Princeton: Princeton Univ. Press, 1987), 56; "The Message," *New York Times*, Dec. 6, 1905; "The Man and His Message," *Los Angeles Times*, Dec. 6, 1905.

61. Roosevelt, *The Roosevelt Policy*, 1:322–346.

62. "Elkins' Rate Views," *Washington Post*, Dec. 6, 1905; "Elkins Defines His View," *New York Times*, Dec. 8, 1905.

63. "Another Rate Bill," *New York Times*, Dec. 20, 1905; Theodore Roosevelt, *Theodore Roosevelt, an Autobiography* (New York: Macmillan, 1913), 435; Thomas Richard Ross, *Jonathan Prentiss Dolliver: A Study in Political Integrity and Independence* (Iowa City: State Historical Society of Iowa, 1958), 201, 241.

64. *New York World* quoted in "May Sit in Senate and Dictate Nation's Policy," *Washington Post*, Dec. 26, 1905; "Senate in Huff; Ready for Revolt," *Chicago Daily Tribune*, Dec. 22, 1905; "Mr. Spooner's Warning," *Atlanta Constitution*, Dec. 30, 1905; "Spooner's Original Speech on Government Divisions," *Milwaukee Journal*, Dec. 28, 1905.

CHAPTER 3: THE MUCK RAKE

1. "Cannon Cites the Bible in Anti-Hearst Speech," *New York Times*, Oct. 18, 1906.

2. "Leaves Madison for the Senate," *Milwaukee Journal*, Jan. 2, 1906; "Weather," *Baltimore Sun*, Jan. 4, 1906; La Follette and La Follette, *Robert M. La Follette*, 197; "Shorter Time to Chicago," *Washington Post*, Nov. 20, 1905.

3. James D. Secrest, "Capital of 1877 Was Floundering in Its Newly Assumed Role of a City," *Washington Post*, Dec. 6, 1937; Charles Frederick Weller and Eugenia Winston Weller, *Neglected Neighbors: Stories of Life in the Alleys, Tenements and Shanties of the National Capital* (Philadelphia: J. C. Winston,

1909), 9–12, 66–67; Clay McShane, "Transforming the Use of Urban Space: A Look at the Revolution in Street Pavements, 1880–1924," *Journal of Urban History* 5, no. 3 (May 1979): 289.

4. "Etiquette and Campaign Pleasantries," *Washington Post*, Feb.1, 1905; "To Be Senator To-Day," *Washington Post*, Jan. 4, 1906; "Interest in Senate Feud," *Chicago Daily Tribune*, Jan. 4, 1906.

5. Unger, *Fighting Bob La Follette*, 141–142; La Follette, *Autobiography*, 373; La Follette and La Follette, *Robert M. La Follette*, 199; Ralph M. McKenzie, "Not a Mud-Slinger," *Washington Post*, Feb. 6, 1905.

6. "La Follette Sworn," *Washington Post*, Jan. 5, 1906.

7. "La Follette a Senator," *New York Tribune*, Jan.5, 1906.

8. "La Follette and Spooner in Truce," *Chicago Daily Tribune*, Jan. 5, 1906.

9. Waldon Fawcett, "Envoys at Washington," *Cosmopolitan*, May 1901, 3–14.

10. Ibid., 3–6; Unger, *Fighting Bob La Follette*, 142.

11. "President and Wife Give Reception to Diplomats," *Washington Post*, Jan. 5, 1906; "About People and Social Incidents," *New York Tribune*, Jan. 5, 1906.

12. La Follette and La Follette, *Robert M. La Follette*, 86, 200–201.

13. John Callan O'Laughlin, "Roosevelt Deals Rate Cabal Blow," *Chicago Daily Tribune*, Jan. 31, 1906.

14. John Morton Blum, "Appendix 2: Theodore Roosevelt and the Hepburn Act: Toward and Orderly System of Control," in Roosevelt, *Letters*, 6:1563.

15. "RMLF to A. M. Lewis," Jan. 15, 1906, Library-Archives of the Wisconsin Historical Society; Unger, *Fighting Bob La Follette*, 142; La Follette and La Follette, *Robert M. La Follette*, 200.

16. La Follette and La Follette, *Robert M. La Follette*, 201–202; John J. Daly, "When Senate Hazers Go Into Action," *Washington Post*, Feb. 7, 1932.

17. La Follette, *Autobiography*, 405–407.

18. Ibid., 407; La Follette and La Follette, *Robert M. La Follette*, 203; Justin Kaplan, *Lincoln Steffens: A Biography* (New York: Simon & Schuster, 1974), 160–161.

19. La Follette, *Autobiography*, 407–411.

20. La Follette and La Follette, *Robert M. La Follette*, 203.

21. Steffens, *Autobiography*, 508.

22. Morris, *Theodore Rex*, 434; "To Pass H.R. 12987," *GovTrack.us*, accessed Oct. 17, 2012, http://www.govtrack.us/congress/votes/59-1/h13; "Row Over Rate Bill," *New York Times*, Feb. 10, 1906; "Rate Bill Deadlock," *New York Tribune*, Feb. 16, 1906.

23. Morris, *Theodore Rex*, 434.

24. Lewis L. Gould, *The Most Exclusive Club: A History of the Modern United States Senate* (New York: Basic Books, 2006), 22.

25. Lorine Swainston Goodwin, *The Pure Food, Drink, and Drug Crusaders, 1879–1914* (Jefferson, NC: McFarland, 1999), 15–84; Harvey Young James, "The Long Struggle for the 1906 Law," in *The Food and Drug Administration (FDA)* (Hauppauge, NY: Nova Science Publishers, 2003), 18, 126.

26. "Railroad Rates and Rebates," *The National Provisioner*, Dec. 24, 1904, 37.

27. Henry Beech Needham, "The Senate–Of Special Interests," *The World's Work*, Feb. 1906, 7206–7211; Goodwin, *The Pure Food, Drink, and Drug Crusaders*, 245.

28. Clayton Anderson Coppin and Jack C. High, *The Politics of Purity: Harvey Washington Wiley and the Origins of Federal Food Policy* (Ann Harbor: Univ.

of Michigan Press, 1999), 76; Mark Sullivan, *Our Times: The United States 1900–1925*, 6 vols. (New York: Scribner, 1926–1935), 2:533–534.

29. "Tillman to Lead," *Baltimore Sun*, Feb. 24, 1906.

30. *33 Cong. Rec.*, S2243–2245 (1900).

31. "Tillman to Lead" *Baltimore Sun*.

32. "Thermometer Lying Low," *Washington Post*, Feb. 4, 1906; "Ground Hog Is Vindicated," *Washington Post*, Feb. 28, 1906; "Spooner Asked to Draw Republican Rate Bill," *New York Times*, Feb. 27, 1906; Fowler, *John Coit Spooner*, 344–346; Merrill and Merrill, *The Republican Command*, 218–219; Blum, "Appendix 2: Theodore Roosevelt and the Hepburn Act: Toward and Orderly System of Control," in Roosevelt, *Letters*, 6:1563–1565.

33. TR to Kermit Roosevelt, April 1, 1906, in Roosevelt, *Letters*, 5:204.

34. Blum, "Appendix 2: Theodore Roosevelt and the Hepburn Act: Toward and Orderly System of Control," in Roosevelt, *Letters*, 6:1565–1567; Gould, *The Presidency of Theodore Roosevelt*, 156; Thomas W. Merrill, "The Origins of American-style Judicial Review," in *Comparative Administrative Law* (Northampton, MA: Edward Elgar Publishing, 2010), 395–397.

35. Lincoln Steffens, "Forming New Political Parties," *Baltimore Sun*, Mar. 11, 1906.

36. TR to Taft, Mar. 15, 1906 in Roosevelt, *Letters*, 5:182–183.

37. Baker, *American Chronicle*, 201.

38. Mark Sullivan, *Our Times*, 3:94.

39. Baker, *American Chronicle*, 201–203.

40. "Roosevelt for Tax on Wealth," *New York Times*, April 15, 1906; "Scores the Man with Muck Rake," *Washington Post*, April 15, 1906; "Tax Big Fortunes," *Baltimore Sun*, April 15, 1906.

41. Baker, *American Chronicle*, 204.

42. La Follette and La Follette, *Robert M. La Follette*, 204.

43. *40 Cong. Rec.*, S5684 (1906).

44. La Follette and La Follette, *Robert M. La Follette*, 204–205; "Few in Senate Hear La Follette," *Chicago Daily Tribune*, April 20, 1906; "'Hazing' Senator La Follette," *Atlanta Constitution*, April 24, 1906; *40 Cong. Rec.*, S5688 (1906).

45. La Follette and La Follette, *Robert M. La Follette*, 205–207.

46. Ibid., 206; "La Follette Defends Railway Rate Bill," *New York Times*, April 20, 1906; Roosevelt, *Letters*, 5:341; Roosevelt's irritation is apparent in his letter to Steffens, see Roosevelt, *Letters*, 5:148.

47. Stephenson, *Nelson W. Aldrich*, 267–268, 283; "Rates Stir Senate," *Washington Post*, April 3, 1906; Blum, "Appendix 2: Theodore Roosevelt and the Hepburn Act: Toward and Orderly System of Control," in Roosevelt, *Letters*, 6:1569.

48. Stephenson, *Nelson W. Aldrich*, 310–312.

49. Ibid., 309–315; Gould, *The Presidency of Theodore Roosevelt*, 158.

50. "Allison Denies It," *Washington Post*, May 5, 1906.

51. "'Twas Aldrich's Idea," *Baltimore Sun*, May 7, 1906; "Tillman Discloses Roosevelt Secrets; Senate Hears Story of Surrender on the Rate Bill," *New York Times*, May 13, 1906.

52. "Roosevelt Quick to Refute Charge," *Chicago Daily Tribune*, May 13, 1906; Gould, *The Presidency of Theodore Roosevelt*, 158.

53. "Snub La Follette," *Washington Post*, May 15, 1906.

54. TR to Kermit Roosevelt, May 13, 1906, in Theodore Roosevelt, *Letters to Kermit from Theodore Roosevelt 1902 to 1908* (Kessinger Publishing, 2005; New York: C. Scribner's Sons, 1946), 148–149.

55. Gould, *The Presidency of Theodore Roosevelt*, 159; A. Maurice Low, "Railway Rate Bill Passes the Senate," *Boston Daily Globe*, May 19, 1906.

56. Harrison, *Congress, Progressive Reform, and the New American State*, 77–82.

57. Gould, *The Presidency of Theodore Roosevelt*, 259; Stephenson, *Nelson W. Aldrich*, 266, 312; Bowers, *Beveridge and the Progressive Era*, 226.

58. Beveridge to TR, Aug. 22, 1906, in Bowers, *Beveridge and the Progressive Era*, 228.

59. Beveridge to John C. Shaffer, Mar. 27, 1906, in Bowers, *Beveridge and the Progressive Era*, 223–224.

60. Anthony Arthur, *Radical Innocent: Upton Sinclair* (New York: Random House, 2006), 43–56, 70, 82; Upton Sinclair, *The Jungle* (New York: Doubleday, Page & Company, 1906), 161–162; Bowers, *Beveridge and the Progressive Era*, 227–230; "Meat Inspection Bill Passes the Senate," *New York Times*, May 26, 1906.

61. TR to James Wadsworth, May 26, 1906, in Roosevelt, *Letters*, 5:282–283.

62. John Callan O'Laughlin, "Packers Yield to the Big Stick," *Chicago Daily Tribune*, May 26, 1906; "Beef Trust Beaten, but Escapes Exposure," *New York Times*, May 27, 1906; "President's Fury Falls on Packers," *Chicago Daily Tribune*, May 27, 1906; "Packers Put up Fight," *Washington Post*, May 27, 1906.

63. "Pure Food Bill Doped by Lobby?," *Chicago Daily Tribune*, May 24, 1906.

64. Walter J. Oleszek, "Speakers Reed, Cannon, and Gingrich: Catalysts of Institutional and Procedural Change," in *The Cannon Centenary Conference: The Changing Nature of the Speakership* (Washington, DC: U.S. G.P.O., 2004), 131–132; Christopher M. Davis, "The Speaker of the House and the Committee on Rules," in *The Cannon Centenary Conference*, 144; La Follette, *Autobiography*, 95; Barbara W. Tuchman, *The Proud Tower: A Portrait of the World Before the War, 1890–1914* (New York: Macmillan, 1966; Ballantine Books Edition, 1996), 127.

65. "House Machine Works as the Speaker Wills," *New York Times*, May 28, 1906.

66. Cannon to W. Loeb in Roosevelt Papers, quoted in William Rea Gwinn, *Uncle Joe Cannon: Archfoe of Insurgency* (New York: Bookman Associates, 1957), 109.

67. TR to James Wadsworth, May 31, 1906, in Roosevelt, *Letters*, 5:291.

68. "President's Threat with Meat Report," *New York Times*, June 5, 1906; John Callan O'Laughlin, "Roosevelt Stirs House to Action," *Chicago Daily Tribune*, June 5, 1906; Early leak of the Neill-Reynolds report, see "Report on Meat Converts Cannon," *New York Times*, May 28, 1906.

69. "Second Meat Report," *New York Tribune*, June 6, 1906; "Threat to Veto Packers' Bill," *New York Times*, June 15, 1906; "Warm Reply to the President," *Boston Daily Globe*, June 16, 1906.

70. "Cannon at White House," *New York Tribune*, June 18, 1906; "Agree on Meat Bill; Both Sides Give In," *New York Times*, June 19, 1906.

71. *40 Cong. Rec.*, H8273 (1906).

72. "President Pleased with This Congress," *Boston Daily Globe*, July 1, 1906.

73. TR to Kermit Roosevelt, June 13, 1906, in Roosevelt, *Letters*, 5:148–149.
74. New York, New Haven and Hartford Railroad Co. Evidence taken before the Interstate Commerce Commission relative to the financial transactions of the New York, New Haven and Hartford Railroad Company, together with the report of the commission thereon, S. Doc. No. 543, at 859 (1914). 75. Ibid., 3–4, 695–696, 858–859.
76. Ibid., 859, 862; Charles S. Mellen to Howard Stockton, Oct. 10, 1907, Concord, New Hampshire Historical Society, Charles S. Mellen Papers, quoted in Sternstein, "Corruption in the Gilded Age Senate," 34; *New York American*, April 17, 1915, quoted in Sternstein, "Corruption in the Gilded Age Senate," 34.
77. Unger, *Fighting Bob La Follette*, 146.
78. James R. Schultz, *The Romance of Small-Town Chautauquas* (Columbia, MO: Univ. of Missouri Press, 2002), 13; William L. Slout, *Theatre in a Tent* (Rockville, MD: Wildside Press LLC, 2008; Bowling Green, OH: Bowling Green State Univ. Popular Press, 1972), 62–63.
79. La Follette and La Follette, *Robert M. La Follette*, 212.
80. "La Follette, Kill Joy of the Senate Hazers," *New York Times*, Nov. 26, 1906; La Follette and La Follette, *Robert M. La Follette*, 216.
81. "Good Fight Ahead, Says La Follette," *Minneapolis Journal*, July 4, 1906.
82. Julie Greene, *Pure and Simple Politics: The American Federation of Labor and Political Activism, 1881–1917* (Cambridge, UK: Cambridge Univ. Press, 1999), 109–112; Harrison, *Congress, Progressive Reform, and the New American State*, 106–108.
83. "Theodore Roosevelt: Sixth Annual Message," accessed Aug. 20, 2012, http://www.presidency.ucsb.edu/ws/index.php?pid=29547.
84. Robert F. Bruner and Sean D. Carr, *The Panic of 1907: Lessons Learned from the Market's Perfect Storm* Kindle ed. (Hoboken, NJ: Wiley, 2009), 16.

CHAPTER 4: THE PANIC

1. "Fowler Opens War on Speaker Cannon," *New York Times*, Aug. 24, 1909.
2. Joseph H. Davis, Christopher Hanes, and Paul W. Rhode, "Harvests and Business Cycles in Nineteenth-Century America," *Quarterly Journal of Economics* 124, no. 4 (Nov. 1, 2009): 1682; Marjorie Kahl Lawrence, *This Is the Way It Used to Be in the Early 1900's* (Frankfort, IN: M.K. Lawrence, 1981), 61.
3. "The West's Harvest Money," *Wall Street Journal*, Aug. 1, 1903; A. Piatt Andrew, "The Influence of the Crops Upon Business in America," *Quarterly Journal of Economics* 20 (May 1906): 323–353; Jeffrey A Miron, "Financial Panics, the Seasonality of the Nominal Interest Rate, and the Founding of the Fed," *American Economic Review* 76, no. 1 (1986): 125–140; Charles Albert Eric Goodhart, *The New York Money Market and the Finance of Trade, 1900–1913* (Cambridge: Harvard Univ. Press, 1969), 3.
4. Jackson Lears, *Rebirth of a Nation: The Making of Modern America, 1877–1920* (New York: HarperCollins, 2009), 169–171; Jerry W. Markham, *A Financial History of the United States: From Christopher Columbus to the Robber Barons (1492–1900)* (Armonk, NY: M.E. Sharpe, 2002), 331–332; Elmus Wicker,

Banking Panics of the Gilded Age (Cambridge, UK: Cambridge Univ. Press, 2006), 59–60.

5. James Livingston, *Origins of the Federal Reserve System: Money, Class, and Corporate Capitalism, 1890–1913* (Ithaca: Cornell Univ. Press, 1986), 85; Richard T. McCulley, *Banks and Politics During the Progressive Era: The Origins of the Federal Reserve System, 1897–1913* (New York: Garland, 1992), 66; Richard G. Anderson, "Some Tables of Historical US Currency and Monetary Aggregates Data," *Working Paper Series* (Jan. 2003): 37–45, http://research.stlouisfed.org/wp/more/2003-006/.

6. Jos Ohl, "Fowler Money Bill, Sent in Favorably, First Outlined to Atlanta Bankers," *Atlanta Constitution*, Mar. 23, 1902; Arthur L. Friedberg and Ira S. Friedberg, *Paper Money of the United States: A Complete Illustrated Guide With Valuations*, 18th ed. (Clifton, NJ: Coin & Currency Institute, 2006), 76.

7. Livingston, *Origins of the Federal Reserve System*, 150–154; McCulley, *Banks and Politics*, 66.

8. Charles N. Fowler, *Address of Hon. Charles N. Fowler, of New Jersey, in the House of Representatives, March 31, 1897* (Washington, DC: G.P.O., 1897); "C. N. Fowler Dies; Ex-Representative," *New York Times*, May 28, 1932; "For Asset Currency," *New York Tribune*, Jan. 14, 1903.

9. Merrill and Merrill, *The Republican Command*, 150–151; "A New Banking Bill," *New York Tribune*, Feb. 10, 1903.

10. "Criticise Aldrich Bill," *New York Tribune*, Feb. 27, 1903; Jos Ohl, "Aldrich Currency Bill Being Bitterly Fought," *Atlanta Constitution*, March 1, 1903; "Credit Currency vs. the Aldrich Bill," *Wall Street Journal*, Mar. 2, 1903; McCulley, *Banks and Politics*, 105–107.

11. "Cannon and the Currency," *Boston Daily Globe*, July 12, 1903; "Warning by Aldrich," *Washington Post*, March 4, 1903; Jos Ohl, "Fowler Predicts Greet Panic Without Currency Expansion," *Atlanta Constitution*, Jan. 26, 1903.

12. "Cannon Is Firm with President," *Chicago Daily Tribune*, July 23, 1903; "A Currency Compromise," *New York Tribune*, Aug. 18, 1903; "The Week," *The Outlook*, Aug. 1, 1903, 774; McCulley, *Banks and Politics*, 108–110; Merrill and Merrill, *The Republican Command*, 152–159; "Theodore Roosevelt: Third Annual Message," accessed Aug. 20, 2012, http://www.presidency.ucsb.edu/ws/index.php?pid=29544.

13. "Has Words of Praise for California Pluck," *San Francisco Chronicle*, Dec. 14, 1906; "1906 Earthquake Arson Fires," accessed Dec. 15, 2012, http://www.sfmuseum.org/1906.2/arson.html.

14. Bruner and Carr, *The Panic of 1907*, 13–15; Kerry A. Odell and Marc D. Weidenmier, *Real Shock, Monetary Aftershock: The San Francisco Earthquake and the Panic of 1907*, Working Paper (National Bureau of Economic Research, Sept. 2002), http://www.nber.org/papers/w9176; "Shaw Would Control Reserve of Banks," *New York Times*, Dec. 6, 1906.

15. "Never Again a Big Panic," *Los Angeles Times*, Dec. 17, 1906.

16. "Stock Market in '06," *Washington Post*, Dec. 31, 1906; "Stock Dealings Fell Off," *Baltimore Sun*, Jan. 1, 1907.

17. "The President and the State of the Country," *New York Sun*, Dec. 28, 1906; "The Financial Situation," *New York Sun*, Dec. 31, 1906.

18. TR to Paul Morton, Jan. 2, 1907, in Roosevelt, *Letters*, 5:535–536.

19. "New Year Festivities in Washington," *New York Tribune*, Jan. 2, 1907; "Foraker at Reception," *Washington Post*, Jan. 2, 1907.

20. Gould, *The Presidency of Theodore Roosevelt*, 230.
21. Emma Lou Thornbrough, "The Brownsville Episode and the Negro Vote," *Mississippi Valley Historical Review* 44, no. 3 (Dec. 1, 1957): 470.
22. TR to Brooks Adams, Dec. 12, 1906, in Roosevelt, *Letters*, 5:534; see also TR to George F. Spinney, Jan. 22, 1907, in Roosevelt, *Letters*, 5:559–560.
23. La Follette and La Follette, *Robert M. La Follette*, 218–219; "Law Limiting Hours of Trainmen Passed," *New York Times*, Jan. 11, 1907.
24. TR to William Allen White, Jan. 5, 1907, in Roosevelt, *Letters*, 5.540–541.
25. La Follette and La Follette, *Robert M. La Follette*, 219–220.
26. Samuel P. Hays, *Conservation and the Gospel of Efficiency: The Progressive Conservation Movement, 1890–1920* (Pittsburgh: Univ. of Pittsburgh Press, 1999), 82–87; La Follette, *Autobiography*, 385.
27. "Change in Public Land Policy," *Wall Street Journal*, Jan. 25, 1907; "Fuel Protection Bill," *New York Times*, Jan. 23, 1907; La Follette and La Follette, *Robert M. La Follette*, 221.
28. RMLF to TR, Feb. 19, 1907, in Unger, *Fighting Bob La Follette*, 149; La Follette, *Autobiography*, 388.
29. "Roosevelt-Taft-La Follette on What the Matter Is in America and What to Do About It," *Everybody's Magazine*, June 1908, 728.
30. TR to RMLF, 19 Feb. 1907 in Roosevelt, *Letters*, 5:594.
31. La Follette and La Follette, *Robert M. La Follette*, 223.
32. Bowers, *Beveridge Congress, Progressive Reform*, 245, 250; "Spirit of the Press," *Baltimore Sun*, Jan. 28, 1907; "Child Labor Assailed," *Washington Post*, Jan. 24, 1907.
33. Bowers, *Beveridge Congress, Progressive Reform*, 255; "Attack on Child Labor," *Washington Post*, Dec. 4, 1906.
34. *New York Mail*, quoted in "To Be Put to Sleep," *Washington Post*, Dec. 24, 1906.
35. Bowers, *Beveridge Congress, Progressive Reform*, 250–252; "Child Labor Assailed"; North Overton Messenger, "Young Men in Congress," *Pearson's Magazine*, Dec. 1903, 566; "Beveridge, Boy Orator, Who's Never Grown Up," *New York Times*, Dec. 11, 1905.
36. *41 Cong. Rec.*, S1552–1557 (1907).
37. John Callan O'Laughlin, "States Must Act on Child Labor," *Chicago Daily Tribune*, Feb. 7, 1907.
38. Ibid.
39. "Gridiron in Its Glory," *Baltimore Sun*, Jan. 27, 1907; Champ Clark, *My Quarter Century of American Politics*, vol. 1 (New York: Harper & Brothers, 1920), 444–445; Morris, *Theodore Rex*, 478.
40. "G.O.P. in Turmoil," *Washington Post*, Jan. 18, 1907; "Both Sides Yield," *Washington Post*, Jan. 21, 1907; The Tribune Bureau, "President Defended," *New York Tribune*, Jan. 15, 1907; Stephenson, *Nelson W. Aldrich*, 324.
41. Arthur Wallace Dunn, *Gridiron Nights: Humorous and Satirical Views of Politics and Statesmen as Presented by the Famous Dining Club* (New York: Frederick A. Stokes, 1915), 180; Morris, *Theodore Rex*, 478.
42. "Jar at Gridiron Dinner," *Baltimore Sun*, Jan. 29, 1907.
43. "All Coons Alike to Roosevelt," *Atlanta Constitution*, Jan. 29, 1907; Joseph Benson Foraker, *Notes of a Busy Life*, vol. 2 (Cincinnati: Stewart & Kidd, 1916), 249–251.
44. Clark, *My Quarter Century of American Politics*, 1:446; Dunn, *Gridiron Nights*, 187–188.

45. Dunn, *Gridiron Nights*, 188; Clark, *My Quarter Century of American Politics*, 1:447; "Roosevelt in Tilt," *Washington Post*, Jan. 28, 1907; "Plain Words at the Gridiron Banquet," *San Francisco Chronicle*, Jan. 28, 1907; Henry Luther Stoddard, *As I Knew Them: Presidents and Politics from Grant to Coolidge* (New York: Harper & Brothers, 1927), 330.

46. Gould, *The Presidency of Theodore Roosevelt*, 234; "Army Clears 167 Black Soldiers Disciplined in a Shooting in 1906," *New York Times*, Sept. 29, 1972; "2nd 'Brownsville' Soldier Gets Honorable Discharge," *Baltimore Afro-American*, April 28, 1973.

47. "59th Congress Dies to Music," *New York Times*, Mar. 5, 1907; "Congress Ends," *Baltimore Sun*, Mar. 5, 1907.

48. Stephenson, *Nelson W. Aldrich*, 320; Fowler, *John Coit Spooner*, 366–367; Spooner to E.W. Keyes, Dec. 25, 1904, in James Richard Parker, *Senator John C. Spooner, 1897–1907* (College Park: Univ. of Maryland, 1971), 329; Spooner to S.M. Booth, Mar. 28, 1903, in Fowler, *John Coit Spooner*, 299–300.

49. "Spooner Resigns Seat in Senate," *New York Times*, Mar. 4, 1907; Fowler, *John Coit Spooner*, 369–371.

50. "Congress Ends,"; John Corrigan, "Cannon Turns down Williams," *Atlanta Constitution*, Jan. 16, 1907.

51. "Congress Ends"; "59th Congress Dies to Music"; "Without day" is the English translation of the Latin *sine die*, meaning, "without any future date being designated."

52. "Fowler Opens War on Speaker Cannon."

53. TR to Cannon, Jan. 24, Feb. 6, Mar. 2, 1907, in Roosevelt, *Letters*, 5:563, 5:581, 5:605.

54. Gwinn, *Uncle Joe Cannon*, 126–128; B. Y. Dickinson, "Cannon in 1908, Says Roosevelt," *Washington Post*, Aug. 17, 1906; "Cannon Boom Launched," *New York Tribune*, Aug. 17, 1906.

55. "12 Congressmen on Junket," *Baltimore Sun*, Mar. 6, 1907.

56. J. P. Morgan Jr., March 14, 1907, quoted in Bruner and Carr, *The Panic of 1907*, 20.

57. J. P. Morgan Jr. to J. S. Morgan & Company, March 29, 1907, quoted in *The Panic of 1907.*, 22; "The Financial Markets," *New York Tribune*, Mar. 18, 1907.

58. Goodhart, *The New York Money Market And the Finance of Trade, 1900–1913*, 113–117.

59. Edwin C. Hill, "The Strangest Stock-Market in the World," *Munsey's Magazine*, Feb. 1920, 44–54; "Stock Exchange Seats," *Wall Street Journal*, Aug. 23, 1906.

60. Bruner and Carr, *The Panic of 1907*, 40–45; "The Outside Market," *Wall Street Journal*, Feb. 2, 1906.

61. "Rise of 25 Points in United Mining," *Chicago Daily Tribune*, Oct. 15, 1907; "United Copper Continues Its Sensational Market Decline," *Wall Street Journal*, Oct. 17, 1907; Bruner and Carr, *The Panic of 1907*, 46.

62. "Skyrocket Jump in United Copper," *New York Times*, Oct. 15, 1907.

63. "Crash in Coppers; Heinze Quits Bank," *New York Times*, Oct. 17, 1907; "The Outside Market," *Wall Street Journal*, Oct. 16, 1907.

64. Bruner and Carr, *The Panic of 1907*, 51–54, 59.

65. "Run Closes Its Doors," *Washington Post*, Oct. 23, 1907.

66. "Knickerbocker Trust Co.'s New Offices," *Wall Street Journal*, Nov. 2, 1903; Bruner and Carr, *The Panic of 1907*, 65–68.

67. "Run Closes Its Doors"; "Pays Out $8,000,000 and Then Suspends," *New York Times*, Oct. 23, 1907.

68. "Call Money Loans at 96%," *Wall Street Journal*, Oct. 24, 1907.

69. "Stock Trouble Is No Stay–Roosevelt," *New York Times*, Oct. 23, 1907.

70. Frederick S. Wood, *Roosevelt as We Knew Him: The Personal Recollections of One Hundred and Fifty of His Friends and Associates* (Philadelphia: John C. Winston, 1927), 165.

71. Bruner and Carr, *The Panic of 1907*, 86.

72. Jean Strouse, *Morgan: American Financier* (New York: Random House, 1999), xii, 54; Ron Chernow, *The House of Morgan: An American Banking Dynasty and the Rise of Modern Finance* (New York: Grove Press, 1990), 38, 48; Ray Stannard Baker, "J. Pierpont Morgan," *McClure's Magazine*, Oct. 1901, 512; "Morgan and Morganism," *London Daily Mail*, Dec. 3, 1902.

73. Strouse, *Morgan*, 394–395.

74. Herbert Livingston Satterlee, *J. Pierpont Morgan: An Intimate Portrait* (New York: Macmillan, 1939), 467–468.

75. Strouse, *Morgan*, 578.

76. Satterlee, *J. Pierpont Morgan*, 469–470; Bruner and Carr, *The Panic of 1907*, 89; Thomas W. Lamont, *Henry P. Davison, the Record of a Useful Life, by His Friend and Partner Thomas W. Lamont* (New York: Harper & Brothers, 1933), 76.

77. Satterlee, *J. Pierpont Morgan*, 469–470.

78. Ibid., 472; Bruner and Carr, *The Panic of 1907*, 92–93.

79. Strouse, *Morgan*, xi–xii; Carola Frydman, Eric Hilt, and Lily Y. Zhou, *The Panic of 1907: JP Morgan, Trust Companies, and the Impact of the Financial Crisis*, Working Paper (National Bureau of Economic Research, Mar. 2, 2012), 3–4, http://conference.nber.org/confer/2012/MEs12/summary.html.

80. Bruner and Carr, *The Panic of 1907*, 101.

81. Satterlee, *J. Pierpont Morgan*, 474.

82. Account by George W. Perkins in Samuel Crowther, "The Intimate Story of the Panic of 1907," n.d., 14, Pierpont Morgan Library Archives, New York City.

83. Satterlee, *J. Pierpont Morgan*, 480–481; "Roosevelt Indorses Cortelyou's Work," *New York Times*, Oct. 27, 1907.

84. James T. Sullivan, "Comfortable Once Inside," *Boston Daily Globe*, Oct. 29, 1907; "The Outside Market," *Wall Street Journal*, Oct. 29, 1907; "Millions for Banks," *Boston Daily Globe*, Oct. 29, 1907; Bruner and Carr, *The Panic of 1907*, 110.

85. Account by George W. Perkins in Crowther, "The Intimate Story of the Panic of 1907," 25–31

86. House of Representatives, *Hearings Before the Committee on Investigation of United States Steel Corporation*, 60th Cong., 2nd Sess., 936 (1911).

87. Account by George W. Perkins in Crowther, "The Intimate Story of the Panic of 1907," 41–43; Bruner and Carr, *The Panic of 1907*, 119–120; Kolko, *The Triumph of Conservatism*, 15, 115.

88. Lamont, *Henry P. Davison, the Record of a Useful Life*, 78–83; Satterlee, *J. Pierpont Morgan*, 485–486.

89. Ida M. Tarbell, *The Life of Elbert H. Gary; the Story of Steel* (New York: D. Appleton, 1925), 200; Henry Fowles Pringle, *Theodore Roosevelt: A Biography* (New York: Harcourt, Brace, 1931), 441.

90. Pringle, *Theodore Roosevelt*, 442; T.R. to Charles J. Bonaparte, Nov. 4, 1907, in House of Representatives, *US Steel Hearings*, 1370–1371.

91. House of Representatives, *US Steel Hearings*, 139, 1370–1371.

92. "Bryan Busy with His Salt," *Chicago Daily Tribune*, Nov. 19, 1907; "Financial Sky-Clearer," *Baltimore Sun*, Nov. 11, 1907; "Last Weak Spot Is Made Strong," *Boston Daily Globe*, Nov. 7, 1907; Bruner and Carr, *The Panic of 1907*, 137–140.

93. "Mr. Morgan's Library," *Wall Street Journal*, Nov. 7, 1907; "John Pierport Morgan a Bank in Human Form," *New York Times*, Nov. 10, 1907.

94. Bruner and Carr, *The Panic of 1907*, 135–142; Ellis W. Tallman, "The Panic of 1907," in *The Routledge Handbook of Major Events in Economic History* (New York: Routledge, 2013), 64.

95. "Dr. Woodrow Wilson Defines Material Issues," *New York Times*, Nov. 24, 1907.

96. "Digs at President," *Washington Post*, Nov. 22, 1907; "Toast to Roosevelt Drunk in Silence," *New York Times*, Nov. 22, 1907.

97. Gould, *The Presidency of Theodore Roosevelt*, 239–240; Strouse, *Morgan*, 589–590; Kolko, *The Triumph of Conservatism*, 117–118.

CHAPTER 5: THE MONEY POWER

1. "Speaker Cannon Wacks Uplift," *Chicago Daily Tribune*, Sep. 14, 1906.

2. *42 Cong. Rec.*, S417–420 (1908); "No Financial Inquiry Yet," *New York Times*, Dec. 19, 1907.

3. Gould, *The Most Exclusive Club*, 19; Lewis L. Gould, *Progressives and Prohibitionists: Texas Democrats in the Wilson Era* (Austin: Univ. of Texas Press, 1973), 13–14.

4. McCulley, *Banks and Politics*, 151.

5. Merrill and Merrill, *The Republican Command*, 256; Livingston, *Origins of the Federal Reserve System*, 181; "Preparing a Finance Bill," *Wall Street Journal*, Jan. 6, 1908; "Oppose a Central Bank," *New York Times*, Jan. 5, 1908; Paul Moritz Warburg, *The Federal Reserve System, Its Origin and Growth: Reflections and Recollections*, vol. 1 (New York: Macmillan, 1930), 31–32; Stephenson, *Nelson W. Aldrich*, 332–334.

6. "Discuss Currency Plans," *Washington Post*, Dec. 4, 1907; TR to William Emlen Roosevelt, Nov. 9, 1907, in Roosevelt, *Letters*, 5:836; TR to Elisha Ely Garrison, March 3, 1911, in Roosevelt, *Letters*, 7:236–237; Busbey, *Uncle Joe Cannon*, 209; TR to Henry Lee Higginson, Feb. 19, 1908, in Roosevelt, *Letters*, 6:949.

7. "Money Bill in Senate," *Baltimore Sun*, Jan. 8, 1908; "Plans Passage Currency Bill," *Los Angeles Times*, Jan. 23, 1908; "Aldrich Bill Will Be Rushed Through," *New York Times*, Jan. 26, 1908.

8. Gould, *The Presidency of Theodore Roosevelt*, 235; Lyman Abbott, "Address at Sagmore Hill," in *The Roosevelt Pilgrimage of 1922: Being a Record of the Pilgrimage of Certain Friends of Theodore Roosevelt to His Grave and to His Home on the Third Anniversary of His Death* (Priv. Print., 1922), 15.

9. TR to Charles Joseph Bonaparte, Jan 2, 1908, in Roosevelt, *Letters*, 6:884–888.

10. "Theodore Roosevelt: Message to Congress on Worker's Compensation," accessed April 27, 2013, http://www.presidency.ucsb.edu/ws/?pid=69649; John Callan O'Laughlin, "Roosevelt Flays 'Trust Puppets,'" *Chicago Daily Tribune*, Feb. 1, 1908.

11. "Roosevelt Fires," *Baltimore Sun*, Feb. 1, 1908; J. Hampton Moore, *Roosevelt and the Old Guard* (Philadelphia: Macrae-Smith, 1925), 219.

12. "Press View on the Message," *Chicago Daily Tribune*, Feb. 1, 1908; "Roosevelt Fires"; "The Great Conspiracy," *New York Times*, Feb. 1, 1908.

13. TR to Kermit Roosevelt, Feb. 2, 1908, in Roosevelt, *Letters*, 6:4579.

14. Mark Sullivan, *Our Times*, 4:304.

15. "Taft Silent," *New York Times*, Feb. 1, 1908; "The Message a Burden," *Washington Post*, Feb. 3, 1908; William H. Taft, *Present Day Problems: A Collection of Addresses Delivered on Various Occasions* (New York: Dodd, Mead, 1908), 289.

16. Henry F. Pringle, *William Howard Taft: The Life and Times* (Newtown, CT: American Political Biography Press, 1939, 2008, reprint), 311–317, 347.

17. "Roosevelt Fires"; *42 Cong. Rec.*, S1819 (1908).

18. La Follette, *Autobiography*, 458–462.

19. McCulley, *Banks and Politics*, 153.

20. Merrill and Merrill, *The Republican Command*, 258; Bowers, *Beveridge and the Progressive Era*, 272, 276.

21. Merrill and Merrill, *The Republican Command*, 258–259.

22. *42 Cong. Rec.*, S3421 (1908); La Follette and La Follette, *Robert M. La Follette*, 240.

23. *42 Cong. Rec.*, S3421–3453 (1908); "Spoke to Democrats," *Washington Post*, Mar. 18, 1908.

24. *42 Cong. Rec.*, S3569–3570, 3799 (1908).

25. Stephenson, *Nelson W. Aldrich*, 328–329.

26. *42 Cong. Rec.*, S3803–3804 (1908).

27. "Senate Oligarchy Fighting for Life," *New York Times*, Mar. 30, 1908; Thelen, *Robert M. La Follette*, 65.

28. Merrill and Merrill, *The Republican Command*, 260–262.

29. "Cannon Prods Caucus," *Washington Post*, May 6, 1908.

30. "Vreeland's Bill up to the Senate," *Chicago Daily Tribune*, May 15, 1908.

31. Merrill and Merrill, *The Republican Command*, 264–266; "New Currency Bill Passes the House," *New York Times*, May 28, 1908.

32. "Win on Currency," *Washington Post*, May 28, 1908; "Last Vote Today on Currency Bill," *Chicago Daily Tribune*, May 29, 1908; "Senate Clears Way for Currency Bill," *New York Times*, May 29, 1908.

33. La Follette and La Follette, *Robert M. La Follette*, 246–247; *42 Cong. Rec.*, S7161 (1908); "La Follette Breaks Senate Talk Record," *New York Times*, May 30, 1908.

34. "La Follette Breaks Senate Talk Record."

35. Ibid.; "La Follette Ill; Talks 21 Hours," *Chicago Daily Tribune*, May 30, 1908.

36. TR to Kermit Roosevelt, May 30, 1908, in Roosevelt, *Letters*, 6:1044.

37. "La Follette Ill; Talks 21 Hours"; La Follette and La Follette, *Robert M. La Follette*, 252–253.

38. La Follette and La Follette, *Robert M. La Follette*, 252–253; "Congress Adjourns," *Boston Daily Globe*, May 31, 1908; *42 Cong. Rec.*, S7220–7221 (1908).

39. "Filibuster Is Crushed," *Washington Post*, May 31, 1908; *42 Cong. Rec.*, S7226 (1908); "Congress Adjourns"; "La Follette's Filibuster Breaks All Records," *Boston Daily Globe*, May 31, 1908; Robert C. Byrd, *Senate, 1789–1989: Historical Statistics, 1789–1992* (Washington: Government Printing Office, 1993), 477.

40. "Filibuster Is Crushed"; *42 Cong. Rec.*, S7244–7246 (1908); "Finale of the Filibuster," *Chicago Daily Tribune*, May 31, 1908; "The Long Fight Ended," *New York Tribune*, May 31, 1908.

41. "Pass Currency Bill by Aldrich Strategy," *New York Times*, May 31, 1908; "Filibuster Is Crushed."

42. *42 Cong. Rec.*, S7259 (1908); "Pass Currency Bill by Aldrich Strategy."

43. La Follette and La Follette, *Robert M. La Follette*, 255; "Congress Adjourns."

44. "Congress Adjourns"; "Weary Congress Ends Its Session."

45. Bowers, *Beveridge and the Progressive Era*, 276–277; Merrill and Merrill, *The Republican Command*, 267–268; TR to Kermit Roosevelt, May 30, 1908, in Roosevelt, *Letters*, 6:1044.

46. *42 Cong. Rec.*, S7274 (1908).

47. "Aldrich Is Chairman," *Baltimore Sun*, June 1, 1908; "Aldrich at Head of Money Board," *Chicago Daily Tribune*, June 1, 1908; "In Secret Session," *Boston Daily Globe*, June 12, 1908; Aldrich to Theodore Burton, June 12, 1908, in Livingston, *Origins of the Federal Reserve System*, 188.

48. Historian Daniel Rodgers has ascribed the phrase "progressive movement" to the 1912 election, but La Follette was using it publicly as early as 1906 and introduced it to Congress in 1908. The phrase does not appear to have been used to refer to an American political alliance or ideology before 1906. See *42 Cong. Rec.*, S3450 (1908); "La Follette Takes Ground for Lenroot," *Minneapolis Journal*, July 22, 1906; Daniel T. Rodgers, "In Search of Progressivism," *Reviews in American History* 10, no. 4 (Dec. 1, 1982): 127fn.

CHAPTER 6: THE SMILE

1. Herbert Smith Duffy, *William Howard Taft* (New York: Minton, Balch, 1930), 328.

2. Steffens to Laura Steffens Suggett, Sept. 23, 1908, in Lincoln Steffens, *The Letters of Lincoln Steffens*, vol. 1 (New York: Harcourt, Brace, 1938), 202.; Lincoln Steffens, "An Apology for Graft," *American Magazine*, June 1908, 120; Kaplan, *Lincoln Steffens*, 153.

3. Steffens to Laura Steffens Suggett, Sept. 23, 1908, in Steffens, *The Letters of Lincoln Steffens*, 1:202.

4. Lincoln Steffens, "Roosevelt-Taft-La Follette on What the Matter Is in America and What to Do About It," *Everybody's Magazine*, June 1908, 730.

5. Ibid., 730–732.

6. Ibid., 736, 58 (advertising section).

7. TR to Lincoln Steffens, June 5, 1908, in Roosevelt, *Letters*, 6:1051–1053.

8. Lincoln Steffens to TR, June 9, 1907, in Steffens, *The Letters of Lincoln Steffens*, 1:195.

9. TR to John Graham Brooks, Nov. 13, 1908, in Roosevelt, *Letters*, 6:1343.

10. "Gossip of the Convention," *Washington Post*, June 17, 1908; "Convention Quiet at First Session," *New York Times*, June 17, 1908.

11. "Convention's Second Day," *New York Times*, June 18, 1908; "Second Day's Work of the Convention," *New York Tribune*, June 18, 1908.

12. Joseph Bucklin Bishop, *Presidential Nominations and Elections: A History of American Conventions, National Campaigns, Inaugurations and Campaign Caricature* (New York: C. Scribner, 1916), 72–73; TR to Kermit Roosevelt, June 6, 1908, in Roosevelt, *Letters*, 6:1060.

13. Pringle, *William Howard Taft*, 329–330; Bishop, *Presidential Nominations and Elections*, 73–74.

14. Ibid.; "Secretary Taft Nominated for President on First Ballot," *Wall Street Journal*, June 19, 1908.

15. "Taft Named; First Ballot," *New York Times*, June 19, 1908; Bishop, *Presidential Nominations and Elections*, 74.

16. Bishop, *Presidential Nominations and Elections*, 74–75.

17. "Brings Joy to Taft," *Washington Post*, June 19, 1908; "Taft, Hearing News, Turns to Mrs. Taft," *New York Times*, June 19, 1908.

18. Taft to Charles Nagel, June 1, 1908, in Pringle, *William Howard Taft*, 354; "Says It Is Sherman for Second Place," *New York Times*, June 19, 1908; "'Taft-Sherman'; That's the Ticket," *Chicago Daily Tribune*, June 20, 1908.

19. "Mile-High Convention," *Baltimore Sun*, July 5, 1908; "Crowds Besiege Convention Hall," *Chicago Daily Tribune*, July 8, 1908.

20. "Convention Sidelights," *Baltimore Sun*, July 11, 1908; "Only Woman Delegate," *Baltimore Sun*, July 6, 1908.

21. "Taft Talks of Woman Suffrage.," *Chicago Daily Tribune*, April 11, 1908; "He Angers Women," *Washington Post*, Dec. 5, 1908; Unger, *Fighting Bob La Follette*, 88; "Cannon Talks About Suffrage," *Los Angeles Times*, March 23, 1908; "Gallant Uncle Joe," *New York Times*, Jan. 28, 1908.

22. "Vote, but Fail at Tricks," *Chicago Daily Tribune*, July 7, 1908; John Callan O'Laughlin, "Platform Made; It's Bryan's Own," *Chicago Daily Tribune*, July 9, 1908; "Bryan Suggests," *Baltimore Sun*, July 9, 1908; "Democratic Party Platforms: Democratic Party Platform of 1908," accessed May 13, 2013, http://www.presidency.ucsb.edu/ws/?pid=29589.

23. "Bryan Dictated All the Planks," *New York Times*, July 11, 1908; "From Servant to Master," *Washington Post*, July 10, 1908.

24. Lincoln Steffens, "Lincoln Steffens on the Democratic Convention," *The Public*, July 17, 1908, 374.

25. Michael Kazin, *A Godly Hero: The Life of William Jennings Bryan* (New York: Knopf, 2006), 147–148.

26. "Bryan Plans to Be Roosevelt's Heir," *New York Times*, Jan. 29, 1908; James Morgan, "Fast Drift Bryanward," *Boston Daily Globe*, July 7, 1908.

27. "Bell Stirs Convention to Great Applause," *San Francisco Chronicle*, July 8, 1908; "Convention on; Full of Action," *Chicago Daily Tribune*, July 8, 1908; "Delegates Come from All Points," *Chicago Daily Tribune*, July 6, 1908.

28. Taft to Sir John Rodgers, July 19, 1908, in Pringle, *William Howard Taft*, 337; Taft to Mabel Boardman, July 14, 1908, in Pringle, *William Howard Taft*, 356–357; Taft to C.E. Magoon, July 10, 1908, in Pringle, *William Howard Taft*, 356; TR to Taft, July 15, 1908, in Pringle, *William Howard Taft*, 358; "Taft Has Regrets at Leaving Bench," *New York Times*, July 21, 1908.

29. "Taft to Leave Sylvan Retreat," *Chicago Daily Tribune*, July 19, 1908; "Shifts to Springs," *Washington Post*, June 29, 1908; "Taft a Giant, Not a Fat Man,"

Chicago Daily Tribune, July 26, 1908; "Taft's Speech Is Voluminous," *Los Angeles Times*, July 17, 1908.

30. "President Likes Mr. Taft's Speech," *New York Times*, July 24, 1908.
31. TR to Taft, July 17, 1908, in Roosevelt, *Letters*, 6:1132–1133; Archibald Willingham Butt and Lawrence Fraser Abbott, *The Letters of Archie Butt, Personal Aide to President Roosevelt* (New York: Doubleday, Page, 1924), 143.
32. TR to Taft, July 21, 1908, in Roosevelt, *Letters*, 6:1140.
33. "Make Taft Arbiter," *Washington Post*, July 26, 1908; "Taft at Cincinnati for Notification," *New York Times*, July 26, 1908.
34. "Taft Accepts Nomination," *New York Tribune*, July 29, 1908; "Taft Is Notified; Cincinnati Joyful," *New York Times*, July 29, 1908; "Campaign Slogan, 'Taft's All Right'," *Chicago Daily Tribune*, July 29, 1908; "Home City Pays Honor to Taft," *Washington Post*, July 29, 1908.
35. William H. Taft, "Functions of the next administration" (Hot Springs, VA, 1908), http://www.loc.gov/jukebox/recordings/detail/id/1486.
36. "Home City Pays Honor to Taft."
37. "Mr. Taft's Acceptance," *New York Tribune*, July 30, 1908; "Western Papers Applaud Mr. Taft," *New York Tribune*, July 30, 1908; "Republican Policies," *San Francisco Chronicle*, July 31, 1908; "Neither Bourbon nor Jacobin," *Wall Street Journal*, July 29, 1908.
38. "Taft Back; Plays Golf," *New York Tribune*, July 31, 1908.
39. "Monetary Commission Arrives," *Boston Daily Globe*, Aug. 11, 1908; "On the Way Home," *New York Times*, Oct. 15, 1908; Stephenson, *Nelson W. Aldrich*, 332–335; "W. B. Allison Dead," *Washington Post*, Aug. 5, 1908.
40. "'The Big Five' Who Run the U.S. Senate."
41. "W. B. Allison Dead."
42. "A Bitter Fight in Senate," *Meade County News*, Aug. 13, 1908; "Bristow Defeats Long," *Baltimore Sun*, Aug. 6, 1908.
43. Charles Richard Tuttle, *The New Democracy and Bryan, Its Prophet* (Chicago: C.H. Kerr, 1896), 63–64; William Jennings Bryan and Mary Baird Bryan, "Biographical Introduction," in *Speeches on Taxation and Bimetalism* (New York: Funk & Wagnalls Company, 1913), xxi–xxii; Kazin, *A Godly Hero*, 143.
44. Kazin, *A Godly Hero*, 61–62; Edward W. Barrett, "Bryan Receives an Ovation," *Atlanta Constitution*, July 10, 1896; Robert Adamson, "The Noisy Georgians," *Atlanta Constitution*, July 10, 1896; "Bryan in the Field," *Washington Post*, July 10, 1896; "Bryan Struck the Chord," *New York Tribune*, July 10, 1896.
45. US Democratic Party, *The Campaign Text Book of the Democratic Party: Of the United States, 1908* (Chicago: Western Newspaper Union, 1908), 243; "Mr. Bryan's Speech," *Wall Street Journal*, Aug. 13, 1908; "Mr. Bryan's Acceptance," *Baltimore Sun*, Aug. 14, 1908; "The Caution of Mr. Bryan," *New York Times*, Aug. 13, 1908; "Bryan Is Notified of His Nomination," *New York Times*, Aug. 13, 1908.
46. TR to Elihu Root, Sept. 5, 1908, in Roosevelt, *Letters*, 6:1207; TR to Nicholas Longworth, Sept. 19, 1908, in Roosevelt, *Letters*, 6:1244–1245.
47. TR to Taft, Sept. 5, 1908, in Roosevelt, *Letters*, 6:1209–1210.
48. Stoddard, *As I Knew Them*, 345; TR to Taft, Sept. 11, 1908, in Roosevelt, *Letters*, 6:1231; TR to Taft, Sept. 14, 1908, in Roosevelt, *Letters*, 6:1234; TR to Taft, Sept. 19, 1908, in Roosevelt, *Letters*, 6:1244; TR to Taft, Sept. 21, 1908, in Roosevelt, *Letters*, 6:1247.

49. Helen Taft to Taft, Sept. 24, 1908, in Carl Sferrazza Anthony, *Nellie Taft: The Unconventional First Lady of the Ragtime Era* (New York: William Morrow, 2005), 217.

50. "20,000 Cheer Taft at Ade's Picnic," *Chicago Daily Tribune*, Sept. 24, 1908; "Mr. Taft Begins Speaking Tour," *New York Tribune*, Sept. 24, 1908.

51. "For Taft, Radical," *Washington Post*, Sept. 25, 1908.

52. Ibid.; "Taft Renews Tariff Pledge," *New York Tribune*, Sept. 25, 1908; "La Follette Joins Taft," *Baltimore Sun*, Sept. 25, 1908.

53. "Taft's Invasion Wins Wisconsin," *Chicago Daily Tribune*, Sept. 25, 1908.

54. "Taft Renews Tariff Pledge."

55. Taft to TR, Sept. 21, 1908, in Gwinn, *Uncle Joe Cannon*, 154.

56. Stephenson, *Nelson W. Aldrich*, 338–339; "A Shocking Discovery," *New York Times*, Oct. 13, 1908.

57. Stephenson, *Nelson W. Aldrich*, 337; Edwin Palmer Hoyt, *The House of Morgan* (New York: Dodd, Mead, 1966), 321.

58. Stephenson, *Nelson W. Aldrich*, 322–323; Sternstein, "King Leopold II, Senator Nelson W. Aldrich, and the Strange Beginnings of American Economic Penetration of the Congo," 189–204.

59. Stephenson, *Nelson W. Aldrich*, 336–340; Warburg, *The Federal Reserve System*, 1:59.

60. "The Campaign: Mr. Taft in the West," *The Outlook*, Oct. 10, 1908.

61. "Bryan on the Last Lap," *Baltimore Sun*, Oct. 19, 1908; Robert W. Cherny, *A Righteous Cause: The Life of William Jennings Bryan* (Norman: Univ. of Oklahoma Press, 1994), 112–114.

62. TR to Taft, Aug. 7, 1908, in Roosevelt, *Letters*, 6:1157; Taft to George R. Sheldon, Sept. 21, 1908, in Pringle, *William Howard Taft*, 362–363; "Taft Says 'Never a Cent'," *Chicago Daily Tribune*, Oct. 31, 1908.

63. "Bryan and Taft Confident of the Result in Election," *Boston Daily Globe*, Nov. 3, 1908.

64. Pringle, *William Howard Taft*, 376–377; Anthony, *Nellie Taft*, 11; William Manners, *TR and Will: A Friendship That Split the Republican Party* (New York: Harcourt, Brace & World, 1969), 61.

65. Manners, *TR and Will*, 61; "Mr. Taft Informed of Great Victory," *New York Tribune*, Nov. 4, 1908, "President Gets News," *Washington Post*, Nov. 4, 1908.

66. "Taft Wants a Rest," *Washington Post*, Nov. 5, 1908.

67. "Roosevelt's View of Taft's Election," *New York Times*, Nov. 5, 1908.

68. Taft to H.A. Morrill, Dec. 2, 1908, in Pringle, *William Howard Taft*, 378.

69. "Not Consulting Bankers," *New York Times*, Dec. 29, 1908; Strouse, *Morgan*, 276.

70. Warburg, *Federal Reserve System*, 1:56–57.

CHAPTER 7: THE TARIFF

1. "Let Tariff Alone!" *Washington Post*, November 17, 1905.

2. James Madison to Thomas Jefferson, Mar. 29, 1789, in James Madison, *The Writings of James Madison: 1787–1790* (G.P. Putnam's Sons, 1904), 335; Margaret C. S. Christman, *The First Federal Congress, 1789–1791* (Washington, DC: Smithsonian Institution Press, 1989), 105; *2 Annals of Congress*, H1353 (1790–1791).

3. *1 Annals of Congress*, H102 (1789).

4. Ibid., H105–106, 146, 167–170.

5. Ibid., H149–156.

6. The Tariff Act of 1789, *1 Stat. 24* (1789).

7. *The Tariff Law of 1897* (Washington, DC: Government Printing Office, 1897); Frank Albert Fetter, *Modern Economic Problems* (New York: The Century Co., 1916), 231–232; Frank William Taussig, *The Tariff History of the United States* (New York: Putnam, 1914), 215, 348–352. There is an error in Taussig's sugar schedule. Raw sugar was taxed at 0.95 cents, not 1 cent. See *The Tariff Law of 1897*, 20.

8. Harrison, *Congress, Progressive Reform, and the New American State*, 174–175.

9. Jerome L. Sternstein, "Corruption in the Gilded Age Senate," 15–21, 28–32.

10. "Mr. Havemeyer on Trusts," *New York Times*, June 15, 1899.

11. Taft to Elihu Root, Nov. 25, 1908, in Pringle, *William Howard Taft*, 405; Taft to Philander C. Knox, Oct. 24, 1909, in Pringle. *William Howard Taft*, 409–410; Taft to William Allen White, Mar. 12, 1909, in Lewis L. Gould, *The William Howard Taft Presidency*, American Presidency Series (Lawrence: Univ. Press of Kansas, 2009), 52;

12. Taft to Horace D. Taft, June 27, 1909, in Pringle, *William Howard Taft*, 406.

13. "Taft Plays Harmonizer," *Los Angeles Times*, Dec. 11, 1908; "The Taft Smile," *Wall Street Journal*, Dec. 12, 1908.

14. James B. Morrow, "Representative W.P. Hepburn Tells What Further Railway Legislation Is Necessary," *Washington Post*, Sept. 20, 1908; John Ely Briggs, *William Peters Hepburn* (Iowa City: State Historical Society of Iowa, 1919), 303–304.

15. Briggs, *William Peters Hepburn*, 309–327.

16. Harrison, *Congress, Progressive Reform, and the New American State*, 210–211; James B. Morrow, "Champ Clark, of Missouri, New Minority Leader in the House," *Washington Post*, Dec. 20, 1908; "Who's Who-and Why," *Saturday Evening Post*, 1908.

17. Briggs, *William Peters Hepburn*, 319–320.

18. Taft to H. E. Pollard, Dec. 22, 1908, in Pringle, *William Howard Taft*, 409.

19. "Georgia Ready to Greet Taft," *Atlanta Constitution*, Dec. 17, 1908; "Blacks Can't Rule, Taft Tells South," *New York Times*, Dec. 8, 1908; "Taft Discloses Policy in South," *Washington Post*, Jan. 16, 1909; "Possum Like Taft Too," *Baltimore Sun*, Jan. 17, 1909; Michael L. Bromley, *William Howard Taft and the First Motoring Presidency, 1909–1913*; reprint (Jefferson, NC: McFarland, 2003), 43.

20. Taft to C. N. Bliss, Dec. 24, 1908, in Pringle, *William Howard Taft*, 386.

21. Butt and Abbott, *The Letters of Archie Butt*, 271–272.

22. Stoddard, *As I Knew Them*, 385–386; TR to Taft, Jan. 4, 1908, in Roosevelt, *Letters*, 6:1458.

23. TR to Taft, Dec. 31, 1908, in Roosevelt, *Letters*, 6:1454.

24. TR to Taft, Jan. 4, 1909, in Roosevelt, *Letters.*, 6:1458.

25. Jonathan Lurie, *William Howard Taft: The Travails of a Progressive Conservative* (Cambridge: Cambridge Univ. Press, 2011), 94; Pringle, *William Howard Taft*, 386; Mark Sullivan, *Our Times*, 4:324; Butt and Abbott, *The Letters of Archie Butt*, 338.

26. John J. Leary, "'Why I Broke With Taft': Further Conversations With Theodore Roosevelt," *McClure's Magazine*, July 1919, 18.

27. La Follette and La Follette, *Robert M. La Follette*, 263; Unger, *Fighting Bob La Follette*, 184–185.

28. After La Follette's death in 1929, the name was changed to *The Progressive*. It's still published out of Madison, Wisconsin, over a century since La Follette founded it.

29. John M. Nelson, "The American Frankenstein," *La Follette's Weekly Magazine*, Jan. 23, 1909, 6.

30. Arthur Sears Henning, "Washington a Dull Place in 1909," *Chicago Daily Tribune*, Jan. 2, 1955; "Avenue Blaze of Light for Taft Inauguration," *Washington Post*, Mar. 4, 1925; "Flood of Visitors Pours into Capital," *New York Times*, Mar. 3, 1909; "Washington Ready for Large Crowds," *New York Times*, Mar. 2, 1909; "Inauguration Crush Begins at Capital," *New York Times*, Mar. 1, 1909; "Crowds See Parade Despite Weather," *New York Times*, Mar. 5, 1909.

31. "Crowds March in Snow and Cheer for Taft," *Baltimore Sun*, Mar. 5, 1909; "What Leading Men See in the Coming of Taft," *New York Times*, Feb. 28, 1909; H. M. Hyde, "Taft President; Storm Is King," *Chicago Daily Tribune*, Mar. 5, 1909.

32. Hyde, "Taft President; Storm Is King"; "Ride to the Capitol," *New York Times*, Mar. 5, 1909; Helen Herron Taft, *Recollections of Full Years* (New York: Dodd, Mead & Company, 1914), 328; "Blizzard Forces Change of Date?," *Chicago Daily Tribune*, Mar. 5, 1909.

33. "Crowds See Parade Despite Weather"; "Unique Features of the Taft Inauguration," *Washington Post*, Mar. 5, 1909; "First in 76 Years," *Boston Daily Globe*, March 5, 1909.

34. "Final Scene in House," *Washington Post*, Mar. 5, 1909; *43 Cong. Rec.*, H3825 (1909); Hyde, "Taft President; Storm Is King."

35. Hyde, "Taft President; Storm Is King"; "Taft Impressed Audience," *New York Times*, Mar. 5, 1909; "Sherman First to Take Oath," *Boston Daily Globe*, Mar. 5, 1909.

36. "Ceremony in the Senate," *New York Times*, Mar. 5, 1909; "William H. Taft Inaugurated President," *Washington Post*, Mar. 5, 1909.

37. "Ceremony in the Senate."

38. "William H. Taft Inaugurated President"; "Taft Impressed Audience."

39. "Presidential Inaugurations. William Howard Taft, Inauguration, Mar. 4, 1909," accessed Sept. 27, 2011, http://memory.loc.gov/ammem/pihtml/pi036. html; John Callan O'Laughlin, "Duty Well Done; Roosevelt Glad," *Chicago Daily Tribune*, Mar. 5, 1909.

40. "William Howard Taft: Inaugural Address," accessed June 20, 2013, http://www.presidency.ucsb.edu/ws/?pid=25830; "Taft Impressed Audience."

41. Walter Wellman, "Terrific Blizzard Mars Inauguration," *Los Angeles Times*, Mar. 5, 1909; Taft, *Recollections of Full Years*, 331; O'Laughlin, "Duty Well Done; Roosevelt Glad."

42. "William H. Taft Inaugurated President."

43. Hyde, "Taft President; Storm Is King."

44. "Inaugural Ball a Stately Climax," *Chicago Daily Tribune*, Mar. 5, 1909; "Gorgeous Scene at Inaugural Ball," *New York Tribune*, Mar. 5, 1909; "Gowns at Inaugural Ball," *New York Times*, Mar. 5, 1909; Benson John Lossing, *Mary and Martha, the Mother and the Wife of George Washington* (New York: Harper & Brothers, 1886), 262.

45. "Taft Fireworks Reflected in Ice," *Chicago Daily Tribune*, Mar. 5, 1909; "Great Show for Taft," *Baltimore Sun*, Feb. 28, 1909.

46. "Taft's First Day a Severe Ordeal," *New York Times*, Mar. 6, 1909.

47. "House Rules Warfare," *New York Tribune*, Mar. 9, 1909.

48. "Tariff Must Be First," *Baltimore Sun*, Mar. 10, 1909; Taft to William D. Foulke, Mar. 12, 1909, in Stanley D. Solvick, "William Howard Taft and Cannonism," *Wisconsin Magazine of History* 48, no. 1 (Oct. 1, 1964): 57.

49. Taft to TR, Mar. 21, 1909, in Pringle, *William Howard Taft*, 400–401.

50. TR to Taft, Mar. 23, 1909, in Roosevelt, *Letters*, 7:3; Archibald Willingham Butt, *Taft and Roosevelt: The Intimate Letters of Archie Butt, Military Aide*, 2 vols. (New York: Doubleday, Doran, 1930), 1:367.

51. *44 Cong. Rec.*, H21–22 (1909).

52. Ibid., H26–28. One additional change known as "calendar for unanimous consent" allowed minor bills to reach the floor without going through the Speaker. I have left it out for the sake of brevity.

53. "Taft Keeps to Desk," *Washington Post*, Mar. 17, 1909.

54. La Follette, *Autobiography*, 437–438; Bowers, *Beveridge*, 334; "Tariff Bill Ready for House To-Day," *New York Times*, Mar. 17, 1909; "Taft to the Point," *Baltimore Sun*, Mar. 17, 1909, 226.

55. "Tariff Bill Ready for House To-Day,"

56. "Cannon Hissed Twice," *Baltimore Sun*, Mar. 17, 1909.

57. La Follette, *Autobiography*, 430–434.

58. Ross, *Jonathan Prentiss Dolliver*, 242–243.

59. Stephenson, *Nelson W. Aldrich*, 345.

60. La Follette, *Autobiography*, 432–433.

61. Taft to Frank L. Dingley, Mar. 21, 1909, in Gould, *The William Howard Taft Presidency*, 54; Taft to Horace D. Taft, June 27, 1909, in H. H. Kolsaat, "From McKinley to Harding: Personal Recollections of Our Presidents," *Saturday Evening Post*, Sept. 30, 1922, 44.

62. "Tariff Is Dividing Congress Along Geographical Lines," *Christian Science Monitor*, Mar. 20, 1909; "17 Women's Clubs Denounce Tariff," *Chicago Daily Tribune*, Mar. 23, 1909.

63. Stephenson, *Nelson W. Aldrich*, 337, 347–353. The rubber increases, carefully concealed in schedules for other products that used rubber including automobiles and wires, created a scandal after the tariff bill passed. Contrary to the accusations, Aldrich's investments were in raw rubber production, so he did not benefit directly from the increases. His customers did, however.

64. Harrison, *Congress, Progressive Reform, and the New American State*, 173; "No New Taxes to Be Imposed, Says Aldrich," *Atlanta Constitution*, April 20, 1909.

65. *Providence Tribune*, June 6, 1909, in Merrill and Merrill, *The Republican Command*, 290.

66. La Follette, *Autobiography*, 443–444; Bowers, *Beveridge*, 339, 347.

67. *44 Cong. Rec.*, S1448–1463 (1909); "New Insurgents Attack Aldrich," *New York Times*, April 23, 1909.

68. Harrison, *Congress, Progressive Reform, and the New American State*, 185.

69. La Follette, *Autobiography*, 440; "D.A.R. Offers Hall," *Washington Post*, May 6, 1909; Taft to William Allen White, Mar. 20, 1909, in William Allen White, *The Autobiography of William Allen White* (New York: Macmillan, 1946), 451.

70. Butt, *Taft and Roosevelt*, 1:40.

71. Taft to Horace D. Taft, June 27, 1909, in Kolsaat, "From McKinley to Harding: Personal Recollections," 48.

72. Anthony, *Nellie Taft*, 258–266; Butt, *Taft and Roosevelt*, 1:86–88, 1:99–102.

73. Butt, *Taft and Roosevelt*, 1:38.

74. Kolsaat, "From McKinley to Harding: Personal Recollections," 48; Taft to Helen Taft, July 11, 14, 1909, in William H. Taft, *My Dearest Nellie: The Letters of William Howard Taft to Helen Herron Taft, 1909–1912* (Lawrence, Kansas: Univ. Press of Kansas, 2011), 28, 41; Taft to E. H. Gary, July 12, 1909, in Bromley, *William Howard Taft and the First Motoring Presidency*, 160; Butt, *Taft and Roosevelt*, 1:58.

75. Taft to J. D. Brannan, June 29, 1909, in Merrill and Merrill, *The Republican Command*, 293; Taft to Horace D. Taft, June 27, 1909, in Kolsaat, "From McKinley to Harding: Personal Recollections," 44; Taft to W. L. Fisher, Sept. 25, 1909, in Pringle, *William Howard Taft*, 414.

76. Bowers, *Beveridge*, 343; "Mrs. Taft Still Improves," *New York Times*, May 20, 1909.

77. Beveridge to Catherine Beveridge, June 4, 1909, in Bowers, *Beveridge*, 345; Ross, *Jonathan Prentiss Dolliver*, 257–259; "Beveridge in a Row," *Baltimore Sun*, June 8, 1909.

78. Harrison, *Congress, Progressive Reform, and the New American State*, 179–180.

79. "Long Hours Promised," *Washington Post*, May 24, 1909; Elihu Root to Charles S. Francis, May 31, 1909, in Merrill and Merrill, *The Republican Command*, 292.

80. Bowers, *Beveridge*, 348; Stephenson, *Nelson W. Aldrich*, 357.

81. *26 Cong. Rec.*, S6636 (1894); *44 Cong. Rec.*, S3929 (1909); "High Tariff with Retrenchment," *New York Times*, April 20, 1909.

82. Taft to Horace D. Taft, June 27, 1909, in Kolsaat, "From McKinley to Harding: Personal Recollections of Our Presidents," 46; Stephenson, *Nelson W. Aldrich*, 354–356. Stephenson speculates that Aldrich had broader concerns that a Democratic-Radical-Western coalition would seize control of the Senate, but he cites no evidence. Taft's recollection suggests that Aldrich was specifically concerned about the income tax amendment.

83. *La Follette's Weekly*, June 26, 1909, quoted in "La Follette Raps President," *Los Angeles Times*, June 26, 1909.

84. Taft to Helen Taft, July 8, 9, 11, 18, 1909, in Taft, *My Dearest Nellie*, 23, 26, 29, 48–49.

85. La Follette, *Autobiography*, 448–449; "About People and Social Incidents," *New York Tribune*, July 13, 1909.

86. Taft to Helen Taft, July 22, 30, 1909, in Taft, *My Dearest Nellie*, 52, 61; Butt, *Taft and Roosevelt*, 1:140; Bowers, *Beveridge*, 361–362; John Callan O'Laughlin, "Taft's Big Stick Hits the Tariff," *Chicago Daily Tribune*, July 17, 1909; "Mr. Taft Puts His Foot Down," *Los Angeles Times*, July 17, 1909.

87. Merrill and Merrill, *The Republican Command*, 292–294; Pringle, *William Howard Taft*, 439–441; Solvick, "William Howard Taft and Cannonism," 439–440; Butt, *Taft and Roosevelt*, 1:163–164.

88. *44 Cong. Rec.*, S4932, 4947 (1909).

89. "President Signs Tariff Measure," *Washington Post*, Aug. 6, 1909.

90. Harrison, *Congress, Progressive Reform, and the New American State*, 174.

91. "Cannon All Wrong, Charges Fowler," *Chicago Daily Tribune*, Aug. 24, 1909; "Cannon Disciplines House Insurgents," *New York Times*, Aug. 6, 1909.

92. TR to Henry Cabot Lodge, Sept. 10, 1909, in Roosevelt, *Letters*, 7:28; Theodore Roosevelt, *African Game Trails: An Account of the African Wanderings of an American Hunter–Naturalist* (New York: C. Scribner's Sons, 1909), 271–322.

93. Taft to F. H. Gillette, Sept. 13, 1909, in Pringle, *William Howard Taft*, 457.

94. Ibid., 452.

95. Ibid., 453–454.

96. Ibid.

97. "'Best Tariff Bill We Have Ever Had,' President Taft Tells 'Insurgents,'" *Atlanta Constitution*, Sept. 18, 1909.

98. "Iowa Insurgents Red Hot," *New York Sun*, Sept. 19, 1909; "Turn Against Taft on Tariff Speech," *New York Times*, Sept. 20, 1909.

99. Taft to William Dudley Foulke, Nov. 18, 1909, in Donald F. Anderson, *William Howard Taft: A Conservative's Conception of the Presidency* (Ithaca: Cornell Univ. Press, 1973), 206.

100. Dolliver to La Follette, Oct. 13, 1909, in La Follette and La Follette, *Robert M. La Follette*, 282.

101. "Capitol News," Dec. 17, 1909, in La Follette and La Follette, *Robert M. La Follette*, 285.

CHAPTER 8: THE INSURGENCY

1. Gwinn, *Uncle Joe Cannon*, 190.

2. Gifford Pinchot, "The Conservation of Natural Resources," *The Outlook*, Oct. 12, 1907, 291.

3. Gifford Pinchot, *Breaking New Ground* (New York: Harcourt, Brace, 1947), 27.

4. Ibid., 145; Mark Sullivan, *Our Times*, 4:385–390.

5. Jerry A. O'Callaghan, "Senator Mitchell and the Oregon Land Frauds, 1905," *Pacific Historical Review* 21, no. 3 (Aug. 1, 1952): 255–261; Stephen A. Douglas Puter and Horace Stevens, *Looters of the Public Domain: Embracing a Complete Exposure of the Fraudulent Systems of Acquiring Titles to the Public Lands of the United States* (Portland, OR: Portland Printing House Publishers, 1907), 324–325.

6. Gould, *The Presidency of Theodore Roosevelt*, 192, 196.

7. *41 Cong. Rec.*, S3188, 3869 (1907); For Fulton's attempt to quash the investigation, see TR to Charles William Fulton, May 13, 1905, in Roosevelt, *Letters*, 4:1176–1177.

8. Roosevelt, *Theodore Roosevelt, an Autobiography*, 404.

9. Pringle, *William Howard Taft*, 343, 477–481; Gould, *The William Howard Taft Presidency*, 46, 65–68.

10. Taft to William Kent, June 29, 1909, in Pringle, *William Howard Taft*, 481.

11. Gould, *The William Howard Taft Presidency*, 66–67; "Pinchot on Warpath," *Washington Post*, July 18, 1909; Taft to E. F. Baldwin, Aug. 13, 1909, in Pringle, *William Howard Taft*, 493–494.

12. Pinchot, *Breaking New Ground*, 427.

13. Pringle, *William Howard Taft*, 494–496.

14. Taft to Francis G. Newlands, Sept. 9, 1909, in Pringle, *William Howard Taft*, 491; Taft to Gifford Pinchot, Sept. 13, 1909, in Investigation of the

Department of the Interior and of the Bureau of Forestry, S. Doc. No. 719, at 4:1220–1221 (1911).

15. Butt, *Taft and Roosevelt*, 1:208, 1:235–236.

16. Pinchot, *Breaking New Ground*, 444; "Eight Died in the Storm Here," *New York Times*, Dec. 27, 1909.

17. "Advice by Pinchot," *New York Tribune*, Dec. 28, 1909.

18. Gifford Pinchot to TR, Dec. 31, 1909, in "A Look Ahead in Politics," *Saturday Evening Post*, Oct. 7, 1911, 4.

19. Pinchot, *Breaking New Ground*, 447, 450.

20. Butt, *Taft and Roosevelt*, 1:253.

21. Pinchot, *Breaking New Ground*, 453.

22. Roosevelt, *African Game Trails*, 459–467; Roosevelt, *Letters*, 7:46fn.

23. TR to Gifford Pinchot, Jan. 17, 1910, in Roosevelt, *Letters*, 7:45.

24. Taft to C. H. Kelsey, Jan. 10, 1910, in Pringle, *William Howard Taft*, 509.

25. La Follette and La Follette, *Robert M. La Follette*, 295–296.

26. Gould, *The William Howard Taft Presidency*, 97–98; Harrison, *Congress, Progressive Reform, and the New American State*, 84–85.

27. Taft to C. P. Taft, Mar. 5, 1910, in Stephenson, *Nelson W. Aldrich*, 483.

28. Butt, *Taft and Roosevelt*, 1:272, 301; "National Climatic Data Center–Daily Summaries Station Details: Great Falls, Md." accessed Aug. 14, 2013, http://www.ncdc.noaa.gov/cdo-web/datasets/GHCND/stations/GHCND:USC00183850/detail.

29. Butt, *Taft and Roosevelt*, 1:299–301.

30. Ibid., 1:301–304.

31. John Thomas Salter, *Public Men: In and Out of Office* (Chapel Hill: Univ. of North Carolina Press, 1946), 202.

32. *45 Cong. Rec.*, H3239–3251 (1910); Gwinn, *Uncle Joe Cannon*, 206–207; "Uprising in House," *Washington Post*, Mar. 17, 1910; "Crushing Defeat Humbles Cannon," *Chicago Daily Tribune*, Mar. 17, 1910.

33. George W. Norris, "The Secret of His Power: A History of the Insurgent Movement in the House of Representatives," *La Follette's Magazine*, Jan. 8, 1910, 7–9; "Attacks President," *New York Tribune*, Jan. 7, 1910; "Cannon Defeated by House Vote," *Washington Post*, Jan. 8, 1910.

34. "'Uncle Joe' at Bay; All Night Fight to Depose Czar," *Chicago Daily Tribune*, Mar. 18, 1910.

35. "Cannon, Baffled in 26 Hour Fight, Treats for Peace," *Chicago Daily Tribune*, Mar. 19, 1910; *45 Cong. Rec.*, H3405 (1910).

36. "Cannon, Baffled in 26 Hour Fight, Treats for Peace."

37. Ibid.; *45 Cong. Rec.*, H3416–3417 (1910).

38. "Speaker Cannon, Shorn of Powers, Saves His Crown," *Chicago Daily Tribune*, Mar. 20, 1910; "Cannon, Shorn of His Power Keeps Office," *New York Times*, Mar. 20, 1910.

39. "Cannon, Shorn of His Power Keeps Office"; *45 Cong. Rec.*, H3425–3428 (1910).

40. Richard Lowitt, *George W. Norris: The Making of a Progressive, 1861–1912* (Syracuse, NY: Syracuse Univ. Press, 1963), 177–178; "House Curbs Cannon; Refuses to Expel Him," *Baltimore Sun*, Mar. 20, 1910; "Cannon, Shorn of His Power Keeps Office"; *45 Cong. Rec.*, H3434–3435 (1910).

41. Arthur C. Johnson, "Cannon the Victor," *Washington Post*, Mar. 20, 1910; *45 Cong. Rec.*, H3433–3434 (1910).

42. *45 Cong. Rec.*, H3437–3439 (1910); "House Curbs Cannon; Refuses to Expel Him."

43. Johnson, "Cannon the Victor"; "Cannon Believes, He Was the Victor," *New York Times*, Mar. 20, 1910.

44. "Cannon Lashes His Foes," *New York Times*, Mar. 21, 1910.

45. Taft to Helen Taft, Mar. 19, 1910, in Taft, *My Dearest Nellie*, 120.

46. Taft to Guy W. Mallon, Jan. 13, 1909, in Gwinn, *Uncle Joe Cannon*, 196.

47. *45 Cong. Rec.*, S1426 (1910); "Elkins Turns Rebel Over Tariff Prices," *New York Times*, Feb. 4, 1910.

48. "Democrats Outwit and Defeat Aldrich," *New York Times*, May 14, 1910.

49. Stephenson, *Nelson W. Aldrich*, 364–366.

50. Melvin I. Urofsky, *Louis D. Brandeis: A Life*, (New York: Random House, 2009), 264–266.

51. Investigation of the Department of the Interior and of the Bureau of Forestry, S. Doc. 719, at 7:3865 (1911).

52. Urofsky, *Louis D. Brandeis*, 267.

53. "Says Ballinger Wrote Taft Letter," *New York Times*, May 15, 1910.

54. "Kerby's Charges Denied by Taft," *Washington Post*, May 15, 1910.

55. "Sends Lawler Draft," *Baltimore Sun*, May 15, 1910.

56. *Investigation of the Department of the Interior and of the Bureau of Forestry*, 1:60–62.

57. Norman Hapgood, *The Changing Years, Reminiscences of Norman Hapgood* (New York: Farrar & Rinehart, 1930), 189.

58. Roosevelt, *Theodore Roosevelt, an Autobiography*, 323–326.

59. Taft to TR, May 26, 1910, in Pringle, *William Howard Taft*, 512–513, 543.

60. James Chace, *1912: Wilson, Roosevelt, Taft, and Debs—The Election That Changed the Country* (New York: Simon & Schuster, 2004), 16; Ross, *Jonathan Prentiss Dolliver*, 272–273; Bowers, *Beveridge*, 384.

61. TR to Henry Cabot Lodge, May 5, 1910, in Roosevelt, *Letters*, 7:80.

62. Viscount Edward Grey of Fallodon, *Twenty-Five Years, 1892–1916* (New York: Frederick A. Stokes, 1925); TR to Taft, Jun. 8, 1910, in Roosevelt, *Letters*, 7:388–389.

63. "Give Roosevelt Record Breaking Welcome to U.S.," *Chicago Daily Tribune*, June 19, 1910; "Details of the Great Ovation," *San Francisco Chronicle*, June 19, 1910; "Million Join in Welcome to Roosevelt," *New York Times*, June 19, 1910.

64. "Roosevelt Home, " *New York Tribune*, June 19, 1910. "New York Is Storm Swept," *Chicago Daily Tribune*, June 19, 1910; "Glad to Get Home," *Washington Post*, June 19, 1910.

65. "Sees T.R. Rejoices," *Washington Post*, June 28, 1910; La Follette, *Autobiography*, 487–488.

66. RMLF to Jonathan Bourne, July 11, 1910, in La Follette and La Follette, *Robert M. La Follette*, 302; RMLF to Judson Welliver, July 9, 1910, in Greenbaum, *Robert Marion La Follette*, 99.

67. Butt, *Taft and Roosevelt*, 2:434, 2:461–462; "Ballinger Won't Quit," *Washington Post*, July 6, 1910.

68. Butt, *Taft and Roosevelt*, 1:418–431, 2:434–437.

69. TR to Henry Cabot Lodge, Aug. 17, 1910, in Roosevelt, *Letters*, 7:117; TR to Theodore Roosevelt Jr., Aug. 23, 1910, in Roosevelt, *Letters*, 7:120–121;

Lucius Burrie Swift to Mrs. Swift, July 8, 1910, in Edmund Morris, *Colonel Roosevelt*, (New York: Random House, 2010), 101.

70. TR to Henry Cabot Lodge, July 19, 1910, in Roosevelt, *Letters*, 7:102; TR to Henry Cabot Lodge, Sept. 21, 1910, in Roosevelt, *Letters*, 7:136.

71. "Roosevelt Stirs Throngs on Trip," *Chicago Daily Tribune*, Aug. 26, 1910.

72. "Mr. Roosevelt's Speech," *New York Times*, Aug. 28, 1910.

73. Theodore Roosevelt, *The New Nationalism* (New York: Outlook Company, 1910), 1–33; Robert S. La Forte, "Theodore Roosevelt's Osawatomie Speech," *Kansas Historical Quarterly*, Summer 1966, 187–200; "Roosevelt Expounds New Nationalism," *New York Tribune*, Sept. 1, 1910; "T. R.'s Challenge," *Baltimore Sun*, Sept. 1, 1910.

74. "T. R.'s Challenge"; Richard Henry Little, "Roosevelt Gives a Radical Creed in Kansas Speech," *Chicago Daily Tribune*, Sept. 1, 1910.

75. *New York Post*, Sept. 1, 1910, quoted in Morris, *Colonel Roosevelt*, 110.

76. TR to Henry Cabot Lodge, Sept. 20, 1910, in Roosevelt, *Letters*, 7:134; Morris, *Colonel Roosevelt*, 116–117.

CHAPTER 9: THE PROGRESSIVE

1. James B. Morrow, "Joseph G. Cannon," *Washington Post*, July 8, 1906.

2. Joseph P. Tumulty, *Woodrow Wilson as I Know Him* (Garden City, NY: Doubleday, Page, 1921), 16–22; Ray Stannard Baker, *Woodrow Wilson: Life and Letters*, vol. 3 (Garden City, NY: Doubleday, Page, 1927), 73–81; "Wilson Named for Governor in Jersey," *New York Times*, Sept. 16, 1910; Arthur S. Link, *Wilson, the Road to the White House* (Princeton: Princeton Univ. Press, 1947), 162–168.

3. Link, *Wilson, the Road to the White House*, 149–150, 206–209; William Inglis, "Helping to Make a President," *Collier's*, Oct. 7, 1916, 16; William Inglis, "Helping to Make a President," *Collier's*, Oct. 21, 1916, 14.

4. "The Crisis in the Republican Party," *The Outlook*, Sept. 3, 1910, 11a–12.

5. Bowers, *Beveridge*, 384–400; "Beveridge the Issue," *Baltimore Sun*, Sept. 24, 1910.

6. Butt, *Taft and Roosevelt*, 2:554–556; "Taft Is Silent as to Election," *Chicago Daily Tribune*, Nov. 9, 1910.

7. The name of the island was misspelled with a single *L* during the club's heyday, later corrected by the Georgia legislature.

8. Frank Arthur Vanderlip and Boyden Sparkes, *From Farm Boy to Financier* (New York: D. Appleton-Century, 1935), 213–217; Stephenson, *Nelson W. Aldrich*, 373–377; Samuel M. Williams, "A Millionaire's Paradise," *Munsey's Magazine*, Feb. 1904, 642–646. Vanderlip also recalled Benjamin Strong's presence at the conference, but this account is at odds with other sources. For a full analysis of the question, see Elmus Wicker, *The Great Debate on Banking Reform: Nelson Aldrich and the Origins of the Fed* (Columbus: Ohio State Univ. Press, 2005), 52–53.

9. Stephenson, *Nelson W. Aldrich*, 378–379; Warburg, *Federal Reserve System*, 1:60; Wicker, *The Great Debate on Banking Reform*, 67–69.

10. Stephenson, *Nelson W. Aldrich*, 377.

11. William Bayard Hale, *Woodrow Wilson: The Story of His Life* (Garden City, NY: Doubleday, Page, 1912), 179–182.

12. "Choosing a Leader for 1912!," *Atlanta Constitution*, Nov. 28, 1910; "Woodrow Wilson, Leader," *New York Times*, Nov. 30, 1910.

13. Baker, *Woodrow Wilson*, 3:121–127; Link, *Wilson, the Road to the White House*, 223–235; Tumulty, *Woodrow Wilson*, 59–71; "5,000 Smith Backers to Storm Trenton," *New York Times*, Jan. 23, 1911.

14. "Ratify Election in Joint Session; Ceremony Simple," *Milwaukee Sentinel*, Jan. 26, 1911.

15. Unger, *Fighting Bob La Follette*, 191–192.

16. "Primary Plan Is to Be Considered," *Milwaukee Sentinel*, Jan. 26, 1911. "An Insurgent Landslide," *Baltimore Sun*, August 18, 1910.

17. La Follette and La Follette, *Robert M. La Follette*, 311–312; "The Nomination of Dr. Woodrow Wilson," *The Outlook*, Sept. 24, 1910, 140; Robert Marion La Follette, *The Political Philosophy of Robert M. La Follette as Revealed in His Speeches and Writings* (Madison, WI: The Robert M. La Follette Co., 1920), 177.

18. "Insurgents in Control," *Washington Post*, Sept. 7, 1910; "Cape Cod Greets Foss Cordially," *Boston Daily Globe*, Oct. 27, 1910; "La Follette Takes Ground for Lenroot"; Judson C. Welliver, "The Tottering Political Machines," *Hampton's Magazine*, Nov. 1, 1910; "Editorial," *Springfield Daily Republican*, Nov. 27, 1910; Ray Stannard Baker to RMLF, Nov. 29, 1910, in La Follette and La Follette, *Robert M. La Follette*, 312.

19. Robert Marion La Follette, "The Beginning of a Great Movement," *La Follette's Magazine*, Feb. 4, 1911, 7–9.

20. Variations of this quote have been ascribed to all of Roosevelt's children. For one example, see, "Writes of Roosevelt's Ego," *Chicago Daily Tribune*, January 31, 1909.

21. Biographer Nancy Unger writes that La Follette was eager to add Roosevelt's name to the NPRL but has trouble reconciling this claim with La Follette's snubs and feigned excuses. Her suggestion that La Follette "could not bring himself to meet face-to-face with the man he so distrusted and envied" seems uncharacteristically cowardly for La Follette, and it's contradicted by their Oyster Bay meeting six months earlier. I suggest an alternative interpretation: La Follette didn't really want to Roosevelt to join the league, at least not on Roosevelt's terms—a plausible assumption since he regarded Roosevelt as a rival. La Follette may have been pressured by his colleagues to proffer an invitation, or he may have been personally ambivalent, but either way, his heart did not seem to be in it. He left no record of his deliberations, so any explanation is necessarily speculative. See Unger, *Fighting Bob La Follette*, 194–195.

22. TR to La Follette, Jan. 3, 1911, in Roosevelt, *Letters*, 7:201–202.

23. "Letter from Robert M. La Follette to Theodore Roosevelt," Jan. 24, 1911, Theodore Roosevelt Papers, Manuscripts division, The Library of Congress, http://www.theodorerooseveltcenter.org/Research/Digital-Library/Record.aspx?libID=o63607.

24. Gwinn, *Uncle Joe Cannon*, 241–244.

25. Merrill and Merrill, *The Republican Command*, 318–320; *46 Cong. Rec.*, H4339 (1911); "Cannon as a Czar Again," *New York Times*, Mar. 5, 1911; "Cannon Despot as Power Ends," *Chicago Daily Tribune*, Mar. 5, 1911; "House Ends in Riot," *Washington Post*, Mar. 5, 1911; "Rancor Banished as Members Part,"

New York Times, Mar. 5, 1911; "Tariff Board Bill Killed in the House," *New York Tribune*, Mar. 5, 1911.

26. Stephenson, *Nelson W. Aldrich*, 380–387; Taft to Aldrich, Jan. 28, 1911, in Pringle, *William Howard Taft*, 411.

27. Standard Oil Co. of New Jersey v. United States, 221 U.S. 1 (1911); "Standard Oil Company Must Dissolve in 6 Months," *New York Times*, May 16, 1911.

28. La Follette and La Follette, *Robert M. La Follette*, 336–337, 475; Thelen, *Robert M. La Follette and the Insurgent Spirit*, 85 86.

20. "New Senate Meets," *Washington Post*, April 5, 1911; "G.O.P. Split Hopeless," *Baltimore Sun*, April 29, 1911; Gould, *The Most Exclusive Club*, 50, 54–55; La Follette and La Follette, *Robert M. La Follette*, 326–327.

30. *46 Cong. Rec.*, S2244 (1911); Ralph A. Rossum, *Federalism, the Supreme Court, and the Seventeenth Amendment: The Irony of Constitutional Democracy* (Lanham, MD: Lexington Books, 2001), 208–211; Larry J. Easterling, "Senator Joseph L. Bristow and the Seventeenth Amendment," *The Kansas Historical Quarterly* 41, no. 4 (Winter 1975): 490, 504–506.

31. Unger, *Fighting Bob La Follette*, 297; La Follette and La Follette, *Robert M. La Follette*, 328–331.

32. RMLF to Fremont Older, Apr. 18, 1911, in La Follette and La Follette, *Robert M. La Follette*, 329; La Follette, *Autobiography*, 522.

33. La Follette and La Follette, *Robert M. La Follette*, 527–528; Theodore Roosevelt, "Wisconsin: An Object-Lesson for the Rest of the Union," *The Outlook*, May 27, 1911, 145.

34. La Follette, *Autobiography*, 526; Unger, *Fighting Bob La Follette*, 198.

35. Morrow, "Joseph G. Cannon."

36. "Wants a Bank Inquiry," *New York Times*, July 9, 1911; Henry Beech Needham, "Woodrow Wilson's Views," *The Outlook*, Aug. 26, 1911, 944–946; "Dr. Woodrow Wilson Defines Material Issues."

37. TR to Nicholas Longworth, June 19, 1911, in Roosevelt, *Letters*, 7:290.

38. House of Representatives, *U.S. Steel Hearings*, 1371–1392; "Mr. Roosevelt's Testimony," *New York Times*, Aug. 6, 1911; "The Steel Merger," *Washington Post*, Aug. 6, 1911; "Roosevelt and Steel," *New York Tribune*, Aug. 7, 1911.

39. TR to RMLF, Sep. 29, 1911, in Roosevelt, *Letters*, 7:348.

40. TR to Hiram Warren Johnson, Oct. 27, 1911, in Roosevelt, *Letters*, 7:421–422; See also TR to William Allen White, Oct. 24, 1911, in Roosevelt, *Letters* 7:418.

41. "Suit to Kill Steel Trust Begun by the Government Under the Sherman Law," *New York Evening World*, Oct. 26, 1911.

42. John Hays Hammond, *The Autobiography of John Hays Hammond* (New York: Farrar & Rinehart, 1935), 578.

43. TR to Hiram Warren Johnson, Oct. 27, 1911, in Roosevelt, *Letters*, 7:421–422; TR to Marshall Stimson, Oct. 27, 1911, in Roosevelt, *Letters*, 7:422.

44. Theodore Roosevelt, "The Trusts, the People, and the Square Deal," *The Outlook*, Nov. 18, 1911, 649–656.

45. "Roosevelt Again Declines to Run," *New York Times*, Nov. 27, 1911.

46. Ray Stannard Baker to RMFL, Dec. 9, 1911, in La Follette and La Follette, *Robert M. La Follette*, 363.

47. Ibid., 353; Greenbaum, *Robert Marion La Follette*, 105–106; Fred Greenbaum, "Teddy Roosevelt Creates a 'Draft' in 1912," in *Theodore Roosevelt: Many-Sided American* (Interlaken, NY: Heart of the Lakes Pub., 1992), 435–439.

48. "Pinchot Comes Out for La Follette," *New York Times*, Nov. 28, 1911.

49. La Follette, *Autobiography*, 542–548.

50. "La Follette Won't Withdraw," *New York Times*, Jan. 4, 1912; "Cheer La Follette in Chicago as He Assails Trusts," *Chicago Daily Tribune*, Jan. 4, 1912; "La Follette's Collar Off," *New York Tribune*, Dec. 30, 1911.

51. Follette, *Autobiography*, 593–595; "La Follette Wants No Limit on Recall," *New York Times*, Jan. 23, 1912; "La Follette Launches Boom Here to Crowds," *New York Tribune*, Jan. 23, 1912.

52. Harold Howland, *Theodore Roosevelt and His Times: A Chronicle of the Progressive Movement* (New Haven: Yale Univ. Press, 1921), 210–211.

53. "Now Col. Roosevelt's Stripped to the Buff," *New York Sun*, Feb. 23, 1912. Many historians have erroneously conflated this quote with another unofficial declaration as, "My hat is in the ring, the fight is on, and I am stripped to the buff."

54. La Follette and La Follette, *Robert M. La Follette*, 376–379, 383–387, 395–397.

55. Ibid., 399–408; Unger, *Fighting Bob La Follette*, 202–213; "La Follette Breaks down; Quits Work," *New York Tribune*, Feb. 4, 1912; "La Follette Goes Wild," *Baltimore Sun*, Feb. 4, 1912; "Spoke Over Two Hours," *New York Times*, Feb. 4, 1912; "Taft Fires on His Opponents," *The New York Times*, Feb. 13, 1912; "La Follette Now Out of the Race," *New York Times*, Feb. 6, 1912.

CHAPTER 10: THE BULL MOOSE

1. "Cannon for Harmony," *Washington Post*, Jan. 7, 1910.

2. TR to Walter R. Stubbs, Feb. 8, 1912, in Roosevelt, *Letters*, 7:499.

3. "The Stampede Is Under Way," *New York Times*, Feb. 7, 1912; "New Governor in Roosevelt Ranks," *Chicago Daily Tribune*, Feb. 8, 1912; "Is Out for Roosevelt," *Washington Post*, Feb. 20, 1912; "Roosevelt to Make His Position Clear," *New York Tribune*, Feb. 15, 1912; "Roosevelt to Fight to End—No Deserter," *New York Times*, Feb. 9, 1912.

4. Theodore Roosevelt, "Women's Rights; and the Duties of Both Men and Women," *The Outlook*, Feb. 3, 1912, 262–266; TR to Mary Ella Lyon Swift, Mar. 7, 1911, in Roosevelt, *Letters*, 7:240.

5. John Callan O'Laughlin, "To Take up of Battle with Roosevelt," *Chicago Daily Tribune*, Feb. 23, 1912.

6. TR to Edmond Haggard Madison, Feb. 17, 1911, in Roosevelt, *Letters*, 7:233; TR to Henry Lewis Stimson, Feb. 5, 1912, in Roosevelt, *Letters*, 7:495; "Roosevelt Indorses Recall of Judges," *New York Times*, Feb. 22, 1912. Lewis L. Gould, *Four Hats in the Ring: The 1912 Election and the Birth of Modern American Politics* (Lawrence, KS: Univ. Press of Kansas, 2008), 56–58.

7. "Alarms His Own Followers," *New York Times*, Feb. 22, 1912; "Speech of T.R. Liked," *Washington Post*, Feb. 22, 1912; "'My Hat Is in the Ring,' Says Col. Roosevelt," *New York Tribune*, February 22, 1912. In fact, La Follette did endorse judicial recall in an unpublished interview for *The Outlook*, but Roosevelt's speech occurred before publication. See Oscar King Davis, *Released for Publication* (Boston: Houghton Mifflin, 1925), 261–265.

8. Gould, *Four Hats in the Ring*, 58–59; John Corrigan, "They Open Fire on Roosevelt," *Atlanta Constitution*, Feb. 23, 1912; "Talking of Roosevelt," *Baltimore Sun*, Feb. 22, 1912; "Good Time to Decide Issue," *Boston Daily*

Globe, Feb. 26, 1912; "The Real Roosevelt," *Saturday Review of Politics, Literature, Science and Art* 113, no. 2940 (Mar. 2, 1912): 262; "Calls Colonel a Demagogue," *New York Times*, Feb. 24, 1912.

9. "Alarms His Own Followers"; John Callan O'Laughlin, "Roosevelt Race Brings Division of Republicans," *Chicago Daily Tribune*, Feb. 27, 1912; Gould, *Four Hats in the Ring*, 59–60.

10. Belle Case La Follette to S. H. Clark, Mar. 2, 1912, in La Follette and La Follette, *Robert M. La Follette*, 426; Belle Case La Follette to George Middleton, Mar. 6, 1912, in La Follette and La Follette, *Robert M. La Follette*, 426.

11. *Minneapolis Tribune*, Mar. 17, 1912, in La Follette and La Follette, *Robert M. La Follette*, 427; *Minneapolis Tribune*, Mar. 15, 1912, in La Follette and La Follette, *Robert M. La Follette*, 428.

12. *Fargo Forum*, Mar. 7, 1912, in La Follette and La Follette, *Robert M. La Follette*, 426; *Fargo Forum*, Mar. 15, 1912, in La Follette and La Follette, *Robert M. La Follette*, 427.

13. La Follette and La Follette, *Robert M. La Follette*, 428; "La Follette Wins," *Washington Post*, Mar. 20, 1912.

14. "Political Balm for All Candidates," *New York Times*, Mar. 21, 1912.

15. "Colonel Enjoys Lazy Arkansas Spring Day," *New York Sun*, April 21, 1912; TR to John St. Loe Strachey, Mar. 26, 1912, in Roosevelt, *Letters*, 7:532. In 1930, journalist-historian Mark Sullivan suggested that TR made the famous bull moose remark right before the Chicago convention in June, and historians have gone astray ever since. Biographer Edmund Morris discovered that TR used the term "bull moose" as early as 1894, but the origin of the quote in the context of the 1912 campaign appears to be the *New York Sun* article from April 21. TR repeated the phrase in New York on May 28, which attracted more headlines than the original story. See "Colonel Enjoys Lazy Arkansas Spring Day," *New York Sun*, April 21, 1912; TR to John St. Loe Strachey, Mar. 26, 1912, in Roosevelt, *Letters*, 7:532; "Feels Like Bull Moose," *Baltimore Sun*, May 29, 1912; Mark Sullivan, *Our Times*, 4:506; Morris, *Colonel Roosevelt*, 616fn27.

16. James Chace, *1912: Wilson, Roosevelt, Taft, and Debs*, 109–110.

17. Taft to C. P. Taft, Sep. 6, 1911, in Pringle, *William Howard Taft*, 761.

18. Ibid., 762–766, 771–772; Manners, *TR and Will*, 217–218; Butt, *Taft and Roosevelt*, 2:794, 2:804; Gould, *Four Hats in the Ring*, 59–60.

19. "Taft Snows Colonel Under," *New York Times*, Mar. 27, 1912; Taft to Horace D. Taft, April 14, 1912, in Pringle, *William Howard Taft*, 773.

20. "Taft Opens Fire on Roosevelt," *New York Times*, April 26, 1912; A. J. Philpott, "Big Meeting Held at Arena," *Boston Daily Globe*, April 26, 1912; Pringle, *William Howard Taft*, 775–782.

21. Butt, *Taft and Roosevelt*, 2:852.

22. Taft to Mabel Boardman, Apr. 19, 1912, in Lurie, *William Howard Taft*, 154; Mowry, *Theodore Roosevelt and the Progressive Movement*, 234–235.

23. "Wilson's Hat There, Too," *Baltimore Sun*, Feb. 23, 1912.

24. "To Knock Mr. Bryan Into a Cocked Hat," *New York Sun*, Jan. 8, 1912.

25. "Wilson and Bryan 'Shake' at Banquet," *New York Sun*, Jan. 9, 1912; Link, *Wilson, the Road to the White House*, 356.

26. Wilson's frequent and flirtatious letters to Peck imply an amorous relationship. Though they vacationed together in Bermuda, there is no explicit evidence of a sexual affair.

27. Wilson to Mary Allen Hulbert Peck, Jan. 14, 1912, in Woodrow Wilson and Arthur Stanley Link, *The Papers of Woodrow Wilson*, 54 vols. (Princeton: Princeton Univ. Press, 1966–1994), 24:43.

28. Link, *Wilson, the Road to the White House*, 386–387, 389.

29. Wilson to Mary Allen Hulbert Peck, June 9, 1912, in Wilson and Link, *The Papers of Woodrow Wilson*, 24:466.

30. Mowry, *Theodore Roosevelt and the Progressive Movement*, 237–241; Gould, *Four Hats in the Ring*, 67; "Chicago Roll Completed," *New York Tribune*, June 6, 1912; "How the Delegates Stand," *Washington Post*, June 5, 1912; "Tweedism, Says Colonel," *New York Tribune*, June 11, 1912.

31. "Arrives in Fighting Mood," *New York Times*, June 16, 1912; John Callan O'Laughlin, "Colonel Here to Stop 'Theft' of Presidency," *Chicago Daily Tribune*, June 16, 1912; "Chicago Rushes to See Roosevelt," *New York Tribune*, June 16, 1912.

32. "Roosevelt Warns of Peril to Nation," *Chicago Daily Tribune*, June 18, 1912; "Mr. Roosevelt's Speech," *New York Times*, June 18, 1912.

33. Roosevelt, *Letters*. 7:548fn.

34. La Follette and La Follette, *Robert M. La Follette*, 437–438; La Follette, *Autobiography*, 647–657.

35. White, *Autobiography*, 483; "Police There in Force," *Washington Post*, June 19, 1912; "All Comforts in Coliseum," *New York Times*, June 16, 1912.

36. "Detailed Story of Convention," *Chicago Daily Tribune*, June 19, 1912.

37. Ibid.; *Official Report of the Proceedings of the Fifteenth Republican National Convention* (New York: Tenny Press, 1912), 42–61.

38. "Cheers T.R., Votes for Taft," *New York Times*, June 20, 1912; *Official Report of the Proceedings of the Fifteenth Republican National Convention*, 160.

39. George Henry Payne, *The Birth of the New Party or Progressive Democracy* (Naperville, IL: J. L. Nicholes, 1912), 22–25; Clinton Wallace Gilbert, *The Mirrors of Washington* (New York: G.P. Putnam's Sons, 1921), 250.

40. Payne, *Birth of the New Party*, 26; "Many of Colonel's Delegates Will Not Follow Him from Convention," *New York Times*, June 20, 1912; Stoddard, *As I Knew Them*, 305–306.

41. Taft to M. T. Herrick, June 20, 1912, in Pringle, *William Howard Taft*, 808.

42. Davis, *Released for Publication*, 307.

43. Joseph G. Bilby, "Sea Girt: NJ's Summer Capital," GardenStateLegacy.com, June 2010, http://gardenstatelegacy.com/files/Sea_Girt_NJs_Summer_Capital_Bilby_GSL8.pdf; "Wilson Is Serene as Voting Goes On," *New York Times*, June 29, 1912.

44. "He Sets Convention in Uproar by Attack on Ryan and Belmont," *New York Times*, June 28, 1912.

45. Link, *Wilson, the Road to the White House*, 447–448.

46. "Wilson Is Serene as Voting Goes On"; Joseph P. Tumulty, *Woodrow Wilson*, 119.

47. Tumulty, *Woodrow Wilson*, 120–122; Eleanor Wilson McAdoo and Margaret Y. Gaffey, *The Woodrow Wilsons* (New York: Macmillan, 1937), 161–162; "Break to Clark on Tenth Ballot," *New York Times*, June 29, 1912.

48. "Bryan Denounces New York Delegates as Puppets," *Baltimore Sun*, June 30, 1912.

49. "Wilson Pleased with Bryan," *New York Times*, June 30, 1912; "Wilson Declines to Go to Baltimore," *New York Tribune*, June 30, 1912; Link, *Wilson, the Road to the White House*, 455.

50. "Gov. Wilson Not Elated by Victory," *New York Times*, July 3, 1912.

51. "Hail New Party in Fervent Song," *New York Times*, Aug. 6, 1912; John Callan O'Laughlin, "Beveridge Opens the Convention; Sounds War Cry," *Chicago Daily Tribune*, Aug. 6, 1912; White, *Autobiography*, 482–484; Stoddard, *As I Knew Them*, 410.

52. Payne, *Birth of the New Party*, 283–302; M. E. Hennessy, "Convention of New Party Under Way," *Boston Daily Globe*, Aug. 6, 1912.

53. Morris, *Colonel Roosevelt*, 227; TR to Julian La Rose Harris, Aug. 1, 1912, in Roosevelt, *Letters*, 7:590.

54. Payne, *Birth of the New Party*, 232–282; "Cheers Indorse Colonel's Creed," *Washington Post*, Aug. 7, 1912; Gould, *Four Hats in the Ring*, 139–140.

55. Wilson to Mary Hulbert Peck, Aug. 25, 1912, in Wilson and Link, *The Papers of Woodrow Wilson*, 25:56; in Wilson and Link, *The Papers of Woodrow Wilson*, 24:203; McAdoo and Gaffey, *The Woodrow Wilsons*, 172.

56. "Gov. Wilson Agrees with Mr. Brandeis," *New York Times*, Aug. 29, 1912; Link, *Wilson, the Road to the White House*, 488–489; La Follette and La Follette, *Robert M. La Follette*, 336–337, 475; Louis Brandeis to Woodrow Wilson, Sep. 3, 1912, in Louis D. Brandeis, *Letters of Louis D. Brandeis*, vol. 2 (Albany, NY: SUNY Press, 1972), 686–687.

57. "Ignore Party Labels Wilson Tells Labor," *New York Times*, Sept. 3, 1912; "T.R. Plan Faulty," *Washington Post*, Sept. 3, 1912.

58. Stephenson, *Nelson W. Aldrich*, 407–408; "Out for Good, Says Aldrich," *New York Times*, Aug. 7, 1912; Martha Smith, "Hollywood Calls on Aldrich," *Providence Journal–Bulletin*, June 8, 1997; Richard Salit, "Rhode Island's Forgotten Mansion," *Providence Journal–Bulletin*, May 22, 1996; "Strike at New Aldrich Home," *Boston Daily Globe*, July 10, 1910.

59. Stephenson, *Nelson W. Aldrich*, 389–400, 405–407; "A New Turn in Monetary Reform," *Wall Street Journal*, Sept. 12, 1912.

60. Robert J. Donovan, *The Assassins* (New York: Harper, 1955), 138; Oliver E. Remey, *Henry F. Cochems, and Wheeler P. Bloodgood, The Attempted Assassination of Ex-President Theodore Roosevelt* (Milwaukee: Progressive Publishing, 1912), 93, 200–202.

61. Taft to Helen Taft, July 22, 1912, in William H. Taft, *My Dearest Nellie*, 229, 233; Taft to Helen Taft, Aug. 26, 1912, in William H. Taft, *My Dearest Nellie*, 289.

62. "Taft Opens Attack on the Third Party," *New York Times*, Sept. 29, 1912.

63. Robert Marion La Follette, "Roosevelt's Tactics," *La Follette's Weekly Magazine*, Aug. 10, 1912, 3; RMLF to Rudolph Spreckels, July 12, 1912, in Greenbaum, *Robert Marion La Follette*, 117.

64. La Follette and La Follette, *Robert M. La Follette*, 448–452; Unger, *Fighting Bob La Follette*, 218–219; Greenbaum, *Robert Marion La Follette*, 117–119.

65. Morris, *Colonel Roosevelt*, 236; Chace, *1912: Wilson, Roosevelt, Taft, and Debs*, 203–204.

66. "Roosevelt Hits at La Follette," *Wall Street Journal*, Sept. 7, 1912; "Wilson Worries Col. Roosevelt," *Atlanta Constitution*, Sept. 6, 1912; "Bandanas Wave for Third Party Leader," *San Francisco Chronicle*, Sept. 15, 1912; "Roosevelt's Two Speeches," *Los Angeles Times*, Sept. 17, 1912.

67. Gould, *Four Hats in the Ring*, 168–170; Chace, *1912: Wilson, Roosevelt, Taft, and Debs*, 203–205; Morris, *Colonel Roosevelt*, 236, 240; Patricia O'Toole, *When Trumpets Call: Theodore Roosevelt After the White House* (New York: Simon & Schuster, 2005), 208–209; "Socialists Cheer Debs 29 Minutes," *New York Times*, Sept. 30, 1912; "Thousands Hear Col. Roosevelt at Auditorium," *Atlanta Constitution*, Sept. 29, 1912; "Roosevelt Speech Angered Atlanta," *New York Times*, Sept. 30, 1912.

68. Remey, Cochems, and Bloodgood, *Attempted Assassination*, 117–118.

69. TR to Kermit Roosevelt, Sep. 27, 1912, in Morris, *Colonel Roosevelt*, 239, 240.

70. Remey, Cochems, and Bloodgood, *Attempted Assassination*, 15–23; Davis, *Released for Publication*, 374–387; Morris, *Colonel Roosevelt*, 243–248; "Rushed to Chicago Hospital," *Washington Post*, Oct. 15, 1912.

71. "High Pulse Said to Be Due to His Fretting at Inactivity," *New York Times*, Oct. 16, 1912; "Taft Wires Regret to Col. Roosevelt," *New York Times*, Oct. 16, 1912; "Wilson to Cut Tour," *Washington Post*, Oct. 16, 1912; Remey, Cochems, and Bloodgood, *Attempted Assassination*, 72–73; Robert M. La Follette, "The Shooting of Roosevelt," *La Follette's Weekly Magazine*, Oct. 19, 1912, 3; Morris, *Colonel Roosevelt*, 655.

72. "Roosevelt Gets Star Ovation of All His Life," *New York Tribune*, Oct. 31, 1912; "New Yorkers Cheer Colonel 42 Minutes," *Chicago Daily Tribune*, Oct. 31, 1912.

73. TR to Kermit Roosevelt, Nov. 5 1912, in Morris, *Colonel Roosevelt*, 253; "Battle Just Begun, Says Col. Roosevelt," *New York Times*, Nov. 12, 1912; TR to Gifford Pinchot, Mar. 28, 1913, in Roosevelt, *Letters*, 1954, 7:716.

74. "'Uncle Joe' to Keep Busy," *New York Times*, Nov. 30, 1912.

75. Robert M. La Follette, "Wilson," *La Follette's Weekly Magazine*, Nov. 9, 1912, 3.

76. "Wilson Pleased by Victory," *Chicago Daily Tribune*, Nov. 6, 1912.

EPILOGUE

1. Bolles, *Tyrant from Illinois*, 46.

2. "Sun Bursting Through Clouds Brings Bright Omen to Nation's New Leader," *New York Times*, Mar. 5, 1913; "Fully 100,000 View Ceremony," *New York Times*, Mar. 5, 1913; "Day with Wilson," *Baltimore Sun*, Mar. 5, 1913.

3. "President Wilson's Inaugural Address," *New York Times*, Mar. 5, 1913.

4. John Milton Cooper, *Woodrow Wilson: A Biography* (New York: Random House, 2011), 216–219; *Reciprocal Trade Agreements Program: Hearings Before the Committee on Ways and Means, House of Representatives*, 80th Cong., 1st Sess., 662 (1947).

5. Wicker, *The Great Debate on Banking Reform*, 84–94; Kolko, *The Triumph of Conservatism*, 230–231, 243–247. For one example of Aldrich-related conspiracy literature, see G. Edward Griffin, *The Creature from Jekyll Island: A Second Look at the Federal Reserve*, 4th ed. (Westlake Village, CA: American Media, 1994).

6. Urofsky, *Louis D. Brandeis*, 386–396

7. Cooper, *Woodrow Wilson*, 343–346.

8. "Sharp Words by Wilson," *The New York Times*, Mar. 5, 1917.

9. "One Flag, One Tongue," *Chicago Daily Tribune*, Sept. 27, 1917; Unger, *Fighting Bob La Follette*, 247.

10. Morris, *Colonel Roosevelt*, 431–432, 476, 481, 487–494.

11. Morris, *Colonel Roosevelt*, 452–460, 553; "They Meet, and It's 'Theodore' and 'Will' Again," *Chicago Daily Tribune*, May 27, 1918.

12. Felix Frankfurter and Harlan Buddington Phillips, *Felix Frankfurter Reminisces* (New York: Reynal & Co., 1960), 85.

13. *26 Cong. Rec.*, S6636 (1894); "Aldrich Sees Bryan Back of Money Bill," *New York Times*, Oct. 16, 1913; Michael Wolraich, *Blowing Smoke: Why the Right Keeps Serving up Whack-Job Fantasies About the Plot to Euthanize Grandma, Outlaw Christmas, and Turn Junior into a Raging Homosexual* (Cambridge, MA: Da Capo Press, 2010), 233–237.

14. Peter Hartshorn, *I Have Seen the Future: A Life of Lincoln Steffens* (Berkeley, CA: Counterpoint, 2011), 308–315.

15. Unger, *Fighting Bob La Follette*, 286–300.

16. La Follette and La Follette, *Robert M. La Follette*, 1169.

SELECTED BIBLIOGRAPHY

Acrea, Kenneth. "The Wisconsin Reform Coalition, 1892 to 1900: La Follette's Rise to Power." *The Wisconsin Magazine of History* 52, no. 2 (Dec. 1, 1968): 132–157.

Anderson, Donald F. *William Howard Taft: A Conservative's Conception of the Presidency.* Ithaca, NY: Cornell University Press, 1973.

Anthony, Carl Sferrazza. *Nellie Taft: The Unconventional First Lady of the Ragtime Era.* New York: William Morrow, 2005.

Arthur, Anthony. *Radical Innocent: Upton Sinclair.* New York: Random House, 2006.

Baker, Ray Stannard [David Grayson, pseud.]. *American Chronicle: The Autobiography of Ray Stannard Baker.* New York: C. Scribner's Sons, 1945.

———. *Woodrow Wilson: Life and Letters.* Vol. 3. Garden City, NY: Doubleday, Page, 1927.

Barton, Albert Olaus. *La Follette's Winning of Wisconsin (1894-1904).* Des Moines, IA: Homestead, 1922.

Bishop, Joseph Bucklin. *Presidential Nominations and Elections: A History of American Conventions, National Campaigns, Inaugurations and Campaign Caricature.* New York: C. Scribner, 1916.

Bolles, Blair. *Tyrant from Illinois: Uncle Joe Cannon's Experiment with Personal Power.* Westport, CT: Greenwood Press, 1974.

Bowers, Claude Gernade. *Beveridge and the Progressive Era.* Cambridge, MA: The Literary Guild, 1932.

Bromley, Michael L. *William Howard Taft and the First Motoring Presidency, 1909-1913.* 2007; reprint. Jefferson, NC: McFarland, 2007.

Broz, J. Lawrence. *The International Origins of the Federal Reserve System.* Ithaca, NY: Cornell University Press, 1997.

Bruner, Robert F., and Sean D. Carr. *The Panic of 1907: Lessons Learned from the Market's Perfect Storm.* McFarland, 2003. 1st ed. Hoboken, NJ: Wiley, 2009.

Busbey, L. White. *Uncle Joe Cannon: The Story of a Pioneer American.* New York: H. Holt & Co., Kindle ed. 1927.

Butt, Archibald Willingham. *Taft and Roosevelt: The Intimate Letters of Archie Butt, Military Aide.* 2 vols. New York: Doubleday, Doran, 1930.

Butt, Archibald Willingham, and Lawrence Fraser Abbott. *The Letters of Archie Butt, Personal Aide to President Roosevelt.* New York: Doubleday, Page & Co., 1924.

Caine, Stanley P. *The Myth of a Progressive Reform: Railroad Regulation in Wisconsin, 1903-1910.* Madison: State Historical Society of Wisconsin, 1970.

Chace, James. *1912: Wilson, Roosevelt, Taft, and Debs—The Election That Changed the Country.* New York: Simon & Schuster, 2004.

Cherny, Robert W. *A Righteous Cause: The Life of William Jennings Bryan.* Norman: Univ. of Oklahoma Press, 1994.

Clark, Champ. *My Quarter Century of American Politics.* Vol. 1. New York: Harper & Brothers, 1920.

Cooper, John Milton. *Woodrow Wilson: A Biography.* New York: Random House, 2011.

Coppin, Clayton Anderson, and Jack C. High. *The Politics of Purity: Harvey Washington Wiley and the Origins of Federal Food Policy.* Ann Harbor: Univ. of Michigan Press, 1999.

Davis, Oscar King. *Released for Publication.* Boston, Houghton Mifflin, 1925.

Duffy, Herbert Smith. *William Howard Taft.* New York: Minton, Balch, 1930.

Dunn, Arthur Wallace. *Gridiron Nights: Humorous and Satirical Views of Politics and Statesmen as Presented by the Famous Dining Club.* New York: Frederick A. Stokes, 1915.

Fowler, Dorothy Ganfield. *John Coit Spooner, Defender of Presidents.* New York: University Publishers, 1961.

Goodwin, Lorine Swainston. *The Pure Food, Drink, and Drug Crusaders, 1879-1914.* Jefferson, NC: McFarland, 1999.

Gould, Lewis L. *America in the Progressive Era, 1890-1914.* New York: Longman, 2001.

———. *Four Hats in the Ring: The 1912 Election and the Birth of Modern American Politics.* Lawrence: Univ. Press of Kansas, 2008.

———. *The Most Exclusive Club: A History of the Modern United States Senate.* New York: Basic Books, 2006.

———. *The Presidency of Theodore Roosevelt.* 2nd ed. Univ. Press of Kansas, 2011.

———. *The William Howard Taft Presidency.* American Presidency Series. Lawrence: Univ. Press of Kansas, 2009.

Greenbaum, Fred. *Robert Marion La Follette.* Boston: Twayne Publishers, 1975.

———. "Teddy Roosevelt Creates a 'Draft' in 1912." In *Theodore Roosevelt: Many-Sided American,* 433–441. Interlaken, NY: Heart of the Lakes Pub., 1992.

Greene, Julie. *Pure and Simple Politics: The American Federation of Labor and Political Activism, 1881-1917.* Cambridge, UK: Cambridge Univ. Press, 1999.

Gwinn, William Rea. *Uncle Joe Cannon: Archfoe of Insurgency.* New York: Bookman Associates, 1957.

Harrison, Robert. *Congress, Progressive Reform, and the New American State.* Kindle ed. Cambridge, UK: Cambridge Univ. Press, 2004.

Hartshorn, Peter. *I Have Seen the Future: A Life of Lincoln Steffens.* Berkeley, CA: Counterpoint, 2011.

Howland, Harold. *Theodore Roosevelt and His Times: A Chronicle of the Progressive Movement.* New Haven: Yale Univ. Press, 1921.

Hoyt, Edwin Palmer. *The House of Morgan.* New York: Dodd, Mead, 1966.

Kaplan, Justin. *Lincoln Steffens: A Biography.* New York: Simon & Schuster, 1974.

Kazin, Michael. *A Godly Hero: The Life of William Jennings Bryan.* New York: Knopf, 2006.

Kolko, Gabriel. *Railroads and Regulation, 1877-1916.* Westport, CT: Greenwood Press, 1976.

———. *The Triumph of Conservatism: A Re-Interpretation of American History, 1900-1916.* Kindle ed. New York: Simon & Schuster, 1977.

La Follette, Belle Case, and Fola La Follette. *Robert M. La Follette, June 14, 1855–June 18, 1925.* 2 vols. New York: Macmillan, 1953.

La Follette, Robert Marion. *La Follette's Autobiography: A Personal Narrative of Political Experiences.* Madison: The Robert M. La Follette Co., 1913.

Lahman, Carroll Pollock. *Robert Marion La Follette as Public Speaker and Political Leader (1855-1905).* Madison: Univ. of Wisconsin, 1939.

Lears, Jackson. *Rebirth of a Nation: The Making of Modern America, 1877-1920.* New York: HarperCollins, 2009.

Link, Arthur S. *Wilson, the Road to the White House.* Princeton: Princeton Univ. Press, 1947.

Livingston, James. *Origins of the Federal Reserve System: Money, Class, and Corporate Capitalism, 1890-1913.* Ithaca: Cornell Univ. Press, 1986.

Lovejoy, Allen Fraser. *La Follette and the Establishment of the Direct Primary in Wisconsin, 1890-1904.* New Haven: Yale Univ. Press, 1941.

Lowitt, Richard. *George W. Norris: The Making of a Progressive, 1861-1912.* Syracuse: Syracuse Univ. Press, 1963.

Lurie, Jonathan. *William Howard Taft: The Travails of a Progressive Conservative.* Cambridge, UK: Cambridge Univ. Press, 2011.

Manners, William. *TR and Will: A Friendship That Split the Republican Party.* New York: Harcourt, Brace & World, 1969.

Margulies, Herbert F. "Robert M. La Follette Goes to the Senate, 1905." *Wisconsin Magazine of History* 59, no. 3 (April 1, 1976): 214–225.

McAdoo, Eleanor Wilson, and Margaret Y. Gaffey. *The Woodrow Wilsons.* New York: Macmillan, 1937.

McCulley, Richard T. *Banks and Politics During the Progressive Era: The Origins of the Federal Reserve System, 1897-1913.* New York: Garland Pub., 1992.

Merrill, Horace Samuel, and Marion Merrill. *The Republican Command, 1897-1913.* Lexington: Univ. Press of Kentucky, 1971.

Moore, J. Hampton. *Roosevelt and the Old Guard.* Philadelphia: Macrae-Smith Co., 1925.

Morris, Edmund. *Colonel Roosevelt.* New York: Random House, 2010.

———. *The Rise of Theodore Roosevelt.* Random House Publishing Group, 1979.

———. *Theodore Rex.* Random House Trade Paperbacks, 2001.

Mowry, George Edwin. *Theodore Roosevelt and the Progressive Movement.* New York: Hill & Wang, 1946.

O'Toole, Patricia. *When Trumpets Call: Theodore Roosevelt After the White House.* New York: Simon & Schuster, 2005.

Parker, James Richard. *Senator John C. Spooner, 1897-1907.* College Park: Univ. of Maryland, 1971.

Payne, George Henry. *The Birth of the New Party or Progressive Democracy.* Naperville, IL: J.L. Nicholes, 1912.

Pinchot, Gifford. *Breaking New Ground.* New York: Harcourt, Brace, 1947.

Pringle, Henry F. *Theodore Roosevelt: A Biography.* New York: Harcourt, Brace, 1931.

———. *William Howard Taft: The Life and Times: A Biography in Two Volumes.* 2008; reprint. Newtown, CT: American Political Biography Press, 1939.

Remey, Oliver E., Henry Frederick Cochems, and Wheeler P. Bloodgood. *The Attempted Assassination of Ex-President Theodore Roosevelt.* Milwaukee: Progressive Publishing, 1912.

Rodgers, Daniel T. "In Search of Progressivism." *Reviews in American History* 10, no. 4 (Dec. 1, 1982): 113-132.

Roosevelt, Theodore. *The Letters of Theodore Roosevelt*. Vol. 3-7. Cambridge: Harvard Univ. Press, 1951-1954.

———. *Theodore Roosevelt, an Autobiography*. New York: Macmillan, 1913.

Rosewater, Victor. *Back Stage in 1912: The Inside Story of the Split Republican Convention*. Philadelphia: Dorrance, 1932.

Rosmond, James Anthony. "Nelson Aldrich, Theodore Roosevelt and the Tariff: A Study to 1905." PhD diss., Univ. of North Carolina at Chapel Hill, 1974.

Ross, Thomas Richard. *Jonathan Prentiss Dolliver: A Study in Political Integrity and Independence*. Iowa City: State Historical Society of Iowa, 1958.

Satterlee, Herbert Livingston. *J. Pierpont Morgan: An Intimate Portrait*. New York: Macmillan, 1939.

Steffens, Lincoln. *The Autobiography of Lincoln Steffens*. Berkeley, CA: Heyday Books, 1931.

———. *The Letters of Lincoln Steffens*. Vol. 1. New York: Harcourt, Brace, 1938.

Stephenson, Nathaniel Wright. *Nelson W. Aldrich, a Leader in American Politics*. New York: C. Scribner's Sons, 1930.

Stoddard, Henry Luther. *As I Knew Them: Presidents and Politics from Grant to Coolidge*. New York: Harper & Brothers, 1927.

Strouse, Jean. *Morgan: American Financier*. New York: Random House, 1999.

Sullivan, Mark. *Our Times: The United States 1900-1925*. Vol. 2-4. New York: Scribner, 1926-1935.

Taft, Helen Herron. *Recollections of Full Years*. New York: Dodd, Mead, 1914.

Taft, William H. *My Dearest Nellie: The Letters of William Howard Taft to Helen Herron Taft, 1909-1912*. Lawrence: Univ. Press of Kansas, 2011.

The Cannon Centenary Conference: The Changing Nature of the Speakership. Washington, DC: US G.P.O., 2004.

Thelen, David P. *Robert M. La Follette and the Insurgent Spirit*. Madison: Univ. of Wisconsin Press, 1986.

Tulis, Jeffrey K. *The Rhetorical Presidency*. Princeton: Princeton University Press, 1987.

Tumulty, Joseph P. *Woodrow Wilson as I Know Him*. Garden City, NY: Doubleday, Page, 1921.

Unger, Nancy C. *Fighting Bob La Follette: The Righteous Reformer*. Kindle ed. Univ. of North Carolina Press, 2000.

Urofsky, Melvin I. *Louis D. Brandeis: A Life*. New York: Random House, 2009.

Warburg, Paul Moritz. *The Federal Reserve System, Its Origin and Growth: Reflections and Recollections*. Vol. 1. New York: Macmillan, 1930.

White, William Allen. *The Autobiography of William Allen White*. New York: Macmillan, 1946.

Wicker, Elmus. *Banking Panics of the Gilded Age*. Cambridge, UK: Cambridge University Press, 2006.

———. *The Great Debate on Banking Reform: Nelson Aldrich and the Origins of the Fed*. Columbus: Ohio State Univ. Press, 2005.

Wilson, Woodrow, and Arthur Stanley Link. *The Papers of Woodrow Wilson*. Vol. 24-25. Princeton, NJ: Princeton Univ. Press, 1966-1994.

Wood, Frederick S. *Roosevelt as We Knew Him: The Personal Recollections of One Hundred and Fifty of His Friends and Associates*. Philadelphia: John C. Winston, 1927.

Zinn, Howard. *A People's History of the United States*. New York: HarperCollins, 2010.

INDEX